Seoul Searching

THE SUNY SERIES

HORIZONS OF CINEMA

MURRAY POMERANCE | EDITOR

Also in the series

William Rothman, editor, *Cavell on Film*

J. David Slocum, editor, *Rebel Without a Cause*

Joe McElhaney, *The Death of Classical Cinema*

Kirsten Thompson, *Apocalyptic Dread*

Seoul Searching

Culture and Identity in Contemporary Korean Cinema

Frances Gateward, editor

State University of New York Press

Published by
State University of New York Press, Albany

Printed in the United States of America

Cover photo courtesy of Photofest.

For information, contact State University of New York Press, Albany, NY
www.sunypress.edu

Production by Marilyn P. Semerad
Marketing by Susan M. Petrie

Library of Congress Cataloging-in-Publication Data

Gateward, Frances K.
Seoul searching : culture and identity in contemporary Korean cinema / Frances Gateward.
p. cm. — (SUNY series, horizons of cinema)
Includes bibiographical references and index.
ISBN 978-0-7914-7225-5 (hardcover : alk. paper)
ISBN 978-0-7914-7226-2 (pbk. : alk. paper)
1. Motion pictures—Korea (South) I. Title.

PN1993.5.K6G38 2007
791.43095195—dc22 2006100306

10 9 8 7 6 5 4 3 2 1

This book is dedicated to Kim Eun-im
and to the memory of
Kim Bong-op, Chae Young-soon, and Kim Chung-hak

Contents

List of Illustrations ix

Acknowledgments xiii

Introduction 1
Frances Gateward

Part 1: Industry Trends and Popular Genres 13

1. Korean Cinema after Liberation: Production, Industry, and Regulatory Trends 15
Seung Hyun Park

2. *Christmas in August* and Korean Melodrama 37
Darcy Paquet

3. Storming the Big Screen: The *Shiri* Syndrome 55
Chi-Yun Shin and Julian Stringer

4. Timeless, Bottomless Bad Movies: Or, Consuming Youth in the New Korean Cinema 73
David Desser

Part 2: Directing New Korean Cinema 97

5. Scream and Scream Again: Korean Modernity as a House of Horrors in the Films of Kim Ki-young 99
Chris Berry

6. Forgetting to Remember, Remembering to Forget: The Politics of Memory and Modernity in the Fractured Films of Lee Chang-dong and Hong Sang-soo 115
Hye Seung Chung and David Scott Diffrient

7. Reflexivity and Identity Crisis in Park Chul-soo's *Farewell, My Darling* 141
Hyangsoon Yi

8. *Nowhere to Hide:* The Tumultuous Materialism of Lee Myung-se 157
Anne Rutherford

9. Closing the Circle: *Why Has Bodhidharma Left for the East?* 175
Linda C. Ehrlich

Part 3: Narratives of the National 189

10. Waiting to Exhale: The Colonial Experience and the Trouble with *My Own Breathing* 191
Frances Gateward

11. Crossing the Border to the "Other" Side: Dynamics of Interaction between North and South Koreans in *Spy Li Cheol-jin* and *Joint Security Area* 219
Suk-Young Kim

12. Race, Gender, and Postcolonial Identity in Kim Ki-duk's *Address Unknown* 243
Myung Ja Kim

13. Transgressing Boundaries: From Sexual Abuse to Eating Disorders in *301/302* 265
Diane Carson

14. Taking the Plunge: Representing Queer Desire in Contemporary South Korean Cinema 283
Robert L. Cagle

List of Contributors 299

Index 303

Illustrations

Figure 1.1	*White Badge* (Jeong Ji-yeong 1992).	23
Figure 1.2	*The Ginko Bed* (Kang Je-kyu 1995). Courtesy Pusan Film Festival.	27
Figure 2.1	*Christmas in August* (Hur Jin-ho 1998). Courtesy Pusan Film Festival.	38
Figure 2.2	*Christmas in August* (Hur Jin-ho 1998).	41
Figure 2.3	*Christmas in August* (Hur Jin-ho 1998).	41
Figure 2.4	*Christmas in August* (Hur Jin-ho 1998).	41
Figure 3.1	*Shiri* (Kang Je-kyu 1999). Courtesy Samsung Entertainment.	56
Figure 3.2	*Shiri* (Kang Je-kyu 1999). Courtesy Samsung Entertainment.	57
Figure 3.3	*Shiri* (Kang Je-kyu 1999). Courtesy Samsung Entertainment.	60
Figure 4.1	*Lies* (Jang Sun-woo 1999). Courtesy Pusan Film Festival.	74
Figure 4.2	*Beat* (Kim Sung-su 1997).	76

Figure 4.3 *Taking Care of My Cat* (Jeong Jae-eun 2001). 77

Figure 4.4 *Attack the Gas Station* (Kim Sang-jin 1999). 84

Figure 5.1 *Insect Woman.* (Kim Ki-young 1972). Courtesy Pusan Film Festival. 100

Figure 5.2 *The Housemaid.* (Kim Ki-young 1960). Courtesy Pusan Film Festival. 105

Figure 5.3 *Insect Woman.* (Kim Ki-young 1972). Courtesy Pusan Film Festival. 108

Figure 6.1 *Peppermint Candy* (2000). Courtesy Pusan Film Festival. 117

Figure 6.2 *Peppermint Candy* (2000). 128

Figure 7.1 *Farewell, My Darling* (Park Chul-soo 1996). 142

Figure 7.2 *Farewell, My Darling* (Park Chul-soo 1996). 147

Figure 7.3 *Farewell, My Darling* (Park Chul-soo 1996). 148

Figure 8.1 *Nowhere to Hide* (Lee Myung-se 1999). Courtesy Pusan Film Festival. 158

Figure 8.2 *Nowhere to Hide* (Lee Myung-se 1999). 161

Figure 9.1 *Why Has Bodhidharma Left for the East?* (Bae Yong-kyun 1989). 176

Figure 9.2 *Why Has Bodhidharma Left for the East?* (Bae Yong-kyun 1989). 177

Figure 9.3 *Why Has Bodhidharma Left for the East?* (Bae Yong-kyun 1989). 181

Figure 9.4 *Why Has Bodhidharma Left for the East?* (Bae Yong-kyun 1989). 182

Figure 10.1 *No Blood No Tears* (Ryo Seung-won 2002). Courtesy Pusan Film Festival. 195

Figure 10.2 *My Own Breathing* (Byun Young-joo 2000). Courtesy Pusan Film Festival. 208

Figure 10.3 *My Own Breathing* (Byun Young-joo 2000). Courtesy Pusan Film Festival. 211

Figure 10.4 *Habitual Sadness* (Byun Young-joo 1997).

Figure 11.1 *Joint Security Area* (Park Chan-wook 2000). 220

Figure 11.2 *Joint Security Area* (Park Chan-wook 2000). 234

Figure 12.1 *Address Unknown* (Kim Ki-duk 2001). 244

Figure 12.2 *Address Unknown* (Kim Ki-duk 2001). 256

Figure 12.3 *Address Unknown* (Kim Ki-duk 2001). 257

Figure 13.1 *301/302* (Park Chul-soo 1995). 268

Figure 13.2 *301/302* (Park Chul-soo 1995). 271

Figure 13.3 *301/302* (Park Chul-soo 1995). 272

Figure 14.1 *Bungee Jumping of Their Own* (Kim Dae-sung 2001). 286

Figure 14.2 *Bungee Jumping of Their Own* (Kim Dae-sung 2001). 292

Figure 14.3 *Bungee Jumping of Their Own* (Kim Dae-sung 2001). 295

Acknowledgments

I WOULD LIKE TO THANK THE MANY people who helped make this book possible. First and foremost I thank the contributors for their patience and diligence throughout the entire process. At State University of New York Press, I am grateful to Interim Director James Peltz, who was an absolute dream to work with, and Murray Pomerance, the editor of the Horizons of Cinema series, a damned good editor and a great friend. Travel assistance was provided by the University of Illinois Research Board for what would be the first of several trips to Korea. Thanks are also extended to the staff at the Korean Film Archive in Seoul, generous hosts who permitted me access to their collection, both print and visual: President Chung Hong-taek, Kim Bong-young from the Operations and Reference Department, and Park Jin-seok, Operations Manager; and at KOFIC Lee Keun-sang, Director of the International Promotion Department, and Dustin Yu. Assistance was also provided by the staff of the Press office at the Pusan International Film Festival.

Special thanks in no particular order to Yomota Inuhiko, Lee Kwang-mo, Lee Hyun-kyun, Chung Woo-chung, Hyun Joo Kim, Joelle Collier, a wonderful friend and colleague, and Darcy Paquet, for the many conversations shared over meals and the internet. I am deeply indebted to Gina Marchetti, who fueled my interest in Asian cinema and provided guidance, mentoring, friendship and support over the years. I also want to acknowledge my family for their encouragement and support, especially Mom, for answering my endless questions and supporting all my pursuits, and David Desser for his sustaining belief in this project and tireless devotion to me and my work.

Introduction

Frances Gateward

- A veteran of the Vietnam War cannot escape the horrors of his past. The guilt and alienation caused by the witnessing of atrocities wreak havoc on his present life.
- After failing the exam needed to apply to university, three working-class teens are confronted by their limited life choices.
- After moving into a new abode, a young man finds a love letter in his mailbox addressed to the previous tenant. He answers the correspondence, beginning a love affair that transgresses both space and time.
- By day a depressed, unappreciated bank clerk, but by night, a villainous, masked professional wrestler popular with fanatics of the sport!
- A down-on-her luck taxi driver and a cynical prostitute team up, planning to rob the brutal gangsters who have wronged them.
- A deaf young man resorts to kidnapping a child in order to fund a kidney transplant for his dying sister. When the abduction ends tragically, the bereaved father sets out to get revenge for the death of his kidnapped daughter.

Upon reading the scenarios listed previously, many filmgoers would assume that they describe American features, for they represent a wide range of genres—the war film, teen film, romance, comedy, heist film, and thriller—and a varied approach to cinema production, from the low-budget independent feature to the studio-produced commercial release, from the high-concept blockbuster to the more esoteric art film. The supposition that these are American and, more specifically, Hollywood plots is not a faulty one, given the dominance of the American film oligopoly on screens around the world and the common misconception that only American cinema is diverse. After all, the French make pretentious, cerebral films; Italians make sex comedies; Mexicans make wrestling and horror movies or wrestling/horror movies; Indians make sappy, overwrought musicals; and East Asians (often undifferentiated) make martial arts actioners. Such prejudices fail to recognize the rich and varied film cultures of these national and regional cinemas, including that of South Korea.

The brief plot synopses listed describe *White Badge* (Jeong Ji-yeong 1992), *Three Friends* (Yim Soon-rye 1996), *Il Mare* (Lee Hyeon-seung 2000), *The Foul King* (Kim Jee-woon 2000), *No Blood No Tears* (Ryoo Seung-wan 2000), and *Sympathy for Mr. Vengeance* (Park Chan-wook 2002), respectively—South Korean films lauded by both critics and audiences the world over, including in the United States. (*Sympathy for Mr. Vengeance* received limited theatrical distribution in late 2005, while the American remake of *Il Mare*, *The Lake House*, starring Keanu Reeves and Sandra Bullock, was released in 2006).

The variation represented by these films speaks to the thriving cinema culture in the southern half of the Korean peninsula. In a remarkable act of prognostication, an article published in a 1985 issue of *World Press Review* predicted, "South Korea has the ammunition to blast Japan off the screen,"[1] which in the last decade it has, even in the theaters of Tokyo. Further, Korea has displaced Japan as the center of "cool" popular culture, as evidenced by the titular and setting change of the sequel to Hong Kong's *Tokyo Raiders* (Jingle Ma 2000). It is not *Tokyo Raiders II*; it is *Seoul Raiders* (Jingle Ma 2005). But it was not only the Japanese and Hong Kong industries that experienced the popularity of "kim chic." In less than twenty years, Korean cinema, once a local cinema on the verge of collapse, has emerged as an international economic and cultural powerhouse, becoming the most the dominant cinema in Asia.[2] Today it is common to see Korean films regularly listed among the top ten films in Japan, Hong Kong, Singapore, Thailand, and Taiwan.

At home, Korean cinema is enjoying an unprecedented success, in many ways surpassing the achievements of its Golden Age, a decade of critical and commercial flourishing that lasted from the mid-1950s to the late 1960s. In the 1990s, new filmmakers rescued the industry from the economic disasters of the 1970s and 1980s, wrenching their screens from the grip of Hollywood. In 2003 for example, local productions made up eight of the ten top-grossing films. The following year, Korean-made films accounted for more than 50% of the total box office.[3]

In order to serve this nation of cinephiles, the number of screens has risen with attendance and box-office grosses. As of 2003, the number of screens increased from a paltry 404 in 1982 to 1,324. In addition to the opening of art and repertory theaters such as the Dongsung Cinemateque, the Core Art Hall, and the Cinecube Gwanghwamun in Seoul, construction of new screening spaces grew tremendously in the last decade. The country's first multiplex, the CGV11 in Seoul, the first in a chain of theaters established by CJ Entertainment in partnership with Golden Harvest (Hong Kong) and Village Roadshow (Australia) was constructed in 1998. The venture proved lucrative, and soon other investment groups and corporations followed suit, such as the Tong Yang Group and Lotte. Several of the new multiplexes operate with twenty-four-hour programming, offering amenities many American theatergoers can only dream about, such as all-stadium seating, state-of-the-art sound systems, large screens, and couple seating. Within the CGV megaplex moviegoers can enjoy a function room, game center, cafe, billiard hall, shopping mall, discount store, and restaurants. The massive expansion in exhibition spaces has done little to dilute audiences. According to a *Forbes* news wire, "Korean cinemas are among the most heavily attended in the world, with an average attendance of more than 100,000 per screen, or nearly three times that of U.S. theaters."[5]

One can trace the emergence of such a vibrant national cinema culture in other ways as well—the movement of the Korean Film Archive to the $2 billion Seoul Arts Complex, completed in 1993; the upgrading of the Archive's legal status from a nonprofit to a government affiliated foundation in 2002; and the restructuring of the Korean Motion Picture Promotion Corporation (KMPPC), founded in 1974, into the Korean Film Council (KOFIC) under the Ministry of Culture and Tourism. KOFIC now oversees the Korean Academy of Film Arts, the MediACT Center (a media literacy program for the public), an art theater that screens both new and retrospective films, the Namyangju Studio Complex, and the promotion of Korean films abroad. In addition to these major areas of growth is the continuing expansion of the Pusan International Film Festival, which has overtaken both the Hong Kong and Tokyo international film festivals to become the preeminent festival in Asia.

Held annually in the southern city of Busan, the festival has gone from 173 films from thirty one nations in 1996 to 307 films from more than seventy countries in 2005. Throngs of locals mix with film industry professionals to see the sold-out screenings and attend special events.

More than 80% of the screenings are attended by "guests," where, at the conclusion of the showing, directors, writers, actors, and cinematographers graciously field questions put forth by the audience. It is common to see programmers from other festivals around the globe in attendance, using the Korean venue to aid in their selections for their respective festivals. There is no better place to see Asian films by new cutting-edge directors, under the New Currents designation, or Korean films—either those not seen in decades in the Retrospective category, or new films by emerging directors, under the Korean Panorama. What may appeal most to those who work in the motion picture industry is the Pusan Promotion Plan (PPP), started in 1997, considered the "mecca of the Asian film market."

An integral part of the Festival's offerings, the PPP serves the international film industry by providing seminars and workshops for filmmakers and producers. Every year, more than one hundred projects are submitted in competition, from which a few are selected, based on their artistic strength, potential for coproduction, and director (either noteworthy or promising). The selected directors and producers are given the opportunity to meet with financiers and distributors to secure funding for their proposed works. In only seven years, the Pusan Promotion Plan has assisted in the production of over 160 features, from more than fifteen countries, including the Philippines, Cambodia, Malaysia, Indonesia, Singapore, Afghanistan, Kazakhstan, Kyrgyzstan, Tajikistan, Iran, Thailand, Vietnam, India, Korea, Japan, China, Hong Kong, and Taiwan. Directors who have benefited from the program include Ann Hui, Fruit Chan, Stanley Kwan, Clara Law, Danny Pang, Nan Achnas, Pen-ek Ratanaruang, Imamura Shohei, Kurosawa Kiyoshi, Sakamoto Junji, Kim Ki-duk, Lee Chang-dong, Wang Xiaoshuai, Tian Zhuang-zhuang, Hou Hsiao-Hsien, Riri Riza, Joan Chen, Sudhir Mishra, and Jafar Panahi.

Such a healthy and exciting state of affairs was not always the case. Historically, South Korean cinema was among the most stifled of industries, hindered by the annexation of the peninsula by Japan during the development of the medium through the end of World War II and the fragmentation of the nation and civil war that erupted in 1950. It was not until the mid-1950s that South Korean cinema came of age, entering into what is commonly known as the Golden Age, producing more than one hundred films per year. By the 1960s, the number of releases had doubled. Increased censorship, fueled by heightened Cold War ideology and a series of authoritarian governments, made it increasingly difficult for filmmakers to exercise creative freedom, however. This, coupled with the transformation in Hollywood toward high-concept blockbusters in the

1970s, made it difficult for the lower-budgeted Korean melodramas and family comedies to compete with American spectacles for screening venues. Theaters closed, and the number of Korean features dropped to a low of only seventy-three films by 1982. That same year saw the number of tickets sold drop to 42,737,086, a significant decrease from the figure for 1969, when 173,043,272 tickets were sold.[6]

The miraculous turnaround of the 1990s was initiated by a complex number of developments—changes in trade laws that led to a loosening of censorship, the movement toward a democratic form of government, rapid industrialization and the growth of the middle-class, a shift in finance laws that altered the funding process, and the legacy of the 1980s Korean New Wave.[7] The first-time directors of the New Wave, who were exposed to media production as active participants in the democracy movement, circumvented the old apprenticeship route to directing. Experimenting with style and content, filmmakers such as Park Kwang-su and Jang Sun-woo reinvigorated the national film industry with more complex narrative structures, nonconventional film styles, and content critical of societal structures—changes that would soon be manifest in the more successful commercial releases that followed.

This anthology looks to those later features, examining them from the valuable approach offered by Andrew Higson, which looks beyond close textual analysis to consider the context of film culture *and* national culture.[8] The chapters gathered herein analyze specific films, examining them in relation to the film culture that includes features from other nations, marketing, modes of production, audiences, other forms of popular culture, and wider cultural discourses. It is not intended to be comprehensive, as such an endeavor would be impossible, given that Korean studies, in general, and research on Korean cinema, more specifically, is still a burgeoning area on this side of the Pacific. It is intended to add to the body of research in film studies begun by such pioneering scholars as Ahn Byung-sup, Kim Soyoung, Chungmoo Choi, Kyung Hyun Kim, Hyangjin Lee, and David James.

The chapters have been written with a broad readership in mind, theoretically informed, but without a requirement of intimate knowledge of complex film theory on the part of the reader. Though the chapters included survey a large body of work, the authors have concentrated their efforts on representative features readily available in various video formats in order to facilitate further study.

The book is divided into three distinct parts, organized according to the different approaches and subjects the authors have employed in their interrogation of Korean cinema. Part 1 serves as an introduction to the field of study, concentrating on industry and regulatory structures and the three dominant genres that have led Korean film to the forefront of Asian cinema—the melodrama, the big-budget action blockbuster, and the youth film. In Part 2, "Directing New Korean Cinema," the focus is on close readings of feature films by several noted directors who have emerged at the forefront of the national cinema. The five chapters consider the relation of style and aesthetics to subject, to ideology, to culture, and to Korean film history. The last section, "Narratives of the National," concerns specific films within their sociocultural contexts and the impact of historical events and their legacies—Japanese colonialism, the Cold War and Korean Conflict, and U.S. neocolonialism. Resistance against traditions of sexism, racism, and homophobia are also explored.

The anthology opens with Seung Hyun Park, who carefully traces the trajectory of government policies overseeing the film industry. In his chapter, "Korean Cinema after Liberation: Production, Industry, and Regulatory Trends," Park provides critical data about the management of film as a cultural commodity, detailing the links between changes in regimes to the modifications of the Motion Picture Laws, edicts that covered censorship, the licensing of production companies, import and screen quotas, and ideological imperatives. This chapter makes clear the history of industrial organization that made it possible for Korean cinema to evolve into the global powerhouse it is today.

One of the films that helped establish contemporary Korean film in Asia is Hur Jin-ho's *Christmas in August* (1998), which played in Hong Kong continuously for two months, a rare feat, even for a Hong Kong feature. Darcy Paquet examines this film as representative of what is arguably the most important genre in Korean cinema—the melodrama. In tracing the ideology of melodramatic form and the history of the genre in Korea, Paquet delineates how the film both adheres to and deviates from convention, modernizing both narrative content and style to signal the tremendous changes the industry would experience in subsequent years.

Chi-Yun Shin and Julian Stringer offer a fascinating case study of *Shiri* (Kang Je-kyu 1999), the film that, in many ways, symbolizes the transformation alluded to in the first two chapters. This spy thriller/action film offered Korean moviegoers the spectacle of a big-budget Hollywood summer flick, but within a distinctly Korean context. With the ability to "out-Hollywood Hollywood," besting James Cameron's behemoth *Titanic* to earn its place as the biggest box-office success in Korean history at the time, *Shiri* and the cultural phenomenon it generated—the *Shiri* Syndrome—led to a series of bigger, louder, and more sensational releases. The authors discuss the implications of the blockbuster, highlighting the contradictions inherent in this postmodern form.

Hedonism, immediate gratification, rampant materialism, and the flattening of emotional affect, attributes of the postmodern condition, are perhaps most evident in the contemporary youth film, features both concerned with and targeted to what has now become the most desired demographic of marketing departments globally. Given that the most profitable industries target their products to the group with the most disposable income, it is no surprise that young people comprise the bulk of film characters and film audiences worldwide. Korea is no exception. David Desser, in the essay entitled "Timeless, Bottomless Bad Movies" (a play on Jang Sun-woo's anarchic *Timeless Bottomless Bad Movie* [1988]), provides an overview of the Korean youth film, the third most pervasive industry trend. Desser argues that the global interest in youth subcultures is directly related to the transnational reach of Korean cinema. He supports his supposition by analyzing the tropes of technology, gang membership, prostitution, the crime spree, education, and class difference.

Chris Berry opens Part 2 with a study focusing on the work of the late Kim Ki-young, considered one of the most radical directors in Asia. His work, often compared to that of Imamura Shohei, Alfred Hitchcock, Sam Fuller, Nicholas Ray, Roger Corman, and Ed Wood, offers a unique perspective of modernization on the peninsula. Berry looks specifically at Kim's use of genre blending. The combination of horror and melodrama that Kim innovated in *The Housemaid* (1960) presents a complex deployment of realist styles alongside the fantastic. Berry interrogates the ambivalent and sometimes contradictory themes of Kim Ki-young's oeuvre, with particular attention to issues of gender roles in the midst of modernization.

Modernization is a preeminent theme in Korean art, literature, and film, reflecting the rapid and radical transformation of the nation. As Hye Seung Chung and David Scott Diffrient describe in their contribution to this volume, the country shifted from "post-War poverty to *chaebol*-led prosperity, from chamber pot tradition to mobile-phone modernity." The authors provide close readings of two pivotal films. The first is *Peppermint Candy* (2000), whose narrative unfolds with a regressive temporality, presenting in reverse chronological order, without the use of flashbacks, the life of its aimless and amoral protagonist. Chung and Diffrient demonstrate how this structure exemplifies the dystopian implications of postcolonial modernization. Their explanation of the important historical events alluded to in the film's episodic narrative provides readers a deeper understanding of how director Lee Chang-dong ultimately narrates the story not of a man but of the nation. The second film discussed, Hong Sang-soo's *Virgin Stripped Bare by Her Bachelors* (2000), also presents a structurally complex narrative. Utilizing a more postmodern sensibility, it "straddles an immediate past and present," taking the Korean folk tradition of *pansori* and integrating it with a style of narrative Cubism, hence the allusion to Duchamp's painting *The Bride Stripped Bare by Her Bachelors*. As the authors argue, the aesthetic challenge to the conventions of linear narrative offered by the two noted directors serves as an expression of contemporary Korea's fragmented and disjunctive cultural condition.

Hangsoon Yi continues the discussion of style, narrative, and social crisis in her study of director Park Chul-soo, with a focus on his use of reflexivity. Yi provocatively contends in her close reading that *Farewell, My Darling* (1986) represents a bold break from both mainstream, traditional Korean films and the New Wave, confounding the boundaries of the diegetic and nondiegetic to simultaneously validate *and* critique filmmaking as process, while also deconstructing the genre of the family melodrama and examining the changing status of the family unit.

In "*Nowhere to Hide*: The Tumultuous Materialism of Lee Myung-se," Anne Rutherford takes on Lee's genre-exploding, visually stunning tour de force in an analysis of its appeal to sensory pleasures. Like the directors noted previously in this section, Lee Myung-se goes against Korean cinematic tradition in this work by attempting a film based on materiality rather than emotional identification. Using the montage theories of Eisenstein, the genre explorations of Steve Neale and Marcia Landy, and Miriam Hansen's work on mimesis, Rutherford offers a compelling study of how Korea's leading visual stylist constructs *Nowhere to Hide* (1999) as true cinematic spectacle.

The independently produced *Why Has Bodhidharma Left for the East?* (1989) is the subject of Linda C. Ehrlich's chapter, a treatise on the aesthetics and significance of Zen Buddhism in Bae Yong-kyun's most noted film. Careful attention reveals how the film's recurring motifs—complicating juxtapositions, varying light, circular camera movements, and symbolism of the journey, and the overall film style—serve as a reminder of the continuing importance of traditional religion and culture in postmodern Korea.

Part 3, "Narratives of the National," opens with my chapter on the recent trend of action films concerned with the historic relations between Japan and Korea. The recent turn away from melodrama toward violent blockbusters revisiting national trauma is attributed to a complex intersection of industry concerns, gender anxieties, neo-Confucianism, the rise of the nation as an economic powerhouse, and the return of the repressed. I argue that these commercialized texts construct nationalism and national identity in narrow terms, as exclusively male projects. It is the independently produced documentary, with its tradition of social progressivism, that serves as intervention in this process of mediated nation building. The example focused upon in this chapter is Byun Young-joo's remarkable trilogy of documentaries—*Murmuring* (1995), *Habitual Sadness* (1997), and *My Own Breathing* (1999)—about the lives of former "comfort women."

No discussion of narratives of the national in South Korean cinema would be thorough without including an examination of the Cold War, the unresolved Korean Conflict, and the tensions between the Republic of Korea and its neighbor to the north, the Democratic People's Republic of Korea. Suk-Young Kim offers a detailed study of the construction of North Korea, its citizens, and Communist ideology, linking these images to South Korean government policy, American portrayals, and the shifting attitudes of the populace. Kim looks beyond the clichéd stereotypes of spies and villainy in her close analysis of *Spy Li Cheol Jin* (Jang Jin 1999), noting the narrative strategies that allow, perhaps for the first time, a sympathetic, more humanized depiction of an agent sent across the border into the South. Her analysis of *Joint Security Area* (Park Chan-wook 2000) links the film's transgressive friendships between the soldiers stationed on the DMZ to issues of postmodern identity.

Identity is also the central concern in the next chapter, a revealing analysis of Kim Ki-duk's *Address Unknown* (2001). A maverick director, Kim Ki-duk is revered as much as he is reviled (in recent years he has been acclaimed at a number of prestigious festivals such as Berlin and Locarno, as well as attacked for his controversial depictions of the darker, seamier aspects of Korean society). The author takes one of Kim's most complex, and in many ways, difficult films, deciphering the specific cultural codes and metaphors that critique marginality constructed on the basis of race, gender, class, sexuality, neocolonialism, and national identity. As the chapter informs us, the historical specificity and location of the film (an impoverished postwar village dependent on the neighboring U.S. military base); the themes of miscegenation, sexual exploitation, and cruelty; and the starkly beautiful cinematography make for a truly compelling work that refuses to turn away from the despair and degradation caused by social hierarchies.

One of the most compelling aspects of contemporary Korean society is the ongoing shift in gender roles and the growth of the feminist movement. In all grassroots struggles for democracy and social justice, the participation of women is integral in the push for progressive change. It is common to find feminist groups working in coalition with other NGOs, such as student organizations, labor unions, and others. Such was case of the democracy movement in South Korea. Hence gender issues are intimately related to issues of the nation. Diane Carson's contribution to this collection focuses on the compelling, and sometimes disturbing, *301/302* (1995), a film that links national crises to gender oppression, eating disorders, sexual violence, and trauma. The film, as sensuous as its subject—food—handles its unsavory issues with what Carson describes as "a courageous, even astonishing, presentation." Park Chul-soo's dynamic use of the camera within the coldly impersonal and often claustrophobic space of the two third-floor apartments (to which the title refers) provides an unflinching view of the effects of patriarchal privilege. As Carson reminds us, such films are rare within South Korean cinema, especially during a period of industrywide "remasculinization."

As journalist Stephen Short reminds us, contemporary Asian cinema, including that of Korea, is full of action, and "we don't mean car crashes."[9] With the loosening of censorship regulations, most notably in 1996 when the Supreme Court ruled forced editing illegal under the constitution, filmmakers eagerly, and with reckless abandon, began to explore what had previously been judged taboo—excessive violence and explicit sexuality. Some of the more striking examples include the depiction of female desire in *An Affair* (E. J. Yong 1998), which features an alienated middle-aged housewife involved with a younger man, her sister's fiancé; a brutal attempted rape committed by the teen protagonist in the opening scene of *Tears* (Im Sang-soo 2000), and another in *Oasis* (Lee Chang-dong 2002), where a social outcast forces himself on a woman with cerebral palsy; and in *Happy End* (Jeong-Jiwu 1999) the display of uninhibited sex between an adulterous wife and her lover. The controversial *Too Young to Die* (Park Jin-pyo 2002), a fiction film about the sexual pleasure enjoyed by a real-life septuagenarian couple, was originally banned from release and later given an 18+ rating because of ambiguous sex scenes in which audiences could not determine if the intercourse presented is simulated or real. In *Desire* (Kim Eungsu 2002), a woman beds a man after she finds out he, a male prostitute, is her husband's lover. In the concluding chapter of this book, Robert L. Cagle takes on one of the most contentious issues in contemporary Korean society, homosexuality. His analysis of *Bungee Jumping of Their Own* (Kim Dae-seung 2001) proves the film to be one of the first to treat same-sex romance seriously and sympathetically, marking a radical move away from staid stereotypes and the use of gay men as comic relief. In a particularly cogent argument, Cagle notes how the themes are communicated through both the mise-en-scène and the nonlinear narrative structure. Whereas several authors have argued that the fragmented narratives so characteristic of Korean cinema function as a trope representing postmodern crises and trauma, Cagle asserts that the structure of this film, built around a series of ellipses and repetition, opens up a space for homosexual desire.

The contributors to this work have utilized approaches, theories, and methodologies as varied as the films themselves in an attempt to aid in the understanding of the international phenomenon that is New Korean Cinema. It is particularly imperative to examine South Korean cinema at this critical moment, to provide a context for newly exposed audiences. Korean cinema is now positioned at the nexus of the globalizing film industry. While the major filmmaking centers of Asia have all engaged in coproductions with Korean media corporations, the Hollywood industry has sought to profit from the popularity of Korean features by obtaining the rights to remake several films. Lee Hyeon-seung's romance *Il Mare* (2000) was purchased by Warner Brothers; Cho Jin Kyu's 2001 action/comedy *My Wife Is a Gangster*, by Miramax; and *My Sassy Girl* (Kwak Jae-yong 2001), a light-hearted romantic drama, by Dreamworks. There is also the gangster comedy *Hi, Dharma* (Park Cheol-kwan 2002), bought by MGM, and the ultraviolent drama *Oldboy* (Park Chan-wook 2003), acquired by Universal. In 2006 the first Korean film was released theatrically with wide distribution by a Hollywood major in the United States, the action film *Typhoon* (Kwak Kyung-taek 2005), distributed by Dreamworks. The significance of South Korea to the American film industry also can also be measured by the number of column inches in Hollywood trade publications. The Pusan International Film Festival is covered annually, internal industry developments are noted, and films are reviewed regularly. Since February 2005, *Variety* has included South Korea in its weekly international box office report.

The industry fascination and critical accolades heaped on Korean films at prestigious international festivals such as Berlin, Cannes, and Venice have garnered the attention of the public. Feature films (and TV melodramas) capture the interest of audiences beyond the specialty cinemas, unlike Hindi films for instance, which, though regularly appearing among *Variety*'s compilation of top-fifty box-office earners in the United States, play mostly to NRI's (Non-Resident Indians) and South Asian Americans. Moviegoers in North America can experience Korean films in retrospectives (such as at the Lincoln Center or Smithsonian), at local festivals (like Seattle, Toronto, and Philadelphia) or in their neighborhood theaters, as several have enjoyed theatrical distribution. DVDs no longer have to be purchased or rented from specialty Internet sites, as they are readily available at mainstream outlets such as Blockbuster and Hollywood Video. This book is intended for those who have yet to venture into this exciting terrain and for those who may have sampled Korean cinema and wish to savor more thoroughly the delights of what many consider the most dynamic national cinema in the world today.

Korean names are listed throughout the text as they are rendered in Korean, with surname first and given name second. Because given names are not linked with a hyphen in Korean, when Romanized they are commonly added. The exceptions here are those transliterated as preferred by the persons concerned. In an effort to appeal to nonspecialist readers, the McCune-Reischauer system is not used, as the use of diacritical marks and specific coding may render this book difficult to read and unwieldy. Instead, the revised Romanization system, adopted by South Korea in 2000, is utilized.

Notes

1. "South Korea's Splash," which opens with a description of Korean films at European festivals, most notably *Village in the Mist* (Im Kwon-taek 1983) at Berlin and *The Spinning Wheel* (Lee Doo-yong 1984) at Cannes, gives a brief introduction to the state of the film industry. Excerpted from *The Economist*, it can be found in *World Press Review* 32.10 (October 1985): 59–60.

2. The editor would like to make clear to the readers that there is no ideological motive for the use of *Korea* and/or *Korean* in reference to the Republic of Korea, commonly known as South Korea. It is merely done for the sake of convenience and brevity in this introduction and throughout this collection.

3. The actual statistic, provided by the Korean Government via KOFIC, the Korean Film Council, is 53.31%. *Korean Cinema 2004 Annual Report* (Seoul: KOFIC) 295.

4. These statistics can be found in *Korean Cinema 1993 Annual Report* (Seoul: KOFIC), 36, and *Korean Cinema 2004 Annual Report* (Seoul: KOFIC) 298.

5. "Imax Signs Four Theater Deal with Largest Distributor in Korea." April 13, 2005, http://www.forbes.com/prnewswire/feeds/prnewswire/2005/04/13/prnewswire200504130730PR_NEWS_B_GBL_HS_TO093.html.

6. These figures are from the *Korean Cinema 1993 Annual Report* (Seoul: KOFIC) 36.

7. The developments listed here are discussed throughout this book. For more on censorship laws, see the opening chapter by Park "Korean Cinema after Liberation: Production, Industry, and Regulatory Trends." The other aspects are covered in Chung and Diffrient's "Forgetting to Remember, Remembering to Forget." For more on the New Wave, see my "Youth in Crisis: National Cultural Identity in New South Korean Cinema," *Multiple Modernities: Cinemas and Popular Media in Transcultural East Asia*, ed. Jenny Kwok Wah Lau (Philadelphia: Temple University Press, 2003) 114–27.

8. Andrew Higson, "The Concept of National Cinema," *Screen* 30.4 (1989): 36-46.

9. Article by Stephen Short from *Time Asia* (2001). www.time.com/time/asia/features/sex/sexfilm.html.

PART 1

Industry Trends and Popular Genres

1

Seung Hyun Park

Korean Cinema after Liberation

Production, Industry, and Regulatory Trends

Before 1988, when Korea opened its film market to Hollywood distribution companies, the government played a crucial role in developing a policy of protection and support for the national film industry, attempting to challenge the dominance of foreign films that displaced local production in its own market. This policy failed, however, for it was centered on the political intention to control cinematic activity through censorship, essentially eliminating controversial ideological content. Because the policy did not grow out of a carefully planned, long-conceived design, it was continually revised, subject to shifting political circumstances and complaints from the industry. In a sense, the history of film industry protections in South Korean cinema is a history of regulation.

The protection system's decline was considered to have begun in 1987. People in the film industry viewed the entrance of Hollywood distribution companies in Korea from a consistently hostile stance. The marketplace was expected to reflect increased competition, and the government, having surrendered its control of the film industry to the industry itself, could no longer secure stable profits for home-based producers. Both the government and once-powerful industry leaders hoped to sustain the status quo of the restrictive system, but U.S. economic pressure prohibited them from doing so. Independent producers, who had been excluded from film production since the early 1960s, looked upon the coming uncertainty as a crucial opportunity, a chance to enter into the system with the possibility of making lucrative profits. The rise of what would become known as a "new wave" reinvigorated the industry, so much so that film critics such as Tony Rayns argue that Korean cinema has been more innovative and surprising than any other national cinema since the end of the 1980s. The formation of the New Wave was related to several factors: the transformation of the Korean film industry, the alleviation of political censorship, and the emergence of young directors. To understand the significance of the movement, we must first look to the period immediately preceding it.

The Depression Period of Korean Cinema, 1973–1986

South Korea had a highly authoritarian political system from the early 1970s to the end of 1986. Park Chung-hee, who took political power in 1961,[1] and his program of *Yushin Kaehyuk* (Revitalizing Reforms)[2] in October 1972, brought the political climate to what many consider the nation's lowest point. After Park's death in October 1979, Chun Doo-hwan initiated a military coup, seizing power in 1980, killing several hundred citizens in Gwangju.[3] Cumings argues that the Chun government was fundamentally Park's system in a new guise (46). Between 1972 and 1986, state power precluded dissent through censorship and managed the mass media to consolidate its doctrine. Like other media, cinema functioned to shape political opinion to favor the centralized government's designated political and economic goals. The censorship board operated as a means to block controversial narratives and representations that threatened political stability and unity, with support from the state that limited private competition in film production.

Censorship became more oppressive during this period, influenced by the political hardline. There were restrictions on films that might disrupt the existing order by violating good taste or customs, harming the interest and dignity of the country, praising North Korea and Communism, or criticizing the president and government policies in South Korea. Filmmakers were placed in the position of self-regulation, forced to always consider censorship when engaging in production. As Lee Young Il describes:

> The films in the 1970s lacked artistic spirit in filmmaking and the attitudes of filmmakers were too easy going. In particular, even if

> the films did not contain ideas on problem consciousness and if the films had contained social matters or had described social facts very truly and critically, those screenplays were regulated by the censorship authorities according to the then existing "Emergency Measures." If the films were not in line with what we call the ideology of "Renovation" or national integration, they were regulated. By enforcement of the film policy for so many years, the film directors and producers realized that to make popular films in line with the then film policy or low class entertainment films for countryside theaters was much wiser and the only way they could survive. (188)

This oppressive situation continued into the 1980s. The president of the Korean Motion Picture Promotion Corporation (MPPC), Lee Jin-keun, defended censorship in an interview conducted in 1982, stressing that film should be a medium that portrayed the bright visions rather than the dark side of Korean society. He contended,

> Among the guidelines the government sets are these: That our traditional culture should be mixed with foreign cultures to create a more brilliant culture; that motion pictures are not for individuals or certain groups but for the public interest and, therefore, they should make everyone happy. In censorship, generally, security of the nation is most important. Second, films should not hurt our cultural heritage. Third, they should not criticize or disregard certain groups in society, such as religious organizations. The trend of movies is toward humanity, emphasizing our life in Korea; both good and bad aspects. Joking with the government officials is not important. I'm not saying they are banned, but just saying that we have more important humanity topics to portray than the government. (Lent 138)

To a great extent, strict censorship determined subject matter. Working as a decisive mechanism regulating content, censorship also exerted an influence on production trends, together with the very adroit management of import quotas. Not only did the authorities have the exclusive right to select who could and could not make films, but also they encouraged certain kinds of films while banning others. Under the period of the import quota system, domestic producers rarely protested against censorship since the government guaranteed them stable profits by limiting competition. Local film companies seldom cared about film production because it was just a way to maintain their primary business—film importation.

The Park government passed the Fourth Revised Motion Picture Law in April 1973, placing the Korean film industry completely under the control of political authorities. The Chun government retained the amended law and its central elements: (1) the establishment of strict censorship; (2) the introduction of a license system for the establishment of film companies, reducing competition in the industry; (3) the formation of a protectionist system in the film industry through reorganization of import quotas and screen quotas; (4) the establishment of the Motion Picture Promotion Corporation (MPPC) to manage film policies; and 5) the encouragement of the production of wholesome movies following political goals.

After dissolving several companies in 1973, the Park government afforded only twelve companies the privilege of releasing both domestic and foreign features. The number of licensed companies increased slightly to fourteen in 1974 and twenty in 1981. These licensed companies circulated about ninety domestic films and thirty foreign ones yearly from 1973 to 1985. Referring to the production of films during this period, Lee Taewon, the most popular producer of the 1980s, admits that every producer made domestic films just to get an import quota (570). According to him, only two of the twenty companies had a genuine interest in the production of domestic films. Using domestic films as a means to obtain import quotas, most producers made several movies a month, even within fifteen days (571). In fact, those selected companies had no incentive to care about the production of domestic films because the stable profits came from the distribution rights to foreign films. Some domestic features even went to warehouse shelves right after completion, while others were sent directly to second-run theaters. Recognizing this degeneration of domestic industry, Jang Sun-woo refers to the production during this period as "the winter of prostitution" (cited in Joo 62). The import quota system required a company to make four domestic films to earn an import quota.[4] In addition to this requirement, supplementary quotas were given each year to film companies when their films either won the awards in the Grand Bell Film Festival[5] or were selected as "quality films" by the MPPC.

The MPPC was established in April 1973, dissolving the existent Union of Korean Film Promotion. The government stated that the purpose of the MPPC was to promote domestic films and to support the Korean film industry. The actual role of this corporation, however, was to regulate the film industry, manage the Grand Bell Awards Festival and select "quality films" in order to encourage the production of politically favored films. It issued the Film Policy Measure every year to publicize what the authorities wanted from the film industry. This practice lasted until 1986. Under Article 1 of the Film Policy Measure, the MPPC specified that Korean cinema should adhere to the political and social guidelines set by the authorities. Filmmakers were compelled to reveal the bright side of social reality and highlight cultural traditions to school the public in the virtues of their ancestors. The authorities tried to teach the audience traditional morality—especially that which involved obedience and respect to authority. They also tried to lead the audience to "do the right thing," as they saw it.

Since the government gave most of the Grand Bell Awards and quality film selections to films that followed official guidelines, companies produced "policy films" to earn another importation quota. This kind of financial reward policy mobilized film companies to make a number of what were deemed wholesome movies, irrespective of whether these films could attract audiences or not. Film importation was almost never a financial risk due to the scarcity value of foreign movies in the market. Each foreign film was considered to be "a goose bearing golden eggs." Thus, production of domestic films was primarily aimed at earning the quota (Son 269).

The production of wholesome films was guided by a unified social goal designed to promote the political legitimacy of the authorities. This goal displayed its ideologies through the representation of the following themes: (1) anti-Communism; (2) heroic historical figures whose deeds saved the nation in times of difficulty; (3) the dedication of the individual to the public interest; and (4) cultural heritage and traditional norms such as fidelity, perseverance, and loyalty. These aspects were essential to indoctrinate citizens to the belief that the authoritarian political was the best way to develop the nation and to protect South Korea from potential enemies, most often represented as invasion by Communists.

The theme of anti-Communism was extremely popular, crossing beyond military films into a variety of genres such as action, detective films, and melodrama. The MPPC produced five anti-Communist propaganda films, including *Testimony* (Im Kwon-taek 1973), *The Battle Field* (Lee Man-hee 1974), *I Will Never Cry Again* (Im Kwon-taek 1974), *The Remaining Spy* (Kim Si-hyun 1975), and *Taebaek Mountains* (Im kwon-taek 1994), while licensed companies endeavored to make many others, like *The Flame* (Yu Hyun-mok 1975), *The Hidden Hero* (Im Kwon-taek 1979), *The Final Witness* (Lee Doo-yong 1980), *Avengo Flying Rangers* (Im Kwon-taek 1982), and *My Last Memory of Heungnam* (Ko Young-nam 1983). Most of these films focus on the psychological and behavioral changes of men in a vortex of bloody struggle between Communism and liberal democracy—from ideologically disinterested men into ardent anti-Communists when they recognize the cruelty of Communists.

Officially backed policy films were used either to enliven patriotism or to stress individual sacrifice for the public interest. *The General Who*

Wears Red Clothes (Lee Du-yong 1973) and *Diary of the Battle Field* (Jang Il-ho 1977) deal with heroic figures in the Chosun-Japan War (1592–1595), while attributing the division of public opinion of the political system to Japan's invasion. *Yu Gwan-sun* (Kim Ki-dok 1974) and *Like an Everlasting Pine* (Lee Jang-ho 1983) present fearless resistance against Japanese colonial rule. *A Daffodil* (Choi Hun 1973) and *The Mother* (Lim Wok-sik 1976) highlight a woman's dedication to social reform in an agricultural village and in an orphanage, respectively. *Policeman* (Lee Du-yong 1978) and other films deal with public officials and their service to the common good.

The authorities also urged films to rekindle pride in the cultural heritage and traditional values. Most films of this theme were categorized as literary films in Korea because their stories were adaptations of novels. *The Soil* (Kim Soo-yong 1974) and *The Old House* (Cho Mun-jin 1977) deal with tragic stories of *yangban*, the noble class during the Chosun Dynasty, as their families struggle amidst the collapse of the traditional morals such as filial piety and loyalty to the community. They describe Western values as destructive to the society's moral structure, persuading audiences to recover traditional morals for national dignity and unity. While keeping pace with the guidelines of the authorities, film companies achieved commercial success with the production of these films because the novels were already familiar to audiences. However, this trend generated a side effect—an indifference to original scripts.

Low-budget action films were also a dominant trend, made with very formulaic narrative structures that transported viewers into a world of fantasy where a swordsman or martial artist would sacrifice everything to kill an adversary. More than twenty movies produced from 1978 to 1983 had titles with variations on the word *Sorim* (Shaolin), the temple that is famous for martial arts in China. Usually blessed with a happy ending, these action films concerned resistance against Japanese colonial rule or Communist oppression. These were typical "quota quickies," popular in the 1970s and the early 1980s, though rarely screened in the first-run theaters.

Melodrama was still the most dominant genre between 1973 and 1986, but the central themes were totally different from those of earlier periods. Melodramas of the 1960s had targeted mainly female audiences, but those of the 1970s were aimed at males. In previous decades, melodramas highlighted the control of women's sexual desire, focusing on sexual affairs, while of course taking into account given social norms. From the early 1970s to the mid-1980s, melodramas paid almost no regard to existing social morals of chastity. Such films as *Heavenly Home Coming to Stars* (Lee Jang-ho 1974), *The Winter Woman* (Kim Ho-sun

1977), and *The Glory of Night* (Kim Ho-sun 1979) depict women's virginity as a burden, placing young women in successive engagements in search of true love. The melodramas during this period generally dealt with three themes: the story of prostitutes and bar hostesses, the love affairs of young college coeds or similarly aged women, and the extramarital affairs of women, most often in their thirties.

Like that of the political system, the period between 1973 and 1986 is viewed as the most depressed period in the history of Korean cinema. Though the nation experienced intensive industrialization and became a highly developed country, emerging as one of Asia's four tigers together with Hong Kong, Taiwan, and Singapore, human rights were curtailed, and for the film industry, decline was inevitable. Economic prosperity created the growth of a middle class who could afford to buy more movie tickets, but Koreans gradually became tired of watching domestic films full of female nudity, sentimentalism, sleazy action, and government propaganda. Scholars generally feel that most Korean films of the time were cheaply produced hostess movies, low on plot and production values and high on nudity and eroticism (Joo, Lent, Rayns). The film industry's collusion in the dubious import quota system conspired to stifle the quality of domestic films.

The film market showed a rapid decline in almost every area: the number of films produced, admission figures, the average attendance per individual, and even the number of theaters. The average number of films attended per individual was 3.7 in 1972; 2.9 in 1974; 1.7 in 1978; and 1.2 in 1981. From 1981 to 1987, this number fluctuated between 1.1 and 1.2. Total admissions in 1986 became approximately one-third of those in 1973, although the population increased by more than 9 million during this period. Film production nose-dived; 122 features in 1973, and 73 in 1986. With lessened product, movie theaters closed regularly after 1971, when the number of theaters peaked at 717. By 1981, only 423 remained open. Full-sized theaters continuously decreased, from 376 in 1983 to only 280 in 1987. The only exception is in total revenues, resulting from an increase of ticket prices from 300 won in 1973 to 2,500 won in 1983.

Young people, the primary targeted demographic of feature films, avoided the theaters. College students and young intellectuals prided themselves on not going to see films made in Korea. In addition, the growing popularity of television began to slice significantly into the film market. Audience apathy, strict censorship, producers' indifference to the production of domestic films, and resulting artistic and technological stagnancy put the Korean commercial film industry in a rather helpless position, completely dependent upon screen quotas for its survival.

The Transformation of the Korean Film Industry 1987–1997

The trade agreement with the U.S. government, allowing Hollywood companies to distribute their films directly to the Korean market beginning in July 1987, caused the Korean film industry to radically change every sector—production, distribution, and exhibition. The government began to lose its regulatory mechanism from the beginning of 1987, when the import quota system was finally invalidated. Anyone could take part in the production of domestic films without depositing a portion of anticipated production funds.[6] Film companies were also allowed to import foreign films without limit as long as they produced one domestic film per year.

As a result, the number of production companies showed a rapid growth—from 20 in 1984 to 113 in 1991. The number of films produced also rose—from 81 in 1984 to 87 in 1988 and 121 in 1991. In a situation where no barriers to importing films existed, most companies carried out their business lavishly without any regard to the production of domestic films. Therefore, the number of imported films soared from 25 in 1985 to 405 in 1996.

With the surge of imported films, foreign movies began to lose their scarcity value during the late 1980s. After the revocation of import quotas, the import of foreign films had become as much of a risky business as the production of domestic films. Under this new circumstance, some film companies concentrated their efforts on the production of domestic films. Their newborn enthusiasm provided a number of young directors with the chance to make films, directors whose work became known as the Korean New Wave. This new generation of filmmakers, who were mostly in their thirties, brought fresh spirit to the industry; reviving domestic production with their innovative and challenging films.

Between 1988 and 1997, many directors came to make their debuts without having worked as assistant directors under the Chungmuro[7] (studio) system, a career progression previously unheard of. Some came from a background exclusively in 16mm production, while others emerged from other art sectors.

No matter what their origin, these new filmmakers marked a turning point in Korean film, generating a more serious approach to filmmaking. Jang Sun-woo, one of the vanguard, viewed film as the most powerful political and social weapon because it could reach a mass audience while also enabling him to express himself through the artistic medium (Joo 153). Others saw film as a device of pure artistic expression, a chance to experiment with innovative ideas and film language. Lee Myung-se, one of the most creative filmmakers of the movement, viewed filmmaking as an individual expression dealing with what he presumed to be real—thoughts, dreams, and fantasies, as well as things that could be seen—without political implications (Rayns 41).

The initial impulse motivating the Korean New Wave was the realistic manifestation of contemporary society. The films were sincere, insightful reflections of what the directors perceived as the existential realities of the nation. They dealt with contemporary social issues such as political oppression, anti-Americanism, labor, and student movements. They were also concerned with the changing lives of Korean people in an increasingly modernized and industrialized society. Seoul, the largest city in the country, was portrayed by such iconography as buildings, streets, and billboards, a city of stray people whose traditional values had been rendered obsolete by the end of the agricultural era. People were presented as living in a moral vacuum where anxiety and uncertainty pervaded the atmosphere. The bleakness of the city was reflected, for example, in *A Rooster* (Shin Seung-soo 1990), the story of a middle-aged married man who is incompetent economically as well as sexually. The film presents the disappearance of meaningful interaction between family members and the dispersion of prostitution throughout the city. *The Day a Pig Fell into the Well* (Hong Sang-soo 1996) mirrors ordinary people's psychological problems of frustration, loneliness, and alienation resulting from the emptiness of interpersonal relations in modernized, metropolitan cities.

Figure 1.1. *White Badge* (Jeong Ji-yeong 1992), ordinary people and the Vietnam War.

The movement also created another trend—critical depictions of the recent past from perspectives that differed from the official history. Korean history had been either distorted by government propaganda or mystified by political taboos. Affected by *minjung*[8] literature and theology during the 1980s, historical studies became the first movement to provide the public with alternative versions of post–Korean War history. The New Wave inherited that tradition and created images of the recent past according to the experiences of ordinary people. Films such as *Southern Communist Guerrillas* (Jeong Ji-young 1990) and *The Silver Stallion* (Jang Gil-su 1992) concern forgotten stories of the Korean War, while *The Song for a Resurrection* (Lee Jung-gook 1990) and *A Petal* (Jang Sun-woo 1996) reflects on the memory of the Gwangju Uprising. *White Badge* (Jeong Ji-young 1992) and *Blue Sleeve* (Kim Yoo Vin 1993) focus on Korea's involvement in the Vietnam War.

The New Wave also concerned the lives of women within a radically transient context. The status of women mirrored the paradoxical aspects of Korean society, which is basically Confucian, but also Westernized, strongly influenced by the processes of industrialization and modernization. Films like *Because You Are a Woman* (Kim Yoo-jin 1990) and *A Dog's Afternoon* (Lee Min-yong 1995) portrayed the reality of women's oppression, as well as the struggles and dilemmas of their search for new identities. Romantic comedies like *Marriage Story* (Kim Eui-suk 1992) became extremely popular, portraying the relations between husbands and wives as egalitarian, depicting the conflict resulting from these new relationships. However, the films seldom gave radical challenge to sexual relations with a more feminist consciousness.

In addition to the shift in content, the movement also changed film form in commercial feature releases. Narrative flow was more elliptical and the connection between storylines more irregular. Plots became more ambiguous. The use of long takes, the conscious manipulation of composition in space and depth, and the mixture of dramatic fiction with documentary footage made the films even more interesting. Directors also began to develop their own diverse styles. Im Kwon-taek, actually a veteran of the cinema, developed a "Korean style" of poetic visual expressions through his depictions of bucolic and pastoral scenery of nostalgic images. In *Sopyonje* (1995), he uses a nine-minute take to follow the characters. In *The Day a Pig Fell into the Well*, director Hong presents documentarylike images of urban life with a cool detachment from the emotional identifications common in melodrama. Lee Myung-se presents dreams within dreams, crossing the border between banality and fantasy in *Gagman* (1988), as well as direct address and the connection of sequences by chapter headings in *My Love My Bride* (1990).

The New Wave made Korean films more competitive, pushing the evolution of Korean feature films. With considerable success, the directors of the movement did not have much difficulty in making films until the early 1990s. Without sacrificing intelligence or integrity, they could make commercially viable movies while raising serious political and historical issues. Their participation in the industry resulted in an excessive rise in film supply. Though it was increasingly difficult for domestic films to be screened in Seoul's first-run theaters, despite the screen quota system that reserved 121 days per year for them, the competition forced producers of domestic films to make their releases attractive works that audiences wanted to watch, because there was now no way to compensate for the loss. Kang Woo-suk, one of the leading producers as well as a popular director in the 1990s, argues that competition helped improve the quality of domestic films (Darlin 81). As a way to get good box office results, film companies began to invest more money in domestic production.

The average production cost per film grew yearly from approximately $140,000 in 1984 to $206,086 in 1990 (Kang 46).[9] In 1990, For the first time more than $1million was invested in the making of three domestic films: *Southern Communist Guerrillas*, *The General's Son* (Im Kwon-taek), and *Mayuni: The Female Terrorist from North Korea* (Shin Sang-ok). The producer of *The Taebaek Mountains*, Lee Tae-won, invested about $4 million in 1994 for the film. In the late 1990s, the average production cost per film was considered to be more than four times as much as that cost at the beginning of 1990.

After the disappearance of barriers on the importation of films, the market share of foreign films continued to increase from sixty percent in 1981 to a little higher than seventy percent in 1988. Revenues of foreign films became more than eighty percent of total box-office receipts in 1989 for the first time after the 1950s, and rose to around eight-five percent in the early 1990s. In a desperate situation where foreign films took over a sizable portion of total revenues in the film market, Korean films became more competitive without following the path of low-budget, small-risk production. The market share held by domestic films gradually began to grow from around sixteen percent in 1993 to more than twenty-five percent in 1997. Also, the number of domestic films attracting more than 100,000 admissions in Seoul went from four in 1987 to a yearly average of seven in 1989–1993, eleven in 1996, and thirteen in 1997. This new enthusiasm revived the appeal of domestic films as in the best days of the 1960s Golden Age.

In the 1980s, domestic films were generally financed by personal investments from the company owner and funds from regional distributors and, since the late 1980s, partly with money from video companies.

Supplemental money from video companies has given production companies new revenue and a chance to garner income, even when films fail to make a profit in the theater. The major financial difficulty was an inability to solicit production capital from outside investors. As a way to animate the film industry, the government transformed the film business from a service industry into a manufacturing enterprise in 1993. This created a legal base for Korean producers to finance film production by borrowing from banks. Since that year, however, banks have seldom invested in film production as their unfamiliarity with the film business makes involvement a kind of speculative enterprise.

Filmmakers then attempted to obtain money from well-endowed Korean corporations, some of which own video subsidiaries. These corporations such as Samsung, Daewoo, and Hyundai began to participate in domestic films production in the early 1990s. For instance, Samsung Entertainment Group started producing films in 1992 with *The Marriage Story*, a romantic comedy that became a number one box office success that year. This company, either partially or entirely, played a role in the production of twenty-two feature films between 1992 and 1996. Followed by Samsung, other two corporations, Daewoo and Hyundai, also became involved with the production of domestic films. As a result, these three, the largest corporations in Korea, competed for film markets, as they did in other economic areas. They never worked together for film production. Considering film production an attractive business, they just tried to initiate it in a new situation. These corporations financed nearly sixty films between 1994 and 1996. They became the primary sources for production capital until 1998, when they withdrew from film production because of economic crisis resulting from the deficiency of foreign currency.[10]

However, a few filmmakers have begun to consider film export as a crucial revenue source, starting with the success of *Why Has Bodhidharma Left for the East?* (Bae Yong-kyun 1989) in Japan and *The Gingko Bed* (Kang Je-kyu 1995) in Hong Kong. *The Gingko Bed* was the first Korean movie to become a big hit in Hong Kong and opened in more than three hundred theaters in China (Koh 51). The total revenue from film export was approximately $210,000 in 1995. It grew yearly from approximately $1,700,000 in 1996 to $3,100,000 in 1998 and $6,000,000 in 1999. *Shiri* (Kang Je-kyu 1999) was the first Korean movie to earn more than $1 million from export.

The "liberation" of the film business also changed the distribution system. Previously, the production companies generally furnished their films directly to first-run theaters in Seoul and sometimes to those in Busan. Regional distributors circulated domestic and foreign films throughout the country, except for the first-run theaters in Seoul, mostly provid-

Figure 1.2. A promotional still from the fantasy *The Ginko Bed* (Kang-Je-kyu 1995). Courtesy Pusan Film Festival.

ing advance money, called a "flat fee," to production companies. Giving a flat fee to producers, regional distributors circulated films within a designated area among six divided regions. Some distributors competed in the bounds of a region, but no single distributor circulated films over the country as a whole. Big pricing differences existed between domestic and imported movies. In the Honam and Kyungbuk areas, for instance, a foreign film earned at least $92,000, whereas domestic ones received a maximum of $16,000 (Lee 1984, 214). This method of distribution allowed the maintenance of stable profits for producers, distributors, and exhibitors.[11]

In the 1990s, however, these mechanisms were no longer sustained because the number of releases skyrocketed from 107 in 1985 to 470 in 1996. Regional distributors could not afford to take every movie released and in the process changed the pattern of business. They seldom provided producers with advance capital as they had in the 1980s and almost never bought movies before completion. The power of regional distributors was also challenged by Hollywood's direct distribution, as well as by a crop of new production companies that attempted to seek direct-distribution channels throughout the country. Although these companies did not build a firm base like that of the major Hollywood companies in the 1990s, some of them, along with foreign distribution companies such as UPI and 20th Century Fox, had already set up their lines in the six largest cities (Lim 59). Thus, the possibility of national distribution chains became more real in the late 1990s. In order to get access to more theaters, domestic companies endeavored to import more foreign films, increasing their prices. Korea was evaluated as the second largest importer in the world, buying Hollywood films with the most expensive prices in 1996 (Lim 62).

Until 1987, the most dominant pattern of distribution involved exclusively opening a film in only one theater in each metropolitan city. The government had restricted the number of prints of each film to eight, but this was invalidated in 1994 as a result of the trade negotiation with the United States in the mid-1980s. Since the late 1980s, when film releases grew to more than three times what they were in the mid-1980s, a day-and-date pattern developed, permitting the simultaneous exhibition of a film in two or three big theaters within a single metropolitan area.

Film censorship became more lenient, particularly in 1988, after the abolishment of laws requiring censorship of all scripts in the preproduction stage. Isolde Standish notes that Korean cinema was freer to address and interpret social realities through serious representations of political oppression or formerly suppressed working-class culture. The freer social and political atmosphere provided filmmakers the opportunity to rediscover a type of realism that had disappeared after the emergence of the military regime in 1961, portraying subject matter previously forbidden. Drawing on contemporary society and recent history, Korean films featured a wide range of voices within the discourse of social and political change. However, the wave of reform subsided before long; meaningful revisions to previously restrictive legislation on expression began to fade by the end of 1989.

The Public Performance Ethics Committee (PPEC)[12] continued to impede filmmaking in the late 1980s and 1990s. It approved the screening of only fifteen uncut films among 113 domestic films in 1990, fifty-one uncut films among 121 domestic films in 1991, and forty-five of ninety-six features in 1992. The stipulations of film censorship were legitimated postproduction cuts, contained in Article 13 of the Motion Picture Law, Article 18 of the Enforcement Ordinance of the Motion Picture Law, and Article 6 of the Enforcement Rule. By these stipulations, the PPEC dictated the content of domestic films. The stipulations listed in Article 13 were as follows: (1) when a film impairs the spirit of the Constitution and the dignity of the state; (2) when a film impairs social order and morals; (3) when a film impairs friendship between Korea and another country; 4) when a film impairs the soundness of the people. Other stipulations also used as the basis of censorship included the following: (1) when a film insults the president of Korea and shows contempt for the national anthem or flag; (2) when a film abets people by depicting antigovernment behavior; (3) when a film impairs social order by depicting a riot or genocide; (4) when a film vindicates the mistreatment of family members; (5) when a film impairs the spirit of the Constitution; (6) when a film does not respect judicial authority; (7) when a film depicts sexuality lasciviously through using implicit symbols such as music, costume, other performances; (8) when a film fosters sexuality through depicting sexual behavior of animals or genitalia; and (9) when a film has a vulgar title or dialogue and uses a title unrelated to the content of the film.

These stipulations were so broad and ambiguous that the censorship committee could interpret each however it wished. Most filmmakers argue that the government used censorship in order to regulate films that contained political critique rather than sensational or violent subject matter. Korean cinema was forbidden to offer sympathetic portrayals of Communists and could not present criticism of government bodies and significant political figures. Censorship prohibited domestic films from touching on the same subject matter that it approved in imported films such as *State of Siege* (Costa-Gavras 1973), *The Official Story* (Luis Puenzo 1985), or *Salvador* (Oliver Stone 1986). Whereas Koreans could watch foreign experiences of political oppression, they were not allowed to see the political oppression that existed at home. This kind of restraint made audiences consider domestic films inferior to foreign ones.

In 1997, when the majority of the Korean population adamantly demanded direct presidential elections, the PPEC forced the cutting of forty-four sections of a romance film, *What Are You Going to Do Tomorrow?* (Lee Bong-won 1987). They were especially incensed in regard to a scene between lovers, where the couple's dialogue was interpreted as antigovernment behavior because it alluded to direct elections.

Censors also endowed favored ratings to foreign films. Imported films received more generous ratings than domestic ones, mostly because the censorship committee was already hypercritical of local products. For example, most foreign action films, including *Terminator* (James Cameron 1984), *Terminator 2* (James Cameron 1991), *Total Recall* (Paul Verhoeven 1990), and the *Die Hard* series earned an "over 15" rating in Korea, although all of them had R ratings in the United States. Unlike these imported action movies, domestic action films, even with a comic approach to the world of gangsters, automatically received an over 18 rating, regardless of violence level. Hollywood films such as *Indecent Proposal* (Adrian Lyne 1993) also received an over 15 rating, although it presented much more graphic sex and female nudity than domestic films such as

That Man, That Woman (Kim Eui-suk 1993) and *Corset* (Jeong Byung-gak 1996), both rated over 18.

The PPEC proclaimed that it would expurgate sexual or violent films in order to protect juveniles, hiding its political agenda. It censored movies showing offenses against public authority or the head of the government. The PPEC deleted a scene portraying police torture of the main character in *Human Market* (Jin Yu-young 1989), in which a hero takes on American soldiers and corrupt Koreans. The PPEC also erased the face of a man in a poster for *Rachu* (Lee Bong-won 1989) even after previous approval. A politician from the ruling party, who saw the poster in the street, required the face to be erased because it mocked the former president by using an actor who looked like him. This case demonstrates the nature of film censorship in Korea where personal decisions of political authorities turned into official guidelines for film regulation.

Film censorship was officially repealed at the end of 1996, when the Supreme Court judged that postproduction cuts are illegal under the Constitution. The invalidation of film censorship resulted from the endeavors of the New Wave directors as well as the more recent filmmakers who made 16mm films about contemporary social problems. After being released from prison, they began legal struggles with the censorship committee, submitting petitions to the Supreme Court. After the revocation of forced postproduction cuts, the government transformed the PPEC into the Public Performance Promotion Association (PPPA) in 1997. Although the PPPA does not have the right to cut any part of a film, the nature of film regulation seems to be unchanged because other stipulations were still effective. In addition to four categories by age, the PPPA can give "no rating" to movies that are considered unfit for public screening, a category often used to tame filmmakers.

Conclusion

The transformation of the Korean film industry since the late 1980s has been viewed a rupture, a crisis so grave that it forced most production companies to abandon many of the practices that had virtually defined film production and distribution from the early 1960s. Not only did those companies throw away old business practices, but they also changed trends of film production to create more popular domestic films, which previously had been considered of low quality. Until the end of 1986, Korean films failed to achieve broad acclaim both within and outside of Korea. Owing to the fact that the protectionist policy was politically adulterated, the economic crisis of the industry had affected every area of the industry since the early 1970s. Even though the number of films produced was an average of more than sixty from 1973 to 1986, Koreans turned their interest away from local products. Most films did not attain box-office success and critical attention, but producers did not care about this failure because they were able to supplement their losses through their privilege to import foreign films. A film's viability as an entertainment product depends, at least in the capitalist context, on its potential to attract a fairly wide audience in the marketplace. The marketplace for Korean films did not function as a place where producers competed for financing for their film projects.

State protection and assistance had been considered necessary because of Hollywood's domination of local markets. However, the period from 1987 to 1997 shows that this continued protection would have been harmful if it had been accompanied by state intervention in production. The introduction of competition involved an active process in which producers and filmmakers were forced to make movies good enough to attract local people to the theaters, while haggling with distributors and exhibitors in a new relation. During the 1990s, they experimented with various types of films through the production of blockbusters and low-budget movies and with diverse subject matter seldom dealt with previously.

In a situation where producers could not get government-subsidized funding, the industry started to free itself from political guidelines. Even though censorship had an influence on what could be seen in public, political authorities no longer played a role in creating propaganda movies favorable to their own political agendas. Furthermore, filmmakers struggled to present more diverse portraits of life in Korea, whether it was the dark side of Korean society or the representation of social outcasts at the economic or political level.

Finally, Korean filmmakers and companies realized film's value, both as an entertainment commodity and as a medium for symbolic expression. Even though people go to be entertained, it cannot be denied that film as a cultural text is a primary arena of social contest in the production of cultural meanings. Dealing with commercial pressure and popular criticism, filmmakers presented a variety of narrative strategies, struggling to decide what to tell, how to narrate stories, and how to entertain. In a situation where they achieved an unprecedented degree of freedom in dealing with their stories, filmmakers cultivated the cultural value of Korean cinema through diverse cinematic themes.

Notes

1. General Park Chung-hee carried out a bloodless coup on May 16, 1961. He accused the civilian leadership of being corrupt, incapable of defending the

country from internal and external threats of communism, and unable to bring about economic and social transformations. Park once pledged to transfer political power to the civilian sector after the tasks of the revolution had been completed in two years, but he searched for an ideological position that would provide long-term justification for his power to extend into the future. Through oppressing democratic claims, Park succeeded in holding political power until 1979, when he was assassinated by his chief aid.

2. Realizing that there was little possibility for him to win the presidential election again through direct election, Park revised the existing constitution and set up the Yushin Constitution to make him "president for life" in 1972. The Yushin Constitution removed the limitations on his presidential terms and empowered him to make political appointments, to nominate one-third of the National Assembly members, and to issue any emergency decree he deemed necessary. It also provided for an indirect election of the president by the locally elected members of the National Conference for Unification (NCU). Since most members of the NCU came to the office under the influence of the government, his election was inevitable. The Park regime maintained power by a judicious combination of terror and privilege. The Yushin reforms pervaded almost every social sphere. Under the Emergency Decree on National Security, Park was granted power to ban any disorderly activity, such as student demonstrations and labor strikes. Practically any citizens could be arrested and jailed without a warrant if a public agent suspected them.

3. Gwangju, a city with a population of 1 million, is the capital of Jeolla province, located in the southwestern portion of Korea. Jeolla province was largely excluded from the industrialization process that took place in the 1960s and 1970s under the Park regime. Park Chung-hee, from Kyungsang province, preferred men from his own province and filled the top political and military posts with them. Chun Doo-hwan, Roh Tae-woo, and most military members who played central roles in helping Chun to take political power in 1979–1980, came from Kyungsang province. Because of already existing regional discrimination, Gwangju citizens became more critical of the emergence of the new hardline military clique, led by Chun. The Gwangju Uprising occurred in the course of General Chun Doo-hwan's seizure of power in the vacuum situation created by the assassination of President Park. Expanding emergency martial law to the entire nation on May 17, 1980, General Chun shut down the universities, intensified political censorship of the mass media, and detained most prominent political leaders. The following day, after proclaiming emergency martial law, Special Paratrooper Forces used excessive force to control the people of Gwangju City, where citizens initiated popular demonstrations against the new military regime. Faced by a series of violent civilian-military confrontations, the military finally crushed this prodemocracy movement on May 27, 1980, killing its own country's people. Gwangju's nine-day bloody riot was the most serious domestic uprising in Korea since the Korean War, because citizens had never taken up arms against their government even in the most repressive days of Park Chung-hee. Also, it was the first time since the end of the Korean War that Korean troops had turned guns against their own civilians under government order. A variety of contradictory

accounts and analyses of the incident have appeared since 1980, but a day-by-day recounting of the uprising, drawn from previously unpublished eyewitness accounts, contradicts both the official government report and many of the contemporary press accounts. Therefore, the exact number of people who died in the period of the Gwangju Uprising is still unclear. According to the government, 191 people lost their lives during this civil uprising. Other sources report from 300 to 2,000 deaths (Warnberg 46). By this incident most Koreans revealed the emotional disapproval of the Chun government throughout his presidency. Also, the Gwangju Uprising in 1980 has been perceived as a turning point for questioning American roles in Korea. By the end of the 1970s anti-Americanism was virtually invisible, and the Korean people were engrossed with an absolutely positive view of the United States, because of the U.S. role both as protector of Korea in the Cold War confrontation and as its main source of economic aid. However, this image changed at the beginning of the 1980s, because most dissidents in Korea thought the U.S. government to be complicitous in the Gwangju Massacre and to be the active supporter of Chun's military regime. In the street, therefore, it was common to see antigovernment protesters yelling, "Yankee, Go Home!" throughout the 1980s. On the Gwangju Uprising and its relation to anti-Americanism, see Clark, Cumings, and Jaekyung Lee.

4. Through the revision of the Enforcement Ordinance in the 1970s and 1980s, the government continued to relax the conditions necessary for the maintenance of companies' licenses. The minimum production number of domestic films was ten in 1975; eight in 1976; six in 1978; three in 1979; four in 1981; three in 1985; one in 1986.

5. The Golden Bell Film Festival has been regarded as the most prestigious film festival in Korea since 1962, the year when the Park regime organized it to encourage and financially reward domestic films.

6. The Korean government promulgated the Fifth Amended Motion Picture Law on December 31, 1984, after promising to open the film market for direct distribution by Hollywood companies in the next three years. The new, revised film law allowed independent filmmakers to make domestic films, but film production was not fully liberated in 1985. Production companies not only were compelled to deposit 50 million won at a time when they got a license, but they also had to deposit 10 percent of anticipated production money with the MPPC before shooting a film.

7. *Chungmuro* is a term referring to Korea's version of Hollywood.

8. *Minjung* literally denotes ordinary people but becomes a symbolic term for oppressed people. For a discussion of the characteristics of the *minjung* discourse, see Nancy Abelmann (20–38).

9. It is very difficult to calculate the average cost for the production of films in Korea because most companies just make one or two movies per year, and producers are reluctant to give exact figures because they are related to taxes. Tax evasion seems to be a natural phenomenon for film production companies as well as theater owners. In 1996, two powerful people in the film industry were jailed for tax evasion and bribery. Koh commented that this might put the entire Korean film industry on trial (32–33).

10. Faced by the possibility of national default owing to the deficiency of foreign currency, the Korean economy faltered and finally requested a bailout from the International Monetary Fund (IMF) on November 23, 1997. Using a $134 billion U.S. loan borrowed from the IMF in the following year, the newly inaugurated government under Kim Dae-jung helped Korea to recover economic stability and finally succeeded in repaying every penny to the IMF in September 1999.

11. When the fourth amended film law was in effect, producers usually compensated regional distributors' losses if a film did not make an adequate profit. One Korean producer called this operation "faithful behavior." This was regarded as a natural action before the invalidation of legal regulations on film production and importation (Lee 570).

12. Emphasizing the PPEC as a civilian body, the government claimed that it did not control the PPEC. Analyzing the Korean film industry in the 1980s, John Lent mentions that the PPEC was "autonomous, even though it was subsidized by the Ministry" (137). Like any other bureaucratic apparatus in Korea, however, the PPEC was operated under the control of the government (Joo 86–91). The president of the PPEC was selected by the Minister of Culture and Arts. The PPEC was administered by the Ministry of Culture and Arts. It was required to submit its reports on operations to a department in the Ministry of Culture and Arts. Out of eleven members responsible for film censorship, four members were public officials. As a bureaucratic apparatus, the PPEC was just a body of civil servants who were employed to help administer the affairs of the state. Its duty was to augment official power.

Works Cited

Abelmann, Nancy. *Echoes of the Past, Epics of Dissent: A South Korean Social Movement.* Berkeley: University of California Press, 1996.

Article 19 (The International Center on Censorship). "South Korea." *Information Freedom and Censorship*. Chicago: American Library Association, 1991. 187–92.

Berry, Chris. "Introducing "Mr. Monster." *Post-Colonial Classics of Korean Cinema.* Ed. Chungmoo Choi. Irvine, CA: Korean Film Festival Committee at the University of California at Irvine, 1998. 39–47.

Clark, Donald N. *The Kwangju Uprising: Shadows over the Regime in South Korea.* Boulder: Westview, 1988.

Cumings, Bruce. *Divided Korea: United Future.* Ithaca, NY: Foreign Policy Association, 1995.

Darlin, Damon. "Hollywood on the Han." *Forbes* October 10, 1994: 81–82.

Joo, Jinsook. "Constraints on Korean National Film." Doctoral dissertation, University of Texas at Austin, 1990.

Kang Bying-kyu. "A Study of the Change on the Korean Film Industry in the 1980s." Master's thesis, Seoul National University, 1991.

Koh, Chik-mann. "Korea Launches Probe into U.S. Distribs." *Variety* February 17, 1997: 32–33.

———. "Korea's Profile Raised by SEG (Samsung Entertainment Group)." *Variety* May 12, 1997: 51–52.

Korea Cinema Yearbook. 1989–1999. Seoul: The Korean Motion Picture Promotion Association.

Lee, Jaekyung. "Anti-Americanism in South Korea: The Media and the Politics of Signification." Doctoral dissertation, University of Iowa, 1993.

Lee Myung-won. "A Study of Structure of Distribution and a Reformation Plan." *The Thesis Collection of Korean Academy of Fine Arts*. Seoul: Motion Picture Promotion Corporation, 1984.

Lee Tae-Won. "Chungmuro People as Visionaries Holding Great Self-respect." *ShinDong* July 1995: 568–81.

Lee Young-il. *The History of Korean Cinema*. Trans. Richard L. Greever. Seoul: Motion Picture Promotion Corporation, 1988.

Lent, John A. "South Korea." *The Asian Film Industry*. Austin: University of Texas Press, 1990.

Lim Hye-won. "A Case Study on the Production of A Local Film by the Big Corporation." Master's thesis, Jung Ang University, 1997.

The Public Performance Ethics Committee, censorship minutes on *Naeileun Mueol Halgeoni and Guro Aryrang*, submitted to the annual supervision of the legislator to the government in 1989.

Rayns, Tony. *Seoul Stirring: 5 Korean Directors*. London: Institute of Contemporary Arts, 1995.

Son Young-moon. "A Personal Note on Chungmuro." *The Course of Korean Film Policy and Its New Prospect*. Ed. Jin-Yong Choi. Seoul, Korea: Jipmundang, 1994. 261–76.

Standish, Isolde. "Korean Cinema and the New Realism: Text and Context." *Colonialism and Nationalism in Asian Cinema*. Ed. Wimal Dissanayake. Bloomington: Indiana University Press, 1994. 65–89.

Warnberg, Tim. "The Kwangju Uprising: An Inside View." *Korean Studies* 11 (1997): 33–57.

2

Darcy Paquet

Christmas in August and Korean Melodrama

In early 1998, as the Korean film industry was experiencing the first stirrings of what was to develop into a creative and commercial boom, director Hur Jin-ho released a muted, tragic-themed melodrama titled *Christmas in August*. The story of a photographer with a terminal illness, the film was characterized by its director as a meditation on death in "warm tones." Eschewing the high drama and suspense of typical melodrama, the film sought instead to move audiences with its minute observations of ordinary scenes. In this and other ways the film's style and narrative departed from the traditional formulas employed by local melodramas; nonetheless the film proved an enduring popular and critical success. As Korean cinema entered the twenty-first century, it was apparent that this film's influence had helped to transform the aesthetic of contemporary Korean melodrama.

Melodrama, in all its various forms, has long been a staple of Korean film, and indeed Asian cinema as a whole. Audiences have supported the genre with consistency, while film studios have made it a cornerstone of their output, due in part to the low cost of producing such works. Although often undervalued by critics, melodrama has nonetheless contributed to Korean cinema some of its most challenging and unique works,

Figure 2.1. *Christmas in August* (Hur Jin-ho 1998). Courtesy Pusan Film Festival.

from the manic family dramas of Kim Ki-young[1] to epic histories directed by Im Kwon-taek. Yet even the more simplistic, commercially driven Korean melodramas serve to illustrate some of the defining features of Korean films and the societal context in which they are produced.

For many viewers, *Christmas in August* may come across as a moving but uncontroversial portrait of a man grappling with knowledge of his impending death. As the protagonist spends time with family, meets with friends, and prints photographs for customers, the audience sees nothing discordant and little out of the ordinary. Yet it is precisely in its embrace of the ordinary that *Christmas in August* has proved to be so influential. For a genre defined in part by hyperbole and the explicit foregrounding of good and evil, Hur's film has provided a soft-spoken challenge.

Christmas in August: An Introduction

Christmas in August is the debut work of director/screenwriter Hur Jin-ho, who had worked previously as an assistant director under Park Kwang-su for such films as *To the Starry Island* (1993) and *A Single Spark* (1996) and as a co-writer for *A Single Spark*. Hur locates the inspiration for this film in a visit to the funeral of a musician, where the traditional memorial photograph[2] featured the deceased in a broad smile. It was this juxtaposition between death and happiness that led him to write the screenplay, he said.

After completing the screenplay, Hur requested the collaboration of his former teacher at the Korean Academy of Film Arts, cinematographer Yoo Young-kil. The focus of a retrospective at the 1998 Pusan International Film Festival, Yoo had worked extensively in the industry and acquired a reputation for his attention to detail. As cinematographer, Yoo reportedly contributed a great deal to the aesthetics of the film, foregrounding the collaborative nature of this work. Yoo passed away shortly after viewing the finished print, but anecdotal evidence suggests that he was pleased with the outcome.

The film features two of Korea's most marketable actors, Han Seok-gyu, who had starred in previous box-office hits *The Gingko Bed* (1996) and *The Contact* (1997), and Shim Eun-ha, who was well known for her roles in television drama. This star power likely influenced the film's successful run at the box office, where it sold 422,930 tickets in Seoul, placing fourth among Korean films released in 1998.[3] After its successful theatrical run the film was invited to screen in the International Critics Week section of the 1998 Cannes International Film Festival, followed thereafter by sales deals to Japan and Hong Kong. In the latter territory the film opened in the Hong Kong Art Center on August 13, 1999, at one screening per day, but its popularity led to a full commercial release at Broadway Cinematheque from September 30 to November 24. The total fifty-six days of screening, quite high for a non-Hollywood, nonlocal feature, amounted to $795,000 H.K.[4]

The film opens with a shot of the protagonist, Jung-won, waking up to the sounds of a school loudspeaker in the background. After cutting to a scene of him driving past the school on his motor scooter, we find ourselves in a hospital waiting room, where he makes faces at a sick child, trying to cheer him up. Although the nature of the protagonist's terminal disease is not revealed at any point in the film, death is invoked early in a first-person voiceover in which Jung-won tells of his mother's passing when he was a child. These juxtapositions of death and childhood in the film's opening scenes establish early mortality as one of the story's key themes. This mortality, further reinforced by a subsequent scene at the funeral of a father's friend, is also reflected in the film's title (the director likens an early death to the disorientation one would feel if one year Christmas were to fall in August).

Having established this theme, the film then introduces the other of its two main characters. Dar-im is a meter reader who comes to Jung-won's photo shop to develop pictures of traffic violators. She becomes a regular at his studio, and the two gradually become friends. Although

Jung-won and Dar-im become increasingly close throughout the film, Jung-won shields her from knowledge of his illness, and she never finds out that he is sick.

The film's narrative follows a simple progression, consisting mainly of Jung-won's time spent with Dar-im interspersed with scenes with family, friends, and customers at the photo shop. Particularly crucial are the scenes with Jung-won's father and sister. Both know of his disease, and their concern is implicit in their actions, although seldom spoken outright. In contrast to the scenes with Dar-im, these episodes foreground Jung-won's mortality and place his illness in the context of the family and his mother's death. Another noteworthy scene occurs when an old woman comes to Jung-won's studio for a portrait. She tells him that the portrait will be used for the memorial photograph in her funeral, and Jung-won's efforts to make the portrait a success recall his own mortality.

As the film nears its end, Jung-won is suddenly taken ill and rushed to the hospital. Dar-im, meanwhile, learns that she is to be transferred to another district, and unaware of Jung-won's situation, she waits in vain for him in front of his studio. After several days she leaves without seeing him, and an undetermined amount of time later Jung-won returns to his studio and discovers a note from her. Now conscious that he is about to die, he prepares himself before catching one last glimpse of Dar-im through the window of a cafe. In his last scene, he takes a self-portrait, the image of which dissolves into the memorial photograph at his funeral.

The final scene of the film takes place in the winter, when Dar-im stops by Jung-won's studio once again. The doors are locked, but when she looks in the window display she sees a portrait of herself, taken by Jung-won earlier in the year. The film ends with Dar-im's smile, together with a voiceover from Jung-wan, thanking her for her unspoken love.

Melodrama and Asia

Christmas in August does not strike the viewer as an unconventional film; yet on closer reflection it is difficult to find other works that are quite like it. If one were to compare it to Hollywood melodramas, one would likely find that many of the film's stylistic and narrative elements set it apart from dominant traditions. Yet in many ways, *Christmas in August* can be read as a specifically Asian form of melodrama.

The word melodrama originally stems from the Greek word *melos*, meaning music. Although definitions of melodrama differ, most would characterize it as a genre that employs hyperbole and emotional excess to evoke pathos in its viewers. Traditionally the form concerns itself with

Figure 2.2. Jung-won's self portrait . . .

Figure 2.3. . . . dissolves into . . .

Figure 2.4. . . . his memorial photograph.

explicit portrayals of innocence and evil, often in the realm of heterosexual romance, family troubles, or scandalous behavior. They have long been viewed as catering to women more than men, leading to derogative terms such as "weepies" or "women's' films."

In Western countries, one of the most influential academic studies on film melodrama is Thomas Elsaesser's "Tales of Sound and Fury: Observations on the Family Melodrama." Elsaesser notes two primary sources for the developments that would lead to melodrama: the late medieval morality play, grouped together with oral narratives and fairy tales (primarily in their use of the story's action to create an overall narrative structure, rather than foregrounding the characters' psychological motivations); and more significantly, the postrevolutionary romantic drama, which in turn grew out of the eighteenth-century sentimental novel. The romantic drama's focus on private feelings and questions of morality form the basis for a kind of restrictive "pressure" that is placed on the characters in the story. This pressure drives the characters to certain actions, but what is more important, it shapes the manner in which the melodrama interacts with its viewers. Elsaesser contends that melodrama, with its inherent links to music, is primarily a question of style and punctuation. Utilizing dramatic reversals in mood and the characters' yearnings for the unattainable, melodrama manipulates its narrative pressure to punctuate the actions of its plot and to bring out longing and pathos in its viewers.

More recently, Linda Williams has argued convincingly for a reconceptualization of melodrama, maintaining that rather than being a minor genre, melodrama is in fact a dominant influence in Hollywood film. Although family melodramas and so-called woman's films have remained at the fringes of American cinema, Williams argues that the emotional and moral registers embedded in mainstream Hollywood film make up part of an overarching melodramatic mode. Although Hollywood films may employ seemingly realistic effects, they are melodramatic in the sense that audiences are made to feel sympathy for protagonists (victims) who struggle with forces that overpower them. At the same time this mode is greatly concerned with the staging of innocence, and it finds resonance in an American cinema that, often hypocritically, portrays its host culture as a wellspring of virtue and innocence.

In Asia, meanwhile, filmmakers have generally utilized different traditions to shape the genre they call "melodrama." Although Western melodrama has exerted a major influence on Asian film, the differences between Western and Asian melodrama are worthy of mention.

In his introduction to *Melodrama and Asian Cinema*, Wimal Dissanayake observes that no Asian language contains a native equivalent to the literary term *melodrama*. Those words that do exist today are based on the Western word, or, like the Korean term *choeryumul* (weepies),[5] were coined in the twentieth century. Nonetheless many of Asia's ancient literary and theatrical genres bear a resemblance to Western melodramatic forms. Through contact with the West, Asian languages have come to adopt the foreign word, and Asian filmmakers have since found it to be a useful term to describe their works. Nonetheless, the word 'melodrama' invokes a different set of associations in Asia than it does in Europe or North America.

One such difference observed by Wimal Dissanayake involves the issue of suffering. He argues that Asian films and other artworks portray suffering as being integral to life, a necessary condition for individual enlightenment. When film protagonists find salvation, it is often through the insights and understandings brought about by suffering:

> [T]he concept of suffering is pivotal to the discourse of film melodrama in Asian cultures. We need to bear in mind the fact that most Asian cultures valorize human suffering as a pervasive fact of life and that salvation is a liberatory experience emanating from the insights into the nature and ineluctability of human suffering. Hence the metaphysical understanding of suffering becomes the condition of possibility for participating in the meaning of life. Suffering and the ensuing pathos are commonly found in Western melodrama as well; however, their place in and significance to Asian film melodrama are considerably different. (4)

Thomas Elsaesser also broaches the issue of suffering in his essay, "Tales of Sound and Fury"; however he describes it as a diminishing force in the Western melodrama. "Melodrama confers on [its protagonists] a negative identity through suffering, and the progressive self-immolation and disillusionment generally ends in resignation: they emerge as lesser beings for having become wise and acquiescent to the ways of the world" (177).

Within Korean culture the concept of 'suffering' is partly captured in the word *han*, which is difficult to translate into English, although it bears some similarity to the Russian word *toska*. Essentially han is the suffering or hardship that accumulates over time and that remains unexpressed in the speaker's heart. The emotion is perhaps most famously portrayed in Im Kwon-taek's 1993 film *Sopyonje* about a singer who is taught the local art of *pansori* by her stepfather. "Your *pansori* is smooth, but it lacks *han*," he tells her. "A person's *han* is accumulated in the chest through living. The act of living is to accumulate *han*, and *han* cannot be separated from life." Many Koreans consider *han* to be a distinguishing characteristic of Korean culture.

Dissanayake argues that another crucial aspect of Asian melodrama is its portrayal of the self in relation to the family. Generally in Western melodramas the family is of interest inasmuch as it provides a context for the portrayal of the individual. In Asian melodramas, however, the family is often the focus of interest. "To phrase it differently," Dissanayake writes, "in Western melodramas it is the individual self in relation to family that is explored, whereas in Asian melodramas it is the familial self that is the focus of interest" (4). These are two of the differences we should keep in mind when analyzing melodramas from Asia and from Korea in particular.

An Overview of Korean Melodrama

Ever since production of the first Korean film in 1919, melodrama has served as a dominant genre in the industry. Although little remains of the silent and sound films produced before the Korean War (destruction brought on by the war has eliminated virtually all of Korea's early film history), written and oral records point to a dynamic and popular genre emerging in tandem with the very first Korean films.

In the introduction to her book *What Is Melodrama?* film scholar Gina Yu points to several early influences that led to the genesis and development of Korean melodrama. One is the introduction through Japanese rule of the theatrical form *shinpa* (Japanese: *shimpa*). Originating in Japan in the late 1880s, two decades after the Meiji Restoration, and subsequently introduced to Korea via local theater troupes in 1910, *shinpa* adapted the forms of Western melodrama to appeal to local audiences. This form of theater became widespread by the 1920s, and its popularity continued unabated even after the liberation of Korea from Japan in 1945. Initially, the plots of most *shinpa* lay within the realm of social melodrama, but subsequent development led the genre to concentrate more on romance or scandalous tales. Contemporary intellectuals derided the works for their escapist character and their overly individualistic plots, which often clashed with the tenets of Confucianism;[6] nonetheless, the plays had considerable popular appeal and an enduring influence on early film.

Korean melodrama also drew largely on native Korean narrative and theatrical forms. Many of the most popular early films were adaptations of traditional folk tales and *pansori* (an oral narrative poetry expressed in song, as portrayed in director Im Kwon-taek's films *Sopyonje* and *Chunhyang* (2000). The pansori tale *Song of Chunhyang*, with its sentimental valorization of a wife's fidelity to her husband, has been filmed over a dozen times in the course of Korean film history, notably as Korea's first sound film in 1935, and again as a hugely popular feature in 1955 that was credited with reviving the local film industry after the war. During the early part of the twentieth century a new theatrical form known as *changguk* was adapted from *pansori* to the stage, and although it never rose to the level of popularity enjoyed by *shinpa*, it continued to be staged in various revivals up to the 1960s, when competition from the cinema finally overpowered the form (Kim Hung-gyu, 130)

Last, following the end of World War II, the U.S. occupation of Korea led for the first time to the mass distribution of Hollywood films in Korea. With the works achieving a high level of popularity among viewers, the Hollywood genre system also exerted its influence on a new generation of filmmakers. Chung Ji-young's 1994 film *Life and Death of the Hollywood Kid* provides an interesting depiction of the influence of early Hollywood films on children of this generation.

There existed much common ground between *shinpa* and native Korean narrative forms. Yu outlines some of the key features shared by the two, many of which have proved enduring in the development of local cinema and television: (1) most plots revolved around a heterosexual love story; (2) the key conflict in the narrative was brought about by trouble due to class differences, problems with money, or alternatively by a cruel act committed by a third character; (3) the stories were structured so as to arouse empathy in their viewers; (4) the narrative would end either in triumph (the hero would become a new person, or go to the United States to study) or a fall in the face of adversity; (5) the male protagonist exhibited some form of power (being highly educated or from a powerful family), while the female protagonist came from lower echelons of society: either a poor young woman, a *kisaeng* (equivalent to the Japanese geisha) or a sexually threatening 'modern woman,' who would in the course of the story submit to the power of the male protagonist; (6) the ideological space of the narrative would often occupy the middle ground between modern and traditional values; and (7) most narratives would not actively push for social change, working instead within the dictates of Confucian society (Yu, 19).

As Korean film melodrama developed from the 1920s up to the dawn of the twenty-first century, the form displayed various trends in terms of subject matter and its embrace of social issues, but most works continued to be shaped from the traditions outlined above.

During the Japanese occupation (1910–1945), widespread poverty and the oppressive strictures of Japanese rulers led many viewers to turn toward melodrama as a kind of catharsis. Na Un-gyu's classic silent film *Arirang* (1926)[7] depicted an insane man's killing of an informer to the Japanese police. Contemporary observers describe the crowd's passionate reaction to the film and the anti-Japanese sentiments it stirred. Many of the films of this time period thus dealt with issues of poverty and unjust authority.

The outbreak of World War II and then the Korean War each effectively shut down the film industry for a number of years, but from the mid-1950s Korean cinema began to experience its first boom.[8] Melodramas of this time period focused on two primary themes: modernization and the issue of "free love." Both were portrayed as the result of Westernization, particularly the latter in its depiction of the destructive influence of strong, independent women. *Madame Freedom* from 1956 was one of the top two grossing films of the decade, and its portrayal of a woman who leaves her family to pursue romance sparked widespread notoriety and scandal. It is also worth noting that whereas melodramas of the past often took place in the countryside, by the 1950s they were firmly grounded in the city.

The 1960s led to a time of greater political and economic upheaval, and in this decade family melodramas reached the peak of their popularity. Often highlighting the economic struggles and class differences that divided society, 1960s melodramas showed a much greater tendency to portray social issues. With the advent of the 1970s, a low point for the film industry and the mood of society in general, melodramas often revolved around women who served alcohol or worked as prostitutes.

The 1980s saw a relaxation of censorship, and with it came a trickle of social-themed work as well as a boom in soft pornography. While the latter tended to portray innocent women in compromising situations, social melodramas often focused on contemporary issues such as Korea's rapid development and the effect this had on the poor. By the advent of the 1990s, audiences were turning more toward romantic comedies and action pictures (which nonetheless contained a degree of melodramatic elements), and melodrama as a genre appeared to be languishing in terms of its development. When *Christmas in August* premiered in early 1998, it seemed to be pointing toward a new possible conception of melodrama.

Tales of the Ordinary

In its subject matter—a virtuous hero stricken with disease, forced to part too soon from a loved one—*Christmas in August* differs little from countless melodramas of the past. Yet in terms of its construction, the film has in many ways initiated a new kind of narrative in contemporary Korean melodrama.

In her essay "Melodrama Revised," Linda Williams analyzes D. W. Griffith's *Way Down East* (1920) and notes five features of the film that are as central to melodrama today as they were in the era of silent film. These features, identified by Williams (52–60), have largely remained relevant for Korean cinema as well:

1. Melodrama begins, and wants to end, in a space of innocence.

2. Melodrama focuses on victim-heroes and the recognition of their virtue.

3. Melodrama appears modern by borrowing from realism, but realism serves the melodramatic passion and action.

4. Melodrama involves a dialectic of passion and action—a give and take of "too late" and "in the nick of time."

5. Melodrama presents characters who embody primary psychic roles organized in Manichaean conflicts between good and evil.

While *Christmas in August* incorporates the first three of the above features, it departs from melodramatic tradition in deemphasizing the fourth and fifth elements. In fact, a withholding of the fifth feature had already become common in late-1990s Korean melodrama, due perhaps in part to the collapse of South Korea's authoritarian government, which had long advocated the use of simplistic moral frameworks in film through strict governmental censorship. Beginning with the Korean New Wave of the 1980s, and becoming increasingly common by the late-1990s, filmmakers could give their works a more modern feel by breaking down dichotomies between good and evil. Two popular melodramas released in 1997, *The Contact* (Chang Yoon-hyun) and *The Letter* (Lee Jeong-kuk), both shun the use of an explicit villain in the construction of their narratives.

Christmas in August, however, was groundbreaking in that the film makes very little use of the tension created by near misses and "in the nick of time." From the opening scenes of the film, Jung-won is never given any hope for recovery. There are no failed attempts to cure his (unnamed) disease, nor is the viewer even shown any symptoms or the progression of his illness. With his impending death never in doubt, the film's drama thus operates in the psychological, rather than the physical (or medical), realm.

Yet even in this psychological realm, the makers of the film largely abstain from the emotional drama that can be created by the "nick of time." Dar-im remains ignorant of Jung-won's disease throughout the course of the film, and although Jung-won writes her a letter shortly before his death, he files it in a box on his desk rather than sending it. As viewers, we are denied the emotional release that would exist if Dar-im learned of his illness shortly before or after his death. In contrast to other late-1990s melodramas such as *The Letter*, noted above, or *A Promise* (Kim Yu-jin 1998), *Christmas in August* avoids staging any farewell scenes.

Whereas melodramas of the past often reveled in excess and the high drama of last-minute discoveries, Hur Jin-ho's film finds its strength in the details of everyday life. Many of the film's most memorable scenes revolve around ordinary events or seemingly unimportant details. It is important that the emotion contained within these scenes comes not from the events themselves but from the tension caused by viewers' knowledge of Jung-won's mortality. In one example, Jung-won's frustration in teaching his father how to use a VCR comes to represent for the viewer his pain in facing an impending separation from his father. Thus events of seemingly little importance make up the foundation of the narrative, and major events in the characters' lives can thus be omitted from the plot without any loss of dramatic impact.

Subsequent filmmakers appear to have been greatly influenced by *Christmas in August*'s deemphasizing of plot to focus on the ordinary. In the first third of *Bungee Jumping of Their Own* (2001), director Kim Dae-seung portrays a developing relationship in a piecemeal style that avoids the emotional staging associated with melodrama, instead presenting isolated scenes that reveal aspects of the characters' feelings. The viewer is denied a complete view of the relationship, but in watching these scenes the viewer is given hints of the emotions that hold the two characters together.

In *I Wish I Had a Wife* (2001), director Park Heung-sik, who served as one of four assistant directors for *Christmas in August*, adopts the latter film's focus on detail in presenting a romantic comedy. Main actor Sul Kyoung-gu spoke of his frustration during filming:

> I admit I became annoyed when director Park Heung-sik would fuss over the smallest details. I thought, do I really have to bother with this kind of thing? The major aspects of my role he would say, "Just do whatever you want," but he constantly stressed over details. However, later when I watched the completed film I realized that those trivial moments were the film's real strength." (Kim Yong-eon 145–49)

In comparing contemporary Korean melodramas to their counterparts in other genres, one finds that the features outlined above by Williams can often more easily be found in recent action or fantasy films. Blockbusters such as *Shiri* (Kang Je-kyu 1999) or *Bichunmoo* (Kim Yung-jun 2000) rely much more heavily on nick-of-time escapes and strong dichotomies between good and evil to move viewers. In many ways, the contemporary Korean films that are labeled as melodramas depart much further from melodramatic norms than films in other genres.

Photography as Style

Apart from its narrative elements, *Christmas in August* also broke new ground in Korean cinema in terms of its visual style. The film appeared at a time in Korean film history when increased technology and equipment, together with the completion of a new center for filmmaking, the Seoul Studio Complex, resulted in a newer, more "glossy" look for Korean feature films. With this change noticed and supported by viewers, filmmakers of the time possessed a unique opportunity to create a new aesthetic for Korean film.

The visual style of *Christmas in August* was a collaborative effort among director Hur Jin-ho, cinematographer Yoo Young-kil, lighting director Kim Dong-ho, and art director Kim Jin-han, famous within Korean independent film circles for his award-winning 1997 short film *Crack of the Halo*. In many ways the result of their work appears to have been influenced both by the narrative elements of the film and by the aesthetics of photography.

In an interview conducted in 1998, Hur discussed the look Yoo had wished to achieve in the film. "In *Christmas in August*, cars passed by many times in the scenes where Han Suk Kyu [*sic*] is sitting in his studio. There was a lot of reflected sunlight passing by him. One time when we were drinking, we were sitting by a window and he suddenly said, 'The feeling when light passes by in a flash—we'd better show this heartwarming feeling bit by bit in this film' " (200). Much of *Christmas in August* is suffused with a sort of warm glow, echoing the director's words when he described the film as a meditation on death "in warm tones" (200). As such the film avoids excessive use of high-contrast lighting. In many ways this aesthetic decision also reflects the type of narrative employed. Whereas many melodramas in the past utilized strong contrasts between good and evil, happiness and sadness (for which high-contrast lighting would provide a visual counterpart to the narrative), Hur's film provides more subtle shadings of these themes. The film's visual style thus reflects the film's major departure from traditional melodramas.[9]

Photography provides another overlap between the film's aesthetics and narrative. Hur Jin-ho has located the inspiration for this film in a photograph, and the medium of photography also ties in with the themes of the work. Jung-won works as a photographer, and his interaction with customers (including Dar-im) make up many of the scenes in the film.

Apart from being his profession, photography also extends into his home and personal life. His father used to work as a photographer (which we learn during the taking of a family portrait), and as Jung-won nears death he leaves his father operating instructions for the newer equipment in his shop. Jung-won also takes pictures of friends for his own personal pleasure, and the display in front of his shop contains a photograph of a woman he once loved as a student. Significantly, this photograph is replaced with a picture of Dar-im by the end of the film.

The qualities of photography in general also appear to have served as a model for the film's aesthetics. Photography, like film, is a medium presented in two dimensions, however it is a static form, and one possessing a different relation to time. Whereas film is capable of presenting an event in time, photography freezes and preserves a moment for posterity. Thus photography often serves as a site of remembrance, presented perhaps most vividly in the form of memorial portraits at a funeral.

Hur's insistence on little camera movement reflects in many ways the static qualities of photography. During shooting, Hur resisted pressure from cinematographer Yoo Young-kil to increase the amount of camera movement. "He really had a hard time with it," said Hur. "He told me, 'It's so plain that it isn't interesting' " (204). Nonetheless, the minimal camera movement employed evokes in many ways the stillness of photographs. The film's narrative focus also supports this aesthetic decision, in that a plot focused mostly on details involves a kind of stillness in thematic development. The viewer in a sense becomes like a person scanning a photograph for details. Narratives driven by major events, in contrast, produce thematic movement that is often supported by physical movements of the camera.

The two-dimensional nature of photography is also reflected in the film's style, in that a surprisingly large number of the film's scenes are shot through windows. One example is when Dar-im and Jung-won hold a mimed conversation through the window of his shop. Alternate turns of conversation are filmed by shot/reverse shot through the plate glass window so that each character is always seen from behind a window pane. This gives the impression of the characters each being a living portrait, matted and framed together with a sheet of glass. Other examples include the visit of Jung-won's old girlfriend to his studio (at which time he is washing the window), Jung-won's last view of Dar-im at the end of the film (when he touches her image as seen through the window of a coffee shop), and the final scene with Dar-im, when she sees her photograph through the window. Notably, the scene that represents the end of Dar-im and Jung-won's friendship is punctuated by her throwing a rock through the window of his studio. The image of Dar-im's face in this scene is divided in two by the remaining shards of the window.

In many ways Dar-im functions in the narrative as a photograph, in that by the film's end she comes to represent a visual site of remembrance and meaning for Jung-won. This can be seen in his act of photographing her and eventually in his decision to replace the photograph in his display with her picture. Dar-im also undergoes a gradual transformation in appearance, first by stopping by the studio on her off hours, when she is not wearing her uniform, and then by starting (to Jung-won's surprise) to wear makeup. Her character's visual transformation parallels the added significance attached to her image as Jung-won begins to see her as signifying the beauty of life. If Jung-won's memorial portrait serves as a site of remembrance for the mourners at his funeral, then Dar-im's image serves Jung-won as a memory representing the life he must leave. The final words of the film, spoken by Jung-won in voiceover, echo this sentiment: "I knew that someday love would become nothing but a memory, like the countless photographs left behind in my recollections. But you alone have remained a part of me. I leave these words to thank you for letting me depart with your love."

In this way, many of the film's visual qualities reinforce the narrative elements outlined above. Although the setting of the film in Kunsan, a provincial city on the southwest coast of Korea, provides a somewhat "ordinary" backdrop for the story,[10] the film's warm lighting and meticulous cinematography bring out a beauty in its everyday setting that reflects the narrative's search for meaning in the ordinary.

Conclusion

Christmas in August appeared just as the Korean film industry was experiencing a major upheaval. As the 1997 Asian financial crisis led to the exit from the film industry of Korea's *chaebol* (large conglomerates), Korean cinema was forced to find a way to reinvent itself economically. Venture capital quickly came to replace the *chaebol* as Korean film's main source of finance, and a younger generation of directors and producers moved into the industry, poised to reinvent the style and substance of Korea's film output. *Christmas in August* thus served as one of the first films to push for an aesthetic renewal in the industry.

Korean filmmakers in the late 1990s sought to distance themselves from the films of the previous decade. After the weakness shown by the Korean film industry in the early and midnineties (local market share dipped to as low as 16% in 1993),[11] filmmakers were anxious to create a new look for their products to attract audience members. At the same time, a power struggle was underway in such organizations as the government-supported Korean Motion Picture Promotion Corporation (KMPPC) between younger and older generations of filmmakers. Younger directors were thus given additional incentive to differentiate themselves from the cinematic traditions of the past.

One of the key means of achieving this goal proved to be experimentation with genre.[12] The dominant genres of past years, comedy and melodrama, which had proved both popular with audiences and inexpensive to shoot, were losing ground to increased competition from Hollywood and other foreign features. Thus, Korean filmmakers found that by blending and bending existing genres, they could create works that appealed to audiences who wanted something new. Some prominent examples of this kind of film include *Shiri*,[13] an action melodrama that broke existing box-office records; *The Quiet Family* (1998), a horror comedy by popular director Kim Jee-woon; and *Nowhere to Hide* (Lee Myung-se 1999),[14] an action art film that outgrossed Western blockbusters *Notting Hill* (Roger Mitchell 1999) and *Austin Powers* (Jay Roach 1997).

Christmas in August, rather than blending genres, sought to reinvent the genre of melodrama. It accomplished this in large measure by its departures in narrative and aesthetics from the traditions established by past melodramas. In doing so, the film found meaning and beauty in spaces that Korean cinema had previously overlooked. Thus Jung-won's struggle to accept his mortality, his discovery of life's beauty through Dar-im, and his final attainment of enlightenment serve as a kind of metaphor for the changes wrought by this quiet film on the traditions of Korean melodrama.

Notes

1. For more on Kim Ki-young and his contributions to Korean cinema, see Chris Berry, "Scream and Scream Again: Korean Modernity as a House of Horrors in the Films of Kim Ki-young," chapter 5 in this anthology.

2. In many Asian cultures it is traditional to place in the middle of the funeral display a photograph of the deceased, adorned with two black sashes.

3. Source: Korean Film Commission.

4. Hong Kong Motion Picture Industry Association. Thanks to Ryan Law for providing me with this information.

5. Kim Soyoung discusses the derogatory word *choeryumul* and the term *yosong yonghwa* ("women's film"), invented by feminist critics in the 1990s, in her essay "Questions of Woman's Film: *The Maid, Madame Freedom, and Women*," *Post-Colonial Classics of Korean Cinema*, ed. Chungmoo Choi (Irvine: Korean Film Festival Committee at the University of California, Irvine, 1998).

6. Note that the derision with which the form was met in the early twentieth century also exists in contemporary literary criticism: "The most popular

themes—family conflicts and relationships between men and women—were presented melodramatically, to move the audience emotionally, usually to tears. This pedestrian sentimentality not only kept *shinpaguk* from developing into a meaningful dramatic form, it also distracted audiences from the problems of Korean society under Japanese colonialism. Several more sophisticated versions of shinpaguk emerged in the 1920s and 1930s, but although these works included more references to social problems of the time and were performed in a more realistic manner, they could not overcome the limitations imposed by the inherent commercialism of the form." Kim Hung-gyu, *Understanding Korean Literature*, trans. Robert Fouser (Armonk, NY: Sharpe, 1997, originally published in 1986).

7. This film, like virtually all Korean silent films, has since been lost. In 2002, a project was undertaken by director Lee Doo-yong to remake the film in a form as close as possible to the original. The film was to be shot as a silent feature with intertitles, black-and-white with color only at the end, with the screenplay to be based on oral recollections and published accounts of the original film. The film was released in 2003.

8. For more on the melodramas of this era see *South Korean Golden Age Melodrama: Gender, Genre, and National Cinema*, ed. Kathleen McHugh and Nancy Abelman (Detroit: Wayne State University Press, 2005).

9. In this sense the DVD release of the film in fall 2000 by Edko Video in Hong Kong is disappointing, as the screen appears considerably darker than in the theatrical print. A 2002 DVD release of the film by SRE Corporation in South Korea is more faithfully rendered.

10. Kunsan, a port city of 280,000 located in North Jeolla province, is home to two national industrial complexes that produce mainly automobiles, steel, glass, and chemicals. It is a sister city to Tacoma, Washington.

11. Source: Korean Film Commision. From 1998 to 2001, market share stood at 21.3%, 35.8%, 32.0%, and 46.1%, respectively.

12. I have written briefly on this phenomenon in the March 2000 edition of *TAASA Review: The Journal of the Asian Arts Society of Australia* 9.1.

13. For more on *Shiri* see Chi-Yun Shin and Julian Stringer, "Storming the Big Screen: The *Shiri* Syndrome," chapter 3 in this anthology.

14. For more on *Nowhere to Hide*, see Anne Rutherford, "*Nowhere to Hide*: The Tumultuous Materialism of Lee Myung-se," chapter 8 also in this anthology.

Works Cited

Dissanayake, Wimal. "Introduction." *Melodrama and Asian Cinema*. Ed. Wimal Dissanayake. Cambridge: Cambridge University Press, 1993.

Elsaesser, Thomas. "Tales of Sound and Fury: Observations on the Family Melodrama." *Movies and Methods II*. Ed. Bill Nichols. Berkeley: University of California Press, 1985. 165–89.

Kim Hung-gyu. *Understanding Korean Literature*. Trans. Robert Fouser. Armonk, NY: Sharpe, 1997.

Kim Soyoung. "Questions of Woman's Film: *The Maid, Madame Freedom, and Women*." *Post-Colonial Classics of Korean Cinema*. Ed. Chungmoo Choi. Irvine: Korean Film Committee at the University of California Irvine, 1998. 13–22.

Kim Yong-eon. "Talks: Sol Kyung Gu and Shim Young Seop." *Kino* February 2001: 145–49.

Williams, Linda. "Melodrama Revisited." *Refiguring American Film Genres: Theory and History*. Ed. Nick Browne. Berekely: University of California Berkeley 1998. 43–48.

Yu, Gina. *What Is Melodrama?* Seoul: Mineumsa, 1999.

3

Chi-Yun Shin and Julian Stringer

Storming the Big Screen

The *Shiri* Syndrome

In recent years the South Korean film industry has produced a series of local blockbusters that have achieved critical and commercial success both domestically and internationally. Titles such as *Soul Guardians* (Park Kwang-chun 1998), *Ghost in Love* (Lee Kwang-hoon 2000), *Joint Security Area* (Park Chan-wook 2000), *The Legend of Gingko* (Park Jae-hyun 2000), and *Yonggary* (Shim Hyung-rae 2000) have initiated an intense debate over the value, or otherwise, to a small film-producing nation such as South Korea of big-budget "event" movies. This debate has sought to explore the question of how Korea should respond to the ubiquitous presence of Hollywood within its marketplace, as well as the strategies its film industry should utilize so as to achieve overseas visibility by competing with foreign commercial cinemas. Within the terms of this larger cultural debate, the concept of the *Korean blockbuster* has been a key term in the mobilization of a variety of differing, and often opposing, arguments and positions.

Up until the recent successes of *Silmido* (Kang Woo-suk 2003) and *Taegukgi* (Kang Je-kyu 2004)—successively breaking the box-office records set by *Joint Security Area* and *Friend* (Kwak Kyung-taek 2001)—Kang

Figure 3.1. *Shiri* (Kang Je-kyu 1999). Courtesy Samsung Entertainment.

Je-kyu's *Shiri/Swiri* (1999) had provided a focus, in many ways a starting point, for much of this discussion. Variously described as an action film, an action thriller, an espionage thriller, a Korean-style blockbuster, and a Hollywood-style blockbuster, the film galvanized local audiences by offering a range of attractions apparently never before served up to Korean cinemagoers. Ostensibly a tale of political espionage and assassination, the film combined action and suspense with romance and melodrama, pitting a group of North Korean special agents against their South Korean counterparts. Writes one reviewer

> Unlike other films, which have dealt with the ideological conflict between South and North, *Swiri* does not disappoint audiences with weak plot structure and strong propaganda. Instead, it satisfies with stunning special effects, spectacular action scenes, and very importantly, a sad love story. After the movie is over, viewers are confronted with a myriad of emotions. Some may realize once again how tragic it is to live in a divided country, while others may be struck by the need to be on constant vigil. ("CK's Domain")

Certainly, this was a must-see movie if ever there was one. On initial release in 1999 the film attracted 5.78 million viewers—twenty times the average audience for a local film (Choe), breaking the all-time box-office record for a domestic product and grossing an estimated $27.5 million (approximately 37,500 million won) in the home market alone (Alford). Most famously, *Shiri* surpassed the Korean box-office record held by *Titanic* (James Cameron 1997) and subsequently was dubbed as "the small fish that sank *Titanic*" ("shiri" is a tiny freshwater fish found only in Korea). In addition, the unprecedented commercial success of the film led Korean films to take 35.8% of the domestic market that year (Kim Mi-hui, *The Korea Herald* 2001) compared with a low of 15.4% in the early 1990s. The film, however, was not just a big hit; it was also a cultural phenomenon. According to one report by a national newspaper, anyone who had not seen the film during its spectacularly successful initial run would frequently be left out of social conversations; sales of the tropical fish kissing gourami, which appear throughout the film, skyrocketed at local pet stores; and three thousand to four thousand copies of the Carol Kid album featuring the film's theme song, "When I Dream," were being sold per day at the height of the film's popularity (Hwang).

Such was the magnitude of this success that the mass cultural reception of Kang's film constitutes what has come to be known as "the *Shiri* Syndrome." The very presence of this terminology testifies to the film's *beul-lok-bust-a* status—its nature as a public event. For example, as the

Figure 3.2. An unexpected ancillary product—kissing gourami. Courtesy Samsung Entertainment.

above review implies, the film has been drawn into the discourse of political debate, with national political figures proclaiming, on one hand, that it provides further ammunition in favor of the "sunshine" policy of reunification, and on the other, that it demonstrates once again the continuing threat represented by the North. (The film has also been appropriated by the South Korean military in its media propaganda exercises.) The *Shiri* Syndrome, then, is a highly evocative term, suggestive both of the film's skill in engaging important social and political issues in a timely fashion, but also the significance and power of audio-visual blockbuster culture in contemporary Korea. Indeed, as well as becoming a cultural phenomenon of the first order, *Shiri* came to represent what the local Korean blockbuster could and perhaps should look like, as well as how astonishingly successful it could become.

In terms of the development of a popular indigenous film culture, this is a highly noticeable development. For a start, the blockbuster is often thought of solely as an American product or genre. The result historically of corporate and conglomerate forces, it is only U.S. studios that are typically perceived to possess the financial power to invest in big-budget event movies. The features most commonly held to determine and define a film's blockbuster status—the foregrounding of spectacle, cultural prestige (or its absence), big budget and big box-office returns, special effects, intertextual commodification, contemporary resonance, and historical endurance—preclude entry to all but the most expensive Hollywood products. Certainly, the blockbuster has been perceived as one of the key means by which Hollywood has kept its global dominance. Designed to appeal to huge numbers of moviegoers in most of the world's territories, the blockbuster is commonly viewed as perhaps the most powerful symbol available of Hollywood power and control, as well as the easy pleasures and diverse potential meanings carried by the popular film as an open text.[1]

The indigenous response to the cultural dynamics of the blockbuster can clearly be seen in the case of the reception of *Titanic* (1997) in South Korea. According to reports in the local print media, resistance to James Cameron's epic was heightened in Korea as its release coincided with the International Monetary Fund crisis then blighting the country. Yet even as film industry personnel distressed by this most alarming example of American cultural imperialism picketed the film, it was still breaking box-office records and sending local moviegoers away in floods of tears. Given such varied responses, the designation "blockbuster" needs to be handled carefully; viewed as a moving target, a symbol subject to no agreed-upon definition, a word whose meaning shifts according to how it is being used. Very often in contemporary Korea the term has been employed through a process of othering, wherein the idea of the blockbuster is given value according to what it is not (usually Hollywood) as much as what it is. In the case of *Shiri*, this process of cultural reception can be illustrated through a question. Does the Korean blockbuster represent an imitation of the Hollywood model or a more properly domestic product?

In answering this question, Chris Berry suggests that South Korea, together with other film-producing nations such as China, is currently undergoing a project to de-Westernise the blockbuster. With titles such as *Shiri*, South Korea has attempted to produce a stream of calculated blockbusters, but to do so within the purview of an export-led, ostensibly pan-Asian and arguably youth-oriented market. As such, what Berry variously terms "blockbuster consciousness" and "the blockbuster strategy" has been utilized by drawing upon the Hollywood "model." However, through this process of local reception, the concept of the blockbuster has been indigenized, or injected with local concerns and local subject matter. This strategy is seen as one that can lead to international success by producing a local product culturally distinct yet also familiar through its resemblance to Hollywood's spectacular big-pictures formula.

As Berry further notes, however, the very conceptualization of Hollywood as providing the model for the idea of the local blockbuster is fraught with ambivalence and contradiction. While it would be futile to deny the reality of the economic and cultural dominance of Hollywood movies in recent times, notions of imitation and postcolonial mimicry cannot fully account for the working through of this indigenizing project. Despite all the evidence to the contrary, the U.S. film industry has not historically had a monopoly on the notion of the big or event movie, and it certainly does not in the age of globalization.[2]

As evidence, consider the intense discussion South Korean blockbusters have been subject to in national public life. Promoted as cleverly designed responses to the post-1998 resurgence of the Korean economy, they are widely talked about as a further manifestation of Korean cinephilia in action. Along with the rise of Korean film festivals (in Jeonju, Bucheon, Busan, and elsewhere), film magazines (especially *Cine 21* and *Kino*), and university film programs, the visibility of local blockbuster movies provides evidence of an intense desire for cinema across the nation. This awareness that when it comes to Korea's involvement in global film culture the stakes are stacking up has been heightened with news of the unprecedented selling of two recent titles to North American distributors. After sales negotiations at the Cannes Film Festival, *Bichunmoo* (Kim Young-jun 2000) was sold to Miramax for distribution in the United States. In addition, and after months of heated speculation, it was confirmed in April 2001 that *Shiri* had finally been picked up for distribution in

North America by the Columbia Tristar Motion Picture Group, the mother company of Sony Classics, also responsible for U.S. distribution of the Asian crossover hit *Crouching Tiger, Hidden Dragon* (Ang Lee 2000). (Since then, more recent titles such as *Take Care of My Cat* [Jeong Jae-eun, 2001], *Chihwaseon* [Im Kwon-taek, 2002], *Spring, Summer, Autumn, Winter. . . and Spring* [Kim Ki-duk, 2003], and *Memories of Murder* [Bong Jun-ho, 2003] have been released in the U.K. Furthermore, apart from popular titles such as Lee Myung-se's Korean police thriller *Nowhere to Hide* [1999] and Park Chan-wook's *Sympathy for Mr. Vengeance* [2001] that are readily available in U.S. and U.K. video/DVD stores, numerous contemporary South Korean film titles are available on DVD from the growing number of Internet retailers that specialize in Asian films.) Sold to date to twenty-two other countries (including France), *Shiri* has thus become a symbol of Korea's ability to return the gaze, to make an impact among the truly major players. With an initial run in ten major U.S. cities in August 2001, director and actor appearances on U.S. television shows, and video and DVD that followed, *Shiri* has more than any other recent title been trumpeted as showing the power and potential of the Korean blockbuster as a domestic phenomenon and an international force.

Kang Je-kyu made his directorial debut in 1996 with *The Gingko Bed*, an attractive tale of reincarnation and obsession which, like *Shiri*, offered audiences an up-tempo narrative, state-of-the art special effects,

Figure 3.3. Setting the sights on Hollywood. Courtesy Samsung Entertainment.

and a classic love triangle. For his follow-up title, the New York University film graduate chose to direct an exciting espionage action thriller that would allow for both maximum thrills and the bonus of compelling subject matter, namely, the continuing division of North and South Korea and the prospects for impending unification.

Years after the fall of the Berlin Wall and the supposed end of the Cold War, the division of the Korean peninsula along the thirty-eighth parallel continues to fester as an open wound.[3] *Shiri* is renowned for having intervened in public debate over the reunification issue. As Berry has pointed out, by engaging its themes in such an emotionally charged as well as exciting manner, Kang's film, along with other major recent blockbusters such as *Joint Security Area*, provides a space for examining and possibly exorcising the anxieties associated with the division of the country into North and South. Indeed, blockbuster titles have been appropriated into the contemporary political maneuvrings around this area in a highly suggestive manner. For example, in 2001 South Korean president Kim Dae-jung presented his North Korean counterpart, Kim Jong-il—known to be a huge movie buff—with a gift of four recent South Korean titles as part of the ongoing diplomatic negotiations on this issue.[4] This event is also closely related to the South Korean government's recognition of, and subsequent policies to promote culture as industry, triggered by the Presidential Advisory Council on Science and Technology's report in May 1994 that pointed out revenues from the Hollywood blockbuster *Jurassic Park* (Steven Spielberg 1993) equaled the export revenue of 1.5 million Hyundai cars. This comparison drew Hollywood blockbusters into the debate on the national economy and argued that South Korean artists and cultural workers should learn and strive to make internationally successful films that could be exported and promoted so as to earn foreign currency.[5]

As such, *Shiri* provides a local case study in blockbuster history, or the construction of public understanding of historical events in a media-saturated environment through the exhibition and widespread circulation of big movies with the power to change and shape perceptions of past, present, and ultimately future events.[6] Such movies are often perceived to be open to charges of falsifying, simplifying, and changing history, even while they themselves contribute to the making of history and the delineation of processes of historical understanding. The widespread celebration of *Shiri*'s ability to "out-Hollywood Hollywood" needs to be seen in this context, as well as in the context of ongoing debates over questions of modernization and postcoloniality. As Chungmoo Choi has argued, the contradictions of postmodernity in Korea produce hybrid and discontinuous images across, but also arguably within, individual films. While modernization may be perceived at times to be the way to avoid further colonial subjugation, the very process of adopting models from colonial powers is fraught with ambivalence and refusal. Within this context, the question is partly whether or not examples of the Korean blockbuster may represent, to use Partha Chatterjee's terminology regarding postcolonial thought and the nationalist dynamic, a derivative discourse.

A key point to make in this regard is that any movie blockbuster will unite audiences around a common perception of its special status, even as the struggles over its meaning may divide sharply public and private opinion. One of the reasons why *Shiri* is such a historic movie, then, is simply its felt uniqueness—the perception that here is a movie that provides something new and something special. The argument we would like to make here is that this "specialness" is inseparable from the movie's own implicit critique of itself as a corporate and national spectacle.

Michael Allen has suggested that the blockbuster can be understood as a form of industrial advertisement allowing commercial film industries such as Hollywood to promote themselves through spectacle. However, for Allen, a temporal dialectic of revelation and concealment characterizes this process. The industry will at times reveal its spectacular mechanics—the tricks of its trade—so as to secure attention and ongoing curiosity and fascination but will then go on to smooth this revelation by promoting the values of illusionism once again. This is an observation also of relevance in the case of *Shiri*.[7]

As a way of beginning to explore the film's self-conscious deployment of spectacle, we might start by noting that while, on one level, *Shiri* takes a specifically Korean situation as its subject matter, it retains many of the elements typically associated with the international action thriller, particularly the Hollywood action blockbuster of the 1980s and 1990s. The film calls to mind numerous specific intertexts. For example, the female protagonist Yi Bang-hee (Kim Yoon-jin), trained to kill and maim, resembles the heroine of *Point of No Return* (a.k.a., *The Assassin*, John Badham 1993)—thus extending the extraordinary intertextual passage of this icon from its contemporary French source, *Nikita* (Luc Besson 1990) into Hong Kong's *The Black Cat* series and its numerous big-screen derivatives, as well as the subsequent U.S. television show.[8] Similarly, the liquid bomb and its imminent explosion jeopardizing innocent lives recalls similar scenes from *Speed* (Jan DeBont 1994) or the *Die Hard* series. The science laboratory scene also refers to any number of science fiction films or, appropriately enough given its cold war associations, James Bond titles, while the spectacular shoot-outs on city streets, filmed utilizing hand-held cameras, are also reminiscent of innovative action sequences from *Heat* (Michael Mann 1995). Most tellingly, *Shiri* makes direct reference to a famous "munch-moment" from *The Silence of the Lambs* (Jonathan Demme 1990), wherein antihero Park Moo-hyung (Choi Min-sik) escapes the airplane taken by a South Korean S.W.A.T. team in true Hannibal Lecter fashion.

The references to Hollywood films, however, go beyond mere imitation. In its design and marketing, *Shiri* exhibits not only a high degree of self-consciousness but also an ambition to exceed Hollywood. This is clearly implied in the scene where a chief scientist explains what CTX is to the two main characters, Yu Joong-won (Han Seok-gyu) and Yi Jang-gil (Song Kang-ho). According to the scientist, CTX is a liquid bomb similar to the ones seen in "foreign films." However, the CTX developed in Korea is superior in that its deadly transparency is ultrapowerful. (As CTX has no color or smell, it is impossible to distinguish from plain water when not activated and hence impossible to trace with even the most advanced bomb detector.) In short, "our" weapon is better than foreign ones. Clearly, this diegetic claim ties in very neatly with the wider cultural effort to convince the domestic market in 1999 that "our" blockbuster cinema is worth supporting.

As with any number of Hollywood and Asian action films, *Shiri* provides clear villains more than willing to spawn spectacles of danger and mass destruction. Here it is the Eighth North Korean Special Army Corps terrorists who want to provoke a war, not further peace talks, so as to achieve the unification of the peninsula. Significantly, however, it is not the North Korean leadership that is depicted as evil but rather a particular dissident group. Indeed, not only is the leader of the North Korea Corps determined to work for peaceful unification, but he also needs to be protected from the activities of this dissident terrorist group. It would not have been acceptable (or wise) to describe the North Korean leadership as terrorist when the peace talks between the countries' two leaders were being conducted at the time of the film's initial release.

From its very first scene, *Shiri* spectacularizes the inhumane aspects of this group, depicting their special training involving the killing of real people during bayonet practice and the murderous competitiveness instilled in trainees (whoever assembles a gun first gets to shoot his or her slower rival). Throughout the training sequence, we follow Yi Bang-hee's progress as she learns to become a top-notch sniper: at the same time as we witness the brutality of her training, we cannot help but admire her skills. We cannot hear any discernible dialogue among characters during these moments. Although the onscreen caption clearly identifies the place as North Korea (in the Korean version with no subtitles, there are only visual hints that the events are taking place somewhere in North Korea), we do not know at first just who this woman is or why she is undergoing all this training.[9] As with *Nikita* and *Point of No Return* there is just a hint of an intimate relationship between Bang-hee and the trainer who later turns out to be the top agent of the special corps.

Only when the training is finished and Bang-hee is sent away are we given information about her. In the first of the film's many representations of modern imaging technologies, a South Korean computer file reveals her identity as a secret agent from the 8th North Korean Special Army Corps. The gruesome activities that constitute her life as a sniper are presented in blood-red typed letters over a rapid montage of images of the bodies of her dead victims (largely politicians and scientists). This stunning opening section of the film—wherein the visual spectacle of crime and its investigation is coupled with the audio spectacle and adrenaline rush of a stirring musical soundtrack—employs an editing style similar to the opening credits of the Hollywood detective film *Se7en* (David Fincher 1995). Yet this Korean blockbuster is no clone. It is special. Its vivid presentation of information through up-to-the-minute electronic communications and computer networks provides just one example of a recurrent fascination with modern and mediating technologies: video relay, mobile phones, MP3s, and so on.

Immediately following this scene there follows a sequence introducing the two South Korean special agents, Yu Jung-won and Yi Jang-gil, who have been chasing Bang-hee for several years. The sequence is set in Incheon port as they lead a SWAT team equipped with machine guns and night vision equipment into a suspect ship. Again, the claustrophobic and suspenseful feel of this scene resembles scenes from *The Silence of the Lambs*, while the general tempo and iconography recall similar moments in many thriller and horror films (particularly the *Alien* series). By the end of the narrative, however, these visual references to Hollywood blockbusters have given way to what may be termed a more properly indigenous projection of spectacle. Two paired scenes suggest the potency of this paradigmatic shift.

First, consider the short scene where Yu Jung-won and Yi Jang-gil watch a musical revue after work. Just as signs for the Korean conglomerates Samsung and Hyundai are prominently displayed throughout the diegesis, at this particular moment the stage of the revue is decked out with signs for Daewoo and JVC. In addition, the cut to the next scene takes place on a large red Coca Cola sign as the action moves to the small café in the mall where the protagonists meet for drinks and meals. Two points should be made about these visual references. For a start, and given the movie's relatively large budget (reported at just under $3 million, or approximately 3,900 million won), it is fair to assume that such images are used for reasons of corporate sponsorship. However, their effect is also to raise the spectre of the corporate presence in the putting on of a blockbuster film spectacle, here displaced onto the visage of a musical revue.

But it is the film's climax, the football stadium scene, that most clearly reveals the working through of this revelatory process. This event is clearly staged as an occasion for the deployment of national spectacle. Ostensibly, the event is a football match between North and South teams to mark the staging of the 2002 World Cup in Korea and Japan. Moreover, the event provides the occasion for the public meeting of the two national leaders, united in their aspiration to join sport with political diplomacy. What is particularly noticeable in the cinema verité–style footage shot here is the matching of the spectacle of the football match with the thematic material of the film as a contemporary national blockbuster. In particular, shots taken from the back of the stadium—which is to say, behind the crowd—depicts the crowd in front performing the famous "Mexican Wave," or the spectacular crowd participation stunt performed during major international football matches. Now, the significance of this kind of staging of audience participation is that it is solely dependent upon mediated technology—television, and the ability of its cameras to beam the event globally into millions of people's living rooms—for its meaning and effect. In other words, with the Mexican wave, football spectators acknowledge themselves as props in a wider spectacle than simply a football match; they are part of a show, a public event, staged for outside observers. They provide evidence of the show's existence for both domestic and international spectators.

When the camera positions itself behind these spectators as they perform the wave (the reverse shot, if you like, of how the wave is normally depicted on television, i.e., with the crowd facing the cameras), we get more than just thrilling documentary evidence that the film crew was "really there" in the stadium that day. We also get the enrolment of the crowd in the projection of the spectacle of *Shiri* itself. And pushing this one step further, this might be said to constitute an exposure of the very ideology of spectacle upon which this film itself as a calculated Korean blockbuster depends. As such, *Shiri*'s climax moves toward the stripping away of the illusion of spectacle, or the revelation of the mechanics of its deployment.

Similarly, it is interesting to note that much of the narrative action takes place in a mall, the place arguably most associated in contemporary consciousness with the rise of the blockbuster. Simply put, the mall is the place where blockbusters—or, at the very least, action blockbusters—are most commonly shown and where cultural anxieties and debates about the influence of U.S. movies are most commonly directed.[10] Significantly, one of the key shoot-outs is set in a mall cinema. The gun battles that take place in and around this symbolic space might conceivably be read as an implicit comment upon the Korean image industry's ongoing trade wars with the United States and its powerful mall and audio-visual culture.

Another way of approaching this subject is to view the orchestrated nature of the deployment of public spectacle—with the football match in particular combining the spectacle of commercial sports with that of official politics—as tied to the film's concern with institutions and their workings. To be more precise, on one level, the film follows the trajectory of the international action thriller: it tells stories of individuated subjectivities in which problems are eventually resolved through hand-to-hand combat on a personal level. For example, the South Korean officials', particularly Jung-won's obsession with the unknown sniper is clear in the scene where the main characters are killed by Bang-hee, which then turns out to be Jung-won's dream. This scene establishes the complex interplay between the chaser and chased, at the same time as it implies a romantic relationship that turns out to be traumatic for all concerned. (What do you do when your lover turns out to be the one you have been trying to track down and eliminate?) The possible love triangle then established between Jung-won, Myung-hyun, and Park Moo-hyung provides a personal motivation for irresolvable larger issues concerning reunification.

At another level, however, the concentration on institutions provides another indication of the film's self-exposure as a conglomerate blockbuster. What drives the main characters is their placement within organizations and hierarchies as much as, if not more than, their individual desires and motivations. The institutions of the international action thriller—the police, the army, the military, the corporations—are depicted in all of their high-tech gloss, as are the image technology and surveillance industries.

Yet perhaps the most important institution commented upon and certainly implicated in *Shiri*'s success is *chungmuro*, the commercial South Korean film industry itself. The film has indeed established a trend for a more market-driven product and provided a blueprint for others to follow. As mentioned, the intense success was occasioned in part by the film's unusually high budget. Produced by a production company satellite of the country's major conglomerate, the giant Samsung Group, its engineering as a calculated blockbuster was facilitated by an enormous 700 million won (approximately $5.7 million U.S.) spent on marketing and advertising campaigns alone. Of course, such an amount is relatively small by Hollywood standards, but the film cost an unprecedented three times the average for a Korean production.

Shiri's high production values and extraordinary success fueled an environment supportive of the production and positive reception of a growing number of Korean blockbusters. One by one, these titles stormed the big screen. *Joint Security Area*, the highest grossing film in the country in 2000, ran up a production cost of 4 billion won, a substantial chunk of which went into building a large-scale replica of the Panmunjom truce village. Later that year *Libera Me* and *The Legend of Gingko* were finished at a cost of 4.5 billion won each (Kim Mi-hui, *The Korea Herald* 2001). With the evidence of success came a newfound confidence. In the past few years, ventured capital has emerged as a lifesaver for producers after debt-laden local conglomerates either downsized their entertainment divisions or pulled out of the media sector altogether. These new players have included Samboo Finance (which went bankrupt in 2000, although the impact of this development appears to have been minimal), Ilshin Investment, Mirae Asset Investment, Kookmin Venture Capital, and KDB Capital. Foreign investors have also noticed the boom; for example, Warburg Pictures invested £18 million in Cinema Service in 2000.[11]

With the kind of prestige that accrues to only the most successful of event movies (multiple awards at the Twenty-Second Golden Photography Awards; Best Director and Most Popular Korean Film at Twentieth Chung Ryong Film Awards), *Shiri* has more than contributed to a new high market share for domestic films. Despite the skeptical view that *Shiri* might be a one-hit wonder, the market share of domestic films has not collapsed. Indeed, the biggest news in the Korean film industry over the past two years has been the robust performance of domestic titles. In December 2000, Korean films controlled a 32.8% share of the local film market, falling marginally short of the 1999 figure. And at the end of May 2001, Korean films actually recorded the biggest market share in the industry's history, reaching 42.2%, with nine titles occupying the top twenty box-office positions in the first six months of the year, and in 2002, the market share rose to 48.3%.[12] In the first half of 2004, thanks to the phenomenal success of two blockbusters—*Silmido* and *Taegukgi*—the market share of domestic films reached 61.9% in the Seoul area.[13]

Finally, in true blockbuster fashion, *Shiri* has expanded the international appeal of Korean cinema exponentially. Most notable perhaps is its headline-grabbing performance in Japan, where it opened as the top box-office draw in February 2000 and held that position for several weeks. (Kang's film was actually the first Korean title released theatrically in Japan after the two governments lifted their ban on cultural imports between the two countries.) Other impressive box-office performances have followed. The Korean Film Commission reports that as of December 2000, total exports for Korean film that year reached $6.98 million, an increase of over 100% from 1999's $3.04 million. The total number of films exported in 2000 was thirty-eight, two less than in 1999, and these films went to a greater number of importing countries. *Joint Security Area* was the biggest film export in 2000, fetching $1.5 million for the Japanese rights alone, $500,000 more than the previous record holder, *Shiri*.

Yet for all this, Kang's action blockbuster continues to have an ambiguous or unstable cultural status. Valued as a national triumph yet devalued as "like Hollywood," differentiated as special, a prestige event, yet subject to damnation on the grounds of excessive commercialism (and "just" an action film to boot), the ongoing dialogue over the film's achievement as occasioned by box-office success reveals much about the issues perceived as of pressing importance to the Korean movie industry. These issues are unlikely to go away, and they give birth to strange contradictions.

Take the ongoing battles over the screen quota system. This system requires that local theatres screen Korean titles at least 106 days of the year. The United States has argued that this quota system violates principles of free trade and lobbied hard for its eradication. As part of its reception history, *Shiri* has been enlisted by some Koreans in support of the argument that Korean cinema will survive the relaxation of the screen quota system. At the same time, as an indigenous blockbuster, the film has come to fill up a good portion of that requirement, thus allowing theaters to fill the rest of their screening slots with the latest Hollywood blockbusters. Moreover, Kang Je-kyu—a key voice of Korea's cinephiliac culture who once claimed he took the idea for *Shiri* from the U.S. action title *The Rock* (Michael Bay 1996)—was himself one of the first among a group of filmmakers to shave their heads in protest against the relaxation of the quota system. From such ironies are the cultural resonances of blockbuster movies forged.

Notes

1. For discussions of the corporate and calculated nature of Hollywood blockbusters, see J. D. Phillips, "Film Conglomerate Blockbusters: International Appeal and Product Homogenization," *The American Movie Industry: The Business of Motion Pictures*, ed. Gorham Kindem (Carbondale: Southern Illinois University Press, 1982) 325–35; Thomas Schatz (1993), "The New Hollywood," *Movie Blockbusters*, ed. Julian Stringer (London: Routledge, 2003) 15–44.

2. Aside from Hollywood blockbusters, *Shiri* is also similar to and yet different from one of its regional others—Hong Kong action films, especially the recent vogue for narratives concerning terrorist activity [cf. *Purple Storm* (*Ziyu Fengbao*, Teddy Chan 1999; *Gen-X Cops* (Benny Chan 1999)]. The effects the September 11, 2001 terrorist attacks on the United States will have on international blockbuster and "Asian action" cinema, respectively, is at the time of writing hard to predict.

3. At the end of World War II, which brought Korea's liberation from thirty-six years of Japanese occupation, the victorious Allies decided that Korea would be occupied by Soviet forces in the North and U.S. troops in the South (in accordance with agreements reached after the U.S.S.R.'s entry into the war against Japan.) Regardless of the Korean people's wish to set up a free and united Korea, the division of the country was carried out. In the North the Soviets hastened to set up a Communist government, although led by Koreans, while in the South, a U.S. military government was set up as a temporary arrangement until such time as a Korean government could be formed and national elections held under the supervision of the United Nations.

Three months after the liberation, the Allied Powers decided that Korea was to be ruled by a trusteeship system for a maximum of five years. A provisional government was to be formed under the trusteeship of the United States, Britain, the Soviet Union, and China. Numerous antitrusteeship demonstrations were immediately held all over the country, and every political party issued public statements opposing the system. The Communist groups in Korea, probably on Soviet instruction, then changed their attitude and came out in favor of trusteeship in early 1946. In the midst of the political chaos, two occupying forces, the U.S.S.R. and the United States, had several meetings in Seoul during 1946 and 1947 in order to initiate the setting up of a provisional government. However, these meetings were dissolved before agreement was reached, due mainly to a conflict of interests. The Soviet side insisted that no political group or leader that had participated in the antitrusteeship movement should be allowed to take part in forming the new government, a move obviously designed to exclude the nationalists and set up a leftist government. Soviet ambitions to control the Korean peninsula clearly opposed U.S. interests.

Judging that negotiations must be held at a higher level, the United States placed the "Korean Problem" before the UN in September 1947. Despite Soviet objections, the UN agreed to attempt a solution, starting with the organization of the United Nations Committee for the Unification and Rehabilitation of Korea (UNCURK) responsible for returning the country to Koreans after democratic elections. UNCURK began to function in January 1948, but the North refused to cooperate with the UN. Leftist parties in the South also boycotted the elections and so the right won a majority in the new constitutional assembly. In May 1948, 198 representatives were elected to the National Assembly, 100 seats being left vacant in case of possible future elections in the north. On July 17, the Constitution of the Republic of Korea was promulgated, and on August 15, 1948, the third anniversary of liberation, the newly formed Republic of Korea was officially proclaimed. Meanwhile, in the North, in open defiance of the UN resolution, the People's Republic of Korea was formed in September 1948.

By June 1949, both Soviet and U.S. troops had been withdrawn, although this proved only a temporary measure. On June 25, 1950, North Korean troops crossed the thirty-eighth parallel heavily armed with Soviet tanks and swept down upon the unprepared South. UN forces soon joined in to support the South, and the Chinese intervened on the North's side, thus exacerbating a Cold War conflict with global implications. One year later, the war reached a stalemate roughly in the area along the 38th parallel where it had initially begun. In July 1951, truce negotiations were called for by the Soviets, but the talks were first suspended and then dragged on until agreement was finally reached in July 1953. Against the South's wish to carry on with the war, it was agreed that each side should pull its forces back behind a Demilitarized Zone that traced the line of battle at the time the armistice went into effect. The Korean War may have been over, but most of the country lay in ruins after its three years of struggle. The war had resulted in tremendous loss of life and property on both sides, and unification is still a dream for many. See Woo-Keun Han, *The History of Korea* (Seoul: Eul-yoo, 1970) 498–507.

4. David E. James reports that North Korean leader Kim Jong-il himself expressed concern over *Shiri*, "raising its depiction of the North as a terrorist state and its overall unfaithfulness to reality as an impediment to mutual understanding." David E. James, "Preface," *Im Kwon Taek: The Making of a Korean National Cinema*, ed. David E. James and Kyung Hyun Kim (Detroit: Wayne State University Press, 2002) 16.

5. See the newspaper report by Hong Kim, "Juragi Kongwon 1nyon heonghaeng suip (1 year's revenue of *Jurassic Park*)," *Chosun Ilbo* (May 18, 1994): 31; and Jeeyoung Shin's essay, "Globalisation and New Korean Cinema," *New Korean Cinema*, ed. Chi-Yun Shin and Julian Stringer (Edinburgh: Edinburgh University Press, 2005). Tony Rayns reported that *Shiri* became the all-time box office champion in Korea "thanks in part to an ad campaign which told audiences it was their 'patriotic duty' to see it." Tony Rayns, "*Shiri*," *The Time Out Film Guide*, ed. John Pym (London: Penguin Books, 2002), 1050. Darcy Paquet reported that the film's production was cited as "a blueprint for Korean businesses to follow in the 21st century. Good planning, a strong team effort and attention to detail were but a few of *Shiri*'s strengths that resourceful companies were told to emulate." Darcy Paquet, "Spymaster Branches Out," *Moving Pictures Online*, www.movingpicturesonline.com/nov2000/korea/korea.html.

6. For more general discussion of this subject, see several of the essays in Kevin S. Sandler and Gaylyn Studlar, eds., *Titanic: Anatomy of a Blockbuster* (New Jersey: Rutgers University Press, 1999).

7. We do not pursue here the following question: If Kang's film has helped to inaugurate what David Scott Diffrient calls "a new genre—the blockbuster—for South Korea,"—and as such represents an initial revelation of the workings of spectacle—will subsequent Korean event movies deny this knowledge so as to preserve subsequent blockbuster illusionism? See David Scott Diffrient, "*Shiri*," *Film Quarterly* 54.3 (Spring 2001): 45.

8. Following Jeffrey A. Brown's work on the transformation of the action movie heroine, we suggest that the changes undergone by *Shiri*'s heroine throughout the film (from murderous army cadet to sophisticated urban denizen to frighteningly competent assassin) are worth exploring in terms of her performance of traits of masculinity and femininity. See Jeffrey A. Brown, "Gender and the Action Heroine: Hardbodies and the *Point of No Return*," *Cinema Journal* 35.3 (Spring 1996): 52–71.

9. Apart from the caption, the export version of the film contains a preopening credit briefing of the Korean Peninsula, which has been divided into two nations—Communist North and Democratic South—after World War II, and how the two nations are still under the state of suspended war.

10. See Mark Jancovich and Lucy Faire, "The Best Place to See a Film: The Blockbuster, the Multiplex, and the Contexts of Consumption," *Movie Blockbusters*, ed. Julian Stringer (London: Routledge, 2003) 190–201.

11. See Hanna Lee, "Venture Caps Push Film Biz," *Variety*, August 9, 1999, www.findarticles.com/cf_0/m1312/12_375?55578545/print.jhtml; Kyung-Yoon Suh, "Storming the Big Screen: South Korea's Previously Moribund Film Industry Finally Finds the Spotlight at Home and Abroad," *Far Eastern Economic Review*, July 20, 2000, http://www2.gol.com/users/coynerhm/stroming_the_big_screen.htm. See also Darcy Paquet, "The Korean Film Industry: 1992 to the Present," *New Korean Cinema*, ed. Chi-Yun Shin and Julian Stringer (Edinburgh: Edinburgh University Press, 2005).

12. Christopher Alford, "Korean Pix Get Local B.O.," *Variety*, November 13, 2000, www.findarticles.com/cf_0/m1312/13_380/67492883/print.jhtml; Kim Mi-hui, "Korean Auds Seoul'd on Local Fare," *Variety*, July 16–22, 2001: 14; Statistics are also from www.koreanfilm.or.kr/statistics/statistics01_03.asp.

13. See Jung Hyun-chang, "A Review of the Korean Film Industry during the First-Half of 2004," *Korean Film Observatory* 12 (Summer, 2004): 3, www.koreanfilm.or.kr/kofic/publications.asp.

Works Cited

Alford, Christopher. "Home Is Where the Hits Are." *Variety*, April 14, 2000, http://www.findarticles.com/cf_0/m1312/10_378/61963412/printjhtml.

Allen, Michael. "Talking about a Revolution: The Blockbuster as Industrial Advertisement." *Movie Blockbusters*. Ed. Julian Stringer. London: Routledge, 2003. 101–13.

Berry, Chris. "What's Big about the Big Film? 'De-Westernising' the Blockbuster in Korea and China." *Movie Blockbusters*. Ed. Julian Stringer. London: Routledge, 2003. 217–29.

Brown, Jeffrey A. "Gender and the Action Heroine: Hardbodies and the *Point of No Return*." *Cinema Journal* 35.3 (1996): 52–71.

Chatterjee, Partha. *Nationalist Thought and the Colonialist World: A Derivative Discourse*. London: Zed Books, 1996.

Choe, Yong-shik. "Korean Films Gain Ground on Hollywood to Claim 40 Percent of Local Market Share." *The Korea Herald*, 24 November 1999, http://www.koreaherald.co.kr/data/html_dir/1999/11/24/199911240023.asp.

Choi, Chungmoo. "The Magic and Violence of Modernization in Post-Colonial Korea." *Post-Colonial Classics of Korean Cinema*. Ed. Chungmoo Choi. Irvine: University of California, 1988. 5–12.

"CK's Domain: So What's It Gonna Be?: *Swiri*." http://www.cheekan.com/like/movies/shiri.htm Posted 23 May 2001.

Diffrient, David Scott. "*Shiri*." *Film Quarterly* 54.3 (2001): 40–46.
Han, Woo-keun. *The History of Korea*. Seoul: Eul-Yoo, 1970.
Hwang, Jang-Jin, "*Swiri* Invigorating Local Movie Industry: Record-Breaking Success Heralds Growth in Film Investment, Wave of Big-Budget Flicks." *The Korea Herald*, March 19, 1999, http://www.koreaherald.co.kr/data/html_dir/1999/03/19/199903190002asp.
James, David E. "Preface." *Im Kwon Taek: The Making of a Korean National Cinema*. Eds. David E. James and Kyung Hyun Kim. Detroit: Wayne State University Press, 2002. 9–17.
Jancovich, Mark, and Lucy Faire. "The Best Place to See a Film: The Blockbuster, the Multiplex, and the Contexts of Consumption." *Movie Blockbusters*. Ed. Julian Stringer. London: Routledge, 2003. 190–201.
Jung Hyun-chang. "A Review of the Korean Film Industry during the First-Half of 2004." *Korean Film Observatory* 12 (Summer, 2004): 3, http://www.koreanfilm.or.kr/kofic/publications.asp.
Kim, Hong. "Juragi Kongwon 1nyon heonghaeng suip (1 year's revenue of *Jurassic Park*)." *Chosun Ilbo* (May 18, 1994): 31.
Kim, Mi-hui. "2000: A Year of Profits and Accolades for Korean Films." *The Korea Herald*, http://kn.koreaherald.co.kr/SITE/date/html_dir/2001/01/13/200101130046.asp.
———. "Korean Auds Seoul'd on Local Fare," *Variety*, July 16–22, 2001, 14.
Lee, Hanna. "Venture Caps Push Film Biz," *Variety*, August 9, 1999, http://www.findarticles.com/cf_0/m1312/12_375?55578545/print.jhtml.
Phillips, J. D. "Film Conglomerate Blockbusters: International Appeal and Product Homogenization." *The American Movie Industry: The Business of Motion Pictures*. Ed. Gorham Kindem. Carbondale: Southern Illinois, 1982. 325–35.
Rayns, Tony "*Shiri*." *The Time Out Film Guide*. Ed. John Pym. London: Penguin Books, 2002. 1050.
Sandler, Kevin S., and Gaylyn Studlar, eds. *Titanic: Anatomy of a Blockbuster*. New Jersey: Rutgers University Press, 1999.
Schatz, Thomas. (1993), "The New Hollywood." *Movie Blockbusters*. Ed. Julian Stringer. London: Routledge, 2003. 15–44.
Suh, Kyung-yoon. "Storming the Big Screen: South Korea's Previously Moribund Film Industry Finally Finds the Spotlight at Home and Abroad." *Far Eastern Economic Review*, July 20, 2000, http://www2.gol.com/users/coynerhm/stroming_the_big_screen.htm.

4

David Desser

Timeless, Bottomless Bad Movies

Or, Consuming Youth in the New Korean Cinema

When Romi gives Min a pager about ten minutes into *Beat* (Kim Sung-su 1997) so that he might literally be at her beck and call, we know by all of our inbred film training that this beeper will be a major factor in the film's visual and aural dramatics. And so indeed it becomes in Kim Sung-su's stylish and stylized adaptation of a comic book by Huh Young-man (a name too clearly symbolic of this film's theme!). Shortly thereafter and throughout the rest of the film, Romi pages Min on a number of occasions, and he meets her as requested. When she disappears for awhile, Tae-soo berates his buddy Min for holding onto what now seems a mere relic of a busted relationship. And when, after many trials and tribulations, some of which will be detailed below, Min and Romi are reunited, the pager once again occupies an all-too-dramatic function. Asked by Romi not to go to Tae-soo's aid, Min, of course, must accede to the demands of friendship and male camaraderie in the film's (inevitably) sad and melodramatic climax. Away he goes on his motorcycle, carrying the ever-present pager with him as he rides to Tae-soo's rescue. But he cannot save Tae-soo, already mortally

Figure 4.1. *Lies* (Jang Sun-woo 1999) Youth is subject and theme. Courtesy Pusan Film Festival.

wounded by Scorpio's gang, and he is soon himself similarly slain in the fight. As he passes into unconsciousness he can clearly hear his beeper urgently paging him, a call he will never be able to answer.

The melodramatic use of the unanswered page should alert us to the ever-present and frequently symbolic use of new technology in New Korean cinema. For a host of associations are brought to mind in this simple yet effective dramatic use of a pager. Among the many associations we must acknowledge include those revolving around social class and the structures in Korean society that perpetuate class distinctions. For it is abundantly clear and an integral part of the drama that Romi is solidly middle class; she meets Min at a dance club, winning a dance with him at an impromptu auction. Her bid of 100,000 won (about $100 U.S.) is far higher than most of the revelers at the club can afford. She is rather imperious to this young man whom we readily recognize as strictly working class and have from the moment his voiceover introduces him to us at film's start. Having gotten two pagers for her birthday, one from her mother and one from a friend, Romi presents Min with one of them—her class status enabling her to have purchased Min, as it were, in the first place and enabling her to continue to hold him. The cellular or mobile telephone and the pager are integral parts of Korean society today. It is, in fact, a ubiquitous feature not only in Korea but throughout Asian society whose streets and sidewalks, restaurants, trains, busses, and, yes, movie theaters are constantly abuzz with the sound of melodious chimes and one-sided conversations. That the teenaged Romi has a cell phone and pager hardly marks her, then, as unique, but it does mark her as middle class, just as much as her certainty that she must study hard for the college entrance exam betrays her class status. Min has no phone or pager and, equally, no hope or even dream that college is anywhere in his future. Romi's incredulous reaction when Min tells her what sort of grades he earns and her certainty that such grades will keep him out of college along with her certainty that her "straight A" career guarantees her success only increase the class divide they symbolize. The question of college has earlier been raised, when Min, to Tae-soo's surprise, indicates that he is changing high schools in order to achieve better grades for college. College has never occurred to Tae-soo, but Min's voiceover remarks that it is merely a pipedream of his mother, in any case.

This symbolic use of a technology to signify social class and to delimit the scope of one's horizons is used no less symbolically and sharply in Min and Tae-soo's hopes for a motorcycle. Though not a "new" technology, the motorcycle is nevertheless a symbol of a certain kind of status, in this case an ambiguous one. For at film's start neither Tae-soo nor Min can afford a motorcycle, but they can easily imagine a time when they can. And such a time shortly arrives, at least for Tae-soo, who joins a criminal gang. His participation in the life of organized crime quickly allows him the means to afford a motorcycle. But the relative inexpensiveness of a motorcycle allows it to occupy a liminal status in this film (as it does in many others). For if the purchase of a motorcycle initially compares, say, to owning a bicycle, upon achieving the means to buy a motorized bike, Tae-soo sets his sights higher, as it were, aiming at a car. The motorcycle, then, comes to stand in both for a level of economic success and for a certain kind of attitude against greater success—a symbol of youthful achievement, but also of rebellion.

Yet another kind of technology is highlighted early in *Beat*, this kind a cinematic one. Every fight scene (and there are a handful) has been step-printed to achieve a slow-motion, highly stylized look. Intended to achieve the results of comic book panels (recalling the film's origin in a comic book/graphic novel), this stylization nevertheless very much highlights the specifically technological means to achieve this.

Beat is a particularly apt film to consider the relationship between its thematic concern with youth and the highlighting of technologies that we might claim are favored by youth. But if *Beat* is insistent on linking its youthful theme with youthful technologies, it is hardly alone in the New Korean cinema in both relying on "youth" as subject and theme and

Figure 4.2. The motorcycle as symbol of class and rebellion. *Beat* (1997).

highlighting what I have just called "youthful technologies" to deliver its message to Korea's overwhelmingly young audience. Jang Sun-woo's 1998 *Timeless, Bottomless Bad Movie* (hereafter *Bad Movie*) is no less concerned with technologies of youth, ranging from the motorcycle to video games; in the "grrrl power" movie *AFRIKA* (aka *A.F.R.I.K.A*, Shin Seung-soo 2002) the exploits of the young heroines become popular fodder on the Internet, as teen fans both follow and celebrate their heroics—the acronym stands for "Adoring Four Revolutionary Idols in Korea Area." The cell phone and its attendant technology of instant messaging provides a graphic indicator not only of the girls' conversations (the messages are printed in double exposure over the rest of the image) but also the gradual dissolution of their face-to-face interactions in the youth melodrama *Take Care of My Cat* (Jeong Jae-eun 2001). The army of delivery boys who confront the teen robbers in *Attack the Gas Station* (Kim Sang-jin 1999) significantly appear on their motor scooters—a sign of their job and its status. And in the clearest concentration of youth subject with youth technology, Jang Sun-woo's *Resurrection of the Little Match Girl* (2002) melds the coming-of-age saga with video game and cyberspace technology. Its extensive use of video effects and Hong-Kong style martial arts choreography to tell a story of youthful alienation and the search for love demonstrate the connection between technological presentation and thematic concerns. That the film was the most expensive failure in Korean cinema history only indicates that the producers had a sense of who their target audience was, even if they failed to hit it.

Figure 4.3. "Tomorrow at 7, Club 369." *Take Care of My Cat* (2001).

Because They're Young

I want to claim that it was the reliance on young or youthful protagonists (by which I mean simply characters who are in relative positions of powerlessness, rootlessness, alienation, identity formation, and the like) that propelled New Korean Cinema into both its solid position in the domestic marketplace and onto the international arena. One might also argue that it has been the province of young directors tackling films about youth problems and issues that has aided Korea's entry into the global film scene, especially in Asia. Foundational films of the New Korean Cinema, like *Whale Hunting* (Pae Chang-ho 1984), one of the biggest box-office films of the 1980s (Kim 1), focuses on a naïve college student; *A Fine, Windy Day* (Yi Chang-ho 1980), focuses on three young protagonists—a delivery boy for a small Chinese restaurant, an assistant in a barbershop, an errand boy in a dingy love hotel; *Chilsu and Mansu* (Park Kwang-su 1988) links its protagonists by their feelings of alienation, one due to politics, the other due to youthfulness. The focus on youth is a hallmark of a resurgent Korean cinema in the early 1990s, with films like *The Life and Death of the Hollywood Kid* (Chong Chi-young 1994), *The Day a Pig Fell into the Well* (Hong Sang-soo 1996), and *Two Cops* (Kang Woo-suk 1993), among others, squarely putting the spotlight on young protagonists. By the late 1990s, the youth film became dominant across all modes of filmmaking. *Beat* might also be considered a breakthrough here. It has been called a cult classic and a turning point in Korean cinema. Kim Sung-soo's film was fourth on the box-office chart of Korean films of 1997 and was selected as one of the Best Six Films of 1997 by the KMPPC.

Following this kind of commercial and critical success the youth film became a transgeneric phenomenon. Blockbusters, whether the high-gloss *Friend* (Kwak Kyung-taek 2001) or the high-powered, Hong-Kong style kinetics of *Shiri* (Kang Je-kyu 1999); genre entries such as the horror films *Whispering Corridors* (Park Ki-hyung 1998) or *Memento Mori* (Kim Tae-yong and Min Kyu-dong 2000); low-budget, entries such as *Three Friends* (Im Sun-rye 1996) or *Take Care of My Cat*; or overtly art-house, festival entries such as *Virgin Stripped Bare by Her Bachelors* (Hong Sang-soo 2000) or *Spring in My Hometown* (Lee Kwang-mo 1998) resolutely focus their narratives on young people. Perhaps not coincidentally, then, as Korean cinema began to coalesce around the youth audience, Korean films came to dominate the domestic box-office charts. In 1995, Korean films accounted for only 21% of the market share of domestic film rentals; in 1997 the figure had risen slightly to 25.5%. My claim that the youth film came to dominate all genres and styles of filmmaking after this period translates into the increasing market share of Korean films on Korean screens: 40% in 1999, nearly 50% by 2001 (http://koreanfilm.org/index.html).

Perhaps it was the demise of Hong Kong cinema in Asia that provided the immediate impetus for Korea's international success in this period after 1997 (Kyung Hyun Kim 271–72) or simply the production of high-concept blockbuster films, especially *Shiri*. At this same time, Korean cinema became an increasing presence on the festival/Art-house circuit. A good deal of this twin success must rest with the Pusan International Film Festival (PIFF), which made it a point to showcase both Korean Art films and commercial features amidst its ever-increasing power as a film festival with international pretensions. Begun in 1996, PIFF thus coincides precisely with the rise of Korean cinema in the international arena. Writes the perceptive Stephen Teo in 2001: "It is perhaps no coincidence that in the six years of PIFF, a new generation of Korean filmmakers has carried out its own new wave, winning international recognition for Korean cinema through a forum such as PIFF" ("Pusan International Film Festival"). But I want to claim that it was the ever-increasing success of Korean films at home that paved the way for its success abroad. Kyung Hyun Kim makes the very important point that

> [the] surprising surge of commercial viability of Korean cinema is attributed to the perseverance of a serious film culture during the last two decades of the twentieth century. . . . During the late 1980s and the early 1990s, students were demonstrating in the streets not only for democratic representation through popular vote, but also for free access to media and film beyond the mainstream images.

> The explosion of visual culture and the popularity of alternative filmmaking and cinephile culture in the urban sectors of Korea had deeply affected the generation of people who were going to college at the time. Most of them were in their thirties in 2000 and they are the newer [generation of] filmmakers who made their debuts in the 1990s. (272)

Indeed this is the case. More important, these directors dominate the popular cinema as well as the cineaste culture. A look at the birthdates of the directors responsible for the top ten Korean films (based on admissions in Seoul) since 1990 reveals that virtually all of them, save for *Sopyonje*'s veteran director Im Kwon-taek, were born in the 1960s. The case in the American cinema is exactly the reverse. Save for Peter Jackson (b. 1961) every popular (nonanimated) American film was directed by someone born before 1960.

The preference of Korean audiences for films made by young directors translates to a preference for even younger actors. A couple of reader polls undertaken by *Screen Magazine* (Korea) are especially revealing of what is a marked tendency toward youth on the part of Korean audiences. In a poll taken in 1999, the average age of the favorite actresses chosen by the readers of the film-oriented magazine was almost twenty-seven, with no actress over the age of thirty-two. (Shim Hye-jin, who made her film debut at the age of twenty-three in *Black Republic* [Park Kwang-su 1990] having the perhaps dubious distinction of being the oldest.) The poll of favorite actors found their average age to be thirty-three, but eliminating the venerable Ahn Sung-ki (an astonishing forty-seven at the time) puts the average at thirty-one. A poll by the same magazine in 2002 found the average age of actresses down to twenty-six, while the average age of the actors had dropped to twenty-nine. What this means, besides the obvious decrease in average age of favored movie stars, however, is that between 1999 and 2002, most of the stars from the earlier list had dropped off in favor of new, younger stars. (Only Shim Eun-ha, Jeon Do-youn, and Kim Hee-seon among actresses retained their favored status; among actors the retention rate was the same, with Lee Byung-hun, Jang Dong-kun, and Yoo Oh-seon reappearing on the later list. See appendices 3 and 4.) One might compare this list to the list of bankable stars in Hollywood in 2000. Here, as might be expected, male stars dominate, with only actress Julia Roberts appearing on the chart—significantly, not only the sole woman but also the youngest star. The average age of these above-the-line box-office champs is forty-three.[1]

The point, however, is not simply that Korean audiences prefer the films of younger directors featuring even younger stars than their counterparts elsewhere. The point is, rather, that the youthful audience consuming and appreciating the youth films of young directors in Korea exactly reproduces the pattern of "new waves" throughout recent history and reproduces habits of worldwide film attendance. By any standards films such as *Titanic* (James Cameron 1997), *Star Wars I: The Phantom Menace* (George Lucas 1999), *Spider-Man* (Sam Raimi 2002), *Spider-Man 2* (Sam Raimi 2004), *Harry Potter and the Sorcerer's Stone* (Chris Columbus 2001), *Star Wars II: Attack of the Clones* (George Lucas 2002), and *The Lord of the Rings Trilogy* (Peter Jackson 2001, 2002, 2003) are youth films. And their presence on the top ten domestic box-office chart in the United States is mirrored by their presence on the list of the most successful films worldwide. (See http://www.boxofficemojo.com/alltime/world/) Thus Korean film production not only satisfies the demands of the domestic audience but reproduces the habits of the worldwide audience, as well. This is especially true in Asia, where filmgoing is largely a pastime of urban youth.

By the same token the Art-house/festival success of New Korean cinema—the production of cineastes in their thirties—follows a pattern set by various new waves preceding it. The French New Wave filmmakers (Godard, Truffaut, Chabrol) who dominated the Art-house cinemas of the 1960s were born in the 1930s; so, too, the Shochiku New Wave in Japan of the 1960s was the product of directors (Oshima Nagisa, Shinoda Masahiro, Yoshida Yoshishige) also born in the 1930s. Unsurprisingly, then, the Hollywood Renaissance cinema of the 1970s was the product of filmmakers (George Lucas, Steven Spielberg, Martin Scorsese, Brian De Palma) born in the 1940s. The Korean New Wave itself, the politically engaged, aesthetically vital films of the 1980s, was the product of directors (Jang Sunwoo, Park Kwang-su) born in the 1950s. A cohort of young film directors, targeting their films to youthful audiences with the production of youth films, thus not only found success in the domestic stakes of film consumption but also worked in the established pattern of the production of "new" cinemas over the last forty years. Most striking about the Korean cinema, perhaps, has been both its box-office and Art-film appeal. Unlike, say, the French and Japanese New Wave cinemas, New Korean Cinema has produced box-office bonanzas and not just Art-theater favorites. Contrarily, the global box-office clout of the Hong Kong cinema never translated into Art-film favorites beyond the singular presence of Wong Kar-wai. Of course, freedom from censorship constraints, some protectionism for the domestic industry on the government's part, the decline of more powerful regional film industries (Hong Kong, Japan), and the availability of finance capital were also necessary factors in the rise and success of Korea's New Cinema.[2] Most of all, however, it was the trans-Asian success of Korean cinema that propelled it onto the international arena, and this success was owed entirely to the youth orientation of Korean cinema. In the following sections, I will try merely to outline some of the major motifs of New Korean Cinema and account for their regularity of appearance as a function of the youth orientation of so many films.

Consuming Teenagers

The heading for this section is meant to be taken in two ways: that the Korean cinema highlights teenagers who are consumers and who are consumed. It is the latter idea that is most intriguing and that may account for the popularity of the youth film in Korea today: it showcases the resentment on the part of Korea's youth for their treatment by adult, mainstream culture. Youthful resentment is hardly a unique attribute of young Korean audiences. But the prevalence of rather apocalyptic visions where the young protagonists are driven to extreme acts of violence and are often led to their deaths marks a shift in attitude from the usual association of teen movies with light or gross-out comedies. Here we must appreciate the two most prevalent structures or pursuits into which youthful protagonists are placed: gangs and prostitution. The young male gang member or the young woman bar hostess/prostitute are striking metaphors for the consumption of teenagers in New Korean Cinema.

Gangs

The gang film (sometimes called the "*jopok* film," e.g., *Jopok Manura*, the Korean title for *My Wife Is a Gangster*, Jo Jin-kyu 2001) not only is ubiquitous in the New Korean Cinema, but it occupies a central place in terms of its ability to highlight so many social problems and concerns. The sheer numbers of such films is almost overwhelming, but it is precisely this ubiquity that demands our acknowledgment. Serious, socially engaged films such as *Green Fish* (Lee Chang-dong 1997) and *Failan* (Song Hae-sung 2001) use the gang film to talk about the disintegration of Korean society and the lingering effects of the move to a postindustrial economy. Comedies such as *Hi Dharma* (Park Cheol-kwan 2001) and *My Wife Is a Gangster*, however, simply utilize the structure for entertainment value while often reifying Korean tradition. A film such as *Friend* utilizes the gang structure to differentiate social class where the four friends in the film split up along the lines of those who attend university and those who do not. Torn between a progressive view of the debilitating effects of the class structure and a retrograde vision where male camaraderie substitutes for social analysis, *Friend* occupies a liminal position between the social critique of *Green Fish* and the social nonsense of *My Wife Is a Gangster*. Similarly, *Kick the Moon* (2001), Kim Sang-jin's successful follow-up to his anarchic

Attack the Gas Station, finds the world of gangs and gangsters an appealing structure, but the film, perhaps inevitably, though free-spirited, seems less critical than his earlier effort. A film such as *Die Bad* (Ryoo Seung-wan 2000) uses the gang structure in even more complex ways: to talk about youth, the breakdown of the extended family and the gang family that substitutes for it, and the betrayal of youth by adults. *Die Bad* can also use the mode as a preexisting structure into which the young, dynamic director can inject a variety of stylistic experiments and moods.

The use of this structure in *Beat* shows most clearly what is at stake for the youth audience in the deployment of the gang film: the betrayal of youth by the adult world. Min must ride to Tae-soo's rescue when he learns that Scorpio has betrayed him. Here we learn of the cynical manipulation of Tae-soo by his gang bosses all along. Tae-soo is cruelly stabbed, and Min, though he heroically tries to rescue him, is himself killed in the process. Given the essentially hierarchical nature of Asian gangs, their roots in a twisted kind of Confucianism, this betrayal by the gang superiors is no small thing. The idea that youth is mere fodder for the adult gang members becomes a recurring motif in later films. We see this even more graphically in the ultraviolent climax of *Die Bad*. Seong-bin, himself a victim of authoritarian cruelty and cynical manipulation when he was a teenager, has become a major figure in a gang that Sang-wan, Seok-wan's younger brother, desperately wants to join. Seong-bin cynically allows Sang-wan to participate in what the younger man thinks is a major gang showdown; in reality Sang-wan and his young friends are nothing more than lambs led to the slaughter. While former boyhood friends Seong-bin and Seok-wan attempt to kill each other in the same pool hall where Seong-bin accidentally killed another teenage boy years back (in the film's first sequence), Sang-wan and his friends are mercilessly stabbed to death by older, fiercer gangsters. The sacrifice of Min, Tae-soo, Sang-wan, and many other youthful would-be gangsters in the New Korean Cinema reveals a powerful sense of betrayal and resentment seething beneath the glossy exterior of Korea today.

Bar Hostesses/Prostitutes

In Japanese, Hong Kong, and Korean cinema, the prevalence of gangster films also includes the prevalence of the nightlife in which gangsters exist, that netherworld of violence, crime, and corruption. Such a netherworld inevitably includes the exploitation of women in the form of prostitution. But no cinema has been so insistent on highlighting the young women in this sordid world as has the Korean. In films such as *Beat*, *Bad Movie*, *Tears* (Im Sang-soo 2000) *AFRIKA*, and *Rush* (aka *At Full Speed*, Lee

Sang-in 1999), among others, the image of young, working-class women who pretend to fawn over men in exchange for badly needed money emerges as a potent social critique.

Not surprisingly, *Bad Movie* highlights the motif of adult exploitation of teens (and teen boys' exploitation of teen girls, for that matter) in the most unflinching manner. Many sections were written and filmed by the youth using 8mm film equipment before being intercut into the film as a whole. The image of young women prostituting themselves in rundown nightclubs is particularly piquant for the way in which the older men treat the girls roughly and force them into what turns out to be dispirited, passionless sex. In the section of the film entitled "Give Me One More Chance," Birdbrain is completely turned off by the experience. She regrets getting caught up in the whole idea, but cannot stop, as she needs the money. Birdbrain, in particular, emerges as one of the film's most pathetic characters. An androgynous figure, her participation in the life of a bar hostess/prostitute is made that much sadder. She is continually left to fend for herself. When the group of homeless teens finds they cannot pay for their bowling time, they all leave, except for Birdbrain, who must sneak out later, jumping from a second-story window and landing in a trash bin. This is by no means a heavy-handed metaphor for the ways these teens are perceived by adult society. In another sequence in the film, Birdbrain is caught shoplifting but is rescued by another young customer. Later in the film, however, in the sequence (ironically) entitled "It's a Beautiful World," the shop manager recognizes Birdbrain. Tony Rayns describes the scene as follows: "One boy is caught returning to the scene of a shoplifting; the shop assistant's price for not handing him to the police is a blowjob in the men's toilets." This misidentification is revealing of Birdbrain's androgyny, indeed, but more important, we need to acknowledge this continued exploitation of the most vulnerable of the teens by an uncaring male, adult world.

The pathos of the teen bar hostess is handled with some subtlety in *Beat* in the form of the supporting character of Sunny, a working-class girl who is in love with Min. When Romi has left him at one point, Min sleeps with Sunny, a scene intercut with Min's ascension in the gang's hierarchy. Suddenly wearing sunglasses and a leather jacket, Min is now also willing to have sex with Sunny in order to get revenge on Romi or to prove his manhood. Thus it is no surprise that the actual sex scene is intercut with Tae-soo and Min fighting another gang. What Sunny's feelings might be, Min never considers. The situation also causes a breakup with his friend Wan, who has longed for Sunny all along. Though Min does not sleep with Sunny for money, he nevertheless treats her with the same casualness that her older male customers do. Teen bar hostesses also appear in *Tears*, the most hyperbolic of the youth films, with the character of Ran exploited by older men and by her would-be boyfriend, who prostitutes her late in the film. Even sadder, in a way, is the fate of Sari. A motorcycle-riding free spirit, she becomes a drug addict by film's end and resigns herself to marrying the bar owner for whom the girls have occasionally worked.

The Crime Spree

If youth gangsters and teen prostitutes are common in so much of the young Korean cinema, so, too, are crime films that focus on working-class youth who turn to crime for the oldest and simplest of reasons: they need the money. In films otherwise as varied as *No Blood No Tears* (Ryoo Seung-wan 2002), *Attack the Gas Station*, *AFRIKA*, and *Sympathy for Mr. Vengeance* (Park Chan-wook 2002) young protagonists engage in typically misdirected efforts to make one big score. The class-based nature or the generational disputes between the criminals and their targets is made abundantly clear in these films. The four women of AFRIKA are drawn from different strata of Korean society—two middle-class girls, one working-class girl, and one working girl—yet their eventual joining together revolves around their sense of being exploited by older, authoritarian, and male figures.

The gas station, run by an older, middle-class man becomes the preferred target of the alienated, working-class youth in *Attack the Gas Station*. *Sympathy for Mr. Vengeance* may be read as a (powerful and violent) allegory of the class struggle, with a resolutely working-class youth and his politically engaged girlfriend embarking on an ill-conceived plan to hold the young daughter of an industrialist for ransom. *No Blood No*

Figure 4.4. Anarchy in the R.O.K. *Attack the Gas Station* (1999).

Tears, Ryoo Seung-wan's follow-up to *Die Bad*, also adds a distinctly feminist dimension to the crime spree subgenre with its focus on a young woman and an older, but no wiser, woman attempting one big heist.

Class Difference and the University

The utilization of gangs and prostitution and the focus on youth who believe the crime spree or one big heist will change their lives grounds many of the youth films around the issue of social class. One of the most striking markers of class difference seen in Korean cinema revolves around access to university education. Jon Byohng Je points out that "higher education has been considered the surest basis for well-being in Korea and investment in higher education has been guaranteed with the most lucrative social rewards of various kinds, ranging from the material to the spiritual. According to one study, 'education is proven to be the most important factor in social career advancement in Korea' " (129). Much of the New Korean Cinema seems determined to dramatize this adage. That university education is a given in Romi's life but not for Min or his circle of friends is abundantly clear in *Beat*. As we have noted, the deterioration of the childhood relationships in *Friend* is strictly owed to the university education that two of them receive; failure to go to postsecondary school consigns the other two to a life of organized crime. That none of the protagonists in *Three Friends* will be able to go to university makes their avoidance of military service all the more poignant for the way in which they must otherwise beat the system. The resentment Jih-ah shows toward Ji-won and So-hyun in *AFRIKA* stems precisely from the manner in which their middle-class status and their expected university attendance guarantees their full participation in consumer society. Again, the deterioration of the friendship between the girls in *Take Care of My Cat* is a function of the greater economic status Hae-joo expects to achieve based on her postsecondary education. Of course, that she has attended only a two-year institution and not a prestigious university is what separates her, and always will, from her even more pretentious and snobbish coworkers.

The centrality of university education to the ability to rise in social class is reflected in the many films where the pressures of university exams occupy a central role. And here, too, we see that it is the adult world that has led youth astray. The pressure to score high on the college entrance exams takes its toll on Romi and her friends in *Beat*. A low score prevents In-kyung from attending Seoul National University; as a result she throws herself in front of a subway train. Romi eventually enters a hospital to recover from the strain. In shame, her parents insist she say she has been abroad. In fact, only 3% of high school seniors in Korea make it into the most prestigious colleges, Seoul National, Yonsei, Korea, or Ewha Woman's University (Elaine Kim 99). Failure to score high means the inability to attend a prestigious school and failure to score well removes the possibility of university education. This has fostered a cynical attitude on the part of Korean youth. Jon Byohng Je notes:

> It is true that for most of the students the primary reason for going to school is not to develop selfhood, but to obtain a degree certificate which is imperative for a better social career. Thus, formal education turned out to be a highly competitive process and the contents of study from the primary school up to the high school turned out to be nothing more than the process of the preparation for entrance examination for better and more prestigious colleges. Under this condition, those who reject colleges and in favour of various professional schools of high school level suffer from an intense inferiority complex and frustration. They tend to look upon themselves as social failures. (130–31)

Jon goes on to note, "There have been many cases of suicide by students who failed to meet the high expectations of their parents. . . . The annual increase in the number of those who suffer from various degrees of mental illness resulting from the strains and stresses of the extremely competitive academic life is alarming" (141). Such expectations and pressures placed on students is clearly a social problem that *Beat* wishes to address.

Bad Movie addresses this issue directly, as well. In the scene "Bits and Pieces from Now On," the friends aimlessly stroll across a pedestrian bridge, singing pop songs. Subtitles suddenly appear on the screen announcing "Surprise Quiz. Number of bad teens and high school dropouts: a) one million; b) five million; c) 200,000; d) 100,000. We don't know for sure, but there are many of them." That the answer is not provided is perhaps meant amusingly, to play with the very fact that these kids are among the many that may be considered "bad teens" partly because they are high school dropouts and thus do not have access to the kind of information they might need to succeed.

University students and recent graduates are frequently the protagonists of many films, reflecting the importance of the postsecondary and university-educated audience for New Korean Cinema. Jon Byohng Je notes that enrollment rates after secondary school went from 1% immediately after the Korean emancipation from Japan in 1945 to 20% in 1981 (127–28). He further notes, "Projections done in the early 80s have the post-secondary level enrollment rate at 42%, an astonishing figure if true. Given the increased importance on technology and electronics manufacturing and programming, there is little reason to doubt this figure" (129). Thus films such as *My Sassy Girl* (Kwak Jae-yong 2001), *Kick the Moon, Bungee Jumping of Their Own* (Kim Dai-seung 2001) specifically highlight the social impact of achieving the university degree, and, of course, more generally, many films focus on characters whose vocations clearly reflect their university or other postsecondary degrees.

For the most part, however, the most successful and powerful films focus on the under class, those left behind in the rush to achieve global economic status that Korea undertook starting in 1960. Perhaps the Korean economic miracle had become so ingrained that it was little questioned until lately, especially in the period leading up to the Gwangju Massacre, when student and youth movements were more concerned with democracy and the evils of the military dictatorship. It is perhaps no surprise, then, that the youth film and its social critiques emerge in 1997 and 1998. This is the height of the postwar economic boom and the beginning of the shocking, still-underway economic bust. Put into production before the economic bust, the films are deeply critical of the overemphasis on materialism, economic success, social status, and overachievement. Yet their critiques of materialism and economic/social achievement are remarkably prescient. Thus it is no surprise to see that *Beat* and *Bad Movie* are the most critical of their society and the most insistent on focusing on those left behind. Korea's entry onto the world economic scene is the most recent of the major film-producing powers in Asia, postdating the rise of Japan and Hong Kong. Much as Japan had declared its arrival as a world economic power in the postwar era via the 1964 Tokyo Olympics, so, too, the Seoul games of 1988 highlighted Korea's assumption of the mantle of modern economic power. In subsequent years, with greater political and artistic freedom, filmmakers can question some of the previously taken-for-granted social and cultural aims. *Beat* is a veritable compendium of how and why a marginalized, underclass remains in Korea—the failure to attend a prestigious university, the presence of crime and violence, lack of concern on the part of the authorities, the rush to materialism, and concern for pretense over substance.

Consumerism and the Acquisition of Style

The idea of pretense at the expense of substance is also highlighted by the critiques of consumerism—the acquisition of consumer goods more for their pretense value and not use value—in New Korean Cinema. From the bicycle to the motorcycle to the automobile in *Beat*, many films show a shift not necessarily in life but in the much more superficial notion of lifestyle. The salesgirl, Jin-ah, in *AFRIKA* seethes with resentment, working in a shop that sells clothes she herself cannot afford. When the girls use their gun to go on a crime spree, they indulge in a shopping spree thereafter; most notable is the transformation of the prostitute, Young-mi, through new clothes and hair style. The shopping trip in the middle of *Take Care of My Cat* reveals the growing dissociation on the part of Hae-joo, her increasing alienation from her friends as her economic and social pretensions increase. Birdbrain's attempted theft of electronic goods that she certainly does not need and cannot use in *Bad Movie* also highlights the pressures to buy, to consume. We might see the gas station not simply as a class marker in *Attack the Gas Station* but also as a potent metaphor of consumption—of consuming and being consumed.

Yet there rests an ambivalence at the heart of Korean cinema here, as indeed we might postulate there is in the society as a whole. For we must also consider the high gloss and polish of New Korean Cinema a form of cultural capital, precisely a style to be acquired and displayed. The ability to compete with Hollywood cinema in the production of high-concept blockbusters such as *Shiri*, or to reproduce the high-impact style of films such as *Pulp Fiction* (Quentin Tarantino 1994) or *Lock, Stock and Two Smoking Barrels* (Guy Ritchie 1998) in a film such as *Nowhere to Hide* (Lee Myung-se 1999) is a source of pride to the Korean self-image. By the same token, attempts to compete with Asian film powers such as Hong Kong with the production of martial arts blockbusters such as *Bichunmoo* (Kim Young-jun 2000), *Musa: The Warrior* (Kim Sung-su 2000), *Dream of a Warrior* (Park Hee-joon 2001), and *Volcano High* (Kim Taekyun 2001) show Korea's self-consciousness about its participation in regional if not global cinema. The stylish presentation of the fight scenes in *Beat* and *Shiri* should also be acknowledged. With Chinese star Zhang Ziyi in *Musa* and Hong Kong star Leon Lai-ming in *Dream of a Warrior* this self-consciousness of Korea's ascendant cinematic power is clear.[3] If Hong Kong's image as the premier action cinema in Asia has also been challenged by the young turks of the Korean cinema, so, too, has Japan's reign as the anime king. The festival success of *My Beautiful Girl, Mari* (Lee Sung-gang 2002) and its regionwide commercial distribution is Korea's assertion that it, too, can accrue the cultural capital of anime along with decent box-office returns.

Once Upon a Time(s)

One of the most striking features of New Korean Cinema is its unwillingness to deliver a straightforward story in a straightforward manner, or, to put it another way, its willingness to experiment with cinematic time, to divorce story elements from plot construction. A number of films are told in flashback structure, such as *Friend*, though within the flashback the events are presented straightforwardly. A more complex interweaving of past and present may be found in *Joint Security Area* (Park Chan-wook, 2000), though even here the reconstruction of events is reasonably straightforward, if rather complex. Similarly, *Memento Mori* relies on a structure in which the past is reconstructed in the present where, again, the element of a mystery demands the audience pay attention and work hard to piece together a coherent story. More daringly, *Interview* (Daniel H. Byun, 2000) leaps between registers of past, present, and conditional, where some narrative events may be fantasy or otherwise difficult to place within a coherent story outline. Both *Calla* (Song Hae-sung 1999) and *Il Mare* (Lee Hyeon-seung 2000) toy with narrative time within the otherwise familiar confines of the romance. Whereas an American film such as *Frequency* (2000), to which *Il Mare* may be compared (without a question of influence in either direction as they were released just a few months apart) uses its time travel or time disjunctions within the context of action adventure (the typical genre where this type of thing occurs in Hollywood movies), the Korean film puts it in the context of a youthful romance/melodrama. The same is true of *Calla* where a shy, would-be lover of a flower shop girl tries to thwart events that seem to have already occurred. *Peppermint Candy* (Lee Chang-dong 2000) has already entered the canon of experimental narrative features with its reverse chronological presentation, preceding the critically acclaimed *Memento* by a number of months. (The Korean film premiered in South Korea on January 1, 2002; *Memento*'s American release came one year later.) Most daringly, *Virgin Stripped Bare by Her Bachelors* presents events from two distinct perspectives, but unlike say, the Hollywood *He Said, She Said* (Ken Kwapis and Marisa Silver 1991), where the film announces its dual-perspective and treats the whole thing comically, the shift in point-of-view in *Virgin* is sudden and remains ambiguous.

This is not to claim any "radical" alterations of film form on the part of Korean cinema of the last half-decade. Certainly, reverse chronology had been done before (e.g., *Betrayal*, David Hugh Jones 1983, from Harold Pinter's play), multiple perspectives on the same event, whether like *Citizen Kane* (Orson Welles 1941) or *Rashomon* (Kurosawa Akira 1950), or the ultimate unknowability of the past, as Alain Resnais demonstrated over and over in his influential oeuvre, are familiar to film historians. Yet each time such a film appears, whether *Rashomon* or *Betrayal* or *Memento*, the critical discourse sounds the clarion call of "new," "experimental," or "daring." While I make no such claims for originality or radical experimentation for Korean cinema, it is precisely within the context of mainstream films, such as *JSA*, *Il Mare*, *Memento Mori*, or even *Peppermint*

Candy, and the very regularity of achronological narrative structures, that is striking.

The ability of Korean cinema to work regularly in what seems like the province of the Art film or the experimental film is something I claim is also owed to the youth-dominated audience to which these films are addressed. The urban-based, educated cinephiliac culture of Korean cinema partly accounts for this willingness of filmmakers to work in complex narrative patterns and the equally willing audience to accept this more complex presentation. The cosmopolitan nature of Seoul and Busan, with their festival orientation, also accounts for the knowledge of filmmakers and film audiences. But I would also claim that the willingness of youth audiences to experience nonchronological or interweaving narratives reflects their familiarity with similarly nonnarrative or complexly entwined presentational forms such as video games or other digital media. The very ubiquity of video games, the Internet, cellular phones, and instant messaging seen on Korean movie screens reflects this youthful ability to work outside of analogic forms, that is, to think alogically.

The following lengthy quote from an Internet article on Korea's "wired culture" gives a good picture of the ubiquity of Internet usage and its centrality to youth culture.

> There's none of the high tech visual overload you see in Tokyo, or the clean-scrubbed, old-meets-new urbanism of Scandinavia—nothing to indicate that Seoul is the most wired city on the planet. Burrow a bit, though, down the alleys, up flights of stairs, or into the corners of malls, and you find something that sets Seoul apart and fosters its passion for broadband: online game rooms, or PC baangs, as they are called here. There are 26,000 of them, tucked into every spare sliver of real estate. Filled with late-model PCs packed tightly into rows, these rabbit warrens of high-bandwidth connectivity are where young adults gather to play games, video-chat, hang out, and hook up. . . . They are known as "third places"—not home, not work—where teens and twentysomethings go to socialize, to be part of a group in a culture where group interaction is overwhelmingly important. As elsewhere, technology scratches a cultural itch. It is the social infrastructure, as much as the hardware and software infrastructure, that's driving the statistics. And the numbers are impressive—South Korea has the highest per capita broadband penetration in the world. Slightly more than half of its households have high-bandwidth connections, compared to less than 10 percent in the US. The growth in broadband has surged in the last three years from a few hundred thousand subscribers to 8.5

> million. . . . Not only is South Korea a more wired country than the US, it is also a more gregarious one. Even if most Koreans had an American-style mega home-theater cocoon, they would still go out. These people do not bowl alone, particularly if they're single (most don't move out of their parents' place until they get married). They want to be with their friends. And right now, the place to be with your friends is a PC baang in downtown Seoul upholstered in Romper Room hues. A hundred monitors glow with the candy colors of computer games. There are also a handful of "love seat" stations, outfitted with two computers and a double-wide bench. Theoretically, this is so guys can play videogames while their girlfriends video-chat with pals. (Herz)

As I have been at some pains to try to prove, Korean cinema's rise both domestically and internationally has been related to the structural features of Korea's population as primarily urban and young, relatively well-to-do, and technologically sophisticated. In this respect Korea's young, middle-class filmgoers are paradigmatic of Asian filmgoers in general, and thus the popularity of Korean cinema in Tokyo, Taiwan, Singapore, and Hong Kong is easily explicable.

Conclusion

Filmgoing is an overwhelmingly urban pursuit, and it is an overwhelming young pursuit. Here, once again, Korea is paradigmatic of these two central tenets of contemporary cinema. With a population of around 48 million, Korea is dominated culturally, politically, and economically by the urban centers of Seoul and Busan, which, with populations of around 10 million and 4 million, respectively, account for almost 30% of the population. More impressively, Seoul, Incheon (the near-by city which now houses the international airport that serves Seoul), and the outlying areas around them account for 46% of the entire population. By the same token, the number of Koreans between the ages of ten and twenty-four is estimated as compromising almost 25% of the total population. With an predominately urban and strikingly young population, and with its economic prosperity, extremely high literacy rate (98%), and availability of finance capital, Korea has been structurally poised to produce films for trans-Asian and global consumption. Working in familiar genres such as gangster, horror, melodrama, and comedy and giving them a decidedly youthful bent, Korean cinema has offered up allegories of the ravages of capitalism and the perils of materialism, the decline of the extended family, the hardening of class boundaries, and the transitory nature of relationships within postmodern culture. Striking responsive chords in other urban technological and information centers, like Tokyo, Taipei, Singapore, and Hong Kong, Korean cinema has added cultural capital to the trans-Asian experience, competing in quality with Hollywood cinema while speaking to local and regional concerns. It has both participated in and helped forge a trans-Asian youth culture that also speaks to diasporic Asian audiences and even to the urban youth in Europe and the United States who can also see themselves in Korea's "beat" generation.

Appendix 1

Top Ten Korean Films (Seoul Admissions), 1990–2002

Film	*Year of Release*	*Director*	*Year of Birth*
Friend	(2001)	Kwak Kyung-taek	1966
Shiri	(1999)	Kang Je-kyu	1962
JSA	(2002)	Park Chan-wook	1963
My Sassy Girl	(2001)	Kwak Jae-yong	1961
Kick the Moon	(2001)	Kim Sang-jin	1967
The Way Home	(2002)	Lee Jeong-hyang	1964
My Wife Is a Gangster	(2001)	Jo Jin-kyu	1960
Public Enemy	(2002)	Kang Woo-suk	1960
Sopyonje	(1993)	Im Kwon-taek	1936
Attack the Gas Station	(1999)	Kim Sang-jin	1967

Appendix 2

U.S. Top 10, 1990–2002 (excluding animated films)

Film	*Year of Release*	*Director*	*Year of Birth*
Titanic	1997	James Cameron	1954
Star Wars I (PM)	1999	George Lucas	1944
Spider-Man	2002	Sam Raimi	1959
Jurassic Park	1993	Steven Spielberg	1946
Forrest Gump	1994	Robert Zemeckis	1952
Harry Potter (I)	2001	Chris Columbus	1958
Star Wars II (Clones)	2002	George Lucas	1944
Lord of the Rings (I)	2001	Peter Jackson	1961
Independence Day	1996	Roland Emmerich	1955
Lord of the Rings (II)	2002	Peter Jackson	1961

(adapted from: http://www.the-numbers.com/movies/records/index.html)

Appendix 3

Screen Magazine Readers Poll (October 1999)

Actress	*Year of Birth*
Shim Eun-ha	1972
Ko So-young	1972
Kim Hee-seon	1977
Jeon Do-youn	1973
Shim Hye-jin	1967
Kim Hye-soo	1970
Jin Hee-kyung	1968
Shin Eun-kyung	1973
Choo Sang-mee	1973
Kim Ha-neul	1978

Actor	*Year of Birth*
Jung Woo-sung	1973
Han Seok-gyu	1964
Park Shin-yang	1968
Ahn Sung-ki	1952
Park Joong-hoon	1964
Choi Min-sik	1963
Jang Dong-kun	1972
Lee Sung-jae	1970
Yoo Oh-seong	1964
Lee Byung-hun	1970

Appendix 4

Screen Magazine Readers Poll (April 2002)

Actress	*Year of Birth*
Bae Doo-na	1979
Jeon Do-youn	1973
Lee Young-ae	1971
Jang Jin-young	1974
Jeon Ji-hyun	1981
Lee Eun-ju	1980
Kim Hee-seon	1977
Lee Yo-won	1980
Shim Eun-ha	1972
Lee Mi-youn	1971

Appendix 4 (*continued*)

Actor	*Year of Birth*
Shin Ha-kyun	1974
Jang Dong-kun	1972
Won Bin	1977
Yoo Ji-tae	1976
Song Kang-ho	1967
Sol Kyung-gu	1968
Lee Jung-jae	1973
Lee Byung-hun	1970
Yoo Oh-seong	1964
Jang Hyuk	1976

(Poll results taken from: http://koreanfilm.org/actors2.html)

Notes

The author would like to acknowledge the help of Timothy White in clarifying the situation of Korean film distribution in Singapore and Darcy Parquet for providing information otherwise difficult to obtain, in addition to maintaining a supremely useful and informative Website devoted to Korean cinema. I would also like to thank Frances Gateward for many, many hours of buying, watching, and discussing Korean films and for giving me the opportunity to continue to explore youth films in Asia.

1. The list includes Mel Gibson (b. 1956), Jim Carrey (b. 1962), Tom Cruise (b. 1962), Tom Hanks (b. 1956), Bruce Willis (b. 1955), Julia Roberts (b. 1967), Eddie Murphy (b. 1961), Robert DeNiro (b. 1943), Harrison Ford (b. 1942), Nicolas Cage (b. 1964), Martin Lawrence (b. 1965), and Denzel Washington (b. 1959) (See http://www.boxofficemojo.com/bankability). There is a difference, to be sure, in comparing a list of the "bankability" of stars to a survey of readers compiled by a movie magazine. In the Korean context, there is a real homology between successful films and popular stars, while in the U.S. charts, only *Forrest Gump* features a rated star. However, bankability does mean demonstrable box-office success of films featuring those stars, and thus comparisons are valid. One would simply say that in the case of the Hollywood films, they do not rely on stars particularly, and it is unlikely that, say, the actors in *Harry Potter* or *Lord of the Rings* will ever emerge as stars in the true sense of that term.

2. I can claim no expertise in the workings of finance capital and the ability to sustain a film industry. But it is worth noting that Korea has managed to recover from the Asian economic crisis of 1997 to a larger extent than the problem-plagued economies of Japan and Hong Kong. The decline of the Japanese and Hong Kong industries may also be owed to other factors. The real creativity and influence of Japanese film culture today rests in anime; Hong Kong has been hit by the defections of important directors and stars to Hollywood, among other factors.

3. The production of martial arts films is not new to the Korean cinema. Costume dramas featuring martial arts were an important part of domestic film production in the 1960s and into the 1970s. Korean-Hong Kong coproductions were also very much a part of the landscape of Asian cinema in the 1970s, including the Korean-shot and -themed films of director King Hu and the chop-socky mayhem of Angela Mao-ying. The recent Korean films, however, carefully integrate the wire and martial stuntwork and style formerly associated with the Hong Kong cinema.

Works Cited

Herz, J. C. "The Bandwidth Capital of the World." http://www.wired.com/wired/archive/10.08/korea.html.

Jon, Byohng Je. "Republic of Korea." In *Youth in Asia: Viewpoints for the Future.* New Delhi: New Statesman, 1988.

"Jung Doo-hung: Action Film Wizard." *Asian Cult Cinema* 29 (Winter 2000).

Kim, Elaine, "Men's Talk: A Korean American View of South Korean Constructions of Women, Gender, and Masculinity." *Dangerous Women: Gender and Korean Nationalism.* Ed. Elaine Kim and Chungmoo Choi. New York: Routledge, 1998.

Kim, Kyung Hyun. *The Remasculinization of Korean Cinema.* Durham: Duke University Press, 2004.

Rayns, Tony. "Cinephile Nation" *Sight and Sound* 8.1 (January 1998): 24-27. Rptd. httt://www.cinekorea.com/essay/tony01.html.

Teo, Stephen. "Pusan International Film Festival—Mature and Independent." http://www.sensesofcinema.com/contents/01/18/pusan.html.

PART 2

Directing New Korean Cinema

5

CHRIS BERRY

Scream and Scream Again

Korean Modernity as a House of Horrors in the Films of Kim Ki-young

Mrs. Kim: This is like a scene from a film. I can hardly breathe.

—*Carnivore*

SO PANTS MATRONLY MRS. KIM when a gigolo comes on to her in Kim Ki-young's penultimate film, *Carnivore* (1984).[1] The line always gets a laugh from Korean audiences. But what sort of a film does she have in mind? Is she overcome with delight at the prospect, or is she aghast? And what does it mean to suggest that there might be a resemblance between real life and Kim's films? Anyone acquainted with the weird and wonderful world of the late great Kim Ki-young's horror films will understand why the idea that they reflect real life might make an audience laugh—both at the absurdity of the notion and with discomfort

Figure 5.1. *Insect Woman.* (Kim Ki-young 1972). Courtesy Pusan Film Festival.

at its possible truth. *Carnivore* displays a family set-up that is too fantastic to be literally believable but touches on all sorts of unconscious fears and fantasies, both individual and provoked by the social change accompanying modernization and industrialization. Mrs. Kim is a successful entrepreneur and has taken over the role as the head of the family. Just as this leads her to gigolos, it leads Mr. Kim to impotency—until he overcomes his problem by acting out an infantile regression fantasy with bar hostess Myeong-ja. With Mr. Kim dressed in diapers and cohabiting with Myeong-ja in a huge Western-style house, the film gets steadily more overwrought. Rats crawl up from the basement as though surfacing from the unconscious, and Myeong-ja fantasizes about gaining full possession of Mr. Kim by having his baby. You should not be surprised to hear that it is not only the scene with the gigolo that provokes laughter. This laughter is the product of the ambivalent shuttling between repulsion and attraction that is so characteristic of Kim Ki-young's films, and it is the topic of this chapter.

By focusing on ambivalence in Kim Ki-young's films as an aspect of horror and the fantastic, this chapter counters the common association of modernity and modernization with the realist novel and its offspring, the realist stage drama, and the realist feature film. This common association holds true for much Korean as well as Anglo-American critical discourse, and the films of Kim Ki-young were once proclaimed as part of that realist tradition. Yet their revival since the early 1990s has revealed a very different relation to the modern. Kim's trademarks combine Western-style houses, appliances, food, and other appurtenances of the new bourgeoisie produced in Korea's rush to modernization with jealousy, adultery, ghosts, shamanism, rats, paranoia, sexual dysfunction, psychotic delusions, and gruesome murders. This has led many commentators to imply his films are critical or negative responses to modernization. But this is only part of the picture. Although Kim's representation of Korean modernity hybridizes many different genres, the dominant one is the horror film, which falls under the fantastic mode rather than the realist one. In the examination that follows, the various characteristics of Kim's films can be both considered under the rubric of the horror film and an ambivalent response to the Korean experience of modernization as at once forced and desired. This paradoxical state that defies either realist representation or critical distance prefers direct somatic response and full ambivalence. The chapter concludes by arguing that rather than considering this phenomenon as simply a reflection of an experience of the modern opposite to that of the West, the cinema of Kim Ki-young should join an ongoing rethinking of the assumed link between modernity and realism in general.

The late Kim Ki-young is generally hailed as one of the great directors from the post–Korean War "golden years" of the South Korean cinema. Shockingly, no complete Korean feature films have survived from the Japanese colonial period that ended in 1945. As a result, it has been impossible to make any reasoned judgments about the work of earlier filmmakers. Kim was born in Seoul in 1922 but grew up mostly in Pyongyang.[2] As a young man, Kim divided his professional interests between the theater and medicine, training as a dentist. He first became involved in the cinema during the Korean War, when he got an opportunity to work on American newsreel films. After the war, this led him into feature films. He debuted in 1955 with *The Box of Death*, a film that has not survived but we know was about a South Korean village resisting guerillas infiltrating from the North. However, war films were not to be his usual genre.

His eighth feature, *The Housemaid* (1960), was both Kim Ki-young's breakthrough film and the work that established his reputation for combining horror and melodrama. The film tells the tale of the downfall of an ambitious middle-class family. Both parents work hard to realize the wife's wish that they move into a modern, Western-style, two-story house. They hire a maid to help them with their new, spacious home, but she seduces the husband. When she becomes pregnant, the truth comes out. The family forces her to have an abortion. But she gains revenge, first by causing the death of their little son and then by persuading the husband to commit suicide with her. The film was an enormous box-office hit, playing into the anxieties about rapid social change that was just beginning to make itself really felt.

After *The Housemaid*, Kim Ki-young returned repeatedly to films featuring femme fatale maids and bar hostesses, emasculated traditional patriarchs and intellectual gentlemen, and wives empowered by modernization to run companies and pursue careers. These characters torment each other in settings featuring the most modern of Western-style houses, stacked to the rafters with the latest American household appliances and a range of ostentatious Western luxury goods. Instead of the consumer paradise promised by advertising culture, the opulent settings became gothic dens of lurid bloodletting and perversity—tales from Sigmund Freud by way of Edgar Allan Poe—dramatizing the intense anxieties unleashed by modernization.

During his career, which stretched from 1955 to 1995, Kim Ki-young directed only thirty-two films. In an era when many Korean directors made two or three films a year this is a low figure, especially when one considers that he was a bankable director with many box-office hits to his name. However, Kim also produced and wrote the screenplays for many of his films, struggling to retain control and realize his own vision to a greater extent than was usual at the time. This no doubt helped his critical reputation, as it conforms to the stereotype of the auteur director. In much critical discussion, Kim is mentioned in the same breath as two other major directors from this period: Shin Sang-ok and Yu Hyun-mok. (It is a mark of their reputation that the Pusan International Film Festival staged retrospectives honoring each director as quickly as possible after it was founded.)

Twenty-two of Kim Ki-Young's films were made under the conditions of right-wing military dictatorship that prevailed in South Korea from 1961 until the late 1980s. This was also when South Korea was transformed from one of the world's poorest agrarian nations to an industrial powerhouse. The advent of that difficult period with the coup that brought President Park Chung-hee to power in 1961 coincides with the production of Kim's breakthrough hit, *The Housemaid*. Until recently, Shin Sang-ok, Yu Hyun-mok, and Kim Ki-young were all frequently acclaimed as the fathers of Korean realist cinema, although none of Kim's 1950s features has survived, making it impossible to know for sure if they were indeed realist. But if they were, *The Housemaid* marks a watershed break away from that realism. How could such a drastic revision critical opinion have occurred?

In the 1980s with his career stalled by a string of flops, Kim was largely forgotten until his later films—including *Carnivore*—found fame as cult favorites among a new generation of film buffs. As editor of *Kino* magazine Chung Sung-il recalls, these "over the top" pieces of grand guignol made him an Ed Wood–like figure for them (Lee). These very late films were the only ones available on video at the time, and because old Korean films are rarely shown on television the realist reputation of his pre-1980s works remained undisturbed. When the Pusan International Film Festival was founded in the late 1990s, the organizers were eager to promote greater knowledge and understanding of Korean cinema both locally and internationally with retrospectives. As Korean film programmer of the time Lee Yong-kwan recalls, when Kim Ki-young was chosen for a retrospective, his reputation as one of Korea's realist directors was part of the attraction. Yet, once the films not available on video were screened for programmers and critics at the Korean Film Archives, it became apparent that very few if any of his films made from *The Housemaid* on could really be considered realist.[3]

The idea that realism is the aesthetic expression—or at least the ideology—of modernity is longstanding. Materialism and secularity correlate to mimeticism devoid of the supernatural, science to logical causality, development-oriented ideas of progress to narrative linearity, and entrepreneurship to narratives centered on the drive to triumph of the individual in a material world. Over forty years ago, Ian Watt famously linked the emergence of the novel to the growth of the bourgeoisie. Bordwell, Staiger, and Thompson's study of the Hollywood studio system cinema is the dominant work on realism and the feature film. For those committed to the ideology of modernity, realism in various forms has been espoused strongly. For example, both Andre Bazin's long-shot, long-take realist aesthetic and Soviet socialist realist cinema stand as anti-Hollywood realisms associated with different ideologies of modernity. In South Korea, a liberal-humanist and at times leftist preference for realism has also been dominant for a long time.[4] Others have criticized the realist aesthetic as inherently tied to bourgeois ideology and favored a critical modernism, in regard to both the novel[5] and the film.[6]

Responding to the rediscovery and reevaluation of Kim Ki-young's films since the late 1980s, different critics have focused on various characteristics of his films that diverge from realism. Moon Jae-chol argues that Kim's films "are based on the framework of melodrama" and suggests that an increasing lack of control over production and ever more stringent censorship during the difficult years of the Park Chung-hee regime made the films increasingly erratic and incoherent. Deploying the idea of melodrama makes space for divergence from realism, but understood from within what is still a realist mode overall. In contrast, I would argue that, as Choi Eun-suk writes about Kim's 1978 film *Killer Butterfly*, the fantastic mode is at least as important in Kim Ki-young's works as realism. The increasingly erratic, exaggerated, and "incoherent" quality of Kim's work may be less symptomatic of degeneration than of a shift toward the fantastic mode beginning with *The Housemaid*. The dominant genre that Kim use in this mode is horror, and in what follows, I examine how the oft-noted nonrealist elements in Kim's films relate to the horror genre, and in particular to its ambivalence.[7] This has not been emphasized in existing analyses of Kim's films, yet it is key to understanding the full complexity of their relationship to the experience of Korean modernity.

As Kristeva has noted, the attention to the abject that lies at the center of horror literature is not the same as a repression of that which disgusts or a rejection of it; instead it is symptomatic of simultaneous repulsion and fascination or, in other words, ambivalence.[8] This mode of engagement is also typical of the horror film genre; spectators are attracted by the prospect of seeing the things they fear or find repugnant. In Kim's case, his consistent return to such elements indicates an equivalent engagement on his part as a filmmaker. Most famously, he even remade his most successful films. *The Housemaid* (1960) reappeared as *Woman of Fire* in 1971, and as *Woman of Fire '82* over a decade later. *Carnivore* (1984) is a remake of *The Insect Woman* (1972). The analysis that follows focuses on these five key films, but most of the points could be extended to most of his output.

Like *Carnivore*, the plot of *Insect Woman* is a convoluted tale of psychosis featuring a bar hostess, an emasculated husband, and a wife who runs the family company. Because the bar hostess is able to restore the patriarch's potency, she becomes his mistress. She discovers a baby in an abandoned refrigerator, but it turns out to be a rat-eating monster. She persuades the husband to leave his wife and moves in with him permanently, but when he discovers the corpse of the baby, he leaves her. She then kills him and herself. The wife's chauffeur reveals that he was responsible for all the strange events that happened and tries to persuade the new widow to marry him. When she refuses, he runs her over. Just as in *The Housemaid*, another family rises and falls with modernization.

Most recent accounts of the horror film as a genre have understood its fascination with the repugnant through a Freudian framework. Here, a return of the element once loved and repressed in the establishment of the subject by negotiation of the Oedipus complex is symbolized by that which is abject, monstrous, or horrifying but simultaneously compelling, appealing, and fascinating. Given that this element is the original identification with the mother, the result is a consistent association of the feminine and the horrific (Clover). Such an interpretation is certainly also relevant to an understanding of Kim's films, as extremely violent and often sexually perverse adultery dramas are central to all of them. Each

Figure 5.2. *The Housemaid.* Courtesy Pusan Film Festival.

case, revolves around a triangular relationship featuring a middle-class couple whose lives are thrown into disarray by the arrival of a young working-class woman from the countryside. She starts out as a maid in their household and soon becomes the husband's mistress. In honor of Kim Ki-young's most favored name for these characters, Kim Kyeong refers to them as "the Myeong-jas" and notes they are the monstrous feminine locus of horror in these films and must therefore be eradicated. Although some present-day feminist perspectives may lead to a sneaking admiration for their ghastly power, it is said that contemporary female audiences bellowed for vengeance against these mistresses (Kim Soyoung),[9] so there seems little doubt such a reading must be understood as operating against the grain.

Important though Freudian interpretations of the horror film are, working with Freud's ideas often leads to following his tendency to universalism and loss of sociohistorical specificity.[10] However, by engaging with the specific characteristics of the gender dynamics in these films, it is possible to get a sense of how they use horror's deep-seated psychological patterns to also communicate a relation to their era of production. Kim Jiseok displaces earlier interpretations that emphasized the films' interest in an apparently universal and dangerous female nature, composed of a savage survival instinct manifested in material greed, rapacious sexuality geared toward reproduction, and absence of moral qualms. Instead, he sees this particular representation of femininity as part of a larger picture, in which "losing his position as a patriarch under pressure from his wife's economic strength dwarfs and enervates the husband," to the extent that he "becomes impotent as his wife ignores him to an ever greater degree, and he gradually turns to masochism as an escape mechanism . . . pursues the maternal and realizes the death drive" (Kim Ji-seok).

Kim Ji-seok also notes that "the direct reason for this [situation] is social, because greed spurred by rapid industrialization breaks the traditional family system and makes the wife take over the patriarchal role from her husband." Although Kim is writing about films of the 1970s and 80s and An Jinsoo's focus is on the 1960 film *The Housemaid*, An notes a somewhat similar combination of elements and relates them closely to the specific social and economic changes of the time. He carries out a close analysis of the context and concludes, "The threat to masculinity is . . . a condensed figuration of a deep-seated social anxiety that emerged in a particular historical conjuncture." Just like Kim Ji-seok, An notes the pressure on men created by economic and material ambitions expressed in the films through their wives but notes that in 1960, prior to the coup that put Park Chung-hee in power and began rapid industrialization and economic growth, the economic situation was more fragile.

What can we conclude from observations of this type about the position the films take on modernization and gender? Because these analyses emphasize the negative results of modernization, it might be inferred that the films constitute a distanced critique of modernity. Yet attention to this specific issue reveals that this is not quite the case. First, these emasculated husbands are not traditional patriarchs left behind by modernity. In *The Housemaid* trilogy, the husband is a piano teacher in *The Housemaid* itself, in *The Insect Woman* he is a professor, and in *Carnivore* he is a publisher. These professions are closely associated with modernity and would be considered highly respectable. Yet, while they might be honorable, none is a money-spinner. Kim Kyeong relates these figures to the idea of the *seonbi*, or gentleman scholar: "According to *Songri Hak* (Seong Confucianism), "a seonbi should not be sullied by an involvement with money matters, which were inferior to scholarly pursuits." These new modern professions are attractive to the husbands because they extend neo-Confucian values into the modern, but because they do not bring in enough money, the wives have to work. In the earliest film in the group, *The Housemaid*, the wife sews at home to help pay for the two-level Western-style home she desires. By the time of the *Fire Woman* and its remake, although she is still a homebody, she is running a large battery hen farm out of the house, and in *The Insect Woman* and *Carnivore* she is running a transport business, and a real estate business, respectively. The films seem to be suggesting this state of affairs has dismaying results. However, because the husbands are engaged in modern pursuits, this is seen from within modern values as a difference between high cultural values and materialism, rather than from outside as a traditionalist critique of modernity itself.

Similar ambiguities arise when one considers the monstrous maids—the Myeong-jas. One could try to see them as eruptions of a premodern and even primitive rural culture into the cozy domesticity of the modern nuclear family. The Korean word for "housemaid," *hanyu*, translates literally as "the woman below," a position that places her parallel to the position in which the unconscious is usually imagined and from which the repressed is understood to sometimes return. This deployment of positions carries through to class and perspective. The film itself begins in the middle-class home, then shifts to the factory where the music teacher conducts a class as part of his efforts to raise enough money for the new house his wife wants. His wife also decides she needs a maid to go with her new home, especially when she is given a fright by a rat in one of the cupboards. The piano teacher asks one of his students from the factory, Miss Cho, to find him a maid, and she in turn moves further down the class scale by recruiting one of the factory's cleaning girls for the job. The first of Kim Ki-young's Myeong-jas makes her proper appearance about twenty minutes into the film. (In retrospect, she has appeared twice, shot from the back, in earlier scenes set in the factory.) Not only does the film establish itself in a middle-class milieu from the perspective of which she is an outsider, but also she is clearly associated with the lowest of the lower classes in the film. Finally, class is equated with civilization when the housemaid proves herself so untroubled by rats that she happily kills them and then picks them up by the tail to throw them away. This suggests a kind of animal insensitivity and ruthlessness on the part of the maid herself, which the film then confirms as she schemes to take over the family and the house.

However, the situation is not so clear-cut. First, as has already been indicated, the films depict the modern nuclear families not as cozy but rather as dysfunctional even prior to the arrival of the maids. In the case of *The Housemaid*, striving for a better and more modern home is exhausting the wife, who has taken in sewing for ten years to pay for it, and putting a strain on the marriage. Second, not only in *The Housemaid* but also in the other films, the maids are needed as a result of both parents' income-producing activities, so they are themselves modern rather than premodern figures. And, most ironic of all, despite all the havoc they wreak, they do restore the husband's potency. In a sense, then, as the modern destroys the privileges of the old *seonbi* and the material household that supported him, it provides him with new opportunities in the form of the maid. But even here this is contradiction and complexity. The maid may have an uncanny resonance for the modern patriarch with

Figure 5.3. *Insect Woman.* Courtesy Pusan Film Festival.

the type of household otherwise lost in the transition to the modern. But the modern economy empowers both the wife and the maid in ways that make the sexual temptation represented by the maid dangerous to the husband's new household and his status within it.

The ambivalent and contradictory feelings communicated through these gender dramas suggest a very different relation to the social changes brought about by modernization from those associated with the realist drama. If the realist narrative is associated with the legend and ideology of the emergence of secular humanism and the self-motivated entrepreneur in Western culture, the conditions of modernization in Korea under Park Chung-hee were quite different. This is what makes the horror film a more appropriate genre. For unlike the Euro-American experience, where modernity and capitalism were developed by the emergent middle classes against the state and the monarchy, under Park Chung-hee it was the state that directed, organized, led, and if necessary forced the middle classes into rapid industrialization and modernization. Although modernization promised the middle class material wealth and power on a national scale—making it highly desired—it also turned its would be beneficiaries into pawns who lost their agency and individual autonomy in the process. If certain families prospered running what became the enormous corporations known as *chaebol*, they did so at the pleasure of Park's regime and certainly not by fighting it. The fact that rapid modernization in South Korea under Park Chung-hee was accompanied by the turn away from rather than toward both democracy and the free market is emblematic of this very different experience.[11]

Not only was modernization initiated by the state rather than the middle classes, but also it was copied from overseas rather than originating locally. Perhaps this accounts for the high visibility of Western material culture in modern settings found in the films. The piano teacher's piano is an obvious example, but only the tip of the iceberg. First, as An Jin-soo notes, the house desired by the wife in *The Housemaid* is not just a large one, but a specifically Western-style, two-level house. Moreover, these houses in which the main characters live and the drama is played out are packed with Western-style furniture, including walls full of grandfather clocks and cuckoo clocks, stained glass partitions, and so forth. Mealtimes are particularly good opportunities for the display of Western consumption, both literally when butter and milk are served and in the display of coffee percolators, toasters, and enormous Kelvinators.

Furthermore, this paraphernalia of the modern West is—in the case of Kim Ki-young's films—a threatening and integral part of its reference to the horror genre. Park Jiye has astutely pointed out in her analysis of Kim's films, "Mansions and castles, i.e., houses, function as major horrifying objects in the gothic novel." She notes that, as is customary in the horror genre, the houses in Kim's films are haunted, not only by the maids, but also by mice, rats and other menacing plagues of animal vermin.[12] Furthermore, the space of the stairs—so strongly encoded as signifier of the special two-level quality of the homes—is also the space on which so many of the accidents and murders occur (Park). In *The Housemaid* itself, this pattern is established from the minute the family looks around its almost completed new home. The son calls out, "Behind you! A rat!" and his disabled sister—who is a few steps up the stairs—stumbles and falls. The stairs then become the site for various more serious and even fatal falls later in the film. The cinematographic representation of these spaces and products accentuates both their fetishization and their threatening quality. Consumer objects loom in the foreground of shots. Complicated latticework, chair backs, and stained glass partitions are positioned between the camera and the protagonists, seemingly imprisoning them. Often the camera is positioned low, including the ceilings and rafters in shots so that they loom over the characters, and the angle of the stairs seems particularly steep.

Just as the analysis of gender leads many commentators to produce interpretations that suggest a critique of the modern, so this leads Park Jiye to emphasize the "pessimistic" quality of the films. But again, it would be wrong to deduce that this constitutes a distanced critique of the modern. For the foreign origins of these material objects supports the simultaneous construal of them as threatening *and* as desirable. They have a mysterious and magical quality as things not produced locally but imported. Writing of the arrival of the cinema itself in Korea, Kim Soyoung has noted how early Korean audiences were more fascinated by the machinery itself than the pictures it projected and how they understood its processes as magical rather than material. Furthermore, as she points out, when the first set of cinematographic equipment was left at the court in exchange for bolts of silk, a pattern of exchanging raw materials and light industrial products for desired but mysterious high technology was established (Berry and Kim). Here again, we have the ambivalence of the Korean experience of modernity as imported; it is at once desired and also a submission to the foreign. That which is intended to strengthen Korea is only achieved by submission to the foreign.

What can we conclude from Kim Ki-young's deployment of the horror film genre within the fantastic mode as the privileged aesthetic expression of modernity in Korea under the Park Chung-hee regime? One possibility would be to set up an opposition between a Western experience and aesthetic expression of modernity and the Korean equivalent. However, this may also be too simple. In recent years, scholars in the West have also been challenging the assumption of a relatively straightforward equation between modernity and straightforward realist drama, suggesting that melodrama with its heavy divergence from realism is at least as central to Hollywood studio–era cinema.[13] Therefore, perhaps one should consider not only a number of different modernities but also a number of different experiences of *those* modernities, expressed in different cinematic patterns. This would also accommodate the need to acknowledge that however appropriate Kim's aesthetic may seem to our understanding of modernity in Korea under Park Chung-hee, his films are not only unusual but also unique.

Notes

1. Lee Sun-hwa quotes this line at the beginning of her analysis of the highly mannered language that characterizes Kim Ki-young's films, "Language of Artifice and Exaggeration: *Carnivore*," http://www.knua.ac.kr/cinema/KKY/Stairway/LSH.htm (mirror site: http://www.asianfilms.org/korea/kky/KKY/Stairway/LSH.htm). Lee's essay was written as part of a Korean National University of the Arts project coordinated by Professor Kim Soyoung and me to research Kim Ki-young's films and build a Web site about them. The ideas presented here were generated out of that project, so I would like to thank Professor Kim, Lee Youn-yi, Kim Sung-eun, Lee Kyung-eun, Lee Sun-hwa, Choi Eun-yeung, Park Seung-taek, Lee Jee-eun, and Ahn Min-hwa for the discussions we had during that process. This chapter would have been impossible to write without them. My visit to Korea was partially funded by a Korea Foundation fellowship, for which I am also deeply grateful, and our research would not have been possible without the cooperation of

the Korean National Film Archive and Kim Ki-young's descendants. Finally, I would like to thank Lee Jee-eun for her unstinting efforts as Web master.

2. For filmographical details, see http://www.knua.ac.kr/cinema/KKY/Cabinet/Film%20List.htm (mirror site: http://www.asianfilms.org/korea/kky/KKY/Cabinet/Film%20List.htm). For biography, see Lee Youn-yi, "Biography," http://www.knua.ac.kr/cinema/KKY/Cabinet/Bio1.htm (mirror site: http://www.asianfilms.org/korea/kky/KKY/Cabinet/Bio1.htm).

3. Chris Berry, "Going Global: An Interview with Lee Yong Kwan," http://www.knua.ac.kr/cinema/KKY/What-Saw/LYKINT.htm (mirror site: http://www.asianfilms.org/korea/kky/KKY/What-Saw/LYKINT.htm). Lee points out that the same holds true for the other two directors considered as the founders of Korean realism and as candidates for Pusan's earliest retrospectives, Yu Hyun-mok and Shin Sang-ok, suggesting the need for a wholesale reevaluation of the Korean cinema of this period. However, their films are as clearly part of the fantastic mode as Kim Ki-young's are.

4. For an example of critical writing animated by faith in liberal-humanist realism, see veteran Korean critic and scholar Lee Young-il's 1965 essay on the shift in Kim Ki-young's filmmaking away from realism, "From Melodrama to Realism to Expressionism: The Early Career of Kim Ki-young," http://www.knua.ac.kr/cinema/KKY/What-Saw/LYI.htm (mirror site: http://www.asianfilms.org/korea/kky/KKY/What-Saw/LYI.htm). His cited preference for an early Kim Ki-young film in a more recent interview is also an example of this aesthetic. See http://www.knua.ac.kr/cinema/KKY/What-Saw/LYIINT.htm (mirror site: http://www.asianfilms.org/korea/kky/KKY/What-Saw/LYIINT.htm).

5. For example, Roland Barthes, *S/Z*, trans. Richard Miller (London: Cape, 1975).

6. For example, Noel Burch, *Theory of Film Practice*, trans. Helen R. Lane (New York: Praeger, 1973), and the critical writing associated with the journal *Screen* in the 1970s and early 1980s.

7. In fact, Kim regularly mixes genres. For example, *Killer Butterfly* (1972) mixes science fiction with the cycle of films about students and the horror film. However, the umbrella genre under which this mixing occurs is the horror film. For further discussion, see Chris Berry, "Genrebender: Kim Ki-young Mixes It Up," http://www.knua.kr/cinema/KKY/Stairway/CB2.htm, (mirror site: http://www.asianfilms.org/korea/kky/KKY/Stairway/CB2.htm), and Chris Berry, "*Salinnabileul Ggotneun Yeoja/Killer Butterfly*," in *The Cinema of Japan and Korea*, ed. Justin Bowyer (Harrow: Wallflower, 2004), 111–20.

8. Julia Kristeva, trans. Leon S. Roudiez, *Powers of Horror* (New York: Columbia University Press, 1982). Kristeva's primary source in Freud for this engagement is his essay "The 'Uncanny,' " (1919).

9. See also "The Monstrous Feminine and Class Conflicts in *The Housemaid*," *Rediscovering Korean Classics: The 20th Hong Kong International Film Festival*, ed. Wong Ain-ling (Hong Kong: Urban Council, 1996), 14–16.

10. For example, Sin Chang-heui analyzes the films as expressions of an auteurist vision of "the essential truth about human beings"; Sin Chang-heui, "A Study of the Images of Women in Kim Ki-young's Films *Woman of Fire*, *Numi*,

and *Carnivore*," http://www.knua.ac.kr/cinema/KKY/Stairway/SCH.htm (mirror site: http://www.asianfilms.org/korea/kky/KKY/Stairway/SCH.htm), extracted and translated by Lee Sun-Hwa from the original MA thesis (Hangyang University, 1990).

11. For an account of this process, see for example, Bruce Cumings, "Korean Sun Rising: Industrialization, 1953–1996," *Korea's Place in the Sun: A Modern History* (New York: Norton, 1997), 299–336.

12. For a more detailed analysis of animals in Kim's films, see Kim Sungeun, "Animals in the House of Kim Ki-young: Hens, Rats and Cracks in the Modern Family," http://www.knua.ac.kr/cinema/KKY/Stairway/KSE2.htm (mirror site: http://www.asianfilms.org/korea/kky/KKY/Stairway/KSE2.htm).

13. See, for example, the essays collected in Jane Gaines, ed., *Classical Hollywood* (Durham: Duke University Press, 1992).

Works Cited

An Jinsoo. "The Housemaid and Troubled Masculinity in the 1960s." http://www.Knua.ac/kr/cinema/KKY/Window/AJS.text.htm (mirror site: http://www.Asianfilms.org/korea/kky/KKY/Window/AJS.htm).

Barthes, Roland. *S/Z*, trans. Richard Miller. London: Cape, 1975.

Bazin, Andre. *What Is Cinema?* 2 vols., trans. Hugh Gray. Berkeley: University of California Press, 1967, 1971.

Berry, Chris. "*Salinnabileul Ggotneun Yeoja/Killer Butterfly*." In *The Cinema of Japan and Korea*. Ed. Justin Bowyer. Harrow: Wallflower, 2004. 111–20.

———. "Going Global: An Interview with Lee Yong Kwan." http://www.knua.ac.kr/cinema/KKY/What-Saw/LYKINT.htm (mirror site: http://www.asianfilms.org/korea/kky/KKY/What-Saw/LYKINT.htm.

———. "Genrebender: Kim Ki-young Mixes It Up." http://www.knua.kr/cinema/KKY/Stairway/CB2.htm, (mirror site: http://www.asianfilms.org/korea/kky/KKY/Stairway/CB2.htm).

———. Berry, Chris, and Kim Soyoung. "*Suri Suri Masuri*: The Magic of Korean Horror Film." *Postcolonial Studies* 3.1 (2000): 53–60.

Bordwell, David, Janet Staiger, and Kristin Thompson. *The Classical Hollywood Cinema: Film Style and Mode of Production to 1960*. New York: Columbia University Press, 1985.

Burch, Noel. *Theory of Film Practice*, trans. Helen R. Lane. New York: Praeger, 1973.

Clover, Carol J. *Men, Women and Chain Saws: Gender in the Modern Horror Film*. Princeton: Princeton University Press, 1992.

Creed, Barbara. *The Monstrous-Feminine: Film, Feminism, Psychoanalysis*. London: Routledge, 1993.

Cumings, Bruce. *Korea's Place in the Sun: A Modern History*. New York: Norton, 1997.

Gaines, Jane, ed. *Classical Hollywood Narrative: The Paradigm Wars*. Durham: Duke University Press, 1992.

Kim Ji-seok. "Reinterpreting Kim Ki-young." *Reinterpreting Asian Films*. Seoul: Hanul, 1996.

Kim Kyeong. "Repetition Compulsion in Kim Ki-young's Films." http://www.knua.ac.kr/cinema/KKY/Stairway/KKtext.htm (mirror site: http://www.asianfilms.org/korea/kky/KKY/Stairway/KK/htm) extracted and translated by Kim Sung-eun from *Film Study* 13 (1997): 251–85.

Kim Soyoung. "The Housemaid and the Korean Woman's Film." *http://www.knua.ac.kr/cinema/KKY/What-saw/KSY1text.htm* (mirror site: *http://www.asianfilms.org/korea/kky/KKY/What-Saw/KSY1text.htm*) extracted and adapted from "Questions of Women's Film: *The Maid, Madame Freedom,* and *Women.*" Ed. Chungmoo Choi. *Post-Colonial Classics of Korean Cinema.* Irvine, CA: Korean Film Festival Committee at the University of California, 1998. 13–22.

Kim Sung-eun. "Animals in the House of Kim Ki-young: Hens, Rats, and Cracks in the Modern Family." *http://www.knua.ac.kr/cinema/KKY/Stairway/KSE2.htm* (mirror site: http://www.asianfilms.org/korea/kky/KKY/Stairway/KSE2.htm).

Kristeva, Julia, trans. Leon S. Roudiez, *Powers of Horror*. New York: Columbia University Press, 1982.

Lee Sun-hwa. "Language of Artifice and Exaggeration: *Carnivore.*" http://www.knua.ac.kr/cinema/KKY/Stairway/LSH.htm (mirror site: http://www.asianfilms.org/korea/kky/KKY/Stairway/LSH.htm).

Lee Young-il. "From Melodrama to Realism to Expressionism: The Early Career of Kim Ki-young." http://www.knua.ac.kr/cinema/KKY/What-Saw/LYI.htm (mirror site: http://www.asianfilms.org/korea/kky/KKY/What-Saw/LYI.htm).

Lee Youn-yi. "Biography." http://www.knua.ac.kr/cinema/KKY/Cabinet/Bio1.htm (mirror site: http://www.asianfilms.org/korea/kky/KKY/Cabinet/Bio1.htm).

Moon Jae-chol. "Cinema on the Edge." *http://www.knua.ac/kr/cinema/KKY/Window/MJtext.htm* (mirror site: *http://www.asianfilms.org/korea/kky/KKY/Window/MJC.htm*), extracted from "Aesthetics of Deviation and Contradiction." Ed. Lee Yong Kwan and Lee Sang Yong. *Kim Ki-young: Cinema of Diabolical Desire and Death.* Busan: Pusan International Film Festival, 1997, 32–41.

Park, Jiye. "Gothic Imagination in *Carnivore* and *The Housemaid. http://www.knua.ac.kr/cinema/KKy/Stairway/PJYtext.htm* (mirror site: http://www.asianfilms.org/korea/kky/KKY/Stairway/PJY.htm).

Sin Chang-heui. "A Study of the Images of Women in Kim Ki-young's Films," *Woman of Fire, Numi,* and *Carnivore.*" Master's thesis, Hangyang University, 1990.

———, and Ahn Min Hwa. "The Kim Ki-young Revival: An Interview with Chung Sung Il." http://www.knua.ac.kr/cinema/KKY/What-Saw/CSIINT.htm (mirror site: http://www.asianfilms.org/korea/kky/KKY/What-Saw/CSIINT.htm).

Watt, Ian. *The Rise of the Novel: Studies in Defoe, Richardson and Fielding*. Berkeley: University of California Press, 1957.

Wong Ain-ling "The Monstrous Feminine and Class Conflicts in *The Housemaid.*" *Rediscovering Korean Classics: The 20th Hong Kong International Film Festival.* Hong Kong: Urban Council, 1996. 14–16.

6

HYE SEUNG CHUNG AND
DAVID SCOTT DIFFRIENT

Forgetting to Remember, Remembering to Forget

The Politics of Memory and Modernity in the Fractured Films of Lee Chang-dong and Hong Sang-soo

Being obliged to forget becomes the basis for remembering the nation, peopling it anew, imagining the possibility of other contending and liberating forms of cultural identification.

—Homi Bhabha, "DissemiNation"

HAVING LONG SLIPPED THROUGH THE fingers of Western scholars and historians, Korean cinema has recently entered academia and sparked debates about the role of filmmakers in South

Korea's "nation-building" project. From the auteur-laden Golden Age of the 1960s, which produced such social-problem classics as *Aimless Bullet* (1961) and *The Coachman* (1961), to the rash of tacky—if not outright offensive—"bar-hostess" sexploitations of the 1970s,[1] both the high and low ends of South Korea's cinematic spectrum have proven to be fertile ground for elucidating the country's shift from postwar poverty to *chaebol*-led prosperity, from chamber-pot tradition to mobile-phone modernity. Dominating recent discussions are references to *minjung*,[2] and post-*minjung*—filmmakers with at least one foot outside the Chungmuro-centered film industry, Korean New Wave directors such as Jang Sun-woo and Park Kwang-su, who emerged during the late-1980s and have continued to provide politically charged, counterhegemonic alternatives to the generically formulaic films that blight the box office. The combined work of two latecomers to New Korean Cinema, Lee Chang-dong and Hong Sang-soo, provides an especially fascinating case study in light of this recent focus.

This chapter positions two critically acclaimed films released in 2000, Lee Chang-dong's *Peppermint Candy* and Hong Sang-soo's *Virgin Stripped Bare by Her Bachelors*, at narratological, historical, and ideological crossroads. Both films feature fragmented, episodic narrative structures sprinkled with novelistic chapter titles and/or numbering that demand active participation on the audience's part in assembling bits of incomplete or nonchronological information into a cohesive story. As will be elaborated in greater detail, Lee's film hinges upon the psychological trauma of a middle-aged man whose loss of innocence, accumulated anguish, and apparently irrational acts of violence allegorically reflect the political and/or socioeconomic failings of the nation over a period of twenty years. The character's transformation is visually bookended by two close-ups. The first is of the protagonist committing suicide in 1999. The second is of the same man, only younger, who—in 1979—dreams of a hopeful future. Bracketed by these two images, the film explores the enigma of the protagonist's death as well as the turbulent history of modern South Korea in seven chapters presented in reverse-chronological order.

Similarly, Hong's film consists of five episodes with overlapping, repetitive, supplementary, or even contradictory accounts of everyday events and ostensibly mundane actions. However, unlike *Peppermint Candy*, which is filtered through the consciousness of its male protagonist, *Virgin Stripped Bare by Her Bachelors* presents, in "cubist" fashion, two different interpretations of the central couple's rocky union: one emanating from a male focalization and suggesting a more ideal and innocent romance based on coincidences and happenstance meetings; the other coming from a female focalization and unveiling the crafty machinations of a young woman who seeks social mobility through a lucrative interclass marriage. In the course of our textual analysis, we engage in a dialogical conversation with two often mutually exclusive critical paradigms (narrative theory and cultural studies) so as to showcase their compatibility in uncovering the complex hermeneutic operations of these modernist narratives, which are entrenched in historiographic and sociopolitical details unique to South Korea's compressed modernization and materialist culture.

Opening the New Millennium: *Peppermint Candy* and National Pride

On the opening night of the 4th Pusan International Film Festival (October 1999), novelist-turned-screenwriter/director Lee Chang-dong's sophomore feature *Peppermint Candy* premiered, receiving enthusiastic kudos from over five thousand theatergoers. Domestic newspapers and film magazines unanimously hailed Lee's film as a masterpiece overshadowing the festival's past choices of opening films—Wayne Wang's *Chinese Box* (1997) and Mohsen Makhmalbaf's *The Silence* (1998). Twenty-odd international film festivals hurriedly sent out invitations for *Peppermint Candy*,[3] which garnered high acclaim from members of the foreign press after screenings in the NHK-sponsored Asian Film Festival held in Tokyo prior to its domestic release (fittingly, on the first day of the new millen-

Figure 6.1. *Peppermint Candy* (2000). Courtesy Pusan Film Festival.

nium). It also swept major prizes, including Best Picture, Best Director, and Best Screenplay, at the 37th *Taejong* (Grand Bell) Awards, the highest honors for Korean films. To what can we attribute the film's critical success, volleyed across national borders? More specifically, what aspects of *Peppermint Candy* beguiled critics representing such varied countries as France, Hungary, Ukraine, and Tibet (to name a few) when the film was shown in the Directors' Fortnight during the 53rd Cannes International Film Festival?

Undoubtedly, the very things that attracted these critics are what distinguish *Peppermint Candy* from other crowd-pleasing, festival-targeted films. Employing an experimental narrative framework from which historical and political subtexts erupt, Lee Chang-dong "decolonizes" the narrational system from dominant Hollywood film language, audaciously challenging the propulsive, forward-moving linearity typical of mainstream cinema with a fragmented, regressive temporality. Consisting of seven discrete chapters, *Peppermint Candy* projects in reverse-chronological order a twenty-year period in the adult life of its protagonist, beginning in spring 1999 and ending in fall 1979. With its episodic structure framed by images of railroad tracks and interspersed chapter titles, this pre-*Memento*[6] meditation on memory moves back to the past without resorting to conventional flashbacks. As a flashback film without flashbacks. *Peppermint Candy* concludes without returning to the starting temporal point, capsizing established conventions of narrating the past.

Like Lee's debut film *Green Fish* (1997), *Peppermint Candy* foregrounds the dystopian implications of postcolonial modernization by vividly depicting the violence, inhumanity, and corruption undergirding a development-driven society (marching to the governmental slogan, Growth first, distribution later) in a realistic mode. In an interview with a local magazine, Lee recounts an anecdote about an overseas Korean councilor's reaction to *Green Fish* when it was screened at an international festival: "A film like that, which shows the shame and ugliness of our country to foreign audiences, undermines years of our efforts to promote Korea overseas in the blink of an eye" (Kim Myong-yol 1999). Bureaucratic and jingoistic as this remark may be, it effectively describes the subversive power of Lee Chang-dong's "ugly," truth-telling aesthetics.

Plunging into the Past: A Reverse-Chronology Realist Poetics

According to Teshome Gabriel, in the third, combative phase of Third Cinema, "the past is necessary for the understanding of the present, and serves as a strategy for the future" (344). This description is particularly applicable to *Peppermint Candy*, which sifts through defining moments in recent South Korean history, placing them within a complex narrative economy. Teasing out those narrative complexities necessitates distinguishing between the film's *fabula* (story) and *syuzhet* (plot). According to David Bordwell's redeployment of these Russian formalist terms, the fabula is a chronological chain of events that the spectator's imagination inferentially constructs within a film's given narrative logic of causality. The syuzhet, on the other hand, is the arrangement of the story, its emplotment or orchestration—a system that simultaneously facilitates and delays the spectator's piecing together of the fabula. As Bordwell notes, the syuzhet builds up suspense through diverse strategies (retardation, distortion, and withholding of information) that postpone the completion of fabula construction and provoke the spectator's curiosity (49–53). Narrational principles and hermeneutic configurations of the fabula/syuzhet dialectic are pertinent to the analysis of *Peppermint Candy's* reverse-chronology structure.

The first shot of the film, over which the credits appear, shows a pinprick of light at the end of a train tunnel that gradually engulfs the screen. This telling image sets the stage for enigmas that will slowly emerge out of darkness into light. The film's opening chapter, "Outdoor Excursion: Spring 1999," introduces us to Yong-ho, a frazzled fortysomething who makes an impromptu appearance at a twenty-year reunion picnic held by his former factory coworkers at a riverbank. After his deranged yelling and karaoke singing momentarily disrupt their party, he climbs atop a bridge across which railroad tracks are stretched. This first chapter ends with a close-up still frame of our suicidal protagonist. Faced with the imminent collision of an oncoming train, the enraged, hysterical Yong-ho wails,"I want to go back!"

The first chapter formulates the prime enigma of the film: Why does Yong-ho commit suicide? Why is he so high-strung and downhearted? The chapter that immediately follows provides a partial answer by releasing information about his identity as a bankrupt and divorced businessman. Having granted Yong-ho's wish of going back, the syuzhet presents fabula events that occurred three days earlier in the second chapter, "The Camera: Three Days Ago, Spring 1999." Yong-ho is shown buying a gun, which he puts into his mouth. He pulls the trigger, only to realize with a mixture of disappointment and relief that the weapon has no bullets. Later he visits his exwife, who coldly shuts the door in his face. In front of his makeshift home, Yong-ho encounters a stranger, the husband of his first love, Sun-im, who delivers a message that she is seriously ill and wants to see Yong-ho before she passes away. Arriving at the hospital, Yong-ho finds that Sun-im has fallen into a coma. With tears pouring down his face, he presents a jar of peppermint candy to the unconscious woman and reminisces about the candies packed inside letters she sent to him when he was in the military. As Yong-ho leaves, Sun-im's husband hands him the camera that Sun-im has kept for him, an object that no longer holds value for Yong-ho, who sells it for food. New enigmas are introduced in this chapter, specifically the nature of Yong-ho and Sun-im's relationship, the relevance of the camera, and the meaning of peppermint candy—the cryptic "Rosebud" of this film. As the ensuing chapters progress, narrative time regresses further into Yong-ho's past, gradually solving these riddles, as well as the enigma of his suicide.

The third chapter, though beginning with the utopian words, "Life Is Beautiful: Summer 1994," reveals the grim circumstances of a dysfunctional marriage rocked by deceit and spousal abuse. In marked contrast to his financial destitution in the earlier episodes, Yong-ho is presented as a successful small business owner. Although he beats his wife, Hong-ja, whom he catches at a motel with another man, he is having an affair of his own with his secretary. On a date with his mistress, Yong-ho spots a man from his past, Myong-sik. In the restaurant restroom, Yong-ho asks Myong-sik, "Life is beautiful, isn't it?" The mystery of these men's relationship and the curious remark that hangs momentarily in the air is solved in the next chapter, which begins with the intertitle "Confession: Spring 1987." Yong-ho and Hong-ja are newlyweds. Yong-ho, now a police detective, questions Myong-sik about the whereabouts of a student activist. After several interrogations, which escalate into water torture, Myong-sik surrenders the information. Yong-ho asks the bruised and bawling student if he really thinks "life is beautiful," a phrase scribbled in Myong-sik's diary that the police confiscated. Yong-ho and his colleagues travel to Gunsan (Sun-im's hometown) to capture the fugitive activist. On the eve of the arrest, Yong-ho sleeps with a local bar girl, calling her "Sun-im."

Yong-ho is new to the police department in the fifth chapter, which is labeled "Prayer: Fall 1984." His first assignment is to crack a factory workers' union, a task that forces him to torture a labor activist. That same day, Sun-im, having traced Yong-ho's whereabouts through his parents, comes to meet her long-lost love, accompanying him to Hong-ja's restaurant (where he flirts with Hong-ja to push Sun-im away). Sun-im offers him a camera as a gift, which Yong-ho refuses to accept. Later that night, Yong-ho takes Hong-ja to a motel where she recites a prayer before they sleep together. The questions set forth in the second chapter are partially answered in this episode, which shows Yong-ho and Sun-im's separation, as well as his rejection of her gift, the camera. However, the reasons why Yong-ho cruelly pushes his beloved Sun-im away and why Sun-im wants to present a camera to Yong-ho remain unanswered. The total disclosure of the central enigma, Yong-ho's ruin and demise, occurs in the penultimate chapter, entitled "Military Visit: May 1980."

Sun-im, hoping to see Yong-ho, visits the military camp where he is stationed, but her request is rejected due to martial law, which has suddenly been imposed. In the barracks, Yong-ho frantically assembles his combat gear, spilling a bag of peppermint candy in the process, and is ordered into a military truck. Unknown to the soldiers, their destination is Gwangju, where an uprising is taking place. That night, during a skirmish, Yong-ho is shot in the foot and, while waiting for help, mistakes a high school student emerging from the shadows for Sun-im. Out of panic and confusion, he accidentally shoots and kills the innocent girl. The last chapter, "Picnic: Fall 1979," begins with a group of factory worker friends, among them Yong-ho and Sun-im, gathering at the same riverbank shown at the beginning of the film. Sun-im hands the twenty-year-old Yong-ho a piece of peppermint candy, telling him that she wraps a thousand of them a day. Not only does peppermint candy signify the innocence of first love, but it is also related to Sun-im's identity as a candy factory worker, a sliver of fabula information that had thus far been suspended. Likewise, the enigma of the camera is finally disclosed when Yong-ho confides his dream of becoming a photographer who captures the beauty of wildflowers. Singing a song, the same one vocalized in the opening, together with their friends, Yong-ho and Sun-im shyly exchange tender glances.

When chronologically reordered through fabula construction into a forward-moving narrative, *Peppermint Candy* displays a conventional hero's downfall trajectory that begins during an innocent, hopeful period of youth (fall 1979) and ends, after gradual corruption, with his demise (spring 1999). By delivering the story in a backward fashion, however, Lee turns a relatively straightforward narrative into a plot saturated with multiple enigmas. Following the logic of the hermeneutic code conceived by Roland Barthes,[5] the opening chapters of the film propose, formulate, and thematize a series of riddles, the answers of which are delayed and suspended. While key fabula information about the mystery of Yong-ho's suicide is given in the last stages of the film, partial answers pepper the entire narrative. At first glance, *Peppermint Candy* seems to follow the mystery fiction's delayed hermeneutic structure, yet its tactics and effects sever the film from that generic heritage. In the mystery plot, it is the detective that infers prior events within narrative causality, time, and space and reconstructs the entire fabula in an explication scene that occurs near the end. Along the way, the syuzhet presents distorted information (snares and equivocations) to enhance the viewer/reader's anticipated surprise. In *Peppermint Candy*, the viewer assumes the detective role. The reverse-chronology syuzhet induces a more active mental orchestration of fabula events.

The effect of reverse chronology is not surprise, however, but irony. For example, in the third chapter, Yong-ho's mysterious aphorism, life is beautiful, is given an ironic twist following his financial and moral downfall in the preceding chapters. In the fourth chapter, the maxim is doubly ironic when Yong-ho quotes it from the diary of Myong-sik after severely torturing him. In the final chapter, irony is imbued with a bitter aftertaste, for indeed life was once beautiful for Yong-ho. The subversive power of *Peppermint Candy*'s back-peddling narration lies in the fact that it transforms a drama of total loss (irreversibility) into a drama of return (reversibility). The narrative coils into a circular series, returning to the same picnic location permeated with the same diegetic music of the first chapter. However, this time Yong-ho is young and hopeful. Ironically, he feels that he has been to this picnic site before. Rather than déjà vu, Sun-im surmises, it must be a pleasant dream. Does this dream reflect his nightmarish future? Does he *remember* his future? Or is life nothing but a circular series of repeated events? There are no satisfactory answers to these questions, just as there is no end to this narrative: The end is the beginning, and vice-versa.

The Gwangju Uprising and the IMF Crisis: Narrating Nation, Class, and Gender

In *Peppermint Candy*, personal time is intimately interwoven with national time. Because Yong-ho's tragic life reflects South Korea's tumultuous modern history, it is important that we situate the story within historical, political, and cultural contexts of the 1980s and 1990s so as to lend greater weight to the ideological significance of the film's fragmented narrative structure. When chronologically reconstructed, Yong-ho's story begins in the last chapter set in the fall of 1979, a period of innocence, youth, and first love mirroring the utopian-tinged national time. In October 1979, the eighteen-year dictatorship of President Park Chung-hee screeched to a halt when he was assassinated by his own right-hand man, Kim Chae-gyu, Director of the Korean Central Intelligence Agency (KCIA). After Park's death, South Koreans enjoyed a brief "Spring of Seoul" in ardent hope of dismantling of the late President's *Yushin* regime, which ruled the nation with authoritarian emergency decrees, suppressing fundamental civil freedoms.[6] However, the interim government's democratic reform did not last long, as General Chun Doo-hwan seized power in a military coup. Chun declared martial law, closed universities, prohibited political meetings, and arrested hundreds of oppositional leaders and dissidents.

On May 18, 1980, the approximate setting of the film's penultimate chapter, citizens of Gwangju arose in a democratic revolt, demanding the eradication of martial law and the release from jail of their political leader,

Kim Dae-jung, who would be elected president of South Korea in 1998. The Gwangju Uprising was brutally suppressed by Chun Doo-hwan's paratroopers, who indiscriminately injured and massacred protesters and bystanders with clubs, knives, and guns. According to official records, 154 were killed, 47 missing, and 2,711 wounded during this ten-day clash. Another report puts the figures at 500 dead and 960 missing.[7] At any rate, the Gwangju Uprising served as a guiding spirit for the 1980s *minjung* movement taken up by laborers, students, and intellectuals, and contributed to the surge of anti-Americanism in South Korea (due largely to accounts of the U.S. allegedly authorizing Chun's military operation).

The Gwangju tragedy is at the heart of Yong-ho's moral and spiritual deterioration and represents a repressed trauma for both the individual and the nation. Even though the film does not directly depict the cruelty of the suppression forces, Yong-ho's killing of a high school girl, which stands for the symbolic wiping out of his first love, Sun-im, allegorizes the mass murders of innocent people in Gwangju. Irreconcilable guilt pushes Yong-ho to give up his first love and shoulder the ruthless police duties of torturing student and labor activists. The centrality of this time in both Yong-ho's life and Korean history is demonstrated by the fact that it is the only chapter that specifies the month of events (May) in the chapter title, while other episodes receive only seasonal markers.

The two middle chapters are set during the 1980s, a contradictory era of political unrest, social turmoil, and economic prosperity. Kyung Hyun Kim describes the inherent irony of the decade: "It was a period of political inquietude where millions of people marched in the streets, but also an era of economic prosperity where millions more flaunted its newly found middle-class identity in newly constructed shopping malls, boulevards, and high-rise apartment buildings" (16). This paradox was epitomized in 1987, the year of the fourth chapter, when mass democratization protests (the "June Uprising") and the decade's biggest economic growth occurred.[8] It is not coincidental that Yong-ho cruelly submits a college activist to water torture in the spring of 1987, the same time when real-life student activist Pak Chong-chul was tortured to death by the police, causing nationwide demonstrations on June 10. Soiling his hands with the blood and feces of political dissidents, factory-worker-turned-police-torturer Yong-ho ascends to middle-class patriarch status against the backdrop of the turbulent 1980s.

Yong-ho's elevated socioeconomic status is displayed in the third chapter, set in 1994, when he is the head of both a lucrative furniture store and a middle-class family. His phallic and pecuniary potency is exemplified in a housewarming party scene when his business partners, his wife and child, and his secretary/mistress all assemble to celebrate his acquisition of a new apartment. Yong-ho's prosperity mirrors that of South Korea during the mid-1990s, when the nation enjoyed its status as one of the "Four Dragons" of East Asia and was envied worldwide for its miraculous economic about-face.

Yong-ho nevertheless falls victim to the "IMF Crisis" that shocked the nation in late 1997. Under the sway of the Southeast Asian currency collapse and mounting foreign debts, South Korea—the world's eleventh largest economy and a member of the Organization for Economic Development and Co-Operation—was suddenly confronted with the specter of national bankruptcy. The Korean government resorted to a $57 billion bailout loan from the International Monetary Fund (the largest amount in the IMF's history). As a precondition of the bailout package, the IMF demanded fundamental reforms of the Korean economy and a contractionary economic policy of increased taxes, reduced government spending, and high interest rates. Although the IMF prescription contributed to stabilizing the foreign currency crisis, it resulted in the bankruptcies of numerous businesses and massive layoffs. In 1998, some twenty thousand businesses collapsed, and the number of unemployed skyrocketed to 1.5 million, three times as high as the national average.[9] The same year, South Korea's economy showed negative growth for the first time in more than three decades.[10] The IMF Crisis also ignited serious social problems such as the increase of crimes, divorces, desertions of children, and suicides—the suicide rate in 1998 doubled over the previous year (Shin and Chang 81). Yong-ho portrays an all-too-familiar IMF victim, a divorced, jobless, penniless, middle-aged man who commits suicide as a way out of his misery.

The IMF Crisis injected a new vocabulary into South Korean society: IMF sales, IMF price reductions, IMF discount restaurants, IMF menus, and even IMF movies all entered common parlance after the financial meltdown. The international hit *The Full Monty* (1997)—a British comedy about unemployed, emasculated steelworkers who solve their economic predicaments by becoming strippers—was one of the many import films marketed as an IMF movie in South Korea. In 1999, director Song Il-gon, fresh from Polish film school, made *Picnic*—a winner of the Jury Prize in the Cannes short film section. That same year, Jung Ji-woo's *Happy End* (1999) was released. Both films thematize an "IMF-style home destruction" in which family murders and suicides are spawned from the economic emergency. *Peppermint Candy* is simultaneously a tragedy about first love, a scabrous political-realist drama, an IMF film, and a "Gwangju film."[11]

Yong-ho is a political antihero. As a paratrooper in Gwangju and a police torturer during the antiauthoritarian, prodemocratic movement era, he victimizes the oppressed *minjung*. However, he himself is a victim of the dehumanizing, totalitarian military regime that pits him against people of his own class. It is ironic that, in the film's fifth chapter, as a novice police detective Yong-ho is given the assignment of cracking a labor organization because of his innate familiarity with the proletariat and their problems. A factory laborer himself before donning military garb, police badges, and business attire, Yong-ho's climb up the social ladder is achieved only through self-denial and betrayal of his working-class origins. In addition, his social status is upheld by phallocentric values that punish the wife's infidelity yet endorse his own. He has sexual license to pursue his secretary and buys a bar girl (Sun-im's look-alike). After the protagonist's financial ruin, the patriarchal discourse puts partial blame on his wife, Hong-ja, who coldly shuts the door on him when he visits her for the last time. In the second chapter, when Yong-ho names a list of people who ruined his life, along with a stockbroker, a business partner, and a loan shark, he mentions his wife, who divorced him. In the eyes of neo-Confucian Korean society, virtuous Sun-im, Yong-ho's first love, who continues to yearn for him from afar (even from her deathbed), is a "good" woman; and unfaithful Hong-ja, who refuses to stay with her husband after his bankruptcy, is the "sinful" flipside of the coin.

The IMF Crisis engendered a patriarchal backlash, demanding that women sacrifice their careers and return to the domestic sphere to stand by their discouraged men. Despite the fact that IMF layoffs targeted female workers,[12] IMF-themed films exclusively cast into relief male unemployment and emasculation. While the mass media actively buttressed the depressed patriarchy with "Encourage Men" and "Cheer Up Our Fathers" campaigns, women were often blamed for their overzealous consumption habits and lack of loyalty to their husbands. The film *Happy End*, for example, shows a bread-winning wife who commits adultery after her husband loses his job and takes over household duties. This "IMF *Madame Freedom*" is ultimately punished by a revenging patriarchy when her husband murders her.

Gender conservatism has long characterized Korean nationalism—whether couched within anti-Japanese independence movements or the anti-American *minjung* movement. Despite women's active roles and participation in both movements, their stories have been buried under an all-male cast nationalist history. The most valued women's roles were mothers, wives, and sisters who nurtured revolutionary male activists. Even in the liberal-progressive films of *minjung*-generation directors Park Kwang-su and Jang Sun-woo, women are frequently burdened with crushing body/nation/class metaphors and imaged as rape victims, bar hostesses and *yanggongju* (a term which, literally translated as "foreign princesses," refers to prostitutes for American GIs).

Despite *Peppermint Candy*'s narratologically and politically counterhegemonic discourse, strong female characters remain absent. There are four women sprinkled throughout the narrative: Sun-im, Hong-ja, the secretary Miss Yi (Lee), and Kyang-ah (a bar girl). Each represents a stereotype, respectively: virginal first love; unfaithful bad wife; seductive mistress; and heart-of-gold prostitute. It is also notable that negative, knee-jerk images of women are related to neocolonial discourses. For example, an American pop song, Ray Peterson's melancholic ode to lost love, "Tell Laura I Love Her," plays in the café where Yong-ho meets the bar girl. Although she becomes Sun-im's one-night surrogate, the bar girl represents a "corrupted" body associated, by musical proxy, with U.S. cultural imperialism and capitalistic decadence. She will never completely substitute Yong-ho's idealized image of chaste femininity, Sun-im, who represents an uncontaminated, non-Westernized Korean woman blessed with traditional virtues. Yong-ho's memory of Sun-im is linked to the nostalgically inflected South Korean single, "Na uttukukae" ("What Shall I Do"). Like the bar girl, Hong-ja attempts to seduce Yong-ho with the allure of Western culture. Before their marriage, Hong-ja asks him out for a midnight screening of the romantic Hollywood tearjerker, *An Officer and a Gentleman* (Taylor Hackford 1982). Yong-ho adamantly refuses her date proposal, and in a moralizing, condescending tone tells her that grown women should not go out at night. In a veiled attempt to defend his threatened masculinity, Yong-ho tries to contain and repress active female sexuality, later punishing Hong-ja's "guilty body" with violence when he learns of her infidelity.

The chauvinistic male vigilante, ever present in South Korean cinema, conforms to the despairing tendency to denigrate the promiscuousness and degeneracy of American "free love" as disseminated through Hollywood films. The negative association between an emancipated female agency and a licentious Western culture pervades South Korean cinema from Han Hyong-mo's *Madame Freedom* (1956), a postwar melodrama in which a professor's wife flirts with playboys in Parisian cabarets, to the aforementioned *Happy End*, a Schubert-drenched, post-IMF drama in which the adulterous wife of an unemployed exbanker supports her family by running an English-language institute.

Peppermint Candy exudes numerous historical, political, and cultural references to 1980s–1990s South Korean society: the Gwangju Uprising, the *minjung* movement, the 1997 financial meltdown, class and gender oppression, and implicit antiforeign sentiments. Reverse chronology is not only a narrative maneuver to undermine the hegemony of a linear progressive temporality but also a subversive ideological apparatus to retrofit two decades of Korean social history from a contemporary, critical perspective. *Peppermint Candy* is a productive case study through which to examine the imbrication of two critical models often thought to be mutually exclusive—narrative studies and cultural studies. A more comprehensive, recondite understanding of the film is made possible through a strategic conjunction of these two critical paradigms. Any exclusive approach (whether strictly narratological or purely cultural) risks delimiting the complexity of *Peppermint Candy*, a film which is neither a narrative curio (a text without a context) nor a lifeless political allegory (a context without a text), but rather a profound meditation on time, mortality, and society told through an unconventional journey into the past. The postcolonial narrative lurches down the railroad tracks of "reversed time" and "perverse history" to the final destination of innocence, hope, and happiness—a destination that, for many Koreans, still appears as an unreachable pinpoint of light at the end of a long tunnel.

A New Train of Thought

At this "whistle stop" between the first and final sections of the chapter, we all turn our attention momentarily to the roles played by the train and railroad in narrating postcolonial memories of the nation. Throughout *Peppermint Candy*, the recurring images of railroad tracks receding toward the horizon at the conclusion of each chapter congeal into a connective tissue linking the fragmented temporal and spatial nodes of the film's self-sustained episodes. Much more than a narratological token, however, the iconicity of the ubiquitous train (which can additionally be seen limning the frame's background every few moments after violence and deceit occur) has less to do with its visual preponderance than its centrality to the framing of an oppressed people's collective memories.

In her groundbreaking treatise, *Parallel Tracks: The Railroad and Silent Cinema*, Lynne Kirby argues that "iron horses" functioned as vehicles embodying modern nation-states in silent films centered around railroads precisely because their tracks, symbolizing the forward trajectory of history, promised both the real and imaginary suturing of far-flung citizens and scattered locales. While in the postindustrial West, the steam engine was pivotal in progressively solidifying national identity in association with modern technology and territorial expansion, the history of the Korean rail system reflects a troubling and not-completely-reconciled colonial history.

Constructed and operated by the Japanese as a medium of intrusion and exploitation from 1899 to 1945, Korean railroads not only facilitated the empire's political, military, and economic invasion but also became a

Figure 6.2. Tracks that lead to the past.

site of conflicts between the colonial forces and their Korean subjects.[13] With the national division initiated by U.S. and Soviet occupational forces at the thirty-eighth parallel, Kyongwison (the railway linking the two Koreas) has likewise suffered a fate of partition, which only recently had begun melting away under the auspices of Kim Dae-jung's "Sunshine Policy." South Korea's much delayed Social Overhead Capital project, the Korea Rapid Speed Rail that opened in April 2004 (linking Seoul and Busan in two hours), was fed by foreign technological interests such as French TGV (Train à Grande Vitesse) and American Bectel Engineering. Hence, the railroad—which in *Peppermint Candy* emblematizes not only the protagonist's plunge into his repressed past but also that of the nation—is a fitting metaphor for modern Korean history, its tracks unfurled against a landscape of personal pain and publicly inscribed trauma. With the locomotive as its narrative engine, the film manifests a politicized discourse by stitching critical events that aroused antiforeign, nationalistic sentiments to the uncanny images of railroad tracks, ghostly palimpsest of Japanese colonialism. Ironically, *Peppermint Candy* is one of the first postcolonial Korean films to be partially financed by a Japanese producer (NHK)—a distant echo, after decades of official separation from Japanese culture and film, of the colonial period of filmmaking.[14]

As Michel de Certeau remarks in *The Practice of Everyday Life*, railway navigation, which the author famously proclaims a traveling incarceration, "guarantees that there is still some history" (113). We now turn our attention to a filmmaker whose abiding interests do not reside in history per se, yet one whose fractured films reveal an acute sense of the spiritual bankruptcy and moral debts exacted in South Korea's rush to modernize—a subtle critique often masked by their outward fixation on frustrated libidinal desires and interpersonal relationships.

Modernity and Cubist Narration in *Virgin Stripped Bare by Her Bachelors*

As a director whose pessimistic portrayal of self-absorbed urbanites betrays an indifference to the concept of a collective Korean identity, Hong Sang-soo's name does not immediately leap to mind when we think of politically charged, counterhegemonic cinema. Nonetheless, his first three films, *The Day a Pig Fell into the Well* (1996), *The Power of Kangwon Province* (1998), and *Virgin Stripped Bare by Her Bachelors*—though ostensibly "apolitical" (insofar as they orbit the "personal")—subtly evoke the repercussions of Korea's emphatic modernization project. In fact, the complex, episodic, and ultimately *Rashomon*like narrative strategies undergirding Hong Sang-soo's films constitute a bracing critique not only of the linear, continuous temporality defined by Homi Bhabha as "pedagogical" but also of the split Korean subject's inability to circumvent class and gender boundaries while in the throes of hypermodernization. Ironically, as Hong gravitates, film-to-film, toward a more explicit realization of what we are calling "narrative cubism," he is implicitly tapping into a performative mode of storytelling that hearkens back to an indigenous oral tradition, which, steeped in episodicity and fragmentation, looks positively postmodern today.

To invoke Homi Bhabha's concept of 'pedagogical time' is to conjure an all-too-slippery theory of postcoloniality that inevitably spills over the rim of this discussion. However, before addressing Hong Sang-soo's films, we feel compelled to provide at least a cursory explanation of what we have gleaned from Bhabha's text and why we think it is applicable to the present discussion. In his essay, "DissemiNation: Time, Narrative, and the Margins of the Modern Nation," Bhabha argues that locating the nation as an enunciated phenomenon necessitates the seemingly contradictory tactics of circumscription and perforation; this entails a conceptualization of what he calls the "double" or "split" time of national narration, a chronoschism ensnarled with counterflows and contestations. The temporality of the pedagogical is a totalizing, horizontal time peppered with people who, when glimpsed from the distant vantage of a "representative" authority, collectively embody a historical object of knowledge—one framed within a nationalist discourse that sandpapers heterogeneous experiences into a smooth surface, leaving only vague striations and grains that suggest the ghostlike voices of marginalized "others."

Counterpoised against the pedagogical is what Bhabha identifies as the performative, a repetitive and recursive time. Performative temporality is contiguous rather than continuous. When hooked to a spatial paradigm, it becomes a dense constellation of pulses and punctuations. The performative emphasizes the process of self-signification emanating from nation-writing subjects—individuals who mobilize "the scraps, patches, and rags of daily life" as material correlatives of those psychic gaps and ruptures that accompany cultural ambivalence and political uncertainty (297). An examination of these gaps and ruptures—so prevalent in Lee Chang-dong's historiographical inquiry—is absolutely vital to our understanding of Hong's multiperspective, cubist narratives.

To couch Hong Sang-soo's films within a "cubist" framework is not to suggest that they are Légerlike abstractions—splices of time and shards of space that reject narrative altogether.[15] Compared to the spastic, synaptic bricolage of *Nowhere to Hide* (2000)[16] and the hyper-kinetic editing of *Shiri*, Hong's films are positively passive—sober reflections of class-entrenched individuals caught in the lens of a sedate, rather than acrobatic, camera. What we are labeling "cubist narration" refers, then, to any film in which a "kernel" story—as seen from various characters' perspectives—is replayed in parallel or obliquely angled episodic form. Kurosawa Akira's *Rashomon* (1950) is indicative of a type of narrative cubism wherein episodes determined by various participants and eyewitnesses collectively render an event more fully while compounding the difficulties in reaching a nonambiguous and permanent resolution. While certain directors, such as Abel Gance (*Napoleon* 1927) and Brian De Palma (*Carrie* 1976), have expanded the syntax of film to show events from multiple viewpoints at once (through triptychs and split-screen effects), Hong relies upon something different: a kind of split-mindscreen effect. For example, in *The Power of Kangwon Province*, when the first scene (set on an overcrowded train bound for the titular travel destination) reappears in the second half of the film, this time from a reverse angle precipitated by the narrative's swivel from female to male perspective, the spectator is called upon to mentally telescope the two and engage in a viewing experience dependent upon recall.

Not for nothing was the Duchampian translation *Virgin Stripped Bare by Her Bachelors* used for *O! Su Jong*'s international release. Like the fractured glasses of Marcel Duchamp, this high-modernist film carries the shattered shingles of Braque and Picasso to a deconstructive conclusion. Each of the film's five episodes begins with a chapter heading. The first episode, a brief scene titled "Day's Wait," is situated entirely inside a hotel room. Here we are introduced to Chae-hun, the thirty-five-year-old manager of an art gallery who anxiously waits for a woman—the considerably younger Su-jong—who will make her first appearance in the second episode. Titled "Perhaps Accident," the second episode, set in the past, shows Chae-hun and Su-jong's first meeting, their subsequent flirtations and quarrels, and is a reflection of Chae-hun's memories. Fragmented into seven numerical subsections, this episode begins outside Chae-hun's art gallery, where their "meet-cute" takes place. Su-jong is with Yong-su, a film director under whose supervision she works as a writer. Chae-hun, a longtime friend of Yong-su, joins the two for dinner. A few days later, Chae-hun accidentally bumps into Su-jong at Kyongbok Palace, where he is looking for his lost gloves (which Su-jong has found on a bench). As she hands him the gloves, Chae-hun asks her if she remembers his name. "I have a good memory," she asserts, to which he replies, "I have a good memory also." These self-confident statements, soon to be weighed against each other when the film later presents the same meeting from Su-jong's perspective, reverberate throughout the narrative, its bifurcated structure of competing accounts visually symbolized in recurring "pillow shots" of ping-pong players and badminton opponents sending a shuttlecock back and forth across a net.

Although Su-jong initially refuses Chae-hun's sexual advances, they begin building a rocky romance—one that is put to the test by frigidity and jealousy. The third episode, "Suspended Cable Car," offers a brief interlude that begins with the same telephone conversation heard in the first episode. This time, however, we see Su-jong calling Chae-hun, who—waiting at the hotel—remains unseen throughout the sequence. Although she reluctantly capitulates to his rendezvous request, Su-jong rides the Namsan cable car for no apparent reason besides her desire to delay the inevitable. She is momentarily stranded in midair when the electricity shuts off due to a mechanical failure. Like the cable car, the narrative grinds to a halt, reorienting itself within the subjective confines of Su-jong's memory before delving once more into the past.

The fourth episode, "Perhaps Intention," reiterates the events witnessed earlier yet, emanating from Su-jong's point-of-view, situates them as contradictory or supplementary angles to an already embellished "truth." While much dialogue is repeated verbatim, discrepancies arise in the details and are perhaps exacerbated by each character's proclivity to drink excessively (inebriation not only circumvents the boundaries of public etiquette but also weakens each person's credibility). For example, the spoon that Chae-hun dropped to the restaurant floor in the second episode is now a fork. Chopsticks have morphed into napkins. More important, the "chance meeting" between the two is planned in advance by a more cunning, less naïve version of Su-jong than the person remembered by Chae-hun. A chaste acolyte in the first half of the film, Su-jong is portrayed as a shrewd, desiring woman who stakes a claim in class mobility after witnessing Chae-hun's display of wealth (she notices him generously tipping the chauffeur of his BMW—an action conveniently omitted from his memory).

The humorously titled fifth episode, "Naught Shall Go Ill When You Find Your Mare," brings this intensely dialogic film to a close: Chae-hun's and Su-jong's perspectives converge as they finally consummate their waning passion in the hotel room. The couple's sexual intercourse engenders a scream not of ecstasy but of pain from the yielding virgin, whose blood stains the bed sheets. The once supplicating, now satiated male jokes that he will take the splotched linen home as a memento mori, a statement that encapsulates both the memory and stain motifs that together play a pivotal role throughout Hong's oeuvre. Like "chapters-in-a-life" films that plot the lives of character-subjects along a narrative path intermittently fissured by chapter headings or intertitles (such as *Vivre sa vie* [1962], *Andrei Rublev* [1966], and *Thirty-two Short Films about Glenn Gould* [1993]), *Virgin Stripped Bare by Her Bachelors* goes beyond the straight-forward recounting of a life story to expose the episodic qualities inherent in one's everyday existence. Nevertheless, the film departs even further from chronological arrangements by casting a series of modifications and outright rebuttals. In fact, the repetitive structure of Hong's film counteracts the forward trajectory of time and, in doing so, disables the fundamental impulse of narrative.

In an interview with the South Korean magazine *Cine 21* conducted after the domestic release of *Virgin Stripped Bare*, Hong Sang-soo stated that his desire to make this, the final film of a thematic trilogy, sprang from his belief that the trajectories formed by characters' converging and departing memories of particular events point toward a palpable yet elusive "objective reality" (Ho and Pak 46–47). The two films produced prior to *Virgin Stripped Bare*, *The Day a Pig Fell into the Well* and *The Power of Kangwon Province*, are equally attentive to the irreconcilable perspectives, the shifting subject positions, and the disjunctive temporal nodes that paradoxically problematize "truth" while hinting at an objectivity ideally equipped to expose the economic and social uncertainties of South Korea's future. As unsentimental portraits of men and women futilely attempting to cross yawning sexual chasms, Hong's first three films link the malfunctioning of language and subsequent breakdown of communication among twenty- and thirtysomethings with the emotional ennui and alienation experienced by those living in Seoul's tenement prisons. The reality of such a dystopian existence, indicative of yet another kind of IMF Crisis, an in-between males and females crisis, is virulent enough to drive Seoulites from their claustrophobic city to the bosom of Gangwon-do, a natural refuge for tourists seeking spiritual rejuvenation. Like the suspended cable car dangling precariously over a field in *Virgin Stripped Bare*, heteroerotic relationships are stunted, or at least locked in a state of perpetual indecisiveness.

This theme, a staple of Hong Sang-soo's work, achieves extraordinary gravity when fastened to a narrational system that, far from upholding conventional principals of straightforward, seamless, causally linked plot progression, radiates a particularly postmodern fascination with multiplicity, plurality, chance, indeterminacy, and negation. Each of Hong's first three films can be broken into autonomous sections, each section rent from the others in a way that suggests social and psychic fragmentation.[17] Because his films exude a textual instability based on narrative repetition, and disjunction, they force us to recognize the contradictions and nonconsensus of a society intent on denying its internal disintegration. In doing so, all three films show Seoul, its surrounding environs, and its inhabitants to be shattered remnants of their former selves.

Gendering Episodicity, Performing Postmodern *Pansori*

If we could snap each of Hong Sang-soo's first three films in half, we would find the same gendered dichotomy: One half of each film is centered on a male perspective, while the other half springs from a female perspective. Narrative voice in this gendered context cannot be spoken of in the singular. As such, Hong's films, with their abrupt shifts from male to female focalization (or vice-versa), mobilize what Mikhail Bakhtin envisioned as a "double-directed" discourse—one in which two contending voices can be heard (180). Although Hong Sang-soo's narratives straddle an immediate past and present, they represent not a recovery of a historically traumatic moment (as does Lee's *Peppermint Candy*) so much as an attempt to rescue "meaning" from a modern milieu by way of repetition and variation—key elements, ironically, of folkloric narratives. Although it seems oxymoronic, we can link Hong's three films to traditional modes of oral storytelling, as well as to literary models that—as collections of independent tales strung together like beads—foreground multiple vocality (from *The Arabian Nights* to *The Decameron* and *The Canterbury Tales*).

Like Scheherazade, who must tell a new story each night to forestall her own death, Hong calibrates his narratives to an existential mode that sees the endless repetition of gendered difference as a transformative, rhythmic, and structural life strategy. And like the four canonical gospels of the New Testament, *Virgin Stripped Bare* essentially tells the same story from different vantages, testifying to how vital the connection between repetition and variation is to sustain a retelling. In his comparison of folk (or oral) art forms and print (or literate) art forms, Teshome Gabriel argues that the performatory effects of the former differ radically from those of the latter. Folk (or oral) art features "multiple episodes that have their own centers." This type of art is distinct from literary forms featuring a "single episode extended through detail" (351).

While it is tempting to forge a stronger partnership between Hong's cubist narratives and a general folkloric tradition, all three of his films are already invisibly tethered to an indigenous tradition that mixes legends, ballads, myths, lamentations, and work songs. As such, one could conceivably perform the unconventional act of contextualizing the first three of Hong's films within South Korea's oral storytelling tradition known as *pansori,* a vocal art that recounts and frames, in episodic song form, popular Korean folktales. *Pansori* sprouted from the general folk cultures of the country's southwest region—specifically the shamanist strains spun throughout Jeolla province during the early eighteenth century. Although the primacy, histrionics, and ultimate catharsis of *pansori* drama are most apparent in films such as Im Kwon-taek's *Sopyonje* and *Chunhyang*, the narratological traits of this musical enunciation act are nevertheless rendered salient in Hong's films.

As Marshall R. Pihl points out, all *pansori* performances are episodic. While the internal ordering of the overall song rarely departs from the linear, chronological system commonly found in Western storytelling, stylistic discrepancies are sure to emerge, episode-to-episode. Moreover, factual inconsistencies between the independent episodes are inherent within the *pansori* form. Pihl, describing this aspect, could very well be providing the frame with which to adduce the contradictory and performative elements in Hong Sang-soo's films: As Pihl states:

> Each episode has a distinct character. . . . [W]hether established as an independent entity by convention or by the authority of some famous kwangdae of the past who made it his showpiece, a given episode often acquired elements of style and content that contrasted sharply with other episodes within the same song. Such a contrast could be furthered by some later kwangdae who might momentarily disregard the song as a whole and concentrate his energy on a given episode in an effort to please his audience . . . .While one may stress ideal moral codes and righteous sentiments, another may present a vivid image of unconforming life as it really is. Unconstrained by the need to maintain strict plausibility, pansori, with its episodic independence, can have a special, inventive liveliness and express, without the distortion of didactic narration, the contradictions inherent in real experience. (6, 84)

The spatio-temporal settings in which group encounters take place in Hong Sang-soo's trilogy are fragmentary and episodic. For social theorist Zygmunt Bauman, episodes appear as self-enclosed and self-sustained encounters

> enacted as if they had no past history and no future. . . . The most important consequence of the episodic nature of the encounter is the lack of consequences—encounters tend to be inconsequential in the sense of not leaving a lasting legacy of mutual rights and/or obligations in their wake. Or, at least, most of the art of fragmentary/episodic encounters is aimed at preventing such a legacy from being left." (49–50)

Impossible to ignore in Hong's films is the theme of an evaporating personal legacy, the trace or residue of someone whose presence is rendered inconsequential in thickly modern urban spaces. This theme, which takes the form of, among other images, stains and blotches, foregrounds the ways in which an individual's words, deeds, and indeed existence are prone to erasure. Although Hong's films do not make sweeping overtures to Korean history, their narrative structures provide a unique spatial and temporal gridwork on which to cognitively map the effects of South Korea's unthrottled modernization. By limiting his palette to the muted tones of personal isolation, by situating his characters within monumentally static and stultifying spaces, and by splintering his narratives into contentious episodes, Hong Sang-soo, like Lee Chang-dong, brushes aside the veil of pedagogical discourse to expose the deeply inscribed political, cultural, and socioeconomic rifts unique to Korea.

Conclusion

The cinema of South Korea—one half of a troubled peninsula divided along the thirty-eighth parallel and victim to the epistemic violence associated with colonialism and neocolonialism—brims with films depicting the disintegration of both the traditionally configured domestic arena and the splintered national sphere. However, even when we consider the outpouring of films featuring fractured narratives and/or flashbacks—for example, sophisticated works as diverse as *Gilsottum* (1985), *Our Twisted Hero* (1992), *To the Starry Island* (1993), *Festival* (1996), and *Taeguki* (2004)—the ideological and phenomenological implications of those films' temporal fissures are not exploited as suggestively as in Lee Chang-dong's and Hong Sang-soo's films. Breaking from the cinematic tradition of forward-chronology narration, Lee's *Peppermint Candy* allegorizes the nation through the backward-told story of a man who is a victim of history, and in the process renders personal and national loss doubly poignant. Similarly, Hong's films—repetitive and recursive, multicharacter dramas whose episodes about futility overlap, clash, and even (in *Virgin Stripped Bare by Her Bachelors*) cancel each other out—are narratologically synonymous with the nation's social upheavals.

Because South Korean history is far from linear and continuous; because it has been pockmarked by violent ruptures, military coups, and revolutionary uprisings; and because its capital city has become increasingly atomized into districts determined by class and social standing, audiences should recognize that the films made by Lee Chang-dong and Hong Sang-soo offer much more than an invitation to speculate on the artifice of cinematic narration. As episodic, fragmented texts imbued with the mutual desires to remember and to forget, they trigger inquiries about the converging forces that form the crosshairs of South Korea's still-fluctuating national identity.

Notes

1. For a discussion of the sexploitation genre of films that predominated throughout the late-1970s and early-1980s, including Jung In-yeop's notorious *Madame Aema* (1982), see David Scott Diffrient, "No Quarter(s), No Camel(s), No Exit(s): *Motel Cactus* and the Low Heterotopias of Seoul," *Moving Pictures/Stopping Places: Hotels and Motels on Film*, ed. David B. Clarke and Valerie Crawford Pfannhauser (Minneapolis: Minnesota University Press, 2006).

2. *Minjung*, which literally translates as "masses," connotes the underprivileged members of South Korea's working class, and is typically linked to the prodemocratic student and labor movements of the 1980s.

3. *Peppermint Candy* participated in international film festivals in Montreal, Vancouver, and Karlovy Vary, where it was awarded the Special Grand Prize, the Netpac Award, and the FICC Award. In 2002, Lee Chang-dong received the Best Director Award at the Venice Film Festival for his third film, *Oasis* (2002).

4. Although *Peppermint Candy* was released prior to the short-term memory loss mystery, *Memento* (2001), and concomitantly with Jean-Luc Godard's twenty-minute retrogressive tour through the twentieth century, *L'Origine du XXIème siècle* (2000), Lee Chang-dong's film was certainly not the first to utilize a reverse-chronology plot structure. Jane Campion's made-for-TV drama *2 Friends* (1986), as well as "The Betrayal"—the notorious "backwards" episode from the hit sitcom *Seinfeld* (1990–1998)—beat Lee to the punch.

5. In *S/Z*, Barthes breaks down Balzac's classic "readerly" text, *Sarrasine*, into 561 lexias according to five codes: the hermeneutic (enigmas), the proairetic (actions), the semic (connotative signifiers), the symbolic (antitheses), and the cultural (extranarrative references). To maintain the linear proairetic progress of the narrative, the discourse perpetually delays the revelation of the enigma until the end. The discourse adopts a series of devices and tactics—what Barthes calls

"dilatory morphemes"—for this hermeneutic delay: the snare ("a deliberate evasion of truth"); the equivocation ("a mixture of truth and snare"); the partial answer; the suspended answer; and jamming ("acknowledgment of insolubility" of the enigma). Bordwell's description of the syuzhet delay mechanism coincides with Roland Barthes's taxonomy of the hermeneutic code. Roland Barthes, *S/Z*, trans. Richard Miller (New York: Hill and Wang, 1974) 75–76.

6. Through the 1972 implementation of the Yushin (or restoration) system, Park made himself a permanent president, wielding absolute powers over both the executive and legislative branches. The dictatorial system suppressed fundamental civil rights—such as freedom of speech, freedom of the press, freedom of assembly and association, freedom of education, and freedom of conscience—under the name of national security.

7. The official figure derives from *The May 18th Kwangju Democratic Uprising*, trans. Lee Kyung-soon and Ellen Bishop (Kwangju: the 5.18 History Compilation Committee of Gwangju City, 1998), 61. The second statistic is listed in Donald N. Clark, ed., *The Kwangju Uprising: Shadows over the Regime in South Korea* (Boulder: Westview, 1988) 13. Chungmoo Choi, however, quotes the massacre figure as being "up to two thousand people" in her essay, "The Discourse of Decolonization and Popular Memory: South Korea," *Formations of Colonial Modernity in East Asia*, ed. Tani E. Barlow (Durham: Duke University Press, 1997) 357.

8. South Korea's GDP growth in 1987 was 13%. Kim In-gol, ed., *Hanguk hyondaesa kangui* (Seoul: Dolbaekae, 1998) 396.

9. These statistics are derived from the LG Financial Research Center's post-IMF financial report, *Towards the Twenty-first Century: Overcoming the Crisis* (Seoul: LG Financial Research Center, 1999) 15.

10. Economic growth plummeted to –5.8%. This figure was given in President Kim Dae-jung's 1999 speech at the International Conference on Economic Crisis and Restructuring in Korea. See *The Korea Herald*, December 4, 1999.

11. Yi Chong-guk's *Song of Resurrection* (1990) was the first theatrically released feature to narrativize the Gwangju events. The film was crippled when the censorship board cut twenty-five minutes, one-fourth of the original running time. Six years later, influential iconoclast Jang Sun-woo made another Gwangju film, *A Petal* (1996), a sympathetic portrayal of a young girl traumatized by the events of May 1980. Gwangju Uprising scenes are intermittently inserted as black-and-white flashbacks that express the girl's repressed memories.

12. According to Chung Ok-nim, the prioritization for corporate lay-offs was, in descending order: married women who have more than two children, married women with one child, married women, unmarried women, senior male workers. See Chung Ok-nim, "The IMF Crisis and its Impact on Korean Women," *Taming Turmoil in the Pacific*, ed. Mohamed Jawhar Hassan and Mely C Anthony (Kuala Lumpur: ISIS Malaysis, 1999) 255.

13. With the rail system at their disposal, the Japanese used Korea as a stepping stone leading to yet another colonial target, Manchuria. For an elaboration of this and other facets of the Korean rail system, see Chong Chae-jong, *(Japanese Colonial Control over Korean Railroads and Korean People's Response [1892–1945])* (Seoul: Seoul National University Press, 1999).

14. Although the Korean government normalized diplomacy with Japan in 1965 (twenty years after the nation's liberation from thirty-six-year colonial rule), it banned the import of Japanese films and other cultural products until as late as 1998.

15. Our notion of "cubist cinema" here departs from that historically linked to works such as Fernand Léger's melange of mechanical objects *Ballet mécanique* (1924) and Marcel Duchamp's hypnotic *Anemic Cinema* (1926). For more information on these films, see Standish D. Lawder, *The Cubist Cinema* (New York: New York University Press, 1975).

16. See chapter 8, Rutherford's analysis of style in *Nowhere to Hide*, in this volume.

17. In emphasizing each film's fragmentation, we do not mean to insinuate that its syntax is in any way altered episode to episode. Hong's films do not feature episodes that radically depart from one another in terms of generic, stylistic, or thematic temperaments. They are not like Humberto Solas' *Lucia* (1969), whose three episodes dip into different generic pools (melodrama, neorealism, and farcical social comedy).

Works Cited

Bakhtin, Mikhail. *Problems of Dostoevsky's Poetics*, Trans. Caryl Emerson. Minneapolis: University of Minnesota Press, 1984.

Bauman, Zygmunt. *Life in Fragments*. Cambridge, MA: Blackwell, 1995.

Bhabha, Homi. "DissemiNation: Time, Narrative, and the Margins of the Modern Nation." *Nation and Narration*. Ed. Homi Bhabha. New York: Routledge, 1990. 291–332.

Bordwell· David. *Narration in Fiction Film*. Madison: University of Wisconsin Press, 1990.

Chong Chae-jung. *Ilche chimryak gwa Hanguk choldo* [*Japanese Colonial Control over Korean Railroads and Korean People's Response (1892–1945)*] Seoul: Seoul National University Press, 1999.

Choi Chungmoo. "The Discourse of Decolonization and Popular Memory: South Korea." *Formations of Colonial Modernity in East Asia*. Ed. Tani E. Barlow. Durham: Duke University Press, 1997.

Chung Oknim. "The IMF Crisis and Its Impact on Korean Women." *Taming Turmoil in the Pacific*. Ed. Mohamed Jawhar Hassan and Mely C Anthony. Kuala Lumpur: ISIS Malaysis, 1999.

Chow, Rey. *Primitive Passions: Visuality, Sexuality, Ethnography, and Contemporary Chinese Cinema*. New York: Columbia University Press, 1995.

Clark, Donald N., ed. *The Kwangju Uprising: Shadows over the Regime in South Korea*. Boulder: Westview. 1988.

de Certeau, Michel. *The Practice of Everyday Life*. Trans. Steven F. Rendall. Berkeley: University of California Press, 1984.

Diffrient, David. "No Quarter(s), No Camel(s), No Exit(s): *Motel Cactus* and the Low Heterotopias of Seoul." *Moving Pictures/Stopping Places: Hotels and Motels on Film*. Ed. David B. Clarke and Valerie Crawford Pfannhauser. Minneapolis: Minnesota University Press, 2006.

Gabriel, Teshome. "Towards a Critical Theory of Third World Films." *Colonial Discourse and Post-colonial Theory*. Ed. Patrick Williams and Laura Chrisman. New York: Columbia University Press, 1994.

Ho Mun-yong, and Ok Un-yong. "Hong Sang Soo Interview." *Cine 21* 256 (June 13, 2000): 46–47.

Kim, Kyung Hyun. *The New Korean Cinema: Framing the Shifting Boundaries of History, Class and Gender*. Dissertation, University of Southern California, 1998.

Kim Myong-yol, "Marathon Interview with Director Lee Chang-dong." *CTL*, December 1999. www.pepeprmintcandy.co.kr/news_19991200_ctl_a.htm.

Kirby, Lynne. *Parallel Tracks: The Railroad and Silent Cinema*. Durham, NC: Duke University Press, 1997.

The May 18th Kwangju Democratic Uprising. Trans. Lee Kyung-soon and Ellen Bishop. Kwangju: 5.18 History Compilation Committee of Kwangju City, 1998.

Pihl, Marshall R. *The Korean Singer of Tales*. Cambridge, MA: Harvard University Press, 1994.

Shin Gi-wook and Chang Kyung-sup. "Social Crisis in Korea." *Korea Briefing, 1997–1999: Challenges and Change at the Turn of the Century*. Ed. Oh Kongdan. New York: Sharpe, 2000.

7

Hyangsoon Yi

Reflexivity and Identity Crisis in Park Chul-soo's *Farewell, My Darling*

In his *Farewell, My Darling* (1996), noted director Park Chul-soo includes the filmmaking process as an integral part of the cinematic narrative. The film treats a family reunion as the main plot, but the presentation of the reunion is constantly interrupted by a metanarrative that involves a film crew shooting the family gathering as a staged event. Park's obfuscation of fiction and reality in the film is a bold break from mainstream Korean cinema, which has been dominated by mimetic representation. Park's formal experiment is also distinct from the Korean New Wave, which, while rejecting the "false" cinematic illusionism nurtured by the commercial film industry and government censorship, derives its principal ideological and aesthetic forces from social realism.

Reflexive art embodies the artist's aspiration to explore a *theory* of fiction through the *practice* of constructing fiction (Waugh 2). In Park's film, this process manifests itself at various narrative junctures when a family drama is momentarily suspended and the audience is visually and/or aurally reminded of the cinematic apparatus behind the unfolding action. Park's critique of cinematic art in *Farewell, My Darling* is a self-conscious

Figure 7.1. *Farewell, My Darling* (Park Chul-soo 1996), funeral procession as staged event.

way of reiterating the magic of film and the power of the film artist. From a more pragmatic point of view, Park uses reflexivity as a device for creating a liminal space in the changing Korean society and culture in which the meaning of family can be negotiated and reconfigured ritualistically. As will be discussed later, family is the mainstay of Koreans' self-identity, and a funeral often becomes an occasion for the complex dynamics of family relations to play themselves out. Focusing on this aspect of a funeral, this chapter is an examination of the various metafictional techniques Park employs in *Farewell, My Darling*, one of the most innovative films in contemporary Korean cinema, and to discuss the aesthetic and sociocultural significance of these techniques.

Farewell, My Darling has a loosely organized plot based on the traditional five-day funeral proceedings. The death of Park Man-dol, the patriarch of the Park clan, brings all the family members to their hometown in the countryside. When Cha-nu, the eldest son of the deceased and a movie director by profession, joins his younger brother, Chang-gil, and Chang-gil's pregnant wife, Kum-dan, in the family home, preparations for a funeral get under way according to the directions of a family elder. Village women gather in the courtyard to cook, while men bring drinks, flowers, and many other items necessary for the house of mourning. Soon Pal-bong, a rich half-brother of the deceased, arrives in a car with his trophy wife and their young daughter and so does Chan-se,

Man-dol's third son, all the way from Los Angeles. With the arrivals of more guests, the rural wake quickly turns into a village festivity. Amid the boisterous wake, Chan-suk also shows up after years of estrangement from her family, accompanied by her boyfriend. Meanwhile, a mysterious little boy named Pau is shown intermittently among the crowd, feeding his pet pig, mimicking drunkards, playing pranks on the guests, and even crying next to the corpse behind the altar screen. When Pal-bong kills Pau's pig for the feast, the boy sets fire to Pal-bong's car for revenge. Shocking as it is, the car explosion eventually forces the grieved matriarch to confess that Pau was born from an extramarital affair her late husband had. In spite of all these twists and turns in the course of their mourning, the family succeeds in conducting the funeral to its last phase, and the film ends with a scene suggesting the birth of Kum-dan's baby.

Farewell, My Darling is an autobiographical piece for Park.[1] He says that he wanted to portray the image of the father in today's Korean society, who has lost much of his authority as the head of the extended family. Park conceived of this film in 1986 inspired by Hwang Chiu's prose poem "The Journey" ("Yojong").[2] Park's project did not materialize until 1992, with the passing of his own father. Park comments that during his father's funeral, he "discovered himself to be in the position of a spectator in the house of mourning." The funeral, he adds, "resembled a feast" but was "tragic and violent" at the same time. In this sacred place of the dead, forgiveness and reconciliation could be achieved easily. In short, it was a human "comedy of an enormous scale" that refused a translation into a film that could resort to a "central narrative thread." Park's notes clarify the episodic structure of *Farewell, My Darling* as a final product, but more important, also illuminate the self-reflexive presence of Park himself as a director within the film text.[3]

All fictions are reflexive to a degree (Siegle 3–4; Stam, Introduction; Waugh 5–7). Although less explicit than in later works, Park's interest in reflexivity can be glimpsed in *301/302* (1995), a film made prior to *Farewell, My Darling*, which is, incidentally, his first production after his declaration of independence from the commercial film sectors in Korea commonly known as *chungmuro*.[4] The use of the intertitle, "Could that be the end of the two women's loneliness?" at the end of *301/302* suggests a temporal ellipsis, implicitly acknowledges the viewers' perplexity at the improbable turn of the plot, and forces viewers to distance themselves from the bizarre story presented, to shift their attention to the storytelling method itself. It prefigures the interrogative mode in which the viewer is invited into the text of *Farewell, My Darling*.

Encased in a black picture frame decorated with a funerary ribbon, intertitles in *Farewell, My Darling* edify spectators on the ancient passage rite for the dead. The funerary rite functions as the film's structuring principle and thematic locus. The central plot is built on an elaborate five-day funeral ceremony; each day is labeled in classical Chinese according to the Confucian funeral tradition in Korea.[5] These daily phases of the ritual sequence are demarcated by intertitles that provide viewers with information about traditional Korean wake customs and mortuary practices.[6] The intertitles are especially informative for today's young urban moviegoers for whom the old-fashioned funeral procedure, prescribed and passed down in arcane terminology, has lost much of its original meaning.

This educational effect, coupled with Park's quasidocumentary style, highlights the film's value as an anthropological study of vanishing cultural heritage in the face of industrialization and urbanization. The ethnographic orientation of *Farewell, My Darling* is fostered by Park's skillful exploitation of the received notion of the camera as a faithful recorder of historical reality. The film's thrust toward realism, however, is constantly checked by the intertitles, which interrupt the autonomy of the story's diegetic universe. Consequently, viewers are first lured into accepting the fictive ritual as realistic and authentic and then are awakened the next moment to the authorial control behind the screen images and sounds.

As pointed out above, one of the most striking strategies of reflexivity in *Farewell, My Darling* is the director's own cameo appearance as the eldest son of the deceased. Park is certainly not the first Korean director who cast himself as a character in his own film, but the centrality of his role in the narrative and the complexity of the thematic implications surpass many precedents of this reflexive technique.[7] In some respects, *Farewell, My Darling* can be viewed as a self-portrait of the film artist as a middle-aged Korean man. Cha-nu, played by Park and specifically given his surname "Park," is an experienced film director making a documentary about his father's funeral. Cha-nu seems to have tasted his share of success as a filmmaker but has also been plagued by chronic financial strain. He remains low key throughout the funeral. His reticence is partly due to the solemn occasion but also due to his self-conscious awareness of the unfulfilled expectations his father had about him as the eldest son. From his unassertive demeanor, it is clear that Cha-nu's chosen vocation as a poor artist has pressured him to relinquish much of the power and authority traditionally accorded to the heir of the clan. During the preparatory stage of the funeral, the clan elder who is the host of the funeral appoints Chang-gil, the second son of the deceased, as the chief mourner, a position normally assigned to the eldest brother.[8] The rationale for subverting the hierarchy between the siblings is that Chan-gil has stayed at the family home in the countryside and thus knows the neighborhood and ritual procedures.

From the family's perspective, Cha-nu is a prodigal son who has drifted away to the city and has lost touch with the hometown.

From the viewpoint of the conservative Confucian patriarchy, Cha-nu is also an emasculated husband. His lack of masculine domination is manifest in his relationship with his wife, who overtly disregards her duties as the eldest daughter-in-law. She acts more like a guest than a host, totally indifferent to the chores at the house of mourning. She also refuses to wear traditional clothes of mourning. Cha-nu attempts to intercede between his wife and the family elders who are annoyed by her behavior, but to no avail. Without a doubt, her thinly veiled irreverence toward her in-laws and their rustic lifestyle causes Cha-nu to lose face in the eyes of his family members. Cha-nu's wife, who runs a restaurant, represents the growing number of married women in contemporary Korean society who are forced to work outside the home to help their family economies. Just as these women tend to acquire strong voices in family affairs, Cha-nu's wife does not hide her business concerns even during the mourning, openly inquiring about family properties to be inherited. By stressing her husband's inability to provide sufficiently for the family, she justifies her aggressive materialistic attitude and also insinuates her right to freedom from the restrictions of a traditional female role.

Cha-nu's meek reactions to her abrasive egotism reflect the changing conjugal relations between husband and wife. He is symbolically deposed as the successor to the patriarchal extended family and as the head of his own nuclear family. Correspondingly, Cha-nu's two children are both female. The film, however, implies that the family bloodline will survive through Chang-gil's offspring. This idea is partly based on the cyclic structure of the narrative, which begins with the grandfather's dreaming of a child's birth and ends with diapers on the laundry line signaling that Kum-dan has delivered a baby. With her ideal combination of modern college education and traditional feminine virtues, Kum-dan constitutes the moral backbone of the family and elevates her baby's stature within the family hierarchy.

Despite Cha-nu's sense of displacement, *Farewell, My Darling* is by no means about his failure as an artist. On the contrary, the upshot of the film is to foreground his alternative, paradoxical way of ensuring the continuity of the family. The camera provides Cha-nu with a means to empower his status by chronicling the ritual and even by imaginatively reconstructing the final moments of his father's life. In other words, Cha-nu's documentary enables him to symbolically carry out his duty as the heir to secure "immortality" for the family lineage. In this sense, his film is an apologia for his forebears. This theme is laid out at the outset of the film in Park's own voice: "In my mind, the camera rolls. I shoot the living and the dead." *Farewell, My Darling* doubles the sense of closure at the end as the birth of a new baby coincides with Cha-nu's completion of the family movie. The metaphoric tie between the two events furnishes grounding for the filmmaker's symbolic reclamation of his place within the family.

Cha-nu's filmmaking becomes a means for Park to contemplate the nature of the cinematic medium and vest *Farewell, My Darling* with reflexivity. Barry Sandywell maintains that reflexivity and reflection should be conceived as a continuum, not as antinomies (xiii–xviii). Indeed, the reflexivity in Park's work relies greatly on his ruminations on filmic images. Park's self-referentiality is suggested by various apparatuses related to film art that appear in the text, metonymically alluding to the director's career in real life: a conventional still camera, a television, a video camcorder, and a movie camera. For instance, the freeze-frames of still photographs, interspersed throughout the film, arrest the flow of the "motion" picture and demystify the cinematic diegesis, directing viewers' attention to its artificiality.

Still photography serves diverse functions in *Farewell, My Darling*. It is Pal-bong's wife who carries a camera in the film, taking tourist pictures against the attractive backdrop of the rural landscape. Because of her camera, she also takes charge of the family photo session after "*songbokche*," the ceremony of the official wearing of mourning clothes on the third day of the funeral. The importance of a photograph is most keenly testified by that fact the funeral itself cannot be official without the formal portrait of the departed on the funerary altar. Through these incidents, Park pays homage to photography's genealogical link to cinematography and to photographic media in general. As an ancestor of cinematic art, photography can preserve the unadorned, raw history of a fleeting moment, as is exemplified by the spontaneous, short bursts of smiles on the weather-beaten faces of the camera-shy peasants.

The dominance of television in Koreans' everyday lives is briefly conveyed in the film when the village women suddenly abandon their kitchen work to rush to watch a soap opera. As some men also want to watch a news broadcast, the two groups keep changing the channels. As a result, two kinds of drama quickly alternate on the screen. The news features General Chun Doo-hwan, who heavy-handedly controlled media during his dictatorship; whereas the "evening drama" depicts a typical family conflict between a mother and a daughter-in-law. This sequence in *Farewell, My Darling* capitalizes on the film-within-a-film structure, evoking concentric circles of analogy between fiction and reality in the fashion of *mise-en-abyme*. The embedded inner circle consists of the world shown on the television and the world populated by Park's characters. The news transmits footage of current Korean political scenes in the spirit of jour-

Figure 7.2. The practice of everyday life.

nalistic transparency, which Cha-nu aspires to have in his documentary, while the television soap opera parallels the tension between Cha-nu's wife and his mother. In the meantime, the outer circle of analogy pairs the worlds that Park's characters and we, the spectators of *Farewell, My Darling*, respectively inhabit. The way in which the villagers in Park's film enjoy the news as well as soap opera corresponds to the film-viewing practices in Korean movie theaters, where spectators customarily watch news reels prior to a feature film.[9]

At first glance, the two television programs appear to be entirely different from each other, particularly in terms of their orientation toward reality; one follows the spirit of nonfiction, and the other, the rules of creative fiction. A closer look, however, divulges that they are not so divergent from each other in that both refract reality. In Korea, news items are subject to government censorship. Similarly, soap operas and feature films are filtered by official and unofficial vigilantes of public morals. These governmental and civic authorities are politically and ideologically allied with each other. Through the villagers' seemingly naïve reactions to the television, *Farewell, My Darling* satirizes familiar social scenes in Korea: the intrusion of television into day-to-day life, people's obsession with the television melodrama, and the plethora of information, verifiable or not, that bombards the television audience.[10] This sequence has an ironic twist for perceptive spectators, who know that Park worked as a producer for both fiction and documentary films in the commercial television industry before he returned to feature films in 1988. Thus, the personal spin he puts on this sequence transpires into a metafictional self-parody.

Among all the self-reflexive signification processes in *Farewell, My Darling*, Park's most strident critique is targeted at Chang Tal-hyo, who runs a video rental shop in the village. Proudly carrying around his camcorder, Chang is a local video artist hired by the employees of the downtown coffee shop that was frequented by the deceased. Park's characterization focuses on Chang's perverse use of the camera with which he claims to "record" the funeral for the memory of the deceased. No sooner do the three women from the coffee shop descend from a car than he starts filming their movements. Irritated by their jovial mood, he tells them to "act" properly for the funeral. At this "directing," the "actresses" walk back and resume their entry into the "set," wailing like disheartened mourners. Their pretentious and exaggerated acting and the video artist's self-styled directing parody filmmaking processes in which Park himself is engaged. Chang's video sequence reflects the relatively recent phenomenon of home video/moviemaking.

With this sequence, moreover, Park tackles more serious ethical issues in the film industry. In the hands of a filmmaker like the self-claimed video artist, the camera can be easily degraded into bait for seducing women and assailing their vanity in self-images. An easy prey is Pal-bong's wife, a young, rich woman stricken with boredom. Their flirtation proceeds in clichés from popular romantic movies. Park's camera traces them walking out of the house, the man taping the women from behind. Park's metacinematic camera then cuts to them in each other's arms in a dark haystack. This development mirrors the tawdry love stories full of sentimental banality and erotic fantasies that profit-

Figure 7.3. Rehearsing the arrival.

oriented moviemakers churn out unscrupulously. Specifically, Park's intertextual censure is aimed at the subgenre of popular women's melodrama of the 1980s that typically dealt with the extramarital affair of a bored housewife.[11]

Chang's sexual escapade marks the lowest point in the film's moral structure. In light of reflexivity, however, it epitomizes the Rabelaisian carnivalesque pervading Park's film. In his seminal study of Francois Rabelais's *Gargantua and Pantagruel*, Mikhail Bakhtin proposes the concept of carnival as "a universal philosophical principle that heals and regenerates" through folk humor (70). The intersection between Bakhtin's theory and reflexivity is their common conception of fiction as a dialogic discourse espousing multiple contending perspectives. Throughout Park's film, the somber ritualistic mood is continuously diffused by ludicrous and farcical situations. The complexity of Park's text stems from the very interplay between funerary grief and festive gaiety that embodies the various opposing forces operating in the text: the tragic and the comic, the sacred and the profane, the official and the unofficial. Bakhtin describes the latter term in each dyad in terms of "a material bodily principle" derived from the marketplace culture (18). The wake often turns into a Bakhtinian carnival, an officially sanctioned occasion for carousal and merriment.[12] The carnivalesque revelry of the body's "lower bottom" abounds in *Farewell, My Darling*: eating, drinking, singing, dancing, merry-making, fighting, copulating, butchering, defecating, selling, buying, and so on. With regard to the significance of these elements, Park states:

> If living is an activity of production, isn't death perchance a release of excrement? The dialectic of life and death must be something like this. "Death" is made loaded and mysterious by human beings, but in fact the gap between life and death is only paper-thin. For this reason, I approached "death" light-heartedly. The natural scenes that were captured thus resulted in a pleasurable film that makes the living laugh. (30)

Some of these "natural scenes" are shown on the screen explicitly, and others are hinted at.

Park's heavy use of a hand-held camera, frenetic jump cuts, and occasional fast motion efficiently cinematize the topsy-turvy world of the rural wake. A compelling visual trope for the chaotic inversion of the established ritual order is a squealing pig that is let loose from its pen and runs around the yard full of guests. To capture it for slaughter, Pal-bong starts chasing the animal. At the tragicomic end of this frantic sequence, the camera juxtaposes the images of the face of the sweaty hunter and the head of the boiled pig. The intriguing close-ups of their facial resemblance—especially their noses—instantly brings to the fore the theme of playful transgression between the high and the low that transcends even the border between life and death. Pal-bong's masculine prowess and wealth—symolized by his gun and car—are interlinked with the swine's powerlessness and filth. With his money, Pal-bong acts like a swaggering braggart among his poor country cousins. There is an irrefutable correspondence between the upstart's vulgarity and the pig's coarseness. As is noted by Peter Stallybrass and Allon White in their book *The Politics and Poetics of Transgression*, the pig has a long and rich history as a symbol of "the lower grotesque, a hybrid creature . . . for the festive and sinister imaginary" (47). While desecration, defilement, and sexuality are not primary associations with swine in Korean folk culture, they reinforce Bakhtin's concept of 'carnival' in elucidating the animal's role in Park's film. The swine is generally perceived as a symbol of wealth in Korean folklore, which sheds an ironic light on Pal-bong's shooting of the animal.[13] After witnessing Pal-bong's wife's promiscuity with the video artist, spectators cannot but entertain an interpretive possibility that Pal-bong's confrontation with the pig is, in fact, a projection of his self-hatred. Hence, his brutal killing of the animal as his bestial other further amplifies the ironic poignancy in their chaser/chased relation.

The swine episode culminates with a fundamental disruption of family relations, divulging an identity crisis faced by contemporary Korean society at large. Family plays a key role in forming one's self-identity in Korean culture. Among various factors that have contributed to this phenomenon, the influence of Confucianism can be counted as the most powerful and enduring. Confucianism was adopted as the state ideology and religion during the Choson Dynasty (1392–1910), and its legacies are still deeply engraved in almost all facets of modern Korean life. In the Confucian worldview, family is the basic unit of society, and an ideal community can be built upon the proper maintenance of the relations between ruler and subject, father and son, husband and wife, elder brother and younger brother, and friends. In this ethical system known as the Five Human Relations, three are directly pertinent to one's family life. It is, therefore, not surprising that a Korean sense of identity is shaped mainly by one's family bonds and that filial piety is deemed a supreme virtue that can even be metaphorically applied to the ruler-subject relation. As is expected, such a cultural milieu encourages people to observe ancestor worship and funeral rites as precious opportunities for strengthening their family ties and thereby reconfirming their identities. Although this practice is by and large rooted in Confucian philosophy, it should be mentioned that indigenous Korean belief systems, such as shamanism, also attach tremendous importance to kinship and blood ties as the foundation of one's selfhood (Hahm 65–68).

It is inevitable, however, that the family as the seedbed of the Korean value system would face challenges in the advent of modernity. In *Farewell, My Darling*, the problems of the Confucian family structure and its ethical mores unravel through Pau, whose relationship to the family remains a mystery during almost the entire course of the film. He appears to be a mere urchin pestering the visitors with small pranks, but he calls for serious attention when he destroys Pal-bong's car. Because the film yields no clue as to his background, the spectators are inclined to speculate that he is Chan-suk's son and that he was probably raised by Chan-suk's mother when her angry father cast her out of the family for her illicit, premarital liaison with a servant. The spectators' misperceptions and misinterpretations are compounded by the characters' equally erroneous conjectures about the boy. To their great astonishment, however, the mother dramatically reveals that he is an illegitimate child by her late husband. A "bastard," the boy turns out to be in the same woeful lot as Pal-bong, a half-brother to the deceased; both are denied full membership in the Confucian familial order.[14]

The mishap involving Pau signifies a hermeneutic quandary that is explored by Park's self-reflexive film. Because of his social status, the young boy is identified with the pig (nonhuman) and then with his uncle (human). Correspondingly, his understanding of the world around him erases any absolute divisions of the human/subject versus nonhuman/object. Also, fact and fiction cannot be lucidly separated with regard to the secret of his birth. At various moments of the film, Park sympathizes with the boy's station in life, and so do the viewers because Pau and Kumdan are the most truthful in grieving the loss of the father. The betrayal of both elusive reality and illusive realism is confirmed by other ills and conflicts similarly repressed and concealed underneath superficial everyday life. For example, Pal-bong's adulterous wife mocks the ideal image her husband tries to project of his family. Such "cracks"—as Jean-Luc Comolli and Jean Narboni would call them—point to the failures of the Confucian patriarchy as a dominant ideological system (817). Given his own fallibility, the father's moral condemnation and ostracizing of Chan-suk vividly lay bare the tyranny of Confucian patriarchy and the hypocrisy of its ethical foundations.

Farewell, My Darling tragicomically addresses the petrified values of traditional family mores in changing society. What is noteworthy here is the ethical dimension of Park's playfulness. His critique of the family is devoid of a cold, detached, and judgmental attitude. His approach embraces rather than eliminates discordant voices in the complex dynamics of family life in modern times. This explains the affirmative note with which Cha-nu's family ultimately reconciles with the forces antagonistic to their received ways of life. They sanction Chan-suk and her live-in boyfriend as a legitimate couple. Their public acceptance of the estranged daughter is dramatically declared when the family elders permit her "lover" to take his turn and ritualistically lead the bier as a son-in-law, on par with the sons.[15]

In *Farewell, My Darling*, the funeral provides a symbolic space in which the community confronts contradictory elements and latent problems in the established social order and then peacefully overhauls its structure. According to Victor Turner, a rite of passage contains a stage called "limen" ("threshold" in Latin). This phase is full of ambiguous, paradoxical, and confusing features, but it is also "a realm of pure possibility whence novel configurations of ideas and relations may arise" for a life and society in transition (97). Liminality, as formulated by Turner, accords with reflexivity to the extent that both celebrate the heterogeneity of voices in a social drama and the positive outcome of their intercourse. A concrete example of this argument can be drawn from the family's eventual acceptance of Chan-se's Christian way of mourning as well as the other signs of "American" culture, by which he has been living. The carnivalesque wake provides the optimal social conditions for the confused and irritated family elders to accept Chan-se's conversion to the alien religion, for the sake of a harmonious community life. So the viewers bear witness to the hilarious scene of Chan-se invoking biblical passages side by side with his brothers' Confucian wailing, followed by the chanting sounds of a Buddhist monk from a tape-recorder. Reluctant as it may be, elders' approval of the Western-style mourning clothes worn by Chan-se and Cha-nu's wife can also be understood in terms of the community's self-conscious attempts to accommodate the changing times and redefine its collective identity accordingly.[16]

Farewell, My Darling is a film about the epistemic crisis in the postmodern age.[17] This theme is humorously and yet pointedly rendered in the swine episode through the blurring of Pal-bong's and the pig's images from Pau's perspective. The film dramatizes the predicament of a stable, monolithic meaning-production system. Park's viewers are forced to travel constantly between the inside and outside of the story world in order to distinguish reality from its representation. In the last scene of the film, Park nearly merges himself and Cha-nu, the creator and the created, bringing his reflexive art to a delightfully provocative finale. The camera first shows a close-up of Cha-nu on the right-hand, frontal plane of the frame, with the funeral procession in the far background. The only reason that we can tell the man is Cha-nu—and not Park—is because he wears a mourner's cap. But it is impossible to distinguish the two figures in the ensuing scene at the family courtyard, in which the director's voiceover suddenly intrudes, telling the characters to stop acting. Over their *tableau vivant*, credit scenes are superimposed, and the voiceover continues in a telephone conversation, explaining that he has finished filming and is returning home soon. The director's one-sided voiceover ends by requesting the telephone interlocutor to contact a writer for him, connoting his on-going engagement with the world of art. The credit sequence pressures viewers to exit from the fictional world with a crucial question: Is the voiceover Cha-nu's, Park's, or perhaps both? Likewise, the director's final message—"Cut! You did a good job."—could have been addressed to the actors (Chu Chin-mo, Pang Eun-jin, Mun Chong-suk, and Kim Pong-gyu) for their hard work during the shooting; the characters (Chang-gil, his wife, his mother, and Pau) for their successful undertaking of the funeral and also for their cooperation with Cha-nu during his documentarymaking; and finally, the viewers of the film (us) for completing our taxing task of disentangling the complicated text.

Farewell, My Darling handles various social and cultural issues related to the disintegration of the traditional family structure in contemporary Korea. These are yet intricately bound up with Park's private reflection on his role as a filmmaker. The film is Park's ritualistic search for his identity as an artist through the exquisite use of reflexive techniques such as intertitles, cameo appearances, films-within-a-film, parody, and carnival, among others. His soul searching in the rapidly changing social and cultural climate is delegated to his double, Cha-nu, whose responsibilities as the eldest son and as the filmmaker are, more often than not, incompatible with each other. His cinematic dissection of his family, therefore, opens up the sources of his existential plight both as an insider and as an outsider. Park deploys Cha-nu's dual positioning as a masterful strategy that comments on the nature of film and filmmaking. In *Farewell, My Darling*, Park constructs and at the same time deconstructs the filmic world, defining his role as an artist in the complex relation between reality and illusion. However, Park's work is not merely an intellectual exercise of artistic technique. What makes this film unique and valuable is the superb combination of cultural criticism, aesthetic experiment, and ludic spirit. In this respect, Park's departure from conventional realism merits critical applause as yet another prominent sign of the maturity of Korean cinema.

Notes

1. To avoid confusion between the director of *Farewell, My Darling* and his director-character in this film, they are indicated as "Park" and "Cha-nu," respectively throughout this chapter.

2. Hwang's poem describes the funeral of the poet's own grandfather. It seems that Park's characterization of the younger sister of the deceased as an insurance agent was borrowed from Hwang's poem.

3. "Director's Notes," http://www.parkchulsoo.co.kr/html/Farewell/f_dnote.html.

4. This is the name of a street in downtown Seoul where both small and large production companies are concentrated.

5. The Chinese terms for the funeral are presented in Korean transcription in the film. It should be noted that although the funerary rite in contemporary Korea cannot be described as strictly "Confucian," it largely follows customs inherited from Confucian Chosun society. As C. Dredge points out, the rite is rather syncretic, incorporating elements of Buddhism, shamanism, and other indigenous folk beliefs (74). For more details on the procedure of the traditional Korean funeral see Im Chae-hae's *Chontong sangnye* (*Traditional funeral rites*) and Dredge's "Korean Funerals: Ritual as Process." For the historical development of the rite see Chong Songmo's "Sangjang chedo ui yoksa wa sahoejok kinung: shin yuhakchok karye chegye rul chungshim uro" (History and social functions of funeral institutions: Focusing on neo-Confucian family rituals) and Lee Hyun Song's "Changes in Funeral Customs in Contemporary Korea."

6. The use of intertitles for the funeral progress is also found in Im Kwon-taek's *Festival*, another film about a Korean family gathered for a funerary rite. Interestingly, *Festival* and *Farewell, My Darling* were released in the same year. Juzo Itami's 1985 film *The Funeral*, which depicts Japanese funeral customs, deserves attention as a possible model.

7. For instance, Yi Chang-ho often appears in his own films. In *A Declaration of Fools* (1983), Yi features himself briefly in the opening sequence, protesting the financial difficulties of being a filmmaker.

8. In her book *The Confucian Transformation of Korea: A Study of Society and Ideology*, Martina Deuchler provides an excellent explanation of why and how neo-Confucianism elevated the eldest son's status to the position of the ritual heir in Choson, Korea (129–78).

9. Until recently, Korean movie theaters were required to show news before a feature film. This practice is presently optional.

10. This genre of evening soap opera is called "drama" or "*yonsoguk*" (serial drama) in Korean. Popular subject matters for this genre tend to deal with inter- or intrafamily conflicts. Their stories are in general apolitical.

11. For historical and sociopolitical contexts of the so-called women's melodrama genre, see Lee Hyangjin, *Contemporary Korean Cinema: Identity, Culture and Politics*, 57–59.

12. The Irish wake is a well-known case. For more detail on merry-making customs at an Irish wake, see Seán Ó Súilleabháin's *Irish Wake Amusements*.

13. For the social meanings of serving pork at Korean funerals, see Dredge, 78.

14. Ironically, however, Pau is ranked in a higher position than Pal-bong in the funeral procession to the burial site. The boy is placed with his half-brothers on the front line of the procession; they are followed by other male members of

the family, including Pal-bong. The positional discrimination between them visually demonstrates the carnivalesque reversal of their initial power relation.

15. Park's film shows that on the fourth day of the funeral, each son goes up to the front of the bier supported by a group of male pallbearers while the corpse is still kept indoors behind a folding screen at the funeral altar. This phase of the funeral is appropriately called "*pin sangyo ollugi*" (comforting the empty bier). Customarily, the deceased's son-in-law is mounted on the fully decorated bier, and the pallbearers walk to and fro chanting. The main purpose of the ritual is to rehearse the final procession to the burial ground the following day. For the playful aspects of this custom see Im's *Chontong sangnye*, 46–51.

16. Chan-se wears a black Western suit, and Cha-nu's wife wears a black traditional Korean dress. In style and color, both deviate from the traditional Korean funerary dress code. The color of mourning in Korean culture is either white or the natural brown of hemp with which the traditional mourning clothes and cap are made. A mourner also puts on straw sandals and carries a cane.

17. Here the term *postmodern* is used in a broad sense. Patricia Waugh associates metafiction with postmodernism. Conversely, Mark Currie argues that metafiction is "neither a paradigm nor a subset of postmodernism" (15).

Works Cited

Bakhtin, Mikhail. *Rabelais and His World*. Trans. Helene Iswolsky. Bloomington: Indiana University Press, 1984.

Chong Song Mo. "Sangjang chedo ui yoksa wa sahoejok kinung—shin yuhakchuk karye ch'egye rul chungshim uro" (History and social functions of funeral institutions: Focusing on neo-Confucian family rituals). *Han guk sangjangnye (Korean funeral customs)*. Ed. National Folk Museum. Seoul: Mijinsa, 1990. 173–86.

Comolli, Jean-Luc, and Jean Narboni. "Cinema/Ideology/Criticism." *Film Theory and Criticism: Introductory Readings*. Eds. Leo Braudy and Marshall Cohen. 6th ed. New York: Oxford University Press, 2004. 812–19.

Currie, Mark, ed. *Metafiction*. London: Longman, 1995.

Deuchler, Martina. *The Confucian Transformation of Korea: A Study of Society and Ideology*. Cambridge: Council on East Asian Studies, Harvard University, 1992.

Dredge, C. Paul. "Korean Funerals: Ritual as Process." *Religion and Ritual in Korean Society*. Ed. Laurel Kendall and Griffin Dix. Berkeley: Institute of East Asian Studies, 1987. 71–92.

Hahm Pyong-choon. "Shamanism and the Korean World-view, Family Life-cycle, Society and Social Life." *Shamanism: The Spirit World of Korea*. Ed. Chai-shin Yu and R. Guisso. Berkeley: Asian Humanities Press, 1988. 60–97.

Hwang Chiu. "Yojong" (The journey). *Saedul to sesang ul Tunun guna (Birds also leave the world.)*. Seoul: Munhak kwa chisŏngsa, 1993. 54–58.

Im Chaehae. *Chontong sangnye (Traditional funeral rites)*. Seoul: Taewonsa, 1990.

Lee Hyangjin. *Contemporary Korean Cinema: Identity, Culture and Politics*. Manchester: Manchester University Press, 2001.

Lee Hyun-song. "Changes in Funeral Customs in Contemporary Korea." *Korea Journal* 36.2 (1996): 49–60.

Ó Súilleabháin, Seán. *Irish Wake Amusements*. Dublin: Mercier, 1967.

Park Chul-soo. "Being a Movie Director." *Text and Context of Korean Cinema: Crossing Borders*. Ed. Young-Key Kim-Renaud, R. Richard Grinker, and Kirk W. Larsen. Sigur Center. *Asia Paper* 17. Washington, DC: The Sigur Center for Asian Studies. 29–35.

———. "Director's Notes." http://www.parkchulsoo.co.kr/html/Farewell/f_dnote.html.

Sandywell, Barry. *Reflexivity and the Crisis of Western Reason: Logological Investigations Volume I*. London: Routledge, 1996.

Siegle, Robert. *The Politics of Reflexivity: Narrative and the Constitutive Poetics of Culture*. Baltimore: Johns Hopkins University Press, 1986.

Stallybrass, Peter, and Allon White. *The Politics and Poetics of Transgression*. Ithaca: Cornell University Press, 1986.

Stam, Robert. *Reflexivity in Film and Literature: From Don Quixote to Jean-Luc Godard*. Ann Arbor: UMI Research Press, 1985.

Turner, Victor. *The Ritual Process: Structure and Anti-Structure*. Ithaca: Cornell University Press, 1969.

Waugh, Patricia. *Metafiction: The Theory and Practice of Self-Conscious Fiction*. London: Methuen, 1984.

8

Anne Rutherford

Nowhere to Hide

The Tumultuous Materialism of Lee Myung-se

> There is . . . great violence and humor as a tumultuous materialism is ushered into modernity's epistemological fold . . . [T]he new form of vision, of tactile knowing is like the surgeon's hand cutting into and entering the body of reality to palpate the palpitating masses therein.
>
> —Taussig, *Mimesis and Alterity*

When Siegfried Kracauer and Walter Benjamin attempted to write the foundations of a materialist theory of cinema spectatorship, they looked to the potential of cinema to restore the mimetic faculty: "a mode of cognition involving sensuous, somatic and tactile forms of perception" (Hansen 1999, 5). For Kracauer, film does not just record the material world, it "puts the material world into play," and he believed that this material dimension engages the viewer on the physi-

Figure 8.1. *Nowhere to Hide* (Lee Myung-se 1999). Courtesy of Pusan Film Festival.

ological level of the senses: "film [. . .] addresses its viewer as a 'corporeal-material being': it seizes the 'human being with skin and hair.' " (Hansen 1993, 458) This understanding of spectatorship emphasises the potential of film to awaken mimetic experience—a type of perceptual experience that brings the viewer into close contact with the image or sound in a way that blurs the boundaries between the viewer and the film.[1]

Nowhere to Hide, directed by Lee Myung-se, is an action film that has been acclaimed for its work on the cutting edge of contemporary genre hybridization and at the forefront of innovative developments with film style. However, the challenges the film makes to contemporary cinema extend beyond questions of style or genre to the very nature of cinema. In its vigorous awakening of the corporeal aspects of cinema spectatorship, *Nowhere to Hide* charts the sensuous and somatic potential in cinema like a relentless mimetic machine.

Lee Myung-se was one of the original three directors of the Korean New Wave (with Park Kwang-su and Jang Sun-woo), who, according to film critic Im Hyun-ock "broke down many barriers politically and aesthetically with their early films, which went on to pave the way for younger directors to work with the political and aesthetic freedom they now have."[2] Lee has spoken of the ways his films were originally seen by critics as "individualistic," separate from the social realist work of the other New Wave Korean directors. (Rutherford 2001). According to Im,

Lee's films were initially disregarded as not serious because they were "not transparently social or political," and she argues that the early disinterest was due to the reluctance or inability of critics to "approach cinema on stylistic and formal grounds and to discuss cinematic language."[3] She points out that "the stylistic breakthrough that Lee Myung-se has made to film style in Korean cinema is only recently being recognized." Lee has talked of the difference between his approach and the approach of people who "look at film primarily in socio-political terms, or with the standards of literature or other arts." He says,"I jumped into cinema itself and questioned cinema on its own terms. You can say that I answer the basic question 'what is film' in each of my films, film after film" (Rutherford 2001).

"You Don't So Much See as Be Hit"

Nowhere to Hide is a virtuoso rollick through a detective's seventy-two-day pursuit of a ruthless gangland assassin. By the time the opening titles assault the viewer with a hard-edged metallic clunk, *Nowhere to Hide* has already set itself up as a hard-boiled gangster/detective film that is slick, fast, and furious. From the moment the film rips open with a rapid iris out, it is all about surface: a stark bleached-out black and white industrial wasteland; a lumbering, thuglike pair of shoulders in horizontal stripes lurching across a vacant lot to the driving beat of a synthesizer; a tough, streetwise character confronting a gang of extortionists whose faces glide into frame and into focus one by one like choreographed physiognomies of criminality. Bodies and body parts freeze in midflight in a high-velocity fight scene set up as a study in movement, rhythm, and stasis: cryptic poses, the energy of a moment or a movement are condensed in a single frame like living figures captured in the disjointed sequences of a cartoon and then released back into motion. Action is segmented into its component parts, transitions between the parts excised, and camera speed shifted to leave a blur of rapid, disjointed movements. Slick, smooth, and tough. Already the film has stretched and reinvented the principles of how to break up a scene and how to hold it together, how to inject lines of force that shatter the harmony, and lines of cohesion that hold the disintegration in check. From here the tone is set, bullets fired, and the camera zooms in through one of the bullet holes onto the titles. "Corporeal understanding," as Michael Taussig writes, "you don't so much see as be hit" (Taussig 30).

After the titles, the rhythm shifts with a series of short, fluid fragments, one after the other like liquid blips—a motorbike rides into frame and halts, a man walks a pace and freezes, a car window lowers halfway and pauses, the camera pans across a windscreen and stops, a man looks forward and freezes—movements interrupted but not truncated as the rhythm is carried on by the next fragment. Clued in by the high-voltage energies of the pretitle fight scenes, the viewer waits for the gangster film to kick in as the fragments pick up pace, and the uneasiness intensifies with the sense of anticipation, watching, waiting. Who is the man in the car, the two on the motorbike, the man on the step? There is a sense of disorientation, fragments in a puzzle with no hierarchy to organize them. As we wait for the pieces to fall into place, the camera moves away and we are lured into a scene of extraordinary sensory pleasure: leaves blow in slow motion in the wind—the intense, almost edible golden yellow of autumn leaves—and a melody picks up a wistful, melancholy lilt, the sweet dreaminess of The Bee Gees "Holiday." As the viewer is lulled by the music, the camera shifts to a set of steps washed in a hazy blue light—the Forty Steps. A little girl jumps down the steps in slow motion, one by one, like a wind-up doll; it starts to rain; people run through the hazy rain, and the music carries the viewer into a sense of eerie unreality. There is a sense that we are simply witness to the passing of time, the passing events of a day.

Across this scene of almost unprecedented sensory richness and saturation, we watch the face of the victim as he stares into the eyes of the man who has just (will have just) killed him. A sword slices through his umbrella and pauses in a freeze-frame, his hand raises and halts. As blood streams in rivulets down his face, he watches expressionless, his eyes barely flicker and then he tumbles in slow motion down the stairs, grasping after his open umbrella. It is a pared back, dispassionate, most businesslike assassination. A frantic chase erupts up the stairs in a chaos of running figures and slashing swords. It is five minutes before a word is spoken in this first sequence after the opening titles. After the murder, the melody carries on as if nothing has happened, and the day goes back to its impartial witness. Cars drive off through the autumn leaves. The viewer is left speechless.

The violence is not so much in the action—the slicing sword, the hand drenched in blood that turns the whole frame red—but in the way the scene splits the viewer in two. One part drifts with the melody into a dreamy, lyrical nostalgia, a sense of suspended animation, while the other is carried by the fragmented editing, glimpses of a building tension with no clues, no explanation, into an unnerving uncertainty, suspense.

Montage and the Sensory

In the Forty Steps sequence, as you watch the umbrella tumble in slow motion down the steps, the sequence evokes echoes of another scene,

Figure 8.2. From the famous "steps sequence."

from Sergei Eisenstein's *Battleship Potemkin* (1925).[4] The strong horizontal lines of the steps recall the Odessa steps, the victim's slow motion tumble down the stairs after his umbrella evokes the baby's pram as it bumps down the steps, and the diagonal lines of force of the gangsters running chaotically up the stairs echo the Cossack's pursuit. Each element reinvents the dynamic energies of conflict in direction, movement, and rhythm that animate Eisenstein's shot construction but reinterpret those principles within an utterly contemporary idiom.

The resonance of Eisenstein is felt not only in the quotation, but also in the way Lee animates the energy of montage, the juxtaposition of discordant associations, rhythms, and moods. It is the way Lee mobilizes the sensory qualities of sound and image, to slide the viewer across untenable links, that echoes Eisenstein's understanding of the nature of the montage fragment. Eisenstein writes of the "sensual nuances," the "collateral vibrations" of a fragment that render viable the "perfectly impossible montage joinings in [his film] *Old and New*" (Einstein 68). He envisages the physiological qualities of each montage fragment as vertical layers, like the various instruments in a symphony, and links fragments together based on what he describes as these "visual and aural overtones" (Leyda, 70).[5] Eisenstein's method of "overtonal montage" draws linkages. These palpable qualities themselves form bridges that release the sequence construction from the stranglehold of the horizontal chain of meaning and free it to proceed along mimetic lines.[6] It is this kind of disruptive sequence that Lee puts to the service of generic play or to the exploration of the cinematic, of movement, of light in *Nowhere to Hide*.

Taussig has linked Eisenstein's theorization of the "totally physiological sensation[s]" of the fragment explicitly with Benjamin's understanding of the visceral quality of mimetic perception, its ability to evoke a "palpable sensuous connection between the very body of the perceiver and the perceived" (Taussig 21).[7] Kracauer has also written of the ways that film "addresses its viewer as a corporeal, material being," arguing that film "stimulates the material layers of the human being . . . [I]t brings the material world into play . . . the material dimension assumes a life of its own and triggers in the viewer associations, memories of the senses" (Hansen 1997, xxvii). This sensory, material aspect of spectatorship holds the key to understanding the impact of *Nowhere to Hide*. In its work with the potential of images to "engage not so much with the mind as with the embodied mind," and its exploration of the energy erupting from the "physical, tactile dimensions of film spectatorship" (Taussig 23), *Nowhere to Hide* could be seen as a mimetic machine par excellence.

Genre and Mimesis

It is the ability to bring together apparently incongruous elements and to play them for the energies that erupt from the juxtaposition that marks many of the elements of Lee Myung-se's film—the capacity to turn the edges, where disparate fragments meet, into edginess. The play with these incongruities has led Darcy Paquet to describe this film as "genre-bending" (Paquet 12).[8] *Nowhere to Hide* is a detective/gangster film that slides at times into a romantic, almost saccharine subplot. The hero, Woo (Park Joong-hoon), is a ruthless, brutal, and streetwise detective who breaks out into a cheeky, childlike playfulness as easily as he gives way to a melancholy loneliness, hankering after the assassin's girlfriend. It is a comedy with a violent edge. Fight scenes break into farce as Woo leaps up and down with bells ringing, and as he wrestles with a suspect after a series of brutal punches, the music breaks into a tango, and the embrace of combat becomes a dance. It is an unabashedly popular, fast-paced music video with an arthouse sensibility; it is a cartoon with live actors.

Lee points out that *Nowhere to Hide* is the first time he has used the action genre, and the film has been hailed as one "that twists its genre in new and interesting ways" (Paquet 12). Paquet discusses the ways the film shifts the expectations of a detective film, with the depiction of the "menial aspects of a detective's life." The core of his discussion of this "genrebending" is the "displacement of narrative and action itself to "focus [viewers'] attention on the more cinematic aspects of the work" (Paquet 13). However, as pivotal as this level of genre twisting is, the broad brushstrokes of a genre criticism that addresses these challenges to narrative convention, character type, or film category cannot fully address the innovativeness of Lee's play with genre. Lee puts genre into play not only on this macrolevel, but also on the microlevel of the sensory experience of each moment. It is in the ways that he works with the experience of viewers moment by moment—in the timbre of a sound, the shape of a shadow, the hue of a light, or the rhythm of a movement—that the core of Lee's work with genre must be understood.

Lee works with genre like a digital paintbox program—color, rhythm, light, shadow, movement, music, sound effects, and cinematic reference all become tools in a tool kit of experiential moments. Lee has said that he "likes to get close to [his] audience" (Dupont), and it is often through the ability to evoke a generic trace in the sensory nuances of a sound or image that he achieves this. Genre is enacted mimetically: the recognition that triggers generic associations or expectations in the film is a mimetic recognition. The generic play between the familiar and the unfamiliar is enacted on the visceral level of the sensuous qualities of sound and image.

The impact of Lee's paintbox approach is in the transitions, as the familiar qualities of a sound or image are used as a pivot to vault the spectator into unfamiliar territory. The humor and pleasure often lie in the unexpected—the surprise that the viewer has been seamlessly transported by an aural or visual link across the boundary between action and musical, between narrative causality and carnivalesque extravaganza. A certain tinniness in a ringing bell catapults a fight scene from realism into farce; a bilious tinge to the green of a street light flips a chase scene over from drama toward a cartoon; the floating, soft rustling of autumn leaves slides the spectator from action to suspension. The affiliation has been registered, experienced, and accepted on a corporeal level before the viewer has caught on to being duped. Much more than the transformation or renewal of character type or narrative lines, this is play with genre in the fullest sense and redefines what generic play can be and how far it can go.

Genre theorists such as Steve Neale and Marcia Landy have argued the need to abandon an understanding of genre as a classificatory system and to think of genre as a process, as "a contract between the audience and the film" (Landy 20).[9] Neale has emphasized the centrality of the spectator to this understanding of genre, arguing that "genres do not consist only of films: they consist also, and equally, of specific systems of expectation and hypothesis which spectators bring with them to the cinema, and which interact with films themselves during the course of the viewing process" (Neale 46). However, in *Nowhere to Hide*, the ways in which genre is played out in this interaction between film and audience cannot be grasped if these "expectations or hypotheses" are understood as an intellectual template, as ideas about the film. Genre is experienced viscerally: it is not located somewhere prior to or floating above the performative unfolding of a film across time and the materiality of the spectator's experience of the film. The generic expectations of the spectator—their establishment, renewal, repudiation, or transformation—are experienced as they unfold in the material resonances of a film.

The capacity to fling together disparate elements in unpredictable ways gives *Nowhere to Hide* a wit and a raucous playfulness. Just as in the Forty Steps sequence we are given glimpses, fragments, actions that seem peripheral but then fly together in unexpected ways, the surface of the film also becomes a fragment to be put into play, to be flung into action. It might be a pool of colored light that takes off onto a bravura progression through garish washes of color—a chase scene through the industrial port-side lit as a progression through hot orange-red, a cold hazy blue, and a lurid green. As Woo's combat/dance with the boxer-suspect spreads out across a cluttered rooftop, the clutter itself takes over: the scene becomes black and white, shot in silhouette, as turrets, chimneys, aerials, and gas cylinders take over the shadow play of slogging combatants.

Nowhere to Hide's cryptic, energetic sequences, which Lee explains in terms of a search for a universal language—clearly assimilate principles of construction from outside a more conventional film language. Lee has spoken of his voracious consumption of comic books during his childhood and youth and the inspiration he has found in comics for his filmmaking methodology and theory:

> I started to think that the comic strip had the capability of going where film couldn't go, and so I started to pull at the art of comics because I saw that the use of the cartoon image is a method whereby film language can be expanded . . . I asked myself questions about the method of expression that the comic uses, such as why is the expression so exaggerated? And what would happen with film if we applied the rules of omission that are used in comics? So I came to experiment with all of these ideas and images. (Rutherford, 2001) [10]

If you think of a film as a set of problems about energy—how to create it, amplify it, sustain it, what shape it might take, how to push it to the limit—the solutions *Nowhere to Hide* invents and the astonishment they evoke draw strongly on this unpredictability. Any moment, any stylistic element, any generic clue or hook can become a point of departure for the film to take off into exuberant flights of fantasy and play, leapfrogging more conventional narrative transitions and picking up a wild momentum that can leave the viewer gobsmacked at the daring, laughing aloud at the unrestrained, almost slapstick humor, or in awe of the technical virtuosity of the editing.[11]

Visual Style and Corporeality

A similar sense of a palette or paintbox underpins the visual style of *Nowhere to Hide*. Color itself is used in this way—applied in whichever way it has most impact on the audience. In the initial conflict with the gangsters, as a body is sliced, the whole screen bleeds red in a wash of color that sums up the scene in a cartoonlike epigrammatic moment. Lee talks of the noir characteristics of Incheon, the port city locations he uses in *Nowhere to Hide* (Im, 2000). It is this noir aesthetic that he reinvents as a study in color cinematography with the stylized sculptural use of colored lighting and shadow. Surfaces take prominence as much of the film is shot through moving barriers—car windows, windshield wipers, slats, bicycle wheels—that continually reshape the frame, make it malleable, fluid, dynamic. The surface of the image itself is complex, textured: candy-colored neon lights ripple across car windows; perspective is confounded as the hero chases the assassin through Escheresque neighborhoods of undulating reflecting glass, lanes, and staircases that seem to lead only in circles. It is noir reinvented in Korean neon.

The sophistication of this "surface dazzle" of Lee's work has enthralled critics and reviewers of *Nowhere to Hide*, who have talked of its "explosive visual style" (Gilmore), and the sense that his work had "no obvious precedent anywhere in world cinema" (Rayns 20). Lee has been acclaimed as a "production design genius," as Korea's "premier stylist" and its "most innovative director."[12] There is no question that *Nowhere to Hide* sets new critical benchmarks for cinematography (as well as for editing, performance, humor, and sheer conceptual energy). However, any discussion of "visual style" as surface, as the "look" of the film, is inadequate to explain the corporeality of the experience of the film, the way the film is imprinted across the sensorium of the viewer.

One of the primary elements of the visual style of the film is the dynamic, fluid work with the frame. The frame is in no sense a "quadrilateral cage": there is no stability for the viewer as the restless, malleable frame is on the move through the entire film, is itself a shape-shifter, just like the villain of the narrative, continually masked, blurred, obscured, and divided. Freeways squeeze the frame from above, moving windscreens contort it, and rippling lines of light disrupt its surface. Across this elastic field of vision, space is compartmentalized, broken into endless panels, boxes, building blocks of urban conglomerate made up of lanes, staircases, tenements, and alleys. There is a sense of urban space infinitely denser, more cluttered, and more fractured than the wide screen would normally allow.

There is a profound understanding here of the nature of the frame and its impact on the embodied viewing of the spectator. The frame itself is a conceptual entity, embedded with cultural significance: the "look" of *Nowhere to Hide* is no more received by a disembodied eye than is the expansive visionary freedom of cinemascope in the American Western. This compartmentalizing of the frame, the composition in panels, is familiar in a more classical form in Japanese cinema in the work of Mizoguchi.[13] In contemporary Hong Kong cinema, Wong Kar-wai has fractured the frame in discordant planes in a similar way to Lee, in *Fallen Angels*.[14] With *Nowhere to Hide*, perhaps we are seeing the fullest expression yet of the assault of the urban sensibilities of the tiger economies on the conventional spatiality of the rectangular frame.[15]

Mood, Affect, and Materiality

The mood of *Nowhere to Hide* does not derive only from color and the frame—rain and snow at times so dominate the image that it is as though we are watching the film through a texture of moving, beating rice paper thatch. Rain carries the burden of mood more often delegated to music: whole segments of the film are wet, saturated, the pounding downpours of rain more articulate than a melody as they alternately mute and mask the action, smother it in melancholy or add a kind of desperate edge to the pursuit of the murderer. The final showdown takes up the silent structure of the Forty Steps sequence—ten minutes of pursuit, cornering, and the final punch-up with not a word spoken, no voice, just the relentless drumming of the rain pummelling the actors and drenching the scene in a feeling that is almost epic, almost akin to awe. (The assassin himself has no voice, only a formidable presence; he has not spoken a word onscreen through the entire film.)

How can an action film do this? How can it take a fight scene and spin it off into this haunting mesmerism? In a film like *Raging Bull* we have seen a structure built around a series of fights that punctuate the film, where each one of the fight scenes takes off as a new experiment in choreography and cinematography.[16] However, whereas *Raging Bull* works through the affectively/libidinally charged fight scenes to plumb spiritual, catholic depths, *Nowhere to Hide* plays the surface to transport the viewer into the kind of feeling that, while not necessarily as emotionally profound, is no less intense—an overwhelming mood that washes over us, sweeps us up, and carries us along. Indeed, feeling is at the center of Lee's description of his own filmmaking practice: "[M]y working style is only to go forward with one's feeling" (Rutherford 2001).[17]

What kind of deep feeling are you having when you're not having a deep feeling? This is one of the paradoxes of *Nowhere to Hide*, that it somehow manages to access an intensity that you don't expect to be there. Hooked into the expectations of a gangster/detective film, you don't expect to be transported into a hypnotic sensory reverie. When you read Lee Myung-se talking of this hard-boiled action film in terms of how Monet would paint a water lily, it comes as a surprise, just as when he talks of the action genre, narrative, and character as a ruse, a decoy that allows him to explore the properties of movement and the filmic. "The story and the characters are not the main focus of my film. Movement is," says Lee, "[T]his is a film about movement and kinetic energy" (Im 2000).[18] Lee talks of studying dance, animal movement, and World Cup soccer to distil these kinetic principles, and he says that "rain is a good medium for showing how movement is essentially about stillness. And stillness contains movement waiting to be released" (Im 2000).[19]

Lee's affinity with Monet, whose water lily paintings explore the qualities of "light-filled water" to evoke "a vision of immaterial light" (Spate and Bromfield 59), is clear in the rain sequence. Just as Lee talks of the painterly use of light, there is a translation of this painterly awareness into principles of cinematography and editing, a cinematic sophistication that would be the envy of many arthouse directors. In his work with "the play of light" (Spate and Bromfield 5), Monet's goal was to capture "not the landscape but the sensation evoked by the landscape" (Inaga 66). Lee's own description of the way he works suggests an affiliation with the impressionist focus on appearances aimed to "penetrate other forms of experience" (Spate and Bromfield 56). He says, "all I show you is no more than a mere impression. This is because what I genuinely want to show you is over there, and then also beyond" (Rutherford 2001).

Impressionist painters such as Monet exalt a way of seeing, of perceiving, which takes the viewer out of him/herself, which "[breaks] down the boundaries between the self and nature" (Spate and Bromfield 60). This impressionist credo is a precursor to contemporary theories of mimetic experience, which define mimesis as a form of "reception of the external world . . . which transcends the traditional subject-object dichotomy" (Hansen 1999, 5). Taussig highlights this breakdown of the boundaries between the viewer and the object viewed in Benjamin's understanding of mimesis, with its recognition that "sentience takes us outside of ourselves" (Taussig 38).

In his description of his method of working, Lee's approach seems clearly to work through the material, to draw out the resonance of the experience of an object. He says: "When I work, I'm in a deep fog, following something vague off in the distance. The form, whatever object you're trying to find is there—it's a matter of capturing it" (Dupont). Lee evokes Gustav Flaubert, Henri Cartier Bresson, and Zen Buddhism to explain the way he approaches images:

> [Flaubert stated that] that there is exactly one word for every object that exists. Along with the photographer Henri Cartier-Bresson who took pictures with this philosophy, I understand this idea as well. For me, the Buddhist methodology is well suited to describe this approach in terms of how to create that one shot. So if there is a methodology at all, I can say it is close to that of Zen (Korean: son). In order to obtain just one shot, I must throw away all thoughts. To obtain what that object is saying to me, I throw away all knowledge and whatever prejudices I have. A more accessible way of understanding this is to think of the poetics of T. S. Eliot. Eliot's poetics proposes that "in order to draw a billiard ball you need to go inside of the ball." This is exactly what I mean by Buddhist methodology. (Rutherford 2001)[20]

Whereas Ahn Byung-sup has written of the central role of sentiment in much of Korean cinema (Ahn), Lee has explicitly located the goal of his work as outside the realm of emotional expression: "I'm going to investigate an object by intuition: it's not an emotional thing, but more akin to Impressionism" (Dupont). He says that "what you seek to gain with the Zen-like method is the viewer's sympathetic response. Only through methods of the Buddhist 'non-action' and non-actions of human agency do you get to the true heart of the viewer's response" (Rutherford 2001).

Lee has talked of the understanding of emotion in the "School of Consciousness-only" Buddhist school of thought, saying that

> countless varieties of human emotions have been identified. According to this classification system, what we commonly think of as emotions being actions inside of a person can in fact be classified as the action of the body. In other words, emotion itself is a material thing. What we call art does not give movement to the material, but rather it gives movement to the spiritual. Then the question arises as to what is the thing that touches the spirit of the person who is doing the looking? But that question concerns that which cannot be understood through words. (Rutherford 2001)

Despite Lee's filmmaking method, which works through the materiality of the object to generate experience, he defines his goal in nonmaterialist terms. Lee's framing of his central concern in this way challenges a materialist understanding of cinema spectatorship to attempt to articulate that which "touches the spirit of the person who is . . . looking." Is this a fundamental challenge to a materialist aesthetics: is his aesthetics incommensurate with a materialist theory of cinema?

In her discussion of Benjamin's understanding of mimetic experience as a mode of perception that "reconnects with the discarded powers . . . of mimetic practices that involve the body," Miriam Hansen has emphasized the affective charge inherent in Benjamin's concept of 'mimetic innervation' (Hansen 1999, 5–6). Hansen explains this innervation as a form of "mimetic perception of the external world that is empowering" (10). She describes it as a two-way process, encompassing both a movement away from the sensorium into the world, and an "ingestion or incorporation" of the world.'[21] As such, it envisages a "greater mobility and circulation of psychic energies [. . .] between organism and the world." (Hansen 1999, 5). With this concept of mimetic innervation, a mimetic appropriation of the material world that, in the moment of contact, generates an "affectively charged, excentric perception," as Hansen describes it (10), we come to understand this double-edged materiality, which is both material and energetic at the same time.[22]

A similar attempt to conceptualize a sensuous, embodied affect, and the potential of cinema to arouse this heightened experience, emerges in Eisenstein's later work in the concept of 'ecstasy,' which he explains as "an awakening, which puts the spectator's emotional and intellectual activity into operation to the maximum degree . . . a movement lifting one out of oneself" (Aumont 59).[23] Eisenstein seems to struggle toward a nondichotomous framework for thinking this movement. As Eisenstein scholar Jacques Aumont understands the concept of ecstasy, there is no contradiction between transcendence and materialism: the spectator is lifted in a frenzy into a union with a transcendental object in a process that is also material. The pleasure that this engenders is described as a movement to a type of "ecstatic vibration" and again as "a move beyond the rudiments of consciousness to enter the purely passionate sphere of pure feeling, sensation, being" (Aumont 60–61). So what is this transcendence that is also material, this sensation that is also being, this nervous excitation?[24]

It would be too easy to assimilate Lee's film into a depth/surface schema that has a long history in Western thought. One pole of this dyad could be exemplified in a depth metaphor of representation in the expressionist understanding of the image. The expressionist image (or sound), as Peter Brooks has described it in the tradition of melodrama, represents a deeper layer of experience, which cannot be contained in language: the image works to dredge up intense affect from the depths of repression

(Brooks 1994).[25] The trend away from this depth model of representation in contemporary culture has been critiqued by scholars such as Fredric Jameson, who associates a shift to surface with "the waning of affect," the devaluing of the imperative to express feeling or emotion, both in contemporary life and in cultural production (Jameson 62)[26] However, Lee's work with the surface of the image and sound, his exploration of the materiality of the object, is not the obverse of depth, as a surface/depth dichotomy is not applicable to understanding either his method or the experience it generates. Through his play with the elements of the surface of the film, Lee has prised this surface loose from the expectations of an expressive mode, but this is not to say that the film lacks affect. In *Nowhere to Hide*, the embodied experience generated in the spectator does not stand in for something else—its affect is not in that which is absent. It is the sensory that Lee captures through his exploration of kinetic energy, and it is in or through the materiality of that experience, the energetic, mimetic connection with the spectator—the mimetic innervation—that the affect is generated. This is the challenge that Lee's "tumultuous materialism" throws out to the understanding of cinema spectatorship, and its epistemological foundations.

Notes

I would like to thank Im Hyun Ock for facilitating and translating my interview with Lee Myung Se and for sharing her own critical insights on *Nowhere to Hide*, Sinead Roarty for extensive editorial comments on this piece, and Juanita Kwok, codirector of the Sydney Asia Pacific Film Festival, for assistance in accessing resources on the film.

An earlier version of this chapter was published as "Arrested Motion: Leaps and Bounds in the Korean Detective Film," in the online film journal *Senses of Cinema* 7 (June 2000): <http://www.sensesofcinema.com>.

1. This concept of "mimetic" is different from a more conventional understanding of mimesis as resemblance. As Taussig elaborates the concept of mimetic experience in Benjamin, it has two parts: the first, the idea of imitation or copy, as in the capacity to mimic, and the second, the idea of contact, this much more complex visceral experience of a relation, a porousness between one's self, one's own body, and the objects or images of the world. It is this second aspect of mimesis that I am most interested in (Taussig, 21).
2. Private correspondence with Ock Im Hyn, May 20, 2001.
3. Private correspondence with Ock Im Hyn, May 20, 2001.
4. While other viewers have also made this association, Lee emphasizes that this similarity is coincidental, rather than an intentional quotation.
5. Eisenstein describes these overtones, on which he bases his method of "overtonal montage" as a "filmic fourth dimension" (69).

6. For an extended discussion of Eisenstein's "vertical montage," see Jacques Aumont, *Montage Eisenstein*, trans. Lee Hildreth, Constance Penley, and Andrew Ross (London: BFI & Bloomington and Indianapolis: Indiana University Press, 1987). Aumont has highlighted the challenge of this "vertical montage" to the conventional understanding of montage along the "filmic chain," which he describes as "horizontal" (31–32).

7. Taussig describes this overtonal montage as an understanding of "the interdependence of montage with physiognomic aspects of visual worlds" (p. 28). The "physiognomic aspects of visual worlds" is the term which Benjamin uses to describe mimesis (Taussig 24).

8. See <www.sapff.com.au> for details of the first Sydney Asia Pacific Film Festival (SAPFF) publishers of this article.

9. See also Alan Williams, "Is a Radical Genre Criticism Possible?" *Quarterly Review of Film Studies* 9.2 (Spring 1984).

10. Lee emphasizes that his use of comic book techniques in filmmaking is part of his search for "the enlightened road to universal language." In order to explain this, he draws an analogy with Picasso and Rimbaud: "Something that may help to explain what I do is to look at Picasso and African art. Picasso used simple forms from African art in his striving to find a universal language. Comics are a definitive means of finding a universal language. Rimbaud discusses the concept of a universal language in his writings on poetics. In 1850 he shouted out that it was the advent of the age of universal language, declaring that universal language can be found in the melody of a current pop song, on the cover of an old magazine, and inside of a comic book. And for me as well, I selected the comic book as my [mode] of universal language." Rutherford, unpublished interview.

11. It comes as no surprise that Lee cites Chaplin and Keaton as filmmakers with whom he shares an affinity (Im Hyun-ock, private correspondence).

12. *Nowhere to Hide* has been described as "a completely new kind of movie," Geoffrey Gilmore, 2000 Sundance Film Festival review, cited on <http://www.cinekorea.com/Recent_Film/Nowhere.html>.

The film has also been described in reviews as "exhilarating," "artistic and commercial perfection." See reviews by Darcy Paquet, <http://myhome.shinbiro.com/~darcypaq/koreafilm.html> and <http://koreanfilm.org/> and by Kwak Kyung-hee, <http://korea.insights.co.kr/webzine/cinetaste/web/index.html>.

13. See for example *The Story of Last Chrysanthemums* (1939).

14. A similar compact density in the compartmentalization of the frame has been discussed by Christopher Doyle, cinematographer of Wong Kar-wai's *In the Mood for Love* (2001), as a solution to shooting in cramped locations, as well as being a metaphor for the "confined nature of the characters' existence," cited in Rachael K. Bosley, "Infidelity in the Far East," *American Cinematographer*, February 2001: 26. In *Fallen Angels*, the claustrophobia and fragmentation are largely constructed through the relentlessly moving camera, with the addition of rippling textured light across the frame. In *Nowhere to Hide*, Lee draws on a broader range of techniques and a more complex relationship between the mobile camera and the set design to establish the dynamism of the frame itself.

15. Kim Kyung Hyun has written of the long-standing lack of interest in the West in Korean films that explore this urban sensibility: "[T]he genres that use the backdrops of the city are normally considered 'too popular' and unsuitable to the taste of the art film community in the west," Kim Kyung Hyun, "The New Korean Cinema: Framing the Shifting Boundaries of History, Class, and Gender," doctoral dissertation, University Microfilms, 1998, <http://eee.uci.edu/99s/20655/metropolis.html>. The enthusiastic responses to screenings at Sydney Asia Pacific Film Festival, Sundance Film Festival, Museum of Modern Art, and others clearly signal the crossover success of Lee's film and its potential to draw audiences outside Korea into a closer exploration of the heritage of Korean cinema and its reinvigoration since the end of the 1980s.

16. *Nowhere to Hide* is in parts like a synthesis of *Raging Bull* and a Jackie Chan actioner—the sheer formal aesthetic pleasures that stir the audience into a heightened sensory awareness in *Raging Bull*, combined with the innovativeness of Jackie Chan's play with martial arts traditions, each action sequence exploring new moves in the combination of slapstick and the martial arts/action traditions.

17. Lee writes all his own screenplays, but claims that "until I shoot there is nothing decided. I'm only constructing plans in order to finally destroy everything. . . . It's not just to shoot as laid out in some pre-arranged plan. So I tell my staff and actors that my working style is only to go forward with one's feeling. I work after making this sort of premise. Until now I have made all my films by doing the lighting design, set design and many other aspects of [production] design—but the major premise is always there which is to destroy any preconceived thoughts or final decisions."

18. Lee mobilizes the pace and inventiveness more familiar from Hong Kong cinema: only in Wong Kar-wai's works *Ashes of Time* (1995) and *Chungking Express* have we seen a fast, fragmented editing style with jump cuts, "jump dissolves" (as Darcy Paquet calls them) and shifting camera speeds to achieve such mesmerizing results.

19. This intrinsic relationship between movement and stillness perhaps gives a conceptual foundation to the dynamic Lee sets up between the fixed dimensions of the frame and their undoing. He has said that he "[thinks] of film as a living organism" (Rutherford 2001).

20. Lee says that "in order to do so, I first close my eyes. Then there is nothing left but darkness. And then it is waiting until the scene I want comes to me on its own. So rather than thinking of myself as a creator I think of myself as a translator. At times. However not all scenes are gained through this method. Sometimes I write and make films with the use of conventional film rules." Rutherford, unpublished interview.

21. In Hansen's account, mimetic innervation encompasses both "a decentering and extension of the human sensorium beyond the limits of the individual body/ subject into the world . . . and an introjection, ingestion or incorporation of the object or device." (1999, 10)

22. This argument about "double-edged materiality" is developed more fully in Anne Rutherford, "Precarious Boundaries: Affect, Mise en Scène and the

Senses in Theodorus Angelopoulos's Balkans Epic," in *Art and the Performance of Memory: Sounds and Gestures of Recollection*, ed. Richard Candida Smith (New York and London: Routledge, 2002).

23. Aumont quotes Eisenstein's collected works in six volumes: *Izbrannie proizvedeniia v chesti tomakh* (Moscow: Izdatielstvo Iskusstvo, 1964–71). Here Eisenstein refers to the etymology of the term *ecstasy*, in the Greek, *ek-stasis*, a "movement lifting one out of oneself."

24. This argument about Eisenstein's concept of ecstasy is explored in Anne Rutherford, "Cinema and Embodied Affect," in *Senses of Cinema*, no. 25, <www.sensesofcinema.com/ contents/03/25/embodied_affect.html>.

25. Peter Brooks, "Melodrama, Body, Revolution," in *Melodrama: Stage—Picture—Screen*, ed. Jacky Bratton, Jim Cook, Christine Gledhill (London: BFI, 1994). See, for example, Brooks' discussion of silent cinema's reliance on an "aesthetics of embodiment" (19) which "[uses] the body in expressionistic ways, as the vehicle of meanings that cannot otherwise be conveyed" (11).

26. Jameson critiques a focus on surface in the prevailing models of contemporary critical theory, with their attention to "practices, discourses and textual play."

Works Cited

Ahn Byung-sup. "Humor in Korean Cinema," February 21, 2001. <http://www.cinekorea.com/Essay/Humor.html>.

Aumont, Jacques. *Montage Eisenstein*. Trans. Lee Hildreth, Constance Penley, and Andrew Ross. Bloomington & Indianapolis: Indiana University Press & London: BFI, 1987.

Bosley, Rachael K. "Infidelity in the Far East." *American Cinematographer* 82.2 (2001): 22–30.

Brooks, Peter. "Melodrama, Body, Revolution." *Melodrama: Stage—Picture—Screen*. Ed. Jacky Bratton, Jim Cook, and Christine Gledhill. London: BFI, 1994. 11–24.

Dupont, Joan. "Lee Myung-Se: Painting Action on the Screen." *International Herald Tribune*. February 27, 2001, <http://www.cinekorea.com/Recent_Film/Nowhere.html>.

Eisenstein, Sergei. "The Filmic Fourth Dimension." *Film Form*. Ed. Jay Leyda. New York: Jovanovich, 1949. 64–71.

Gilmore, Geoffrey. "2000 Sundance Film Festival." February 27, 2001, <http://www.cinekorea.com/Recent_Film/Nowhere.html>.

Hansen, Miriam Bratu. "Benjamin and Cinema: Not a One-Way Street." *Critical Inquiry* 25.2 (1999): 306–43.

———. "Introduction." *Theory of Film*. Siegfried Kracauer. Princeton, NJ: Princeton University Press, 1997. vii–xlv.

———. " 'With Skin and Hair': Kracauer's Theory of Film, Marseille 1940." *Critical Inquiry* 19.3 (1993): 437–69.

Im Hyun-ock. "An Interview with Lee Myung-se." Taewon Entertainment press kit, cited in Sydney Asia Pacific Film Festival 2000 publicity material.

Inaga Shigemi. "Claude Monet, Between 'Impressionism' and 'Japonism.' " *Monet and Japan*. Ed. Pauline Green. Canberra: National Gallery of Australia, 2001. 64–76.

Jameson, Fredric. "Postmodernism, or the Cultural Logic of Late Capitalism." *New Left Review* 143–46 (1984): 53–92.

Kim, Kyung Hyun. "The New Korean Cinema: Framing the Shifting Boundaries of History, Class, and Gender." Doctoral dissertation, University Microfilms, 1998. February 27, 2001 <http://eee.uci.edu/99s/20655/metropolis.html>.

Landy, Marcia, ed. *Imitations of Life: A Reader on Film and Television Melodrama*. Michigan: Wayne State University Press, 1991.

Neale, Steve. "Questions of Genre." *Screen* 31.1 (1990): 45–66.

Paquet, Darcy. "Genrebending in Contemporary Korean Cinema." *New Directions in Asian Cinema*. (Catalogue of the first Sydney Asia Pacific Film Festival, March, 2000. Also published in *TAASA Review, Journal of the Asian Arts Society of Australia* 9.1 (2000): 12–13.

Rayns, Tony. *Seoul Stirring: 5 Korean Directors*. Ed. Simon Fields. London: Institute of Contemporary Arts, 1994.

Rutherford, Anne. "Cinema and Embodied Affect." *Senses of Cinema* 25 (2003), <http://www.sensesofcinema.com/contents/03/25/embodied_affect.html>.

———. "Precarious Boundaries: Affect, Mise en Scene and the Senses." *Art and the Performance of Memory: Sounds and Gestures of Recollection*. Ed. Richard Candida Smith. New York and London: Routledge (Memory and Narrative series), 2002. 63–84.

———. Unpublished interview with Lee Myung-se. Trans. Im Hyun-Ock, March 5, 2001.

Spate, Virginia, and David Bromfield. "A New and Strange Beauty: Monet and Japanese Art." *Monet and Japan*. Ed. Pauline Green. Canberra: National Gallery of Australia, 2001. 1–63.

Taussig, Michael. *Mimesis and Alterity: A Particular History of the Senses*. New York and London: Routledge, 1993.

9

Linda C. Ehrlich

Closing The Circle

Why Has Bodhidharma Left For The East?

Nothing really takes place in *Why Has Bodhidharma Left for the East?* (1989) by Korean director Bae Yong-kyun, but the movement of the everyday in all its ordinary splendor and monumentality. *Bodhidharma* tells the deceptively simple tale of three generations of monks at a remote Buddhist temple on top of Mount Chonan in Korea. Three main characters—the venerable Zen master Hye-gok (Yi Pan-yong), the young disciple Ki-bong (Sin Won-sop), and the orphan and novice, Hae-jin (Huang Hae-jin), adopted by Hye-gok—embark, individually and communally, on spiritual paths that pass through breathtaking scenes of the five elements: earth, water, fire, air, and ether.

As an official selection of "Un certain regard" at the Cannes Film Festival in 1989 and winner of the Golden Leopard award at the 1989 Locarno Film Festival, *Why Has Bodhidharma Left for the East?* marks the first director's award in the history of Korean cinema. Bae Yong-kyun spent ten years as screenwriter, cinematographer, director, and editor of the film.[1] (Only the music is composed by someone else: Chin Kyn-yong.) The title comes from the journey of Bodhidharma (AD 460–534), the Indian monk considered to be the founder of Ch'an (Zen) Buddhism.

Figure 9.1. *Why Has Bodhidharma Left for the East?* (Bae Yong-kyun 1989).

According to legend, he traveled from India eastward, supposedly arriving in China in AD 520.[2]

Links in a Chain

In this richly textured film, unexpected juxtapositions and fragmented sequences call on the viewer to try to complete the puzzle. Temporal and spatial leaps remind us how difficult it is to understand the world in some totalizing sense.

Near the beginning of the film, the camera moves from a reflection of Hae-jin's face in a pool to a close-up of the mouth of a golden Buddha statue. These links are legible, but then a close-up of a toad walking laboriously across the road suddenly appears on the screen, followed by a close-up of the hands of Ki-bong chopping up a tree branch. How can we read this kind of seemingly unconnected montage? One way is to realize that—visually and thematically—this is a film about interconnectedness and about the transformation of one event, object, person into another in a regenerative chain of causality.

After throwing a rock at a bird (who later dies), Hae-jin is haunted by its mate. Later, Hae-jin himself almost dies in a chain of events somehow connected with the bird—a chain that sends him plunging into the river and later crashing through the forest. An ox that had earlier escaped from its pen reappears and starts to lead him back to the temple, in a manner reminiscent of the ox-herding pictures of Zen Buddhism. (These pictures present a model of the path toward discovering the true nature of the mind and the true nature of Emptiness [*shunyata*]. The pictures in the series are frequently marked as follows: searching, seeing the traces, seeing the ox, catching the ox, leading the ox, riding the ox home, ox forgotten/ self alone, both ox and self forgotten, return to origins, entering the village with bliss-bestowing hands.)[3] Only afterward do we realize that this ox might be another form of Hae-jin's mother, represented by a woman drenched in the waters of the river.[4] As she opens her mouth to awaken the sleeping boy who lies exhausted by his ordeal in the forest, the ox bellows. As film scholar Cynthia Contreras reminded: "The film does not suggest reincarnation but, rather, the continual flow of one thing into another."[5]

Images of Light

Variations in the quality of the light help differentiate locales in this slow-paced story. The sepia-tinted city slum room contrasts with the temple courtyard flushed with sunlight. In particular, the elderly master, Hye-gok, is associated with images of light, especially the moon. The Temple Superior who sends Ki-bong to the remote monastery speaks of the venerable master as a light for all, overcoming any distance. Hye-gok's first words in the film are: "The universe is deep in the shadows. Light the fuse in your heart to light the way." The *koan* he gives to Ki-bong to help quiet his restless mind is: "When the moon rises in your heart, where does the master of my being go?" (In the same way, the koan of the film's title (in its slightly altered form) has revealed to Zen masters over the centuries the depth of a disciple's path toward enlightenment.)

Figure 9.2. Hye-gok and enlightenment.

Hye-gok dies during the time of the full moon, leaving behind only his shoes, teacup, and the bold calligraphy he had painted. (All of these possessions are given to the child, Hae-jin, who, with his newfound awareness of nonattachment to material things, decides to burn them.)

The film is suffused with images of light, yet each of the film's three main characters also encounters violence and shadows—Hae-jin with a group of children from the lower areas of the mountain who try to push him under the water (filmed in a painful slow motion), Ki-bong with his internal struggles over his abandonment of his family. Even the old master, seemingly so unshakable, is seen pacing back and forth and pitting his frail body against the fiercest of rapids when his disciples go astray.

Images of Fire

Following his master's precise instructions, Ki-bong cremates Hye-gok's body in a carefully tended fire and then scatters the ashes through the countryside. He is observed secretly by a shivering Hae-jin, by the solitary bird on a nearby limb, and by the ox (shown in a startling close-up of an eye filled with tears). As if immersed in the profound silence of another world, the image of the young monk, covered with ash, is reflected in a still pool as he empties the bag of ash and pounded bones. The next day Ki-bong leaves the temple, promising to send someone to look after Hae-jin. The young boy, alone, tends the cooking fire and gazes into the flame.

Journeys

Bodhidharma is a film of journeys, of losing and finding one's way. Slow-motion close-ups of the feet of Ki-bong as he approaches the master's temple for the first time emphasize the journey theme. Ki-bong's subsequent trip back to the "dusty world" to beg for funds for the master's herbal medicine reveals in the sharpest detail the journey he has undergone and what still remains ahead of him.

Bodhidharma presents disturbing images of urban slum life that go beyond a simple exhortation for us to abandon city life and escape to a temple in the hills. When Ki-bong returns to the city in his monk's robe, he sees a claustrophobic scene full of flashing red lights, vendors hawking blue jeans, the misery of a young man literally harnessed to a cart of snacks and cheap liquor that he pulls through the streets at night. The two images of the same man—then and now—are more than contrasts: they are two inevitabilities that—like the earlier montage sequence of tea bowl, hands, and toad—are intrinsically interconnected. In this remarkable scene, which may be hard to decipher on first viewing, the monk Ki-bong "sees" his former self emerging from the dust of the streets.

Later, in an interior monologue brilliantly staged in silhouette and spoken by two figures, a man perched on a ledge listens to another man explain his reasons for returning to the needs of the quotidian world. Are these men two distinct figures, a dialogue between two sides of Ki-bong's psyche, or both? If attachment to desire is the root of all suffering, as the Buddha taught, where does a passionate desire for enlightenment fit in the order of the universe? The "other" monk announces he is returning to the "dusty world" and then walks toward the camera, by implication involving us in his decision. If Ki-bong and his fellow monk actually return to the world by the close of the film, they are following the path of the Bodhisattva of Mercy, whose practice toward enlightenment is to assist others along the path to salvation.

In the early life of the Buddha, the overly protected prince Gautama journeyed out of the royal compound and encountered illness, poverty, and despair. In a similar fashion, Ki-bong, returning from the city to the temple along a narrow path, passes an old man and his retarded child peering curiously from the window of their worn-down farmhouse. Life, with all its weight and fragility, can be seen in the face of this resigned elderly man as he rests for a moment. The lesson is not lost on the fledgling monk.

Trapped between a desire for enlightenment and ties to the suffering of the mundane world, including the suffering of his blind mother (widowed at an early age), Ki-bong attempts to silence the voices within him through his austerities. He is aware of his need for his master's teachings, and yet it is the master's death that proves the ultimate koan. But this is not a film about endings. As Rhim Hye-kyung writes in a review of the film in *Cinemaya*:

> There is no room in this film for the superfluous; there is a mathematical precision of dramaturgies—of story, light, sound, music. The overwhelming scenic beauty is indeed contemplative, but unlike Ozu, where tranquility implies a sadness at the transitory nature of human existence, Bae's film is a vivid and affirmative engagement in the recognition of this reality.[6]

Roundness

In his *Poetics of Space*, philosopher Gaston Bachelard writes of "the phenomenology of roundness" as a means of offering lessons on solitude and calmness. These images of roundness, which can be experienced as a kind of jolt of awareness, are ones that he calls "metapsychological" and as not necessarily stemming from past experience.[7]

Images of roundness reflect the circular nature of the historical Buddha's journey—from royal palace to forest and then back to the world. Many writings on *Why Has Bodhidharma Left for the East?* cite the famous Zen saying: "Before practicing Zen, rivers were rivers and mountains were mountains. When I practiced Zen, I saw that rivers were no longer rivers and mountains no longer mountains. Now I see that rivers are again rivers and mountains are again mountains."[8]

In the making of the film, even the camera assumes a circular path at times, especially in the long sequence in which the Temple Superior is telling Ki-bong how Hye-gok needs assistance in the isolated monastery after suffering from chillbains brought on from his spiritual austerities. The camera completes almost a 360° pan around the elder monk before revealing the person he is addressing.

The circular format of the film appears as well in round objects such as the moon, the mouth of the tea bowl, the bowl Ki-bong carries to beg for funds for his master's medicine, and the circle of beads of the rosary in the monk's hand. Near the beginning of the film, the roundness of the shaven heads of the monks is paralleled in matched shots with the beautifully rounded proportions of the head of the statue of the Buddha in the mountain temple. Later there is another more, discordant image of the round head of the mannequin of a boy (with Western features) in the shop window in the city and the round shape of the clock Ki-bong's blind mother winds—one of her only ties to the outside world. As unconnected as all of these images might seem, they are all part of the same whole, reminding us perhaps of the Chinese phrase *the circle of heaven*. It could also remind us of the circle of rebirth, suffering, and death in Buddhist cosmology or to Zen paintings and calligraphy of the circle (*enso*). The round shapes of clouds, considered symbols of abundance in Korean art, frequently fill the screen in long, contemplative sequences. The soft mountain scenes evoke the gentle natural environment of the Korean countryside.

A circle of caring continues throughout the film, adding a note of intimacy to the geographical isolation of the temple. Particularly harmonious are three shots of the main characters assembled, engaged in activities such as writing calligraphy, pulling out Hae-jin's infected baby tooth, and drinking tea. These shots stress the three generations and how each one is necessary to provide harmony.

Shots of Hae-jin nursing the injured Ki-bong after his extreme austerities on the river are crosscut with the earlier scenes of Hye-gok's attempts at rescue in the raging water. In these shots, the director experiments with mixing asymmetrical images with those of greater balance. In

Figure 9.3. Making room for growth. The three-shot of tooth removal.

the same way, Ki-bong's ghostly appearance following the cremation, as he wanders the hills covered with ash, ties him to the death of the master.

The sense of roundness also ties into the way the director fails to provide one consistent narrative point of view. As Francisca Cho notes, this policy "impugns the viewer's expectation of mastery and demands a very different version of perceptual fullness."[9]

In contrast to a sense of roundness, there are sharply angular images that reflect a lack in the character's spiritual attainment. At the beginning of the film, images of the city—of blinking traffic lights, roundness encased in angularity—show a man entrapped in the harsh angles of the cart he pulls through the city streets like a human ox—similar, and yet distant, from the ox who figures into the monastery tale. The trajectory of the rock Hae-jin throws at the bird is another suspiciously straight, and injurious, line.

There are almost no straight lines associated with the elderly master Hye-gok. Even his walking cane—(also the instrument he uses to berate the wavering Ki-bong)—has noticeable curves in it.

Monumentality

In a film where disturbances to the balance of nature form a central theme, it is appropriate that the camera would also help construct images of balance. A unique camera placement for the scenes of the meditating monks introduces a sense of monumentality. Frequently the director will place the camera behind, and at a low angle to, the meditating figure until it fills the frame. Sometimes the monk, seated in meditation, is even shown framed in red, as if a guardian figure encircled by flames.

Figure 9.4. Begging amidst umbrellas in the market.

In contrast, the most asymmetrical shot in the film is the one of Ki-bong with his begging bowl, set off-center amidst the umbrellas in the city marketplace. The crowded shots of the urban world contrast with the open framing of many of the temple scenes. Later in this sequence, Ki-bong stands in the doorway of his family's slum dwelling, his face divided—half in light, half in shadow.

Sounds and Stillness

As Zen teachers, like the Japanese Buddhist priest Kukai (774–835), have stated, Suchness transcends forms, but without relying on forms it cannot be realized. The three main characters all engage in this dance of form and formlessness, in a studied alternation between light and darkness. Yet along with this stillness is an underlying tension that, as Michael Gillespie writes, is built on "an urgent feeling that something is happening, growing and building."[10]

The vaguely shamanistic Buddhist dance in the lower temple near the end of the film unites the five elements as it also unites light and shadow, life and death.[11] The undulating spirals of the sleeves of the temple dancer free our minds from linear thought. Crosscuts between the sound of the drum and shots of Ki-bong and Hae-jin—first attracted to the beauty of the dance and then returning to their temple through tall grasses as day dawns—underscores the urgency of their return. As Hye-gok passes away in the mountain temple, the pure white garb of the dancer reenters the darkness with a quiet, sliding motion.

On second or third viewings of this film—viewings that yield new riches—it is intriguing to concentrate on the sounds. In addition to the music composed for the soundtrack, there is the compelling beating of the *moktok* (wooden instrument used during meditation or the city begging scene) contraposed to the staccato cries of the city vendors hawking their wares. There are discordant sounds—the bird's squawking cry for its lost mate, the cruel yelling of the rural boys "playing" with (attempting to drown?) Hae-jin. There are ambiguous sounds, such as the ox's lowing. At times the "one note" aspect of the master's teaching can be off-putting, but it too adds a regularity to the sounds, as does the intermittent ringing of the temple bell. Even the other-worldly dance music performed at the ceremony at the lower temple quiets down to just the sound of crickets and the rustling of grasses. In a careful viewing of this film, all of our senses are invoked, and many scenes appeal to various senses at once. For example, when Ki-bong and Hae-jin return from the temple ceremony, it is the smell of burning herbal medicine that warns the young boy that something is amiss.

Bae Yong-kyun is not afraid of long silent sequences, most notably the one following the master's death up to the return of Ki-bong to the temple at the completion of the cremation process. Hae-jin's childlike voice, chanting the sutras in place of his master, leads into the final phase of this evolving story.

Child's Play

The trajectory of Hae-jin's apprenticeship as a monk passes through paradoxical images of play—both constructive and destructive—as he is taught by the two older monks how to assume that lifestyle. In child's play we find the acts of imitating, rehearsing, assuming power, coping with difficulties, problem solving, and the creation of something new. Children learn by "pretend play"—the use of fantasy, make-believe, and symbolism.[12] In his *Homo Ludens*, Dutch scholar Johannes Huizinga reminds us that play absorbs the player totally.[13]

Some of the very first images of the cinema were those of children playing—playing tricks on the gardener, being fed by parents, interacting with the camera.[14] These images are at once revelatory and contrived. Bae Yong-kyun never sentimentalizes Hae-jin; rather, he tends to present him as a *tabula rasa*, a blank slate, onto which the Buddhist teachings can be inscribed. This process is shown as an easier one than that of the adult Ki-bong whose spiritual journey is more tortuous.

There have been a few cinematic attempts at linking childhood to a sense of faith, as in Carl Dreyer's *Ordet* (1955) and Jacques Doillon's

Ponette (1996). *Why Has Bodhidharma Left for the East?* offers fleeting glimpses into the steps a child takes to explore the parameters of the life of faith he sees around him. Hae-jin's explorations of his new landscape are both natural and perilous. We explore with him; at times we fear for his life. As all of the films listed above show, children immersed in an inner religious vision can be marked as "different" and "other," and even put their lives at risk.

Closing the Circle

For a film like *Bodhidharma*, it is helpful to consider the description of religion as "imagistic, participatory, performative, and world-creating." As film and religion scholar S. Brent Plate reminds: "Films are not religious simply because of their *content* but they become religious due to their *form* and *reception*."[15] Some feature films with Buddhist themes—*Kundun* (Scorcese 1997), *Little Buddha* (Bertolucci 1993), *Siddhartha* (Conrad Rooks 1972)—focus on the life of the historical Buddha or on other prominent Buddhist figures. The Korean cinema has its own offerings in this area—in addition to *Bodhidharma*, we can find Im Kwon-taek's *Mandala* (1981) and his *Come, Come, Come Upward!* (1988), Chang Sonu's *Passage to Buddha* (1994), and Chung Ji-young's *Beyond the Mountains* (1991), among others. *Bodhidharma* is distinct in the meditative stance that underlies the entire style of the film.

Frequently discussions of religion on film turn to depictions of the lives of religious figures or even to popular films such as *Star Wars* (1977), *The Godfather* (1972), and *E.T.* (1982), to examine the sacred on screen.[16] Another approach is that of screenwriter/director Paul Schrader or film scholar David Bordwell, who set out specific characteristics for a kind of film that Schrader called "transcendental" and Bordwell called "parametric"—a film whose mysterious, yet oddly precise, style seem to defy easy classification even as an "art film."[17] In *Transcendental Style in Film*, Schrader looks at the films of Ozu, Bresson, and Dreyer in terms of what he defines as the three steps of transcendental style: (1) a focus on the everyday, (2) a disparity (an actual or potential disunity between humans and their environment that culminates in a decisive action) and (3) a stasis that does not resolve the disparity but rather transcends it. Films with this overall tone tend to feature an aesthetics of sparseness, simple editing, austere cinematography, and acting that does not look like acting. They leave questions unanswered.

So *Bodhidharma* presents a series of paradoxical liminal spaces, both within the story and as a film itself. The isolated monastery is so deep in the mountains that few come to visit, yet the Temple Superior who sends Ki-bong there compares Hye-gok, the elder monk, to a beacon of light. As director and theoretician Victor Turner points out, liminality is associated with a passage from one basic human state or status to another, and with a separation form one's antecedent life.[18] This liminal mode could be either individual or collective. Tuner cites the three-phrase pattern of "rites of passage" noted by Arnold van Gennep: separation/detachment, margin (or *limen*, a realm with none of the attributes of the former life), and aggregation/consummation of the passage.[19] In *Bodhidharma*, the elder monk has completed this three-part passage, the child Hae-jin jumps from stage one to stage three, and we embark on the total journey with Ki-bong, the character who most closely reminds us of our own struggles.

Momentous events take place in *Why Has Bodhidharma Left for the East?* A man decides to leave his destitute mother in the city and become a monk; an older monk adopts an orphan and takes him to live in a remote monastery; the older monk dies, and the man tends to the burning of his master's body. Yet, in a way, nothing takes place in this film but the movement of the everyday in all of its ordinary splendor and monumentality. As Hye-gok affirms near the close of the film, "I am insubstantial to the universe. But in the universe there is nothing which is not me." The inconclusive ending—where Ki-bong looks up to the heavens in response to Hae-jin's query about where he is going—ties into the tradition in Chinese poetry where the poet encounters the absence of the recluse and develops spiritually through this absence.[20]

In an earlier scene in which the child Hae-jin accidentally falls into the water, he struggles and appears to be drowning. When he gives up and just floats, he reaches the shore safely. As Hae-jin floats to safety after falling into the cold mountain lake, the diffused light on the water shines like jewels. This message of nonattachment to what is transitory and in flux is what the old master instructs when the child remains curious about the diseased tooth that had been pulled from his mouth (and, following an old custom, is tossed up on the temple rooftop). The message of nonattachment—difficult as it may be—is not lost on the attentive viewer as well.

The director of *Why Has Bodhidharma Left for the East?* has stated that Zen Buddhism is the setting for the film, not its final meaning, and that the viewer can approach the film without prior knowledge of the kinds of questions or answers intended.[21] At the close of the film, a solitary bird flies up into the heavens. Our eye follows the track of the wings as they disappear from sight.

Notes

A shorter review of this film by the author appeared in *Film Quarterly* 48:1 (Fall 1994): 30–31.

1. Bae Yong-kyun, born in 1951 in Taegu, Korea, received his doctorate from the Faculty of Fine Arts in Korea and presently teaches painting there. His second film *Gum eu na thang ae hee na pae sung* (1955) has not appeared in video format in either Korea or the United States. It is about a middle-aged man named Alex Kauffman who comes back to Korea after being adopted as a baby forty years earlier.

2. In Chinese, Bodhidharma is known as *Pú-tí-ta-mo*, or just *Ta-mo*, and in Japanese as *Daruma*. He is a frequent subject of paintings in both countries and is also considered a popular deity in Japan.

3. The representation of the "ox-herding pictures" began as early as the Southern Sung period (1127–1279). A famous example of a handscroll of ten *sumi-e* (inkwash paintings) based on this theme is attributed to the fifteenth-century artist-monk Shubun and is owned by the Shokoku-ji temple in Japan.

4. The fact that few women appear in this film reflects the setting (a remote Buddhist temple) rather than any political statement on the part of the director (personal correspondence with the director, September 1993).

5. Cynthia Contreras, "Depicting the Buddha, Teaching the Dharma," *Asian Cinema* 10.1 (Fall 1998): 176–92.

6. Rhim Hye-kyung, *Cinemaya* 5 (Autumn 1989): 33.

7. Gaston Bachelard, *The Poetics of Space* (*La poétique de l'espace*), trans. Maria Jolas (Boston: Beacon, [1958], 1969) 233–34.

8. Note Michael L. Gillespie, "Picturing the Way in Bae Yong Kyun's *Why Has Bodhidharma Left for the East?*" in *The Journal of Religion and Film* 1.1 (April 1997, online journal).

9. Francisca Cho, "Imagining Nothing and Imaging Otherness in Buddhist Film," *Imag(in)ing Otherness: Filmic Visions of Living Together*, ed. S. Brent Plate and David Jasper (Atlanta, Georgia: Scholars, 1999) 188.

10. Gillespie, *Journal of Religion and Film* (online).

11. Buddhism was introduced into Korea from India, via China, in the late fourth century AD and spread among the common people. Although Korea received Confucianism and Taoism from China as well, it has always retained its own unique national identity. One aspect of this identity is the way in which shamanism has retained an intimate relationship with Buddhism in Korea and how it continues to be vital in the popular culture. It is believed that the shaman *(mudang)*, in a state of possession, is able to communicate with a deity during shamanistic rites *(kut)*.

12. Sandra Russ, *Play in Child Development and Psychotherapy* (Mahwah, NJ: Erlbaum, 2004) 2.

13. Johannes Huizinga, *Homo Ludens: A Study of the Play-Element in Culture* (London: Routledge, 1949).

14. For example, in the Lumière operators' film in Indochina, entitled *Namo*, the unseen cinematographer is seated on a rickshaw, and for fifty seconds

children run toward the camera as it retreats before them. Also note one of the earliest moving picture sequences by the Lumière brothers *The Gardener Gets Watered* (1895).

15. S. Brent Plate, *Representing Religion in World Cinema: Filmmaking, Mythmaking, Culture Making* (New York: Palgrave, 2003) 1.

16. The interplay between religion and film has been examined in such books as *Screening the Sacred, Image and Likeness, Seeing and Believing, Film as Religion: Myths, Morals, and Rituals* , *The Hidden God: Film and Faith*, and others.

17. Paul Schrader, *Transcendental Style in Film: Ozu, Bresson, Dreyer* (Berkeley: University of California Press, 1972); David Bordwell, *Narration in the Fiction Film* (Madison: University of Wisconsin Press, 1985), especially pages 274–79.

18. Victor Turner, "Betwixt and Between: The Liminal Period in Rites of Passage," *Betwixt and Between: Patterns of Masculine and Feminine Initiation*, ed. Louise Mahdi (Le Salle, IL: Open Court, 1987) 3–19.

19. Ibid, 5. Turner draws from A. van Gennep, *The Rites of Passage* (Chicago: University of Chicago Press, 1960).

20. Note Cho 173–74.

21. On a practical note, Gillespie comments on the reactions of (American) students to the film: reactions ranging from "resistance (maybe childcare authorities should be called in to stop the old man from raising the orphan that way)" to subtle questions about subtext and motivation. I have also found this film a "hard sell," even among the most willing of students. In addition to the articles cited above, other critical writing on the film includes Frank Tedesco, "A Conversation with Bae Yong-kyun," *Tricycle* 3.4 (Summer 1994): 103–06; Michel Ciment, "Entretien avec Yong-kyun Bae," *Positif* 344 (October 1989): 2–6; Tony Rayns, *Sight and Sound* 1.5 (October 1991): 47 (review); Stephen Holden, "Zen and the Art of Making Its Tenets into a Movie, September 25, 1993: B2; Philippe Niel, "'No Ideas but in Things' *(Pourquoi Bodhi Dharma est-il parti vers l'Orient?)* in *Positif* 350 (April 1990): 25–26; and Max Tessier, "*Pourquoi Bodhi-Dharma est0il parti vers l'orient?* Une majestueuse entrée en Zen," in *La revue du cinéma* 459 (April 1990): 19.

Works Cited

Bachelard, Gaston. *The Poetics of Space* (*La poétique de l'espace*). Trans. Maria Jolas. Boston: Beacon, (1958), 1969. 233–34.

Cho, Francisca. "Imagining Nothing and Imaging Otherness in Buddhist Film." *Imag(in)ing Otherness: Filmic Visions of Living Together*. Ed. S. Brent Plate and David Jasper. Atlanta: Scholars, 1999. 169–96.

Ciment, Michel. "Entretien avec Yong-kyun Bae." *Positif* 344 (October 1989): 2–6.

Contreras, Cynthia. "Depicting the Buddha, Teaching the Dharma."*Asian Cinema* 10:1 (Fall 1998): 176–92.

Gillespie, Michael L. "Picturing the Way in Bae Yong-kyun's *Why Has Bodhidharma Left for the East?*" *The Journal of Religion and Film* 1.1 (1997), http://avalon.unomaha.edu/jrf/gillespi.htm.

Holden, Stephen. "Zen and the Art of Making Its Tenets into a Movie," *The New York Times*, September 25, 1993: B2.
Niel, Philippe. " 'No Ideas but in Things' (*Pourquoi Bodhi Dharma est-ïl parti vers* l'Orient?)" *Positif* 350 (April 1990): 25–26.
Rayns, Tony. "Why Did Bodhi-Dharma Leave for the East?" *Sight and Sound* 1.5 (October 1991): 47.
Rhim Hye-kyung. "*Why Has Bodhi-Dharma Left for the East*?" *Cinemaya* 5 (Autumn 1989): 33.
Tedesco, Frank. "A Conversation with Bae Yong-kyun." *Tricycle* 3.4 (Summer 1994): 103–06.
Tessier, Max. "*Pourquoi Bodhi-Dharma est0il parti vers l'orient?* Une majestueuse entrée en Zen." *La revue du cinéma* 459 (April 1990): 19.

PART 3

Narratives of the National

10

FRANCES GATEWARD

Waiting to Exhale

The Colonial Experience and the Trouble with *My Own Breathing*

> [W]henever I think about it and talk about it, fire blazes inside of my body and I can't extinguish it. . . . Tears flow in my chest. As long as I am alive, this sadness will always be with me like a knot tied around my chest.
>
> —Yoon Doo-ri, *Silence Broken*

THE INTENSE FEELINGS OF discomfort described above by Yoon Doo-ri,[1] an elderly woman living in a government-subsidized apartment complex in Ulsan, South Korea, are classic symptoms of *hwa byung*, a culturally bound psychiatric disorder most commonly experienced by Korean women beyond middle age with little education, who are from rural areas and of low socioeconomic standing. Literally translated as "fire disease," it is a suppressed anger syndrome, developing when individuals experience anger caused by external events. Because those of lower economic status are left with little recourse, and because angry outbursts are not socially sanctioned for women (they are expected to bear misfortune, misery, and maltreatment silently), the anger is directed inward, resulting in a number of somatic manifestations—headaches, indigestion, heart palpitations, a sensation of heat in the body, and most commonly, respiratory difficulties caused by oppressive and heavy feelings in the chest. These physical symptoms usually coincide with anxiety, clinical depression, a pessimistic worldview, loss of interest, an inflammatory temper, rage, hate, resentment, frustration, mortification, regret, shame, and thoughts of suicide.

It is not surprising that *hwa byung*, considered an archaic disorder, persists in modern South Korea. The economic miracle that placed the nation among the Asian "tigers" of Hong Kong, Singapore, and Taiwan was not experienced by everyone. As the once agriculturally based "hermit kingdom" became an industrial powerhouse, earning its place among the vanguard of global technological innovators, the concurrent social and cultural upheaval left several population groups displaced and disregarded. Class differentiation became more distinct as incomes rose along with consumerism and materialism. With increased urbanization and the growth of Seoul into a megalopolis, whole shantytowns were razed to make way for high-rise apartment buildings.[2] In turn, these virtually indistinguishable concrete towers contributed to the loss of extended family households, leaving the elderly disheartened, since tradition dictated they would spend their twilight years living with their children and grandchildren. Parents eager to see their children succeed in the global marketplace have placed an undue emphasis on the ability of their children to speak fluent English. Billions of dollars are spent annually by the middle and upper classes on tuition for English-language kindergarten and grammar schools, tutors, and after-school programs. Frenulotomy, a surgery performed in the West to correct severe speech impediments and tongue immobility, is treated in Korea as elective cosmetic surgery on children under the age of five, with an expectation that it will enhance their ability to speak unaccented or, more specifically, American-accented English. Babies are exposed to hours of English-language videos, and children as young as eight are sent overseas to academies in Australia and Canada so that they may rise above their competition. This obsession with the global capitalist and techno-enhanced future has rendered those unable to keep pace, and those associated with the past, invisible and inconsequential—people like Yoon Doo-ri, who is not only old, undereducated, and poor, but also a reminder of the nation's degraded past.

This chapter explores the cinematic treatment of history in Korea, specifically, the recollection of the colonial past and its legacies. How is the memory of this period constructed? Why is this commercial cinema, helmed by young directors with no personal experience of Japanese rule, so invested in the reimagining of a period fraught with the trauma of oppression and exploitation suffered by their forebears? What is the role historical representation plays in the cinema in the production of popular memory and Korean national identity? And last, whose vision of the past is legitimized, and whose is consigned to oblivion?

The Past Isn't Dead—In Fact It's Not Even Past

One of the most intriguing aspects of New South Korean cinema is its treatment of time, in terms of both historical representation *and* narrative structure. A review of the literature, ranging from film reviews to retrospective programs, interviews with industry professionals, historical surveys, and in-depth textual analyses reveals the defining characteristic of contemporary Korean cinema to be fragmentation. The majority of feature films, regardless of genre, rely on narrational strategies that deviate from the paradigm of linear progression. Audiences that watch Korean films have learned not to expect a plot structure organized by forward causal momentum. Instead, they are more likely to experience the refusal of a unified narrative presented in a linear form. Films offer a repetition of events from varied perspectives, parallel-time structures, regressive causal momentum, violations of the space/time continuum, time travel, and most common, and perhaps most telling, a reliance on flashbacks to explicate the present.[3] The dominance of the flashback further complicates the narrative order in that it is frequently presented in complex forms. Rather than the simplistic cut or dissolve cued by a character's memory so that we may witness an expository event occurring earlier in the story, Korean directors favor parallel flashbacks, contradictory flashbacks, open-ended flashbacks, and sometimes even flashbacks within flashbacks.

The formal emphasis on temporality, as evidenced by the prevalence of the flashback and the other time-rupturing techniques, coincides with the story focus, as an unusually large number of films are concerned with issues of history and memory. Though interrogations of the past can take many forms, Korean filmmakers often utilize the peculiar trope of amnesia. How pervasive is this phenomenon? The motif is manifested in almost every genre: the supernatural thriller *Secret Tears* (Park Ki-hyung 2000); the *jopok* (gangster) comedy *My Wife Is a Gangster 2* (Chung Hung-soon 2003); big-budget science fiction spectaculars such as *Rub Love* (Lee Seo-goon 1998), *Nabi: The Butterfly* (Moon Seung-wook 2001), and *Yesterday* (Jung Yun-su 2002); romantic comedies such as *Over the Rainbow* (Ahn Jin-woo 2002); mysteries such as *Spider Forest* (Song Il-gon 2004); and melodramas, as exemplified by *A Moment to Remember* (John H. Lee

2004). Even the Korean contribution to the transnational omnibus horror film *Three* (2002) makes use of the theme, as the short is aptly titled, *Memories* (Kim Jee-woon). As film scholar Robert Cagle theorizes, "These narrative strategies, of filling in the gaps of the past, are overdetermined, representing an attempt at constructing a seamless and unified tradition. It is a longing for an idealized past."[4]

The nostalgic impulse and desire for a mythic past is often depicted in films of triumph or reconciliation, usually within three distinct historical periods—the colonial period of control by Japan, from 1910, the year of annexation, to the end of the Pacific War in 1945; the outbreak of the Korean War in 1950 to the cease-fire in 1953, and from 1971, when the state of emergency declared by the autocratic government led to the rescission of civil and human rights, to 1987, the beginning of the Sixth Republic, when the struggles of the democratic movement were realized with the election of Roh Tae-woo. References to these eras may be central to the storylines, as in *The Last Witness* (Bae Chang-ho 2001), a drama concerning romantic love and the lives of people swept up in Cold War ideology or *A Petal* (Jang Sun-woo 1996), an unflinching examination of the Gwangju Massacre, or as immaterial as a seconds-long shot of a martial arts grandmaster sucking in tear gas during a 1980s demonstration in *Arahan* (Ryo Seung-wan 2004).

The ubiquity of period films and historical metafictions—what Hayden White describes as fictional films grounded by referents in history (18)—is expressive of the drive to reconstruct the past, be it nostalgic or otherwise, clearly demonstrating that cinema has become central to the national historical memory, providing younger generations engaging and readily available mimetic experiences of the monumental traumas of which they have no firsthand recollection. The films of fragmentation, memory loss, and historical reenactment reveal an anxious nation that, as it looks to the future, is attempting to reconcile tragic historical conflicts while attending to the inevitable return of the repressed. This fixation with history and memory is indicative of what I would characterize as *the* preeminent project of contemporary Korean cinema, the determination of a national identity, moreover one that is becoming increasing defined as masculine.

"You Bitches Have Ruined This Country!"

This line of dialogue, delivered by a frustrated character in the film *No Blood No Tears* (Ryo Seung-wan 2002) might very well serve as an index of the misogynistic gender constructions in a number of extremely popular films, despite the long history of sympathetic female characters who

Figure 10.1. Challenging the social order in *No Blood No Tears* (Ryo Seung-won 2002). Courtesy Pusan Film Festival.

challenged gender roles in such films as *A Bride Born in the Year of the Horse* (Kim Ki-deok 1966), Shin Sang-ok's *Women of Yi Dynasty* (1969) and the much noted *Madame Freedom* (Han Hyong-mo 1956)—all melodramas released during the Golden Age. Women such as actress Lim Eun-joo battled in martial arts epics such as Kim Chung-yong's *18 Amazons* (1979) and *12 Gates of Hell* (Lee Hyuk-soo 1979). A challenge to domestic violence was focused upon in *A Hot Roof* (Lee Mi-yong 1995), while *Because You Are a Woman* (Kim Yu-jin 1990) provided a sharp critique of sexual violence and the patriarchal power of the state.

In the last five years, however, South Korean women have been generally maligned in the cinema, typically depicted as destructive forces threatening the sanctity of the home and the integrity of the nation. No longer just "missys"[5] or "sassy girls," these *michinyuns* (crazy bitches), as they are often referred to in films, are everywhere, engaged in murder and mayhem in the movies to an unprecedented degree, not only in number, but also with increased precision, firepower, and brutality. For example, there is the duplicitous North Korean assassin in *Shiri* (Kang Je-kyu 1999), the sexual molester in *The Butcher's Wife* (Shin Jeong-gyun, 1999), the emasculating adulterer of *Happy End* (Jung Ji-woo 1999), *Tell Me Something*'s (Chang Yoon-hyun 1999) serial killer with a penchant for dismemberment, *Pisces'* (Kim Hyung-tae 2000) vengeful woman scorned, the crafty Communist conspirator in *The Last Witness* (Bae Chang-ho 2002), and the stalker hunting her object of desire in *Oh Happy Day* (Yun Hak-ryul 2003). Though these films feature gender-defined transgressive acts, they are not presented as celebratory feats of feminism or female empowerment. Rather, they are treated as degenerate and depraved, with the restoration of the social order serving as patriarchal fantasies of punishment meted out to women who have overstepped their boundaries. A prime example of this is the 2002 box-office smash *My Wife Is a Gangster* (Cho Jin-kyu 2001), described by one critic as *The Long Kiss Goodnight* in reverse.[6]

My Wife Is a Gangster is an odd blending of comedy, drama, and action, focusing on Chae Eun-jin (Shin Eun-kyung), nicknamed Mantis, the second-in-command in the hierarchy of a crime organization. Presented to us in the precredit sequence as the organization's fearsome champion, the most skilled in hand-to-hand combat, Eun-jin, referred to as "Big Brother," is placed in charge of the group's activity in the absence of the crime boss. Her short hair, lack of makeup, low voice, gruff manner of speaking, and boxy suits disclose an ideology that characterizes femininity and power as mutually exclusive. It even goes so far as to require her to bind her breasts before a duel with a Japanese martial artist. Eun-jin spends the bulk of the film trying to fulfill her dying sister's wish—that she marry—while still trying to maintain her leadership of the gang. The task of matrimony proves the more difficult of the two, for she has no one to represent her in the initial family introduction (an older couple is bullied into posing as her parents) and is so masculinized that a bar hostess must be brought in to instruct her on how to dress and how to be coy and demure. Once a husband is secured her sister reveals a further hope that Eun-jin will become a mother, so the bar hostess is solicited once again, this time for lessons on how to sexually arouse her husband.

Though the film does reveal gender as a social construct through scenes of instruction and gender role reversal—the male gangsters are clumsy and stupid, and the husband, a skilled homemaker and nurturer (he is the caretaker of his ill sister-in-law), is physically incapable of defending himself—the film must exact a compromise. Women like Eun-jin, who are too independent and too efficient at leadership, and thus too manly, must be disciplined. And in action films like *My Wife Is a Gangster*, the punishment is physical, usually occurring in an extended fight sequence highlighting the brutality.[7] Earlier fight sequences are hyperstylized, using slow motion, wirework, expressionistic lighting, extreme angles, and CGI effects. The opening credit sequence, for instance, where Eun-jin saves her crew from a rival gang, is set in the rain so as to add dramatic back-lit trails of water as characters twist and leap, while towering volumes of water splash upward as dispatched opponents hit the ground. In the climax, however, the scene of her comeuppance where she is literally beaten into submission, the visuals transform from a hyperstylized slickness into a more realist mode, detailing the gut-wrenching assault. She loses the fight because she is distracted by the need to protect her unborn child. She is, as Mellencamp so well phrases in her discussion of the protagonist of *La Femme Nikita*, "tough but tamed by femininity" (116). Ultimately, the discourse is a male one, as the title remains, *My Wife Is a Gangster*, and Eun-jin learns that she must not lead men, but work alongside them.

Of course, this is not to say that more docile women are absent from the cinema. They *are* present. But, more often than not, the more traditional the role, the less likely it is to be a Korean woman in the narrative portrayed by a Korean actress. As Kim Soyoung points out, "As South Korean women disappear, other women are summoned to enable the purposes of nostalgia" (17). The parts of distressed damsels in need of rescue and women functioning to affirm the heterosexuality and heroism of the male protagonists are being outsourced. In *Musa: The Warrior* (Kim Sung-su 2001) a small group of Korean envoys battle a horde of bandits in the desert, protecting a Ming Dynasty princess played by PRC actress Zhang Ziyi. Hong Kong's Cecilia Cheung plays the title character of Failan in Song Hae-sung's melodrama released in 2001. As a sickly and impoverished illegal alien from China, she longs for the husband she has never met, a failed gangster who married her only for a one-time payment. Her character is pathetic, laboring at menial jobs in the day and entertaining romantic fantasies about the life with her husband she will never obtain.

Though casting across borders may be attributed to good economic sense, since most pop culture industries are dependent upon foreign audiences to boost potential profit margins, it is, nevertheless, curious. The association of Korean women with the monstrous, the infliction of punishment on those who "need" to be reminded of their place, and the trends of international casting are corollaries to Kyung Hyun Kim's assertion that contemporary Korean cinema is a cinema of remasculanization. The anxiety over male identity, linked to humiliation and emasculation by historical trauma, is renegotiated in narratives of "rejuvenation:"

> a revival of images, cultural discourses, and popular fictions that fetishized and imagined dominant men and masculinity. And the longing for an ideal male hero became integrated in the production of a new symbol for Korea in the era of industrialized, modern, and global subject formation. By the late 1990s, the typical representation of Korean men in cinema as no longer solely composed of self-loathing and pathetic male characters; images of well-proportioned bodies in sleek suits and professional jobs also began to appear with regularity and unprecedented force. No longer merely the targets of

public embarrassment, many screen males emerged instead as objects of desire. (9–10)

I argue further that the remasculinization is occurring not only *on* the screen, but *of* the screen. The industry has turned to a reliance on specific genres, all of which are steeped in ideologies of gender and nation. The changes in trade laws, making Korean films more vulnerable to Hollywood big-budget films, upped the ante for Korean filmmakers.[8] The industry also had to contend with the growth of the home video market, the popularity of cable television, and the gradual opening of the domestic market to Japanese films.[9] The remedy for an ailing box office was discovered with the success of *Shiri*[10] and its subsequent record breakers—*Joint Security Area* (Park Chan-wook 2000) and *Taeguki* (Kang Je-kyu 2004), which affirmed the value of high-concept blockbusters. Audiences are flocking to their local multiplexes to experience time travel with historical epics, obtain pleasure in the illicit allure of gangster thrillers, be excited by heart-pumping action-adventure films, and witness the thrills of victory and agonies of defeat in sports movies. It would seem, then, that the once-staple genre of the industry, the melodrama, has been for the most part relegated to television, and quite successfully so, given the international success of dramatic miniseries such as *Winter Sonata*, popular in eastern Europe, the United States, and throughout East and South Asia. The decline of the Hong Kong film industry is due in part to the rise of the Korean cinema and the fact that Korean directors offer Hong Kong–style fight choreography and high-octane gunplay just as thrilling as their Chinese counterparts, in a localized context with production values on par with Hollywood.

The three most privileged genres, enjoying the largest budgets, biggest stars, and media blitz campaigns are the epic, the actioner, and the sports film. Though films categorized within these genres have the potential to function as what Klinger outlines as "rebel texts," subverting the ideologies of established genres by altering their respective formulas' themes, characters, narrative forms, and visual styles, they are most often emblematic of reactionary ideologies. The epic, action film, and sports film are among the most rigid of genres, as they deal with absolutes. Though the setting, characters, and even focus of the narratives may be divergent, they are similar in that the diegesis is dependent upon the establishment of a precise set of rules. Further, the characters are narrowly drawn, operating from moral codes of honor that prescribe the action.

Epics are objects of fascination for contemporary audiences, because they offer an excess of cinematic spectacle of both scale and violence. In addition, as prestige films they are by default star vehicles, mobilizing all the glamor the cinema can muster. As grand historical narratives, they function as a public site to enact both heritage and history and thus are central to contemporary national mythologies. By highlighting traditional culture through setting, dress, music, and language, these period dramas easily accommodate the mobilization of old moral codes and the historical figures that embody them. The most recurring character of the epic is the hero, defined by his masculinity and his association not only with the national but with the chivalric and the martial as well. *Musa: The Warrior*, for example, is a film of national emergence. In 1375, a Korean emissary is sent with his small entourage to China, seeking official recognition for their newly formed nation. They are rejected, and on their return home through the desert they take on the impossible task of protecting a Ming Dynasty princess from hordes of marauding Chinese bandits. The Korean men overcome their own internal differences, proving themselves to be more righteous than the Chinese, who would attack their own royalty to satisfy their greed. The Chinese refusal to acknowledge Korea as a nation strikes an ominous tone, as the disrespect for the sovereignty of the peninsular country would arise centuries later with the Korean War.

Similar themes are enunciated in the action-adventure film, though with less bombast and fewer melodramatic tendencies. Though denigrated and dismissed as escapist, the car chases, explosions, gun battles, and choreographed fisticuff skirmishes of the action film bring to the fore questions of, as Marchetti informs us, "rights of possession and property; the definition of the national, ethnic, racial self as opposed to 'other'; the propriety of intervening in other nations' or other cultures' affairs; the moral consequences of violence; and the meaning of masculinity and male prerogatives" (188). *Shiri*, noted earlier, blends the spy thriller with the action film, resulting in a tense, suspenseful narrative about terrorism, unification, and the triumph of the masculine against the threatening deceptive feminine.

The emphasis on physical prowess and performances of masculinity so common in the action film are central to the sports film, which draws on all of the preestablished gender-based expectations of both athletes and fans, regardless of the level of competition, professional or amateur. The issue of identity is central, as the monikers of winner and loser define "who is the man," often linked to rivalries of race, class, and region. In the martial arts world of Asian cinema, particularly in films made during and after the 1970s, competition extends beyond issues of individual achievement, style superiority, or school-associated pride. The community within the walls of the martial arts academy is frequently a metaphor for the immediate family, clan, and country, linked to the national through themes of protection and sharing of traditional knowledge, adherence to the tenets of Confucianism, and the invocation of national enmity. One example is the first Hong Kong kung fu feature to enjoy wide release in the United States, *Five Fingers of Death* (1973). Korean director Chen Chang-ho's film used the pretense of a martial arts competition to vilify the Japanese and their Chinese conspirators. The celebrated *Chinese Connection* also known as *Fist of Fury* (Lo Wei 1972) has Bruce Lee's character Chen Zhen defending Chinese masculinity against the Japanese, who have declared them the "sick men of Asia." A recent Korean film that uses the martial arts trope rather interestingly is *Spin Kick* (Nam Sang-kook 2004). As a coming-of-age film set in high school, it uses the national Korean martial art tae kwon do as a tool to define characteristics of acceptable manhood. A group of delinquent miscreants faced with expulsion are forced to join their high school team, with the expectation that they will restore the institution's former glory as champions. Through the sport they learn discipline, perseverance, loyalty, sacrifice, and personal honor. These are important lessons given the nation's concern with its future, made worrisome by increasing levels of juvenile misconduct—alcohol abuse, truancy, hedonism, and crime sprees committed by *chijon pa*, alienated youth who kidnap and kill the well-to-do, not out of greed but out of hate and envy.

The epic, action, and sports film are compelling genres of study in their own right, especially in terms of gender and the national, but what I find particularly intriguing is their continual invocation of the colonial past. Together they work to create a collective Korean identity based on the normalizing of anti-Japanese images, often making use of real historical figures. A short list of popular features in this vein follows:

> *Saulabi*, also known as *Time Travel to the Root of the Samurai* (Mun Jong-geum 2004). This expensive epic, which utilized over three hundred professional martial artists, four thousand extras, and three hundred horses, was the cause of great controversy in Asia. The word used for the title, *saulabi*, is the term for the elite class of swordsmen during the Paekjae Kingdom (18 BC–660 AD). Though the plot seems innocuous—more than four hundred years after the fall of Paekjae two warriors hope to restore the "Spirit Sword" and the spirit of the nation in the midst of Japanese aggression—the assertions made in the film provoked debates between the two nations. It added to already existing disputes about origin: Which martial art is derived from the other, tae kwan do or karate? Are the Japanese actually descendants of Koreans who emigrated during the prehistoric era? This film puts forth a claim that samurai culture originated from that of the saulabi.

Anarchists (Yu Young-sik 2000). This, the first coproduction between South Korea and the People's Republic of China, is set in 1924 Shanghai. A group of Korean freedom fighters, supported by the local Chinese sympathetic to their cause, use guerilla tactics and covert assault methods to resist colonization by Imperial Japan.

2009: Lost Memories (Lee Si-myung 2002). This science fiction/action film presents an alternative future where East Asia has been unified under the Japanese flag. Japan's East Asia Co-Prosperity Sphere has been realized because a real historical event, one hundred years previously, has been altered. The 1909 assassination of Hirobumi Ito, the former Prime Minister of Japan (1892–1896) and Resident-General of Korea, served as the pretext for the annexation of Korea. In the reenactment, which serves as the opening precredit sequence, the assassination attempt failed. In 2009 a detective investigating a terrorist incident learns of, and becomes aligned with, the Chosun Liberation Movement. At the film's climax, a special device permitting time travel leads the film backward to the scene of the 1909 assassination in Harbin, China, where the revolutionaries attempt to alter the future by changing the past, making sure the assassination is successful.

YMCA Baseball Team (Kim Hyun-seok 2002). Like *2009 Lost Memories*, this film is also grounded in real historical events. The formation of the first baseball team in Korea is used as a pretext for anti-Japanese sentiment, as the film is set in 1905, the year of the Japan-Korea Agreement, a treaty that made Korea a protectorate. As depicted in the film, baseball *was* introduced that year, by Christian missionary Phillip L. Gillete, and the first organized team was indeed that of the YMCA The film makes use of the historical context by having a noted member of the resistance movement wanted by the Japanese to play on the YMCA team. In a blatant abuse of power, a Japanese military officer attempts to shut down the team to make more efficient use of the field. The Japanese are met with a challenge by the Koreans, who agree to disband—but only if they lose a game to a team of Japanese soldiers.[11]

Fighter in the Wind (*Barumui Fighter*, Yang Yun-ho 2004). This martial arts epic chronicles a period of the life of Choi Bae-dal (1922–1994), who was also the subject of a popular manga series released in the 1960s, *Karate Baka Ichidai*. Known in Japan as Oyamu Masutatsu, Choi, a Korean who emigrated to Japan during the Pacific

War, was one of Asia's most talented martial artists, winning numerous competitions. He is also revered as the founder of Kyokushin karate. The film highlights Choi's outsider status as he struggles to survive against poverty and ethnocentrism, eventually rising to challenge and defeat the greatest Japanese fighters.

Rikidozan: A Hero Extraordinary (Song Hae-sung 2004). Also a biopic about a Korean athlete in "the land of the rising sun," this film's title is also the appellation taken by Kim Shin-rak (1924–1963), known in Japan as the father of *puroresu* (pro wrestling). He traveled to Japan in pursuit of a wrestling career, but left the sport of sumo after experiencing continuous discrimination because of his ethnicity. He turned to professional wrestling in 1951, and after defeating several Americans, including Lou Thesz in a heavyweight title bout in 1958, became a sensation in Japan. Ironically, he became a source of pride for the defeated postwar nation.

That the Japanese would be employed regularly as the most reviled characters in Korean cinema is no surprise, given the cruel and dehumanizing treatment Koreans endured during nine years of gunboat diplomacy, five years as a Japanese protectorate, and thirty-five years of colonization.[12] Japan's policy of *fukoku kyohei* (enrich the nation, strengthen the military) was realized through the exploitation of the labor and natural resources of Korea and other colonies. Japan established slave labor camps to support their colonial expansion and, according to Schmidt, drafted 6 million Koreans into service as forced labor, military support, sailors, and soldiers, with 1 million sent to Japan (83). The modernization of Korea, under the pretext of civilization and enlightenment, was mobilized first and foremost for the benefit of Japan. The cultivation of the natives entailed a process of obliterating Korean identity. Koreans were forced to worship the emperor and to take Japanese names. Ancient landmarks were destroyed. The Korean language was banned in schools, and traditional folk arts were thoroughly denigrated. The tragedy of the brutal conquest was exacerbated by the fact that the colonization led directly to the outbreak of the Korean War, a conflict that cost more than 4 million lives.

Thus history is being deployed then, in the most "manly" genres—the epic, action film, and sports film—in order to create a public memory and national identity that is essentially hypermasculinist. These films collectively deny tropes of victimization by focusing on narratives of struggle and allowing Koreans to prevail. As Elsaesser points out in his study of film and the Holocaust, these kinds of historical films reveal a "typically postmodern hubris, namely the faith that the cinema can redeem the past, resolve the real, and even resolve that which was never real" (166). Though these Korean features do not change the past by allowing the achievement of the ultimate victory—the liberation of Korea—the characters are afforded moral triumphs and individual successes. This cinema provides Koreans with the opportunity to refight the battle and emerge with its national pride intact, as Susan Jeffords argues the action films of the 1980s such as *Rambo* and *Missing in Action*, did for the United States and Vietnam. Or more correctly, I should say they provide Korean *men* with such opportunities, as women are side-lined to serve the narrative functions of allegory for the subjugated nation, guarantors of heterosexuality in the homosocial texts, or sidekicks who highlight the heroism of the male hero.

Though certainly the cultural, political, and historical circumstances are distinct, the spectacles of masculine power on the cinema screens of Korea feel eerily similar to that of the "Reagan Revolution," which is defined as an ideologically conservative period of reassertion—of American military strength, economic power (for some), and male patriarchy. The "muscularization" of American films of that era is tied not only to an administration interested in a return to an American global hegemony but a culture of antifeminist backlash as well. As Higson suggests in his treatise on definitions of national cinemas, researchers must look inward rather than outward, to the cinema's relationship to already existing national, political, economic, and cultural identity (42). To do that with contemporary Korean films is to look to the recent culture wars and rise of the neoconservatism.

According to Cho, the reinvigoration of the economy in the 1990s fueled a new social movement, *sinsahae udong*, involving a revival of Confucianism, a concentration on issues of global trade, and a renewed value in national traditions. The reassertion in traditional values was purported as *the* fundamental reason for the miraculous economic growth. The country was gripped by "*Sopyonje* fever," a revival in popular folk culture reflected and inflected in the film *Sopyonje* (1993) by Im Kwontaek, a wildly popular melodrama about *pansori* artists struggling to perform and preserve their art in a modernizing world. Though generally seen as positive for Korean culture, especially after decades of deprecation under the Japanese and the continuous inundation of American popular culture, the trend was not without its drawbacks.

The coalition of government and business forces exerted enough influence to give economic concerns precedence over the social justice ideals supported by the coalition of religious, human rights, labor, student, and feminist organizations that led the democratization movement a decade before. The increased visibility and social power of neocons, previously "silenced" by the *Minjung* movement and the concentration on expanding Korea's global market came with a heavy cost. The price was paid by the rural, the poor, and the undereducated. Recent studies, like the work of Leonard Shoppa, have even demonstrated a marked decline in government-sponsored social welfare programs. Writing in 1998, Cho observed that the new nationalist trend "is chauvinistic in its desire to be powerful and totalizing in its adherence to an essentialized tradition. It does not allow room to reflect on power/knowledge/history, and it oppresses minority voices at home. The nationalists are particularly anxious to push women back to the domestic sphere" (89).

The antifeminist backlash supported by *sinsahae udong* is directly reflected in the revitalization of Confucianism, the belief system initially adopted during the founding of the Yi Dynasty (1392–1910). The rigid hierarchal social order, based on age, sex, and inherited social status, further entrenched the society as agnatic (descent defined in terms of a common male ancestor) and thoroughly patriarchal. Though all are expected to live according to tenets of faithfulness, filial piety, wisdom, courage, prosperity, fraternal love, sincerity, and righteousness, the onus falls particularly on women, who are expected to be passive, quiet, respectful, and chaste. Under Confucianism, a virtuous woman is of special value, an honor to the entire family. In the premodern era, it was not unusual for families with virginal daughters to be recognized by the construction of *yollyomun* (monumental gates) in front of their homes or to be exempted from taxes or given pensions or extra rations of rice. Female education was generally limited to female virtues and domestic skills—how to raise children and the required manners of speech and conduct. Given the recent gains in gender equality procured by the *yosong haebang* (women's liberation) movement, it is not surprising that conservative forces would coalesce to undermine the continuing struggle.

The history of the feminist movement in Korea is a long and complex one, much too rich for a detailed discussion in this chapter, with recent achievements ranging from the *yokdong udong* (factory girls movement), which challenged national security laws and labor laws in the 1970s under threats of unemployment, blacklisting, rape, and other forms of violence to unionize and seek humane working conditions, to passage of the Equal Employment Opportunity Act, legislation that went into effect in 1988, establishing job placement and on-the-job training for women, as well as maternity leaves up to one year for each child and equitable promotion, retirement, and compensation packages. Other accomplishments include the addition of women's studies courses on university campuses, the passing of the Special Law on Sexual Violence in 1994 (legislation that adds sexual abuse and harassment to the existing laws on sexual crime, which previously recognized only rape), the Act for the Prevention of Domestic Violence and Victim Prevention in 1997 (which established penalties for the offenders including the limitation of parental rights; responsibility for medical costs, loss or property, and custodial care), and changes in child-custody practices (children no longer automatically go to the father in cases of divorce) and in the provisions of the Civil Code, more commonly known as Family Law. (In 2005, the Constitutional Court ruled unconstitutional the provisions of Articles 778 and 781, which established male primacy with respect to succession to the family headship. The inheritance system now allows all surviving children, regardless of gender, marital status, or birth order, the right to their families' legacies).

Clearly the repercussions of these advances in gender equality, an anxiety centered on a shift in definitions of masculine and feminine expectations, are so profound that the (re)formation of Korean national identity is articulated in the cinema as a crisis of masculinity. By revisiting the colonial past through a rejection of victimization, highlighting patriotism and nonpassivity, these films transform the traumatic social memory of defeat to one of active struggle. Integrated into the wider social context of increased nationalism, they serve as a kind of cultural glue for the "imagined community," aiding in the creation of what the Popular Memory Group describes as "dominant memory." In their formulation, this concept "points to the power and pervasiveness of historical representations, their connections with dominant institutions and the part they play in winning consent and building alliances in the process of formal politics" (207).

The ubiquity of the cinema, with its processes of psychological identification and seductions of spectacle, make the epic, action film, and sports film, in particular, powerful tools in the circulation of dominant ideologies and memories. As Strupples states,

> Images that become internalized as cultural memories, when they become naturalized, implanted as "indigenous" memories, act as instruments of cohesive identity. That sense of cohesion may be exercised both positively to give individuals a sense of belonging and cultural affiliation, to bring groups together for collective endeavor, as well as negatively to exclude, to bracket out the Other. (127)

By not allowing women to be significant and active characters in these historically based blockbusters, the films effectively eliminate women from the national history. And if an entire group is rendered inconsequential in the past, what then is their value in the present? And what is their importance to the future?

New Murmurings

A powerful intervention in the pervasive masculinist historical discourse emerged with the release of a remarkable documentary series by Byun Young-joo. That such politically challenging work would emerge from the field of independently produced documentary is not unexpected, given the contentious nature of documentaries in South Korea. Early committed documentaries were produced in relation to the Minjung movement, against the more typical nonfiction—travelogs, scenic films, newsreels, and government propaganda. Filmmakers dedicated to the use of film as an educational and organizing tool for progressive social change ignored laws prohibiting independent film, risking imprisonment if caught publicly screening their work. One of the most noted is Kim Dong-won, the founder of Purn, a collective of more than 250 members dedicated to the production of social issue documentaries.[13] Kim has been repeatedly arrested and his equipment seized by the police. Others, such as Lee Yong-bae and Kim Myong-gon, members of the Consolidated Fight Committee, a collective of eighteen film organizations, were accused of instigating strikes in 1990, and their film, *Eve of Strike*, was confiscated. In April 1997 Yoo In-taek and Hong Ki-sun were prosecuted for the production and screening of *Oh! Dream Country* and fined 100,000 won for their film about the role of the United States in the Gwangju Massacre. When Sarangbang, a noted human rights organization, attempted a Korean Human Rights Film Festival in 1997, five police squadrons were deployed in a search and seizure operation. They shut down the festival and arrested the chairperson, Suh Joon-sik, under violation of the National Security Law.

Though Byun has not been prosecuted for her work, she has provided a constant challenge to patriarchal ideologies and their implementation in Korean society. A graduate of Ewha Women's University, she is perhaps the most well known Korean documentary filmmaker, both inside and outside the country. She began her career as an independent documentary filmmaker, helping to build a feminist-based film movement. The first documentary Byun directed, *A Woman-Being in Asia* (1993), sponsored by the Association of Korean Women's Unions and shot by an all-woman crew, is a critical treatise on prostitution and sex tourism. While shooting that film she encountered a woman who became a sex worker to earn money for her mother's surgery. The mother, Byun learned, was a "comfort woman" during World War II. This discovery led her to the undertaking that would extend over seven years, to more than eighteen locations all over Korea, and to the Philippines and China—the production of three linked films about women such as Yoo Doo-ri (quoted in the epigraph)—women who survived the horrifying experience of military sexual slavery.

From 1932 to 1945, an estimated 200,000 women and girls, some as young as twelve, were forced into institutionalized sexual slavery by the Japanese Imperial Army. Women from China, Thailand, French Indochina (Vietnam), Singapore, Malaysia, Burma (Myanmar), Indonesia, the Philippines, Taiwan, and largely Korea (80–90%) were shipped like military supplies to camps throughout Asia to serve the Japanese army as *jungan ianfu*, a euphemism that translates as "comfort women." These mostly poor and uneducated women—kidnapped, drafted, and recruited by false promises of factory employment—were sent to camps where they were subjected daily to multiple rapes by Japanese soldiers.

During their internment they suffered brutal psychological and physical tortures. Some were even subjected to medical experiments. The transport of the women to other countries facilitated their imprisonment, as they could not speak the language of their respective surroundings and remained in Japanese territory. More than 70% died before the end of the war, and of those who survived, a large number were never repatriated. Those who did return home did not go on to live "normal" lives. The physical disorders caused by sexually transmitted diseases, malnutrition, and physical abuse were compounded by severe psychological and emotional traumas. In Korea the survivors were no longer considered virtuous under Confucian codes and thus were deemed unmarriageable. Many went on to live destitute and in lonely isolation, while others felt compelled to hide their pasts. They received little support from their families, communities, and government, all of which refused to address their experiences for almost fifty years.

The sense of shame that kept this subject unspoken was complex and multilayered. It involved first and foremost the profound and deep feelings of the women themselves. In addition, the abductions and mass rape effected a wounding of both masculine and national pride. The subsequent tragedies that overtook the nation after World War II—the separation of the country, the Korean War, and a succession of coups and dictatorships—removed comfort women from the national agenda. As the country began rebuilding its economy from the1960s through 1980s, the issue of justice for the formerly enslaved women failed to be raised, as their government administrations feared alienating Japan during on-going trade negotiations and economic conferences.[14] Feminist groups, religious associations, student organizations, and political activists repeatedly urged the government to take action, and by the late 1980s their efforts began to have an impact. On August 4, 1991, one year after the formation of The Korean Council for the Women Drafted as Sexual Slaves by Japan,

Kim Hak Soon publicly recounted her ordeal as a military sexual slave. By the end of the year, three women gave testimony in a lawsuit against the Japanese government. Despite this legal proceeding, and those that would follow, regular protests, open letters to the Japanese government, petitions, the inclusion of the issue on the agenda of several conferences, such as the Vienna World Human Rights Conference of 1993 and the Beijing International Women's Conference of 1995; reports and resolutions from several councils of the United Nations (the Commission on Human Rights, the Sub-Commission on the Protection of Human Rights, the Convention on the Elimination of All Forms of Discrimination against Women), and urging from the International Commission of Jurists, and the International Labor Organization, Japan has yet to offer an official apology, take legal responsibility, or provide reparations.[15]

Byun Young-joo took on the cause of the former military sexual slaves, revealing the intimate details of their lives in three extraordinary documentaries. *Murmuring* (1995), *Habitual Sadness* (1997), and *My Own Breathing* (2000) differ from other most films about historical trauma.[16] Privileging a style never used before in the covering of the subject matter, they stand in stark contrast to the television documentaries produced in both Japan and Korea in that they avoid the clichés and expected voyeuristic pleasures of dramatic reenactments. There are no testimonies by the women of the horrors experienced during their imprisonment given in the mode of the "talking head." No archival footage is edited in, and maps are not used to trace their journeys. The films do not even provide a bevy of facts or historical detail. What these films offer is the rejection of the "poetics of mourning," a treatment that focuses on the *halmunis'* strength as survivors and commitment as activists.[17]

Figure 10.2. *My Own Breathing* (Byun Young-joo 2000). Courtesy Pusan Film Festival.

This critical intervention in the social production of Korea's history makes public the history excluded both in Japan and Korea. They are significantly different from the commercial features set in the past because they are actually not about history. They are about memory. As defined by the Popular Memory Group, "memory is, by definition, a term which directs our attention not to the past but to *the past-present relation*. It is because 'the past' has this living active existence in the present that it matters so much politically" (211). We learn a great deal about the women's experiences as comfort women, but we learn even more about the cost of those experiences, the emotional and physical legacies that the brutality wrought—shame, abandonment, isolation, poverty, the impossibility of marriage, the regret over never having received an education, the inability to bear children, and a longing for lives that might have been.

Each film focuses on different aspects of their lives, featuring different women. *Murmuring* concerns the women's struggle to overcome their shame and to become active participants in the struggle for justice. It introduces us to the shocking daily routines and practices of the comfort stations; the reception of the survivors after repatriation; and for a group of women who were never repatriated, living in Harbin, China, the longing for home and family and the dreadful fear of being forgotten. We are moved to undertake the cause, inspired by the *halmunis'* willingness to stand outside in the cold of winter, participating in the weekly Wednesday demonstrations in front of the Japanese embassy in Seoul. Ultimately, we are taught harsh lessons by the experience of the survivors, who know all too well the discrimination heaped on those who are poor, old, uneducated, female, and survivors of sexual crime.

Habitual Sadness is centered on the House of Sharing, a communal home for the former comfort women, provided by a Buddhist charity and supported by several groups and volunteers. It contains two dormitories, a temple and education center, an office, and a museum, which displays the art we see the women create as therapy. This film, the second in the series, feels more personal, as the camera enters more intimate spaces and makes use of more close-ups. Because we are in the shared living space, we get a better view of the mutual support system that organizes the *halmunis'* lives. We watch them make decisions based on a democratic process, prepare meals for the community, care for those among them who are ill, and work in their vegetable garden. Though the film depicts warmth and some joy, it is not wholly bucolic. Their lives are difficult, their experiences haunt them, their fight for acknowledgement and reparations has not yet been realized, and the need for resolution is more urgent. They are getting older and worry that they will not be alive to witness satisfaction of their demands. (Five women died between the start of the first film and the finish of the third. Since the initial registration of former comfort women in 1991, more than 62% have passed away.) The death of Kang Duk-kyung and her subsequent funeral occur toward the end of the film. We are left with her words at the close of the film, as recorded in a video interview, intercut with scenes of her when she was still healthy and vital:

> I've been thinking about this film. Lots of people may come to see it. I will pray everybody comes. I hope it will get a lot of attention. It may move people to help us. That is my utmost wish. . . . We grannies are old, but we live together as a family. Japan, be warned. You thought we'd break down if you threw money at us. We can survive despite our pain. We are determined. We've demonstrated on two hundred Wednesdays. We'll fight to the last woman. We'll fight you Japanese. I want the world to know our fight. We won't give up easily. We've steeled ourselves, and Japan made us that way. We will become stronger.

The last shot of *Habitual Sadness*, a portrait of Kang looking directly at the camera, is both a memorial and a silent entreaty posed to the audience, asking, "What will you do?"

The last film, *My Own Breathing*, continues the call for immediate action by opening with a memorial service for those former comfort women who have died. Those who remain are even more resolved to their cause and vow to continue the fight, which has expanded to coalition building with survivors from other nations. A public commemoration takes place in the Philippines, attended by Lee Yong-soo, whom we saw briefly in the previous film. She is our point of entry and guide through *My Own Breathing*, which focuses on women who do not live in the House of Sharing and so provides different stories of daily survival. Her travels through Korea, visiting with other *halmunis* to inquire on their morale and physical well-being, remind us of the intimate relationships demonstrated in the last film. We are for the first time given an opportunity to witness a familial relationship, between a young woman and her mother, Kim Yoon-shin, winner of the Chun Tae-il Literary Award for her published memoir recounting her abduction while a young teen and her three-year experience at a comfort station in Harbin, China.[18] It is one of the most astonishing scenes of the trilogy.

Kim discusses in detail, as if it were only yesterday, her life after returning to Korea—her marriage and the guilt and shame at birthing a deaf daughter due to syphilis she contracted while interned, leading her to run with the baby from her home. Later she is interviewed in a long take, with her and her adult daughter together in a two-shot. Using sign language, the daughter reveals, unbeknownst to her mother, that she has known for some time about her mother's past. It is a remarkable scene to watch as the younger woman recounts her knowledge of the details, as her mother pretends not to be listening, moving further to the right of the frame to work on her sewing project. As the daughter's interview continues, we are mesmerized by the continually shifting emotions displayed on Kim Yoon-shin's face as she attempts to remain calm. We find out with her that her daughter discovered her mother's secrets by reading the memoir when her mother was out. Though Kim Yoon-shin is clearly troubled by the exchange, she is a bit relieved as well. And the interaction between her and her daughter is one filled with love and understanding.

The first two parts of the trilogy were shot using a method of filming lengthy continuous scenes in an almost cinema-verité style, cut down later in postproduction. *Murmuring* and *Habitual Sadness*, then, are firmly grounded in traditions of contemporary feminist filmmaking, characterized by the approach Julia Lesage notes as using "cinema verité in a new and different way. They [feminist documentary directors] often identify personally with their subjects. Their relation to that subject while filming often is collaborative, with both subject and filmmaker sharing the project's political goals" (Lesage, 231). Byun treats the women as subjects, not objects, and

Figure 10.3. Mother and daughter reach a new understanding in *My Own Breathing*.

Figure 10.4. *Halmonies* pose with the crew of *Habitual Sadness*.

worked according to three principles: (1) the establishment of a close relationship with the subjects, (2) the importance of understanding that the most important audience consists of the subjects themselves, so they are treated with respect and honesty, (3) and the films serve as a means of personal expression for the women, who have for too long suppressed their memories and feelings and had few outlets available. Byun attempts to have the films, and specifically *My Own Breathing*, function as a journal, "a record of their [the *halmunis'*] seemingly trivial and disorganized daily lives, providing a vivid and detailed description of those lives."

Through the use of narration and white-on-black intertitles in all three, Byun allows us to understand the dilemmas and challenges she faced at every stage of the production, with issues of aesthetics and politics complicated by her role as director and identification as a woman. She shares with the audience the effects the films had on her emotionally and psychologically and the contradictions of her positioning. By placing herself in the documentaries via the use intertitles and direct address on the soundtrack, Byun places herself within the narrative, and yet outside it at the same time, in many ways emblematic of her location. The title of the final film, *My Own Breathing*, for example, refers directly to the shooting style of the film and the director's relationship to her subjects. *My Own Breathing*, unlike the first two installments, was filmed in short bursts that Byun describes as "much like filming an impromptu performance" (*Way of Capturing* 42). She knew she would not be able to record everything, but would instead capture selected brief moments, like the very breathing of the *halmunis*. The use of the possessive in the title reflects her initial frustration with her own identification throughout the process of production. To better understand her subjects, she could become neither a former military slave nor an elderly woman. And the camera could not literally transfer the perspectives of the women to the audience, no matter how intimate the angle of view. But by "breathing" with them, following their rhythms, perhaps we could more deeply comprehend their lives.

The bond of trust that developed between the director and the former comfort women is significant, given the women's initial hesitance to agree to the first film. Their expectations were very low, as their treatment in the press has been problematic. They were featured in documentaries and news stories that reduced them to victims, shortened their comments to sound bites, and concentrated only on the past, most often through testimonials that became rote. Byun succeeded in her attempt to create a cinematic journal, in essence, a "voice" for the women, because they themselves were active in the production of the trilogy. They chose what aspects of their lives—and for Kang Duk-kyung, her death—were filmed. It was in fact the *halmunis* themselves who conceived the idea of a sequel to *Murmuring* and were instrumental in the formulation of *My Own Breathing*. Most of the interviews, like that with Lee Young-sook in *My Own Breathing*, were filmed at their request and, ultimately, were not interviews, but monologs. As Byun recounts of the scene with Kim, "It is hard to even call it an interview as I never said a word or threw a question. She just expressed her will and feelings voluntarily as the camera started rolling" (*Way of Capturing* 43).

Unlike the more widely seen feature films discussed in this chapter, films that use Japan's historical enmity as the basis of high drama, films like Byun Young-joo's documentary trilogy recall an *actual* historical past. Though the historical circumstances are filled with shame and subjugation, it is actually these films that reveal a victory. It is represented by the very survival of the former comfort women. Through their compassion, solidarity, fortitude, and perseverance in the fight for justice, they are the true heroes of history. History is not made solely by "great men," like the warriors of the epic, action film, or sports film. Real social change, like that of the *Minjung* movement, is made from the bottom up, from grassroots movements. Perhaps soon women like Yoon Doo-ri will no longer have to hold their breath.

Notes

1. Yoon Doo-ri gives an accounting of her life in Kim Gibson, *Silence Broken: Korean Comfort Women* (Parkersburg, IA: Mid-Prairie Books, 2000).

2. According to the United Nations, Seoul experienced a remarkable growth rate averaging 7.6% per year between 1950 and 1975, with the population

doubling every nine years. In 1950 the statistic was slightly over 1 million. By 1975 it increased to 6.8 million (UN Population Report, 91). Seoul is now considered one of the world's megacities, with close to 30% of the nation's population living in the city or in the surrounding area.

3. It would be an arduous task to attempt a comprehensive list of Korean features with nonlinear plot development, particularly those involving the use of flashbacks, but here are a few examples: repetition of events—*Attack the Gas Station, Jakarta, Virgin Stripped Bare by Her Bachelors*; parallel and interwoven timelines—*Failan*; backward trajectory—*Peppermint Candy*; violations of the space/time continuum—*Il Mare, Ditto, Calla*; time travel—*2009 Lost Memories* and *My Mother the Mermaid*; and flashbacks—*301, 302, Bongja, No Blood No Tears, Old Boy*, and *Ice Rain*.

4. I shared a conversation about this phenomenon with my colleague Robert Cagle on the afternoon of June 25, 2005, on the campus of the University of Illinois—Urbana Champaign.

5. The term *misi-jok*, first popular in 1994, is attributed to the marketing campaigns of Seoul department stores. It refers to young middle-class housewives with professional jobs who are committed to the conspicuous consumption of fashion and cosmetics, rather than the more conventional values of frugal, diligent housewives.

6. *The Long Kiss Goodnight*, directed by Renny Harlan, is an American action film released in 1996. The lead character—a small-town school teacher, mother, and partner in a committed relationship—recovers from amnesia, discovering that she was previously a spy/assassin. She gives up her feminine identity for that of Charlie Baltimore, her previous tough, hypersexualized, and violent persona.

7. A similar scene occurs in *No Blood No Tears*, where the two female leads are beaten by the pimp/small-time hood they robbed. It is perhaps the most brutal, pornographic violence this author has ever witnessed in a movie theater.

8. For more detail on the changes in the industry see the opening chapter by Park Seung Hyun.

9. Before the gradual lifting of the ban on Japanese cinema, it was illegal for Koreans to purchase Japanese computer games, comic books, music, and copies of live-action movies and anime. Films could be screened, but only at international festivals like the annual fest in Busan. The stages of release from the ban were as follows:

> 1998—Grand prize-winning films from the Cannes, Venice, or Berlin film festivals; films nominated for the Academy Award in the Best Foreign Language Film category, and Korean-Japanese coproductions. Japanese actors were permitted to be cast in Korean films, and for those Japanese films that did receive theatrical release, distribution was permitted in video formats. The first film screened commercially was Kitano Takeshi's *Hana-Bi* (winner of the Golden Lion in Venice).
>
> 1999—Films rated for general audiences and those awarded from a list of seventy film festivals.

2000—Films rated for audiences as 12+ or 15+ and animated films recognized at selected film festivals. Distribution also included those awarded at film festivals or those rated for general audiences that were permitted for broadcast on cable or for satellite systems.

2004—All live-action films, including those rated 18+ or for "limited release only," films already granted theatrical release permitted for broadcast for over-air, as well as cable and satellite; and animated films granted theatrical release were granted access to cable and satellite television.

10. Chi-Yun Shin and Julian Stringer provide an excellent overview of the blockbuster phenomenon in their chapter on *Shiri*.

11. That baseball was chosen for a sports film with an emphasis on Japanese colonialism is significant. Only two years before the release of *YMCA Baseball Team*, South Korea was held in thrall as its national team battled Japan on the diamond for a medal in the Sydney Olympic Games. The South Koreans won a bronze medal, denying Japan a medal for the first time since the sport had been included in the international competition. (Japan won a bronze in Barcelona in 1992 and a silver at the Atlanta Games in 1996).

12. Korea was the first nation-state to fall victim to what would later become known as *dai toa kyoeiken*, the Greater East Asian Co-Prosperity Sphere, Japan's attempt to "protect" Asia from Western colonization by seizing territory and control—the aggression that would result in the outbreak of the Pacific War. Despite political opposition and frequent rebellious outbreaks of violence, Korea was forced to open its ports to Japan in 1876. Korea lost localized government control after the Russo-Japanese War in 1905 and was officially annexed in 1910. Korea was liberated in 1945, at the close of World War II. For more on the subject see Peter Duus' historical account in *The Abacus and the Sword: The Japanese Penetration of Korea, 1895–1910* (Berkeley: University of California Press, 1995).

13. As stated on their Web site, Purn's aim is to participate in social change and give voice to grassroots movements, develop the art of documentary in Korea, and promote media education so the "public can understand visual messages correctly and cultivate a more democratic environment" (docupurn.jinbo.net). Purn has covered a number of critical social issues, documenting subjects as varied as the labor movement, unification, environmental pollution, poverty, and corruption. Other important documentary groups include Labor News Production, which organizes video production groups for the national federation of labor unions and conducts video production workshops, and the Seoul Visual Collective, with a founding principle of "The film movement must make efforts to secure social rights for the masses."

14. The issue of justice for the women and the prosecution of Japanese war criminals who participated in the organization and maintenance of the "comfort stations" were dropped repeatedly from international negotiations, including the bilateral treaty between Korea and Japan in 1965. In 2002, a lawsuit was filed by a group of survivors demanding the release of government documents detailing how the South Korean government promised not to demand compensation for

the surviving comfort women in exchange for $500 million in grants and soft loans in 1964.

15. The only war crime trial that addressed military sexual slavery was the Batvia Military Tribunal of 1948. Several Japanese officers were tried and convicted for human rights violations committed in Indonesia. However, the trial only addressed the violations against white Dutch women, ignoring the crimes against the indigenous women and the other Asian women abducted. The organization leading the cause for the Korean survivors, the Korean Council for the Women Drafted for Military Sexual Slavery, is an umbrella nonprofit made up of more than twenty-two individual groups. It provides medical support, counseling, and financial support for the survivors. They operate several educational programs and coordinate the volunteers who assist the survivors in their daily lives. The demands made by the organization on behalf of the former military slaves include the Japanese government's admission of the crime of compulsory drafting of Korean women as military sexual slaves, a full investigation and exposure of the atrocities, the punishment of those responsible for the crimes, an official apology through a resolution of the Japanese Diet, legal compensation for the survivors and their families, inclusion of the facts in Japanese history textbooks, and the building of a memorial and museum. For more on comfort women see the special issue of *positions*, "The Comfort Women: Colonialism, War, and Sex" 5.1 (1997); Dai Sil Kim-Gibson, *Silence Broken: Korean Comfort Women* (Parkersburg, IA: Mid-Prairie Books, 1999); *Comfort Women Speak: Testimony of Sex Slaves of the Japanese Military*, ed. Sangmie Choi Schellstede (New York: Homes and Meier, 2000); and David Andrew Schmidt, *Ianfu: The Comfort Women of the Japanese Imperial Army of the Pacific War: Broken Silence* (Lewiston: Mellon, 2000).

16. *Murmuring* was the first Korean documentary to receive attention abroad. Awards for the film include the Ogawa Shinsuke Prize at the Yamagata International Documentary Film Festival, the Grand Prix of the Jury at Brussels International Film Festival, Special Jury Prize at the Amnesty International Film Festival, Special Jury Prize at the Munchen Documentary Film Festival, and inclusion on the list of the Worlds Most Important Feminist Films by the New York Women's International Film Festival. The sequel, *Habitual Sadness*, was invited to renowned international film festivals including those in Berlin, Montreal, and Hong Kong. It also won the Merit Prize at the Taiwan International Documentary Festival. *My Own Breathing* was recognized at the Pusan International Film Festival with the Woonpa Award and by the Korean People's Artists Federation with the People's Art Award of the Year.

17. *Halmuni* is the Korean word for grandmother. In common usage it is also extended to refer to all elderly women, irrespective of family relation.

18. Chun Tae-il (2948–1970) is an important figure in the Korean labor movement. His work on behalf of textile workers and his act of self-immolation, after he declared, "We Are Not Machines," inspired the Democratic Union movement.

Works Cited

Alford, C. Fred. *Think No Evil: Korean Values in the Age of Globalization*. Ithaca: Cornell University Press, 1999.

Anderson, Benedict. *Imagined Communities*. New York: Verso, 1991.

Cho Hae-jong. "Constructing and Deconstructing Koreanness." *Making Majorities: Constituting the Nation in Japan, Korea, China, Malaysia, Fiji, Turkey, and the United States*. Ed. Dru C. Gladney. Stanford: Stanford University Press, 1998. 73–91.

Choi Schellstede, Sangmie, ed. *Comfort Women Speak: Testimony of Sex Slaves of the Japanese Military*. New York: Homes and Meier, 2000.

Choi Chungmoo, ed. *The Comfort Women: Colonialism, War, and Sex*. Spec. issue of *positions* 5.1 (1997): 1–323.

Duss, Peter. *The Abacus and the Sword: The Japanese Penetration of Korea, 1895–1910*. Berkeley: University of California Press, 1995.

Elsaesser, Thomas. "Subject Positions, Speaking Positions: From *Holocaust*, *Our Hitler*, and *Heimat* to *Shoah* and *Schindler's List*." *Persistence of History: Cinema, Television, and the Modern Event*. Ed. Vivian Sobchack. New York: Routledge, 1996. 145–83.

Fujitani, T., Geoffrey M. White, and Lisa Yoneyama. "Remembering and Dismembering the Asia-Pacific War(s)." *Perilous Memories: The Asia Pacific Wars*. Ed. T. Fujitani, Geoffrey M. White, and Lisa Yoneyama. Durham: Duke University Press, 2001. 1–29.

Gateward, Frances. "Youth in Crisis: National and Cultural Identity in New South Korean Cinema." *Multiple Modernities: Cinemas and Popular Media in Transcultural East Asia*. Ed. Jenny Kwok Wah Lau. Philadelphia: Temple University Press, 2003. 114–27.

Higson, Andrew. "The Concept of National Cinema." *Screen* 30.4 (1989): 36–46.

How the Camera Waits: Making of The Murmuring. Seoul: Docu-factory Vista, 1998.

Jeffords, Susan. *The Remasculinization of America: Gender and the Vietnam War*. Bloomington: Indiana University Press, 1989.

Kim-Gibson, Dai Sil. *Silence Broken: Korean Comfort Women*. Parkersburg, IA: Mid-Prairie Books, 1999.

Kim, Kyung Hyun. *The Remasculinization of Korean Cinema*. Durham: Duke University Press, 2004.

Kim Soyoung. "The Birth of the Local Feminist Sphere in the Global Era: 'Trans-Cinema' and Yosongjang." *Inter-Asia Cultural Studies* 4.1 (2003): 10–24.

Klinger, Barbara. "Cinema/Ideology/ Criticism Revisited: The Progressive Genre." *Film Genre Reader*. Ed. Barry Keith Grant. Austin: University of Texas, 1986. 74–90.

Korean Cinema 1999. Seoul, Korean Film Commission, 2000.

Lesage, Julia. "Feminist Documentary: Aesthetics and Politics." *Show Us Life: Towards a History and Aesthetic of the Committed Documentary*. Ed. Thomas Waugh. Metuchen, NJ: Scarecrow, 1984. 223–51.

Marchetti, Gina. "Action-Adventure as Ideology." *Cultural Politics in Contemporary America*. Ed. Ian Angus and Sut Jhally. New York: Routledge, 1989. 182–97.

Mellencamp, Patricia. *A Fine Romance . . . Five Ages of Film Feminism*. Philadelphia: Temple University Press, 1992.

Popular Memory Group. "Popular Memory: Theory, Politics, Method." *Making Histories: Studies in History-Writing and Politics*. Ed. Richard Johnson, Gregor

McLennan, Bill Schwartz, and David Sutton. Minneapolis: University of Minnesota Press, 1989. 205–52.

Production Notes: Habitual Sadness. Seoul, Docu-factory Vista, 1994.

Rayns, Tony. *Seoul Stirring: Five Korean Directors.* London: Institute of Contemporary Arts, 1994.

Schmidt, David Andrew. *Ianfu—The Comfort Women of the Japanese Imperial Army of the Pacific War: Broken Silence.* Lewiston: Mellon, 2000.

Schoppa, Leonard. "The Retreat of Social Welfare in Japan and South Korea." Korea Studies Workshop. University of Illinois. Urbana, Illinois. March 4, 2005.

Smith, Anthony D. "Theories of Nationalism: Alternative Models of Nation Formation." *Asian Nationalism.* Ed. Michael Leifer. New York: Routledge, 2000. 1–20.

Strupples, Peter. "Visual Culture, Synthetic Memory, and the Construction of National Identity." *Third Text* 17.2 (2003): 127–39.

Turim, Maureen. "The Trauma of History: Flashbacks upon Flashbacks." *Screen* 42.2 (2001): 205–10.

The Way of Capturing Memories: Making of My Own Breathing. Seoul: Docu-factory Vista, 2000.

White, Hayden. "The Modernist Event." *The Persistence of History: Cinema, Television, and the Modern Event.* Ed. Vivian Sobchack. New York: Routledge, 1995. 17–38.

United Nations Population Division. *World Urbanization Prospects: The 2001 Revision.* Geneva, Switzerland, 2001.

11

Suk-Young Kim

Crossing the Border to the "Other" Side

Dynamics of Interaction between North and South Koreans in *Spy Li Cheol-jin* and *Joint Security Area*

North Korea, often referred to as the "hermit" kingdom, was brought under the international spotlight when George W. Bush designated the nation, together with Iran and Iraq, as part of the "axes of evil" in his State of the Union speech in January 2002.[1] Since then, there has been no shortage of news coverage on North Korea by the U.S. media, which keeps the American public well informed of the possible dangers the hermit kingdom presents to the United States and the international community. At the same time, the American public has been informed by the media of North Korea's devastating economic hardship and starvation. These two faces of the hermit kingdom as illustrated by American media coverage—the irrational threatening power (what Ronald Reagan once termed "nuts with nukes"), and, to a lesser degree, the suffering one, on the brink of collapse without immediate

Figure 11.1. North and South meet at the DMZ in *Joint Security Area* (Park Chan-wook 2000).

humanitarian support—do not easily converge, thereby creating a puzzling question of what to make of this little-known quixotic nation.

Such a bifocal projection of North Korea is found not only in the news media but also in films—made both in the United States and South Korea. In the example of *Die Another Day* (Lee Tamahori 2002), this latest James Bond movie sets North Korea as its opening locale, where James Bond faces hostile enemy attack, after which he is captured, tortured, and jailed in atrocious conditions. Yet, in addition to being presented as the site of military conflict, North Korea in this movie is represented as a site of poverty and hardship. Though introduced in the film by brief shots that flash by rapidly, there are scenes of North Korea's barren farm land and impoverished landscape, which the film adopts as a visual metonymy of a starving nation. Corresponding to this bifurcated sketch of the nation, the representation of North Koreans in this film is twofold: there is a stereotypical evildoer, but also a humanistic character, who provides a counterexample to the general argument that in *Die Another Day* North Koreans represent nothing but evil stereotypes.[2]

The conventional image of North Koreans is of enemy soldiers, terrorists, guerrillas, and snipers. Only rarely have North Koreans been projected as full-blown human beings with the inner capacity to feel, suffer, and fear. One such example is *The Hook* (George Seaton 1963), which starred Kirk Douglas as a U.S. army officer fighting in the Korean War. This film focuses on the moral struggle of an American officer whose assignment is to execute a North Korean prisoner of war. Although the movie's focal point lies in the moral struggle of Americans, the suffering face of the North Korean prisoner is equally an essential point of the film, fleshing out the inhumanity of war. The movie introduces the family picture of the North Korean prisoner through the gaze of his American executioners and thereby makes it difficult for the Americans to treat the North Korean as an impersonal enemy. The movie's poster rather bluntly recapitulates the moral question posed by the film: "It is one thing to drop a bomb and kill an impersonal enemy you will never see. It is quite another thing to kill a man, a human being, face to face! Could you do it?" This approach to North Koreans as human beings, even though presented as a minor backdrop to stage the central issue of the inhumanity of war, casts a rather refreshing light on Korean War films made in Hollywood, most of which reflect the polarized division of the world system in the Cold War era.[3]

In a similar vein, South Korea's film industry during the Cold War also found the Korean War to be a limitless resource for film subjects. However, South Korean films dealing with North Koreans and the Korean War have not, until recently, portrayed North Koreans in a sympathetic light. The presence of the National Security Law, which provided South Korean military dictators with the legal ground for strict censorship,[4] made it extremely difficult to portray North Koreans outside of the official Cold War propaganda and did not leave much room for the humanistic portrayal of North Koreans. Consequently, South Korean films about the Korean War for the most part have been the products of the Cold War imagination, by and large more dogmatic than Hollywood films.[5]

In the few exceptional cases that portrayed Communists in a somewhat positive light, unpleasant troubles emerged. One such example is *Seven Women Prisoners* (Kim Shi-hyeon 1965), a banned film that led to the arrest of the director, Lee Man-hee. During the period of such sociopolitical and cultural repression prior to the downfall of the Berlin Wall and the Soviet Union, South Korean war films produced sets of evil stock North Korean characters—spies, guerrillas, snipers, and terrorists—to instill and reinforce a mass paranoia on the part of South Koreans. Due to such anti–North Korean war films made by South Korea, the Korean War became an ongoing event—if not on the battlefield, then at least on screen.

The Second Korean War and the Turn of Events

The Korean War (1950–1953) left an indelible scar on the minds of Korean people, who share a long history of common language and culture. Yet the two Koreas are the last countries in the world to remain divided by the ideology of Cold War. Since the end of the Korean War, both Koreas have prohibited their citizens from engaging in any level of humanitarian contact outside of government-controlled channels, such as communications between separated family members, intellectual and cultural exchanges, and any type of political discourse. Consequently, the discussion of anything North Korean—unless it took a form of fierce anti-Communist propaganda—was unthinkable for South Koreans for half a century.

Ironically, the division of the two Koreas in the aftermath of World War II[6] and the Korean War was anything but the Korean people's own desire. As Gregory Henderson, a former U.S. Foreign Service officer notes: "No division of a nation in the present world is so astonishing in its origin as the division of Korea; none is so unrelated to conditions or sentiment within the nation itself at the time the division was effected; none is to this day so unexplained" (Oberdorfer 7). In the process of creating two ideologically and politically hostile regimes out of one homogenous nation, the division of Korea was hardened into a structure that has perpetuated the rituals of Cold War and has regulated every aspect of life in both parts of the divided Korea.[7]

In the process of separating the homogenous Korean people into South and North Koreans on hostile terms, the regimes of both Koreas devoted extraordinary effort—for example, by using police and military forces to suppress free speech and artistic expression. The separation of North Koreans from South Koreans required strong governmental control. But equally important, the enforced separation has benefited the regimes of both Korean leaderships to a great extent by legitimizing the two regimes and the power they exercise.[8] To reinforce this sense of legitimacy, various rituals for ostracizing North Koreans were used to consolidate power by the postwar regime in South Korea, carrying out a kind of psychological war against the North. As Vamik Volkan explicates in his book *The Need to Have Enemies and Allies*:

> The more chronic that involvement with conflict with one or more opposing group is, the greater the tendency to "psychologize" it. Concealed or apparent emotional issues and attempts to regressively solve them dominate, modifying real world aspects of the conflict. Whatever the contributing historical, military, economic, or social factors may be, the resultant chronic conflict becomes increasingly difficult to resolve; it becomes embedded in the identity of a group or nation. The enemy is insinuated into the self-image of the group or nation, becoming "the other," a collection of traits that the group itself does not wish to have, the embodiment of taboos vigorously repudiated by the group ethos. (5–6)

As Volkan points out, this waging of psychological warfare by South Koreans against North Koreans during peacetime became an essential part of defining South Korean national identity, which was forged by the total rejection of the "other."

Volkan's aforementioned notion serves as a useful framework not only in thinking about the "psychologized" national self-image but also in accessing the spatial significance of a nation. Because "what has happened on a nation's territory is contained in its self-image," as Jonathan Boyarin points out, the historical events that take place on a nation's territory are intricately related to the way that nation conceives its identity (18). Thus, the collective psychology of rejecting the "other," the semiotic significance of national space, and the formation of national identity merge in a single tangled process to produce cultural expression.

Because South Koreans defined themselves and their culture based on the psychological rejection of anything North Korean, the South Korean government did not allow anything North Korean within its physical and psychological borders. Koreans who defected from the North to the South before or during the Korean War were subjected to open prejudice and discrimination in the South. South Koreans were also conditioned to ostracize the North Korean dialect, vocabulary, and regional customs.

In shaping the South Korean national identity in part based on the rejection of the North, culture and education played important roles.[9] June was declared a month for bolstering anti-Communist spirit, when the entire country of South Korea was inflamed to fever pitch through ceremonies commemorating the outbreak of the Korean War. Elementary schools held competitions in June, during which children submitted anti-Communist posters portraying North Koreans as nonhumans. Students were encouraged to enter anti-Communist speech contests; others wrote anti-Communist essays in which they explained how much they abhorred the North Korean Communist invaders—even though they had no experience with North Koreans and knew them only through state-controlled anti-Communist propaganda. In the course of such massive rituals in South Korea, North Koreans were the archenemy in the imagination of South Koreans.

In my view, the anti-Communist fever in South Korea culminated in Communist witch-hunts to such a degree that they constituted the "second Korean War"—as ferocious a war as the actual military conflict on the battlefield from 1950 to 1953. This type of psychological warfare alienates the most intimate human relationships and produces a collective anxiety about the enemy. The 38th parallel not only divided the territories of North and South Korea, but also severed the natural connective bond among people. The film industry was one of the cultural weapons used to wage this psychological war, which left no room for portraying North Koreans as multidimensional characters.[10]

However, the dynamics of this psychological war changed in the late 1990s with a massive transformation in power structure of global politics. With the downfall of the Soviet Union and the subsequent disintegration of the international Communist bloc, the power equilibrium between North Korea and South Korea shifted rapidly. South Korea normalized its diplomatic relationships with the Soviet Union (1990) and the People's Republic of China (1992), the two powerful countries traditionally seen by the South Korean government as sponsors of North Korea's aggressions against the South.

In this rapidly thawing atmosphere, South Korea's strict measures against North Korea relented accordingly. Gaps and fissures appeared in the stifling Cold War ideology; and intellectual fresh air permeated South Korean society in 1990s, allowing the film industry cautiously to explore some taboo subjects concerning North Koreans. Certain previously forbidden subjects, such as the tragic finale of the guerrilla warfare of the pro–North Korean partisans in the South during the Korean War, became the subject matter for two films, *Partisans of South Korea* also known as *The South Korean Army* (Jeong Ji-yeong 1990) and *The Taebaek Mountains* (Im Kwon-taek 1994), which enjoyed a wide audience among South Koreans.

Nonetheless, the official policy of the South Korean government under President Kim Young-sam's leadership (1993–1997) toward North Korea remained one of containment, which was expected to lead to the ultimate downfall of the regime. Hoping to base the case of Korean unification on a German model, South Korea, in accordance with American foreign policy, adhered to the measures of hostile containment toward the North, while keeping the door open for unification by absorption.[11]

South Korean policy took a dramatic turn with the introduction of the "Sunshine Policy" in 1997, under which South Korea actively took the lead in initiating friendly relationships between the two Koreas, embracing the North instead of isolating it. Taking its concept from Aesop's fable about a contest between wind and sunshine to make a traveler voluntarily remove his coat, the new policy advocated open dialogue instead of military conflict, mutual understanding instead of mutual accusation.[12]

The catalyst for the shift in the Korean political relationship was the summit meeting between the leaders of the two Koreas in the North Korean capital, Pyongyang, which literally created a pro-North Korean cultural fever in South Korean society. After the historic meeting took place, there was an explosive amount of publications about North Korea, high interest in North Korean culture, and numerous occasions for cultural exchange. In 2000 alone, the number of cultural and human exchanges exceeded that of any previous year. According to the South Korean government's *White Paper on Unification* (2000), the number of South Korean citizens who visited North Korea from 1998 to 2000 totaled 16,019, six times the number who visited the North between 1989 and 1997 (Kim 2001, 61).

The North Korean cultural rush served as a motivation for South Koreans to rethink the question of reunification, as well as to reshape the negative stereotypes they had of North Koreans for decades. The cultural exchanges contributed tremendously to the mutual understanding of North and South and reaffirmed the fundamental connection among Korean people. As the *White Paper on Unification* concluded, the social and cultural exchanges between the two Koreas under the Sunshine Policy "contributed to the dissolution of the cultural alienation between the peoples of two Koreas due to the realities of division, and restored the homogeneity of our nation" (Kim 2001, 61).

The Sunshine Policy not only changed the political and diplomatic relations of the South Korean government with the North but also transformed the South Korean people's perception of the North—a transformation that was fundamentally related to the way South Koreans perceived themselves. South Korean national identity, which had been based on the rejection of the other, now faced the inevitable revision during the years of the Sunshine Policy, transforming the strict Cold War binary opposition of the "self" and the "other" into a fluid convergence of North and South.

Just as the film industry during the years of the Cold War took the lead in forging the South Korean national identity, which excluded the North Koreans, it once again stood at the front of rapid social transformation under the Sunshine Policy. The newly emerged countervision to the stereotypical portrayal of North Korea and its citizens included such films as *Shiri* (Kang Je-kyu 1999), *Spy Li Cheol Jin* (Jang Jin 1999) and *Joint Security Area* (Park Chan-wook 2000). To varying degrees, these films reflected the thawing political tension in the Korean peninsula and, for the first time, began openly to explore North Koreans as human beings with inner dimensions.

Furthermore, these films engaged in a radical experiment by redefining the spatial semiotics of both Koreas as open to the other side, thus experimenting with the possibility of whether the other Koreans could enter its own territory and become an integral part of it. As news coverage of the summit meeting in 2000 showed the previously unthinkable image of a South Korean president setting foot in the North Korean capital of Pyongyang, South Korean films began to produce parallel images of North Koreans setting foot on South Korean territory.

South Korean films also reexamined the semiotic significance of the border dividing the two Koreas. Just as the Cold War era had produced films that reduced the meaning of the border to a barrier that blocked the free flow of people and information to the other side, now films produced during the Sunshine Policy began critically to view the border as an unnecessary barrier segregating the two Koreas and preventing natural communication between people. The new South Korean films laid bare the artificial nature of the border and projected it as a Korean version of the Berlin Wall, which should be torn down to promote freedom and joy on the part of both peoples.

These post–Cold War South Korean movies also deconstructed the psychological war and offered "a respite from the relatively closed and rigid historical patterns that dominate ideologies" (Clark and Holquist 302). This humanistic projection of North Koreans in films accentuated the frustration produced by the convincing reality of divided Koreas and created a haven for imagination in a surrogate reality—one uniting both hope for reunification and longing for the lost national half. These films provided South Koreans with festive occasions to celebrate the previously forbidden "other." By seeing the division of Korea as human tragedy, the films successfully present the subaltern point of view in resistance to the metanarrative of the Cold War era.

To illustrate the dramatic change that took place in the South Korean film industry in the late 1990s, I would examine two films that best exemplify the humanistic projection of North Koreans and the tragic reality of division, namely, *Spy Li Cheol-jin*, and *Joint Security Area*. The first was released just before the summit meeting in 2000, and the second just after. These two films reflect the rapidly-changing vision of South Korean society during this time period.

Li Cheol-jin, a Spy Caught in Between

The subject of North Korean espionage has been dealt with exhaustively by South Korean films for decades. Spies have been one of the most exploited stereotypes that easily incited the anti-Communist sentiments of South Koreans.[13] Corresponding to the social anxiety about North Korean spies, representation of North Koreans in films frequently involved espionage as the central plot around which to weave the narrative.

The release of *Shiri* in 1999 marked the point at which South Korean films and audiences started to rethink critically the place of North Koreans in the configuration of Korean national identity. The troubling questions of what to make of North Koreans became the central focus of *Shiri*, since the film presents two contrasting faces of the enemy—a threat to South Korean security but also a human being. By interweaving the traditional taboo subject (humanistic portrayal of North Koreans) and the familiar cliché of anti-Communist propaganda, *Shiri* references numerous South Korean films about the deceptiveness of the North Koreans in a critical mode but does not transgress the conventional boundaries that confine North Korean spies as threatening enemies. In contrast to the carefully measured examination of the projection of North Korean spies in *Shiri*, *Spy Li Cheol-jin* is a rather a free-spirited experiment with the taboo subject. As such, it transfigures the stereotypical face of North Korean spies. As if affirming the Bergsonian thesis of "rigidity is the comic, and laughter is its corrective," the film sustains the majority of its text with human errors, mistaken identities, and betrayed expectations, which all generate elastic comic energy that deconstructs the stringent ideology of the Cold War era (Bergson 74).

Li Cheol-jin, a spy trained in North Korea, is sent to Seoul on a secret mission to steal DNA samples of a "super pig" that could help relieve the starving population of North Korea. The motivation of Li's espionage is unusual if one considers how North Korean spies used to occupy the horrific center of South Koreans' imagination. Li crosses the border and comes to the South with a humanitarian cause, an attempt to save the starving. But as soon as he arrives in Seoul, he is robbed by clumsy gangsters, losing all his equipment and seed money. Hence, the expectations of any South Korean audience for the conventional spy are betrayed, since it is the spy who is threatened and victimized, just like any innocent South Korean country boy who makes his first trip to Seoul.

Moreover, the gang members who rob Li mistakenly conclude that they have ripped off a South Korean secret agent after they discover a gun[14] and electronic equipment in his stolen bag. This serves as a second twist in dismantling the conventional identity of a spy; Li is projected as a South Korean secret agent in the eyes of stolid gangsters thus involuntarily becoming the archenemy in the imagination of petty criminals.

Later in the film, Li even catches an armed bank robber when he accidentally runs into him, after which he is identified as an anonymous young man whose courageous deed is widely broadcast on South Korean television. He projects yet another improbable identity—that of a model South Korean citizen, adding another dimension to complicate the cliché of an evil spy. Such a comic and elastic shift of Li's identity helps South Korean audiences lower their psychological guard against the North Korean spy.

As Li is gradually portrayed as a sympathetic and credible character to the audience, he opens up the possibility of letting the audience identify with him and experience the events in the film from his point of view. By the process of psychological identification, South Korean audiences perceive their own society as a strange land from the perspective of a stranger. Such psychological identification with the conventional enemy, which is diametrically opposed to the Volkanian notion of "psychologizing" the "other" as evil, becomes a critical device to make South Korean audiences rethink the conventional ideas that saturated the national imagination about the evil other.

Li goes into hiding for a time to accomplish his mission of stealing the DNA sample of the super pig. Li seeks to be completely isolated from the rest of the South Korean society in order to conceal his identity and mission. In the meantime, a network of North Korean spies locates Li and sends him secret orders to assassinate another of their spies, whose presence has now become futile for the espionage operation in the South. Demonstrating perfect obedience to the orders he is trained to follow, Li goes to the designated site, only to find out that the North Korean spy he was about to assassinate is none other than his closest friend. After a moment of strong emotional turbulence, Li nonetheless overcomes his hesitation and pulls the trigger. Such a horrific event functions as a device to illuminate Li's multiple inner human dimensions; he suffers from the cruel nature of his own mission, spends that night drinking, and wanders around the nocturnal streets of Seoul, where he experiences a hallucination of seeing North Korean civilians amidst the bustling South Korean crowd.

The turning point from comedy to tragedy in the construction of Li marks an essential moment in the movie, since it is a moment of flux when elements previously forbidden in South Korea, such as the presence of North Koreans on South Korean territory, emerge. The presence of North Koreans in South Korea traditionally has been seen as military aggression of one form or another. But the North Koreans whom Li sees on the streets of Seoul are children, a young woman, and an old man, who do not impose any threat to the viewers. Instead, they appear oddly dislocated, which arises from the juxtaposition of incompatible subjects for both North and South Korean viewers, whose minds have been collectively and systematically conditioned by both governments not to accept each other on one's soil. The two Koreas' coercive rules prohibiting their people from crossing the border are violated in this scene, and it should be noted that the bizarre visual juxtaposition is presented through the eyes of the spy, who crosses the border, has access to both sides of the border, and thereby can question the strict order by which the two Koreas are supposed to be diametrically opposed.

D. Emily Hicks has noted that the one who crosses the border is involved in deterritorialization, that is, moving away from his or her own soil, but at the same time, also in " 'reterritorialization' to the extent that she or he clings to nostalgic images on the other side" (xxii). Consequently, the process of reterritorialization by the border crosser transforms the semiotics of the new soil. In the case of *Spy Li Cheol-jin*, Li's painful experience of reterritorialization corrosively disfigures the conventional image of Seoul as a site of speedy urban modern life. By projecting the images of poor North Korean civilians onto the bustling streets of Seoul, Li not only clings to the nostalgic images he has left behind but also explores the possibility of coexistence between North and South Koreans in the same territory. The improbability of seeing North Korean civilians on the streets of Seoul gains credibility at the cost of dismantling Li's identity, as he convincingly transforms himself from the most threatening kind of enemy to a most humane individual, which makes the audience realize that North Koreans could coexist with South Koreans in a nonconflict situation.

Li's reterritorialization visualized in these striking images unfolds further in the movie. The bizarre feeling of being an outsider in Seoul increases as Li runs into more trouble that same night. Feeling extremely nostalgic, he gets into a taxi and asks the driver to take him to the North Korean capital, Pyongyang. In spite of Li's sincerity, the taxi driver, who just received a moving violation ticket and is in an extremely bad mood, takes this request as a bad joke. The driver asks Li if he meant to say Yangpyong, which is a reversal of two syllables Pyongyang and a small town in South Korea. After some bickering, they end up in a police station where a jaded but kind South Korean officer tries to persuade Li not to sabotage his work when Li keeps insisting that he is a North Korean spy. Nobody believes the truthful confession of Li, and he is simply put into a jail overnight, to be released the next morning.

The subversive nature of this scene, which presents "laughter through tears," may be understood in the context of multiple ironies that challenge the concept of South Korea as the center of anti-Communism. The South Korean police officer does not believe that he is encountering a North Korean spy in the police station. Of course, the probability of such an event as a real spy voluntarily confessing his true identity in the enemy's headquarters is low. Yet it is bizarre to witness how truth is so easily dismissed in this scene, which ironically testifies to the fact that the anti-Communist propaganda, despite its fierceness, has actually disabled South Koreans from recognizing the enemy when he makes an appearance. Like the taxi driver and the police officer in the movie, one refuses to believe the actual presence of the enemy in the society.

When South Korea was caught up in the frenzy of anti-Communism, police and military forces constantly repeated that spies are embedded everywhere in "our" society and that South Korean citizens should be vigilant in identifying them. Posters calling for such vigilance, such as "If one appears dubious, look twice; if you feel suspicious, report to the police," covered the ceilings and walls of the subway, school gates, and billboards of the skyline of South Korea.[15] The level of saturation was so great that any South Koreans who lived through the Cold War era could easily recite such slogans. But as the mechanical anti-Communist slogans were repeated for decades, the real referent of propaganda (dangerous enemies) is lost, and the linguistic signifiers (propaganda themselves) remain as empty shells designating nothing.

The emptiness of the language that composes propaganda, in turn, raises a question of whether the referent, the real enemies, existed in the first place. Were the enemies only products of paranoid South Koreans' imaginations? The police station scene in *Spy Li Cheol-jin* has a biting potency, as the comic energy exposes the indoctrinated character of South Korean society and provides an occasion for interrogating itself and new ways of thinking about North Korea and North Koreans.

The reversal of conventions, functions, and identities culminates in the last moment of the film, when Li successfully steals the DNA sample of the super pig and goes to the site where he is supposed to contact North Koreans to cross the border, which will bring his mission to an end. While Li is waiting in the café for his accomplices, he sees an announcement on the television news that the South Korean government plans to deliver the DNA samples of the super pig to North Koreans. The news broadcast shows the images of starving children of North Korea in the light of a humanitarian crisis, which is a carefully choreographed attempt by the South Korean government to conceal the embarrassing incident involving the theft of the DNA samples by the North Korean spy. Although the film never addresses the motivation of the South Korean government's sudden generosity, the reason for the donation is obvious. The South Korean government now realizes that the DNA samples are in the hands of the enemy and will be flown into North Korea anyway, so they want to make use of the opportunity to propagandize their humanitarian efforts and keep the embarrassing secret of not having been able to defend their important laboratory.

A reversal of events immediately follows, as three North Korean agents, who are supposed to help Li return to Pyongyang, appear in order to eliminate Li. Li realizes that his plans and mission have gone astray in the final moment and desperately fights to protect the DNA samples from the North Koreans. Nonetheless, North Koreans shoot the briefcase holding the DNA samples, which have become an unnecessary embarrassment for them. Like the stolen DNA samples, Li realizes that he himself has become a useless element in the overall relationship between two Korean governments, each of which rapidly exploited the situation for its own political benefits. Faced with his failure to complete the mission and betrayal by his own government, Li is speechless. There is a momentary flash of starving North Korean children, and as this stream of consciousness is prolonged, the audience confronts the face of a failed human being—one who believed in his mission and tried hard to be part of the system but was ruthlessly discarded once his usefulness vanished.

Li moves the gun he has pointed at the head of one of the North Koreans to his own and commits suicide.

Just before crossing the border, Li dies, unwillingly caught between the two regimes. Such a death in liminality tragically asserts the impossibility of transgressing the borders between the North and the South for an individual capable of seeing the fallacy of both regimes. The movie poignantly shows that one living in the reality of the divided Koreas cannot be in between: one must choose between the two regimes in order to survive. But the real irony of Li's death lies in the fact that even though he was totally ready to accept one of the two systems and tried hard to function as part of the system, he was doomed to failure. Against his hope, Li Cheol-jin's life ends in between the two systems and territories, each of which refused him as a person, as a result of which his humanitarian mission failed in a very inhuman way.

Disjointed Utopia, *Joint Security Area*

Joint Security Area begins with the sound of a gunshot in the deep of night on the border between North and South Korea, one of the most heavily armed areas in the world. The setting of the film is a direct reminder of the Korean War as a military struggle, since the establishment of the demilitarized zone was a direct result of the armistice that halted the war in 1953.

The film revolves around the investigation of the incident in which two North Korean soldiers were shot dead on the North Korean post and one South Korean soldier was shot in the leg and left lying over the military demarcation line. The only surviving witnesses of the incident, a North Korean first lieutenant, Oh Kyeong-pil, and a South Korean corporal, Li Su-hyeok, remain silent. The North Korean officials accuse South Koreans of invading the North Korean post, whereas South Koreans accuse North Koreans of abducting their soldiers.

As the investigation reaches a dead end, a third neutral party, a Swiss-Korean named Sophie,[16] is sent by the United Nations to unearth the truth. As the film unfolds, she eventually discovers the amazing story that the two survivors tried to hide. After much detective work and numerous interrogations with both South Korean Li and North Korean Oh, Sophie discovers that, contrary to the hostile accusations of the officials, the South Korean soldiers had befriended the North Korean guards and secretly visited the North Korean post at night many times before the incident took place. She then comes to realize the true motivation for the silence—admitting to their forbidden friendship would endanger themselves as well as their secret friends.

While divulging the truth was a centrifugal force in *Spy Li Cheol-jin* for turning the subversive world upside down (in which the true confession was either ignored or laughed at), it becomes a centripetal force in *Joint Security Area*, as all the elements of the film focus on or contribute to the effort to discover the secret world where enemy soldiers could become brothers. Quite contrary to the truth-speaking spy Li Cheol-jin, neither North Korean Oh Kyeong-pil nor South Korean Li Su-hyeok in *Joint Security Area* wishes to tell the truth, since the world in this film, with its military setting as the simulacrum of an ongoing Korean War, does not allow subversion to take place openly. Thus, the meetings of the friends across the border become a secret, a silenced antiritual, taking place at night when the military rituals of the diurnal world are temporarily set aside.

How could such unlikely encounters have taken place? The film discloses the story of secret friendship through a painful retrospection of the survivors of the gunshot incident. It begins in an improbable situation, when South Korean Li, waiting to be discharged from the army, accidentally steps on a land mine while on night patrol in the joint security area along the border between the two Koreas. He calls out for help, only to be discovered by two North Korean soldiers, bringing a moment of tension as the soldiers face their enemy and react according to their long years of military training. They instinctively point guns at each other, only to learn that they could all die if Li removes his foot from the mine. Upon realizing the risk, the two North Koreans simply leave Li behind and walk away. Li first curses them for leaving him and then begs them to save his life. The two North Koreans return and remove the mine so that Li can escape safely. After this event, the forbidden friendship between North Korean and South Korean soldiers develops, leading the South Korean soldiers to frequent the North Korean post across one of the most heavily armed borders in the world.

The initial fear and suspicion between the enemies are washed away as the soldiers' personal relationships eclipse the external setting of military conflict. The two extreme modes of mutual engagement—secret friendship and military conflict—weave two contrasting time and space zones within the text. The plot of forbidden fraternal affection between South and North plays out at night, when the watchful eyes of the belligerent world are asleep, thereby allowing the enemy soldiers to assume the temporary yet truthful identity of friends.[17] The secret meetings take place in North Korean territory, which is conventionally regarded as a hostile land on which South Koreans cannot set foot. By crossing the forbidden border, the South Korean soldiers reverse their ordinary anticipation of the North and discover a haven in North Korea where humanistic communication with the enemy becomes possible. The spy Li Cheol-jin crosses the border and searches for the possibility of coexistence between North Koreans and South Koreans through hallucinatory visual juxtaposition. By contrast, the South Korean soldiers in *Joint Security Area* actualize the fantasy by crossing the border and socializing with North Korean soldiers. Unlike *Spy Li Cheol-jin*, the juxtaposition of the North and the South in *Joint Security Area* appears neither subversive nor dislocated, but rather natural and just.

However, the nocturnal companionship with enemies in their territory reverts to normalcy in the daytime. Back on the other side of the border, the same participants in this utopian ritual of forbidden friendship return to their permanent conventional roles, assigned by their regimes. They carry out the rigid war rituals of hating and aiming guns at each other. In the film, there are juxtapositions of scenes where the South Korean soldiers Li and Nam go through intensive target practice, aiming and shooting at the wooden figures of North Korean soldiers while secretly whispering about their nocturnal friends whom they are being trained to shoot. In the background of this training scene, there is an anti-Communist poster with a militant slogan, a familiar mise-en-scène for South Koreans who lived through the Cold War, in order to accentuate the schizophrenic status these South Korean soldiers' experience.

According to Christopher Nash, such an experience is part of the postmodern life, in which a single overriding ideology, principle, or ritual is dismantled by competing interests. An individual may assume "dispersed multiple identities of affiliation, and with multiple identity spaces—together with new ways of feeling 'betwix and between' " and as a result, "the world becomes diversified, 'hybridized,' 'creolized' and potentially fractured in heretofore unimagined and presently incalculable ways. The disintegration of relatively unified notions of time, space and person bids to become a universal precondition for living" (169).

Just as Li Cheol-jin's conventional identity as a spy is fractured into multiple identities, in *Joint Security Area* multiple identities are established for the South Korean soldiers in their relation to the North Korean friends/enemies. But the expression of multiple identities in *Joint Security Area* is much more closely connected to the intrinsic relationship between time and space[18] in the sense that various temporal and spatial zones impose various identities for South Korean soldiers. *Joint Security Area* constantly reminds the viewers that engaging in nocturnal friendships for South Korean soldiers is temporal and is doomed to come to an end; before the sunrise, South Korean soldiers have to cross the border and return to their military post. As a result of situating the secret friendship within the large historical context of the everlasting Korean War, the pleasant nocturnal encounter becomes an ephemeral event, which will sooner or later end in destruction. Even at the most humane and intimate moment of friendship between the enemy soldiers, there is an overriding tension, which the soldiers cannot completely resist or eliminate.

When Nam, one of the South Korean soldiers, tries to take a picture of two North Korean soldiers and another South Korean soldier Li inside the North Korean post, he is disturbed by the portraits of the founding father of North Korea, Kim Il-sung, and his son, Kim Jong-il, that appear in the background. The three soldiers whose pictures are being taken cannot see this and thus follow the instruction of Nam, who tells them to put their faces closer to one another so that the portraits of the North Korean leaders can be covered from view. This moment sharply reminds the viewers of the fact that the South Korean soldiers are in enemy territory, even though the soldiers resort to the free-spirited exchange of friendship and temporarily forget the ideologies that divide the North from the South. Nam's uncomfortable feeling of seeing the leaders of North Korea brings back the overriding historical tension created by both Korean regimes to position themselves against each other. Nam's modest effort not to include the portraits of political leaders into the frame of the picture capturing their friendship is a sublimated way of resisting the North Korean regime.

In another moment during their meeting, Li offers a piece of South Korean–made chocolate cake to Oh, who marvels at the taste and questions why the North cannot make such a thing. Upon hearing this, Li asks Oh if he intends to defect to South Korea where he can enjoy limitless amount of delicacies. Oh, who was still enjoying a mouthful of cake, immediately spits it out and mechanically preaches to Li that his dream is to serve his beloved republic and to strengthen it so that it can

Figure 11.2. Overshadowed by ideology.

make cakes a hundred times more tasteful than what he just had in his mouth. Clichéd as Oh's speech may be, the words of Oh ring out at the moment when the soldiers are engaged in the most intimate exchange of human relationship and therefore gain a chilling cogency. If Oh's words were heard from the state media, which repeated such slogans constantly, it would have been dismissed as a part of the conventional political rituals that saturated the daily lives of people in both Koreas. However, when heard from a person such as Oh, who is able to transgress the line of rigid propagandistic rituals, it serves as a powerful and painful reminder of how deeply such propaganda lexicons creep into the subconscious. The moment of tension between Li and Oh succumbs to uncomfortable laughter on the part of Li, who tells Oh that he was just joking; but this brief verbal tension foreshadows the impending physical conflict between them, which ultimately puts an end to the utopian fraternal bond.

The secret meeting tragically ends when another North Korean on patrol discovers the presence of the South Korean soldiers in North Korean territory. The newly arrived North Korean is shocked at the improbable sight of enemy soldiers in his own territory. As a result of long years of military training, the South Korean soldiers instinctively aim at the newly arrived enemy. The newcomer also aims at the South Korean soldiers, and the tension escalates to a miniature war between the two Koreas. Experienced and quick in responding to crisis, Oh, in an effort to avoid a drastic outcome, persuades the newly arrived North Korean to put down his gun since the South Koreans had come to the post in order to discuss the possibility of defecting to North Korea. As both lower their guns at Oh's persuasion, the unbearable equilibrium of tension is broken by a gunshot when the tape in the cassette player is reversed and starts to play South Korean rock music, revealing clearly to the newly arrived North Korean patrol that Oh's incredible story about the South Koreans defecting to the North is a lie. In an uncontrolled state of fear and intimidation, Li and Nam end up firing shots, not only at the newly arrived North Korean patrol but also at their North Korean friends, who saved Li's life.

The director of the movie has commented on the significance of the scene when Li fires explosive shots at the North Koreans: "The North Korean soldiers should be killed extremely violently. Their heads are blown into pieces, and their fingers are cut off, because this is the moment when our subconscious communist-phobia violently explodes. Ironically, violence always emerges out of fear for the other" (Kim 2000, 69). It is exactly the nature of this fear of the unknown other that this scene in *Joint Security Area* explores. By projecting North Korean soldiers simultaneously as a military target and brothers, the film suggests that what

South Koreans have been trained to call enemies is nothing more than the product of their own imagination—a fake target made of a wooden panel for gunshot training. Yet, in this nightmarish accident when the South Korean soldiers shoot at their friends, the fake wooden targets become real people with human faces and hearts. At this moment, the South Korean soldiers' critical ability to think is pushed aside by the mechanical way they have been trained to react, mercilessly destroying the utopian time and space of celebrating fraternity.

Despite the highly unconventional portrayal of the relationship between South and North, the ending of the film returns everything to its original point—the perpetual status of the Cold War. The survivors of the scene, Li and Oh, out of consideration for each other's safety, keep their friendship secret. Sophie suggests to Li that she is aware of the fact that at the night of the incident, Li first shot one of the North Korean soldiers, the benefactors of his life, who removed the mine in the night of the first encounter between them. Unable to sustain the moral burden, Li commits suicide on the day he is discharged from military service. As Li is lying in a pool of his own blood, the film moves on to a still photo, which becomes the last image of the film. It is the photo of the four border guards, two on the side of the South and the other two on the side of the North, which was taken earlier in the movie by an American tourist unaware of the story behind the guards captured in his shot. Even though the photo visually epitomizes the permanent status of the Cold War that divides the two Koreas, the guards in the picture are none other than the two South Korean soldiers and two North Korean soldiers engaged in the secret friendship; but at the moment the picture is taken, they face each other as enemies guarding their nations at the edge of their territory. In a long sequence that highlights their estranged faces, one after another, the faces reveal that they are not allowed to express the true intimacy they secretly built. The tragedy of having to suppress human desires in order to sustain an unchallengeable ideological system is condensed in this last moment of the film, as the enemy's human faces are concealed by the masks already forged for by the tragic historical fate of modern Korea.

Where Do We Go from Here?

Since the commercial and artistic success of *Shiri*, *Spy Li Cheol-jin*, and *Joint Security Area*, a momentum has been created in the South Korean film industry to produce more films about North Korea and the absurdity of division. *Double Agent* (Steve Kim) starring Han Seok-gyu, the same male protagonist of *Shiri*, opened in South Korean theaters in January 2003, again presenting the tragic downfall of a double agent who worked for both South and North Koreas and could not survive in both regimes.

Under the direction of Kang Je-kyu, another Korean War film, *Taegukgi: The Brotherhood of War*, opened in March 2004 and set many new records in the Korean film industry. With twenty-five thousand extras and eight months of shooting, the production costs exceeded $10 million U.S., a record amount for South Korean film production. The film opened on four hundred screens across South Korea, attracting 324,000 viewers on opening day alone. Within nine days, the film set a record, attracting 10 million people. From its inception, the film targeted a global market beyond the national boundaries. With leading actors whose faces are familiar to fans across Asian countries, the film became a commercial success in Japan and received positive reviews in the United States.[19]

Such a boom in promoting North Korean and Korean War subjects in South Korean films owes much to the successful transformation of the stereotypical images of North Koreans and the convincing projection of the tragic realities in divided Korea in the two films analyzed in this chapter. South Koreans' humanistic representation of the North Koreans exposed the anomalous nature of the divided Korea, especially arguing to the viewers that the hostile way in which the North and South Korean political regimes have regarded each other for decades should not be applied symmetrically to the ways North and South Korean people relate to each other. What *Spy Li Cheol-jin* and *Joint Security Area* share as common ground is making audiences critically view the ideologically distorted representation of people of the other side and make them realize that the people of the other side are simply people, just like "us." The presence of border crossers in both films—a North Korean spy who comes to the South in *Spy Li Cheol-jin* and South Korean soldiers who go to the North in *Joint Security Area*—facilitated the understanding of the people of the other side, since "the border crosser is both 'self' and the 'other,' " and his " 'subject' emerges from double strings of signifiers of two sets of referential codes, from both sides of the border" (Hicks xxvi). Nonetheless, the border crossers meet tragic death in both movies, which effectively expresses the absurdity of the current political order in both Koreas.

The commitment to seek mutual understanding on the part of the two Koreas is not limited to the political and diplomatic realms but also concerns the realms of culture and everyday life. In this respect, the South Korean film industry has more responsibility for the representation of the other and the prospect of Korean unification, especially at a moment when the thawing mood between the two Koreas could easily revert to perpetuation of the cold war. Hopefully, more South Korean movies about North Korea and its people will present these issues in a sensitive way.

Notes

1. In October 2002 North Korea declared that it was restarting the nuclear program that was prohibited by the Geneva nonproliferation agreement with the United States in 1994. In the first quarter of 2003, in a desperate attempt to attract the attention of the United States and restart negotiations, North Korea launched two short-range missiles to the East Sea and dispatched two jets to restrain the activities of a U.S. spy plane in international airspace near North Korea.

2. The James Bond movie *Die Another Day* incited a strong anti-American sentiment in South Korea even before the film was released. The majority of South Koreans felt the film was exploiting political tensions in the Korean peninsula and portraying North Koreans as the stereotypical evil enemy for entertainment purposes at a time when the portrayal of North Koreans had become a sensitive issue.

3. There are other exceptions to this stark formula of Cold War–era Hollywood films. *Manchurian Candidate* (1962), for example, shows technical and thematic complexity in weaving out the horrifying nightmares of war and its aftermath.

4. The National Security Law owes its institutionalization to surging anti-Communist sentiment in South Korea. As Kim Sun-hyuk argues, the National Security Law was the favorite anti-Communist weapon devised by the first president of South Korea, Rhee Syng-man, and was passed by the National Assembly in 1948 after an allegedly Communist-led sedition in Yeosu and Suncheon. The National Security Law defined sedition in such a broad and vague way that the Rhee government could use the law to suppress virtually any kind of opposition. Kim Sun-hyuk, *The Politics of Democratization in Korea: The Role of Civil Society* (Pittsburgh: University of Pittsburgh Press, 2000) 30. In the subsequent years of military dictatorship (1960–1991), the importance of the National Security Law was increased because of a growing need to suppress the democratic civil movement, which stood against military dictatorship.

5. Film scholar Lee Hyangjin points to 1960–1979 as the pinnacle of the South Korean anti-Communist policies toward the film industry. See Hyangjun Lee, *Contemporary Korean Cinema* (Manchester and New York: Manchester University Press, 2000) 49–55.

6. Korea was a Japanese colony from 1910 to 1945, and there were a significant number of Japanese Imperial Army troops on Korean territory at the end of World War II. The United States and the Soviet Union divided the task of disarming the defeated Japanese army by dividing Korea into two halves along the 38th parallel, north of which was trusted to the Soviet Union and the south of which was trusted to the United States. According to Bruce Cumings, it was around midnight on August 10–11, 1945, that John J. McCloy of the State-War-Navy Coordinating Committee directed two young colonels to find a place to divide Korea. Bruce Cumings, *Korea's Place in the Sun* (New York: Norton, 1997) 186–87. In post-WWII Korea, the 38th parallel was supposed to serve as a temporary border to separate two zones of bilateral trusteeship in Korea by the Soviet Union and the United States. But as the two superpowers eventually turned into enemies, the 38th parallel became the borderline between the two hostile regimes

of North and South Korea. When the Korean War was brought to a halt through an armistice in 1953, the 38th parallel was designated as the dividing border and still serves that function.

7. Charles Armstrong's article "The Cultural Cold War in Korea, 1945–1950" explains in detail that the cultural conflict between the two Koreas was in large part the outcome of the ideological competition and rivalry between the U.S.S.R. and the United States, the occupiers of North and South, to win the heart and mind of the Korean people on both sides.

8. Paik Nak-chung, a South Korean critic, used the term "division system" to describe the process of perpetuating the division in a permanent system, from which both Korean regimes benefited. The system of division in Korea, according to Paik, is "a *sui generis* system that has survived the Cold War, and is deeply indebted to the latter for its inception and subsequent life." Paik Nak-chung, "The Idea of a Korean National Literature Then and Now," *positions* 1.3 (1993): 574. As Paik notes further, "understanding the system of division in terms of contradiction infers a scientific grasp of the 'contradiction between the division system and the populace of north and south,' rather than a 'contradiction between the northern and southern systems.' Paik Nak-chung, "The Reunification Movement in Literature," *South Korea's Minjung Movement: The Culture and Politics of Dissidence*, ed. Kenneth M. Wells (Honolulu: University of Hawaii Press, 1995) 180.

9. As suggested by Benedict Anderson, nation and its identity are an "imagined political community," into which the idea of the other is inherently built. Benedict Anderson, *Imagined Communities* (London: Verso, 1991) 6.

10. Many South Korean films develop their narratives by portraying North Koreans as evil aggressors. Some well-known examples are *Arirang* (1954), *The Marines Who Never Returned* 1963), and *Last Words of a Battleground Friend* 1979).

11. Martin Hart-Landsberg points out that on the eve of German reunification, "a civic revival [in East Germany] was taking place as growing numbers of people demonstrated their willingness to struggle to create a political system based on the principle of direct democracy and an economic system based on the principles of worker control, social solidarity, and ecological sustainability." *Korea: Division, Reunification, and U.S. Foreign Policy* (New York: Monthly Review, 1998) 212. Unfortunately, such civic participation was systematically ignored by the Western German government, which aimed only at absorption of East Germany.

12. The former South Korean president Kim Dae-jung had been an ardent advocate of the policy before he assumed the presidency in 1998. He credited the nonhostile approach of the Clinton administration toward North Korea in resolving the 1993 nuclear crisis by inviting North Korea to sign the Non Proliferation Treaty in Geneva in 1994. Kim Dae-jung, *Korea and Asia* (Seoul: Kim Dae-jung Peace Foundation Press, 1994) 36–38. During his presidency (1998–2003), Kim Dae-jung consistently committed himself to the nonhostile approach of the Korean conflict, in the process of which he went so far as to send secret funds to the North Korean leader Kim Jong-il. The monetary aid presumably facilitated the summit meeting between the leaders in June 2000, but the secret delivery of the funds to North Korea only became known to the South Korean public when Kim's tenure ended and the scandal erupted, marring the significant steps taken

forward in improving the relationship between the two Koreas. The scandal also tarnished Kim's receipt of the 2001 Nobel Peace Prize, which was awarded for his contribution to bringing peace to the Korean peninsula. Nevertheless, the impact of social changes that the Sunshine Policy brought to South Korea was too significant to be clouded by the political scandals.

13. Among numerous incidents involving North Korean spies, the older generation of South Koreans still vividly remembers the tragic event in 1974 when a team of North Korean spies accidentally assassinated the respected former first lady, Ryuk Young-soo. The real target of the North Korean spies was her husband, President Park Jung-hee. This event inspired both sorrow and anger on the part of South Koreans.

14. South Korean civilians are not allowed to purchase, own, and carry guns. Therefore, the gang members assume that Li Cheol-jin, the owner of the gun, is a noncivilian.

15. The last scene of *Spy Li Cheol-jin* shows Li Cheol-jin riding the subway with Hwa-yi, the daughter of the veteran North Korean spy who is hosting Li in Seoul. Li sees an anti-Communist poster on the wall, promising a 10-million-won ($83,000) reward to those whose reports lead to the capture of North Korean spies. Li asks Hwa-yi what one can do with 10 million won in South Korea, and Hwa-yi tells him that it is not a large sum, but maybe enough for a decent foreign-made car. This moment reminds the South Korean audience of the materialism associated with the frenzy of anti-Communist propaganda in South Korea.

16. The film makes clear that Sophie's father was a North Korean soldier and prisoner of war, who, in the aftermath of the Korean War, chose to settle in a third country, Switzerland. Being half Korean and half Swiss, she personifies the neutral zone between two opposing regimes and ideologies and is free to go back and forth between the two because she does not belong to either.

17. Kim Kyung Hyun notes the peculiar nature of the male bonding between North and South Korean soldiers as follows: "As much as it is difficult to claim *JSA* as a gay film, it is almost impossible to disclaim the same-sex bonding as the film's primary element that derives the desirable and subversive narrative movement. *JSA* is a 'male melodrama' that induces all of the ingredients of pathos, sentimental music score, and emotional experiences of war exercises and camps most Korean men have endured for almost three years of their youth in their military." *The Remasculinization of Korean Cinema* (Durham and London: Duke University Press, 2004) 266.

18. Mikhail Bakhtin recognized the indivisible relationship between time and space, neither of which can be regarded as less important than the other. According to his words, "we will give the name chronotope (literally, "time and space") to the intrinsic connectedness of temporal and spatial relationships." Mikhail Bakhtin, "Forms of Time and of the Chronotope in the Novel," *The Dialogic Imagination*, ed. Michael Holquist (Austin: University of Texas Press, 1981) 84. Gary S. Morson rephrases the term *chronotope* as "a particular complex of socio-historical relations," because Bakhtin understood time as historical and space as social. "Commentary: Chronotope and Anachronism," *Literature and History* (Stanford: Stanford University Press, 1986) 265. The Bakhtinian notion of

chronotope as sociohistorical concept of time and space is useful in accessing the significance of chronotope in *Joint Security Area*, since the artificial binary opposition of night/North Korean territory/friendship and daytime/South Korean territory/hostility can only be understood in terms of the sociohistorical reality of divided Koreas.

19. *Taegukgi* opened in major U.S. cities, such as New York, Washington DC, Los Angeles, and Chicago in September 2004 and attracted many Korean American viewers.

Works Cited

Anderson, Benedict. *Imagined Communities*. London: Verso, 1991.

Armstrong, Charles. "The Cultural Cold War in Korea, 1945–1950." *Journal of Asian Studies* 62.1: 71–100.

Bakhtin, Mikhail. "Forms of Time and of the Chronotope in the Novel." *The Dialogic Imagination*. Ed. Michael Holquist. Austin: University of Texas Press, 1981. 84–258.

Bergson, Henri. "The Comic Element in Forms." *Comedy*. Ed. Wylie Sypher. Baltimore: Johns Hopkins University Press, 1956.

Clark, Katerina, and Michael Holquist. *Mikhail Bakhtin*. Cambridge: Harvard University Press, 1984.

Cumings, Bruce. *Korea's Place in the Sun*. New York: Norton, 1997.

Hart-Landsberg, Martin. *Korea: Division, Reunification, and U.S. Foreign Policy*. New York: Monthly Review Press, 1998.

Hicks, D. Emily. *Border Writing: The Multidimensional Text*. Minneapolis: University of Minnesota Press, 1991.

Kim Dae-jung. *Korea and Asia*. Seoul: Kim Dae Jung Peace Foundation Press, 1994.

Kim Kyeong-uk. "Overcoming Division: The Task of Korean Cinema." *Korean Culture and Arts Journal*. (November 2000): 66–70.

Kim, Kyung Hyun. *The Remasculinization of Korean Cinema*. Durham and London: Duke University Press, 2004.

Kim Sang-hwan. "The Achievements and Problems of Social and Cultural Exchange between South and North Koreas." *North Korea*. (April 2001): 61–69.

Kim Sun-hyuk. *The Politics of Democratization in Korea: The Role of Civil Society*. Pittsburgh: University of Pittsburgh Press, 2000.

Lee, Hyangjin. *Contemporary Korean Cinema*. Manchester and New York: Manchester University Press, 2000.

Morson, Gary Saul. "Commentary: Chronotope and Anachronism." *Literature and History*. Stanford: Stanford University Press, 1986. 263–74.

Nash, Christopher. *The Unraveling of the Postmodern Mind*. Edinburgh: Edinburgh University Press, 2001.

Oberdorfer, Don. *Two Koreas*. Indianapolis: Basic Books, 1997.

Paik Nak-chung. "The Idea of a Korean National Literature Then and Now." *positions* 1.3 (1993): 553–80.

———. "The Reunification Movement in Literature." *South Korea's Minjung Movement: The Culture and Politics of Dissidence*. Ed. Kenneth M. Wells. Honolulu: University of Hawaii Press, 1995. 179–207.

Paquet, Darcy. "Appendix G: South Korean Films about the Korean War." *Korean War Filmography*. Ed. Robert Lentz. Jefferson, NC and London: McFarland. 454–59.

Volkan, Vamik K. *The Need to Have Enemies and Allies: From Clinical Practice to International Relationships*. Northvale, NJ: Jason Aronson, 1998.

12

Myung Ja Kim

Race, Gender, and Postcolonial Identity in Kim Ki-duk's *Address Unknown*

Recently Kim Ki-duk, a young Korean film director/writer/producer, was acknowledged as one of the new stars of world cinema by winning the awards for the best director at two of the most renowned international film festivals. The 2004 Berlin Film Festival honored him for *Samaritan Girl* and The 61st Venice Film Festival (2004) awarded him for *Vacant House*. Since shocking the Venice Film Festival with *The Isle* in 2000, Kim Ki-duk has been expanding his filmography with incredible speed and productivity. After debuting with *Crocodile* in 1996, he completed eleven feature films in eight years: *Wild Animals* (1997), *Birdcage Inn* (1998), *The Isle* (1999), *Real Fiction* (2000), *Address Unknown* (2001), *Bad Guy* (2001), *Coast Guard* (2002), *Spring, Summer, Fall and Winter* (2003), *Samaritan Girl* (2004), and *Vacant House* (2004).

Kim Ki-duk is known as much as a heretic as he is prolific. Unlike most Korean film directors, who are highly educated members of the middle or upper class, Kim Ki-duk has not benefited from a formal institutional education, either generally or in film studies. After working in factories from the age of seventeen and service in the marines, he left for

Figure 12.1. *Address Unknown*'s three wounded, marginalized youth. (Kim Ki-duk 2001).

France in 1990, spending virtually all his money on the plane ticket. There, he continued the painting he started as a child and supported himself for two years by doing odd jobs and selling his paintings.[1]

Upon his return from France, Kim focused on writing film scripts, jumpstarting his film career by winning prizes for two scripts submitted in competition. Since then, he has written and directed of all his films. Kim is renowned for his sweeping style, his use of amazingly low budgets, and his expedient production schedules, as exemplified in the six-week production time of *Address Unknown*. As a social and cultural outcast himself, he distances himself from the bourgeois aesthetics of art and is deeply concerned with issues of social alienation in Korean society.[2] For this director, filmmaking is a way to expose the fallacious reasoning of the mainstream that seeks to marginalize people, revealing the tragic and often fatal results of stigmatizing those regarded as inferior and different from the established norms. His films are considered "autobiographical writing with a film camera," which is why Kim describes each of his films as a "sequence" within his entire body of work (biography). With his inherent sensitivity, direct observation, and personal experience, he attempts to translate the suppressed outrage and explosive tension of marginalized people into images charged with grotesqueness and cruelty. His use of both extreme violence and the sublime beauty of lyricism in coexistence has branded him "a shockingly original filmmaker whose work negotiates the terrain between mainstream appeal and art cinema bravura" (untitled document).

Taking his title from undelivered letters strewn on the ground, the director dedicated *Address Unknown* to the memory of a childhood friend who committed suicide at the age of twenty-eight (interview). Full of gory images of chilling violence and self-destruction meant to shock, it focuses on the issue of miscegenation and mixed-race children through the characters of Chang-gook, a black/Korean youth, and his single mother, who continually writes letters to her son's father, an African-American soldier, enclosing pictures of Chang-gook. However, her efforts are in vain because the letters are always returned, stamped "address unknown." Chang-gook's life is devastated by the prejudice and discrimination he faces in his daily life, causing him to strike back with violence. He finally ends his life in a suicidal motorcycle crash.

Regardless of the scientific fact that the only race is the human race,[3] throughout history people have nonetheless tried to classify human beings into hierarchical racial groups, and under this grouping, miscegenation has been, and remains, a strong taboo in most societies. In his study, *The Secret History of Mixed-Race America*, Gary Nash reveals an American past "in which powerful Americans passed laws, spun scientific theories, judged court cases, wrote tracts, created popular entertainment, and preached the belief that every person has one and only one race and that walls must be built to prevent intimacy, love, and marriage between people who supposedly belong to different races" (viii). The dominant racism in American society rested upon centuries of federal and state sanctions as well as legal segregation, which is attested by the long history of American antimiscegenation laws prohibiting marriage between whites and "others." Such laws were common in the nineteenth century throughout the United States. In 1880, for example, the California legislature extended restrictive antimiscegenation categories to prohibit any marriage between a white person and a "Negro, mulatto, or Mongolian."[4]

The prejudice against miscegenation and mixed-race children in Korean society also has deep historical roots. Without understanding the political and cultural history of Korea, from the period of Japanese colonialism through the Korean War and the neocolonialism of U.S. military forces, it is not easy to understand the deterministic tone underlying *Address Unknown*. This was reflected in the puzzled reactions of some audience members to the premiere at the Venice Film Festival in 2001. It can be summed up as "it is difficult to understand, but . . . ," or "I cannot understand the Korean circumstances under U.S. military, but . . . I could feel the sorrow."[5]

In this chapter, I will trace the various cultural and historical factors that contributed to the construction of the ideologies of race, gender, class, sexuality, and postcolonial identity in Korean society and their relationship to the issue of interracial mixing as presented in *Address Unknown*. This study will also show how Kim Ki-duk problematizes these issues for critical interrogation from the perspective of an outsider.

Miscegenation as Racialized and Gendered Stigma

In this film, a nameless former prostitute, who is only identified as Chang-gook's mother, lives in an abandoned bus on the outskirts of an American military camp town, enduring the villagers' ostracism and her biracial son's trauma in the hope of the American dream she expresses in her letters to Chang-gook's African-American father. As a permanent outsider, Chang-gook makes friends with only two teenagers, Ji-hum and Eun-ok, who are also alienated. As a shy and introverted boy, Ji-hum is humiliated and tormented by his peers. Eun-ok's alienation is symbolized by her scarred eye, which induces her to become a "GI girl" for James, a young, white U.S. serviceman, in exchange for an eye operation. James also suffers from adjustment problems, to both life in the army and life stationed abroad. All four young people are forlorn, caught in a karmic chain that dates back to the legacy of the Korean War.

Kim's concern with historical and political issues is made clear from the initial expository scene. The graphic representation of traditional Korean symbols of yin and yang overlapped by those of an American military field uniform symbolizes the Korean culture overthrown by U.S. colonialism and military culture. By dealing with the lives of the people living in the area surrounding a U.S. military base, the director "ruminates on the history from the Korean War back to the time of Japanese imperialism" (interview). In this film, the camp town functions as a topographical signifier representing the poisonous legacy of war and is portrayed as a prominent force controlling and shaping individual lives. The director uses scars and wounds, such as the crippled leg of Ji-hum's father and Eun-ok's lost eye, as mnemonic devices that tell their stories. It is not just people's faces that tell their life stories, as Gloria Anzaldua perceptively observes, they are " 'written' all over . . . carved and tattooed with the sharp needles of experience" (xv). "The needles of experience" are most vividly inscribed by the tattoo etched on the chest of Chang-gook's mother and on the entire body of her mixed-race son, the color of his skin. As social pariahs, mother and son live in an abandoned army bus on the outskirts of a camp town, alienated and marginalized even in a place that is already marked as a "barred-zone" in Korean society. Essentially rootless, they are meant to be moving (to America) but are immobile, just like the wrecked bus in which they live. In the films of Kim Ki-duk, the means of transportation often lose their original functions and stay still in one place. As with the motorcycle that the nameless female character always gazes upon outside her window in *The Isle*, the bus in *Address Unknown* stands still, sharply contrasted by the planes of the U.S. Air Force constantly flying over Chang-gook and his mother, ridiculing their American dream. The red of the bus implies the possible threat and "danger" Chang-gook and his mother represent to the morals and ethics of the community, serving as a warning to young girls, including Eun-ok, who is cautioned, "Do you want to end up like Chang-gook's mother?"

To understand the discrimination and prejudice against miscegenation in Korea, we have to understand the political and historical circumstances surrounding the issue. It was not a major social concern until the U.S. military forces began to occupy the Korean peninsula after World War II. They withdrew temporarily after the establishment of a Korean government below the 38th parallel, but since the outbreak of the Korean War, American military forces have continued to remain through to the present day, though in much smaller numbers.[6] Throughout Korea's long history of 4,335 years, there have no doubt been quite a number of international marriages with people from neighboring countries such as China and Japan, but they were interethnic rather than interracial, and their descendants were easily dispersed and intermingled among Koreans. Mainly due to the isolationist policy, which lasted nearly until the end of the Yi Dynasty,[7] there was not much history of interchange with the West. We can find a rare record of interracial mixing between Koreans and Westerners before the twentieth century from Donald R. Haffner. In 1653, a Dutch Naval vessel, the *Sparrow Hawk*, was shipwrecked near Jeju Island at the southern end of Korea. Only three out of thirty-six survivors went back to the Netherlands via Japan, and a few of those who remained married Koreans.[8] According to *A Report on the Registered Mixed Race People*, published by the Pearl Buck Foundation, the official record of mixed-race children began in 1947 after American occupation at the end of World War II (Han 10).

The Korean government officially defines mixed-race children as "the second and third generation of children born to American military personnel and Korean women after 1950" (Han, 8). According to this delineation, every mixed-race child is supposed to be born of U.S. soldiers and Korean women, implying that the children are the offspring of military sex workers in camp towns. This is also the prevalent view of the Korean general public. In a globalized world, where exchanges across racial and cultural borders are increasing every day, it is surprising to see that some Koreans still hold this limited view on interracial relationships. I met a student at Boston University who identified herself as "a double" not "a half," she insists, with an American father and Korean mother. She told me: "I hate to go back to Korea, where I lived until I became fifteen, because everybody assumes my father is a soldier and my mother a prostitute."

Kijichon, the setting of this film, is the term for U.S. military bases and their surrounding areas, but it is generally associated with the massive sex industry located around the more than half a dozen American military bases throughout South Korea. The military sex workers are called "*yanggongju*." Hyun Sook Kim explains the etymology and implication of the term as follows:

> Used derogatorily, it means "Yankee whore," "Yankee wife," "UN lady," and/or "Western princess." This epithet "Yanggongju" relegates Korean women working in militarized prostitution with foreign men to the lowest status within the hierarchy of prostitution. Since the end of the Korean War, this category has been extended to include Korean women who marry American servicemen (pejoratively called "GI Brides"). In postwar Korea, the epithet "Yanggongju" has become synonymous with "GI Brides," so that Korean women in interracial marriages are also viewed as "Yanggongju." (Kim 1998, 178)

Such discrimination and prejudice against military sex workers or any Korean woman who has an interracial relationship with a Western man reflects the dominant view of traditional Korean society, which is deeply related to the strong Confucian morality and ethical norms of womanhood that deny female autonomous subjectivity.

The philosophy of Confucianism is basically concerned with ruling policy for the rulers and emphasizes a strict hierarchical order with gender and class stratifications. In the past, the strong patriarchal code that controls women was typically represented in the "three obedience code," where women were expected to follow father when young, husband when married, and son when old. Male and female were not to mix socially from age seven on, after which the living and social quarters were separated, restricting women from the social and public spheres. There were also "seven seminal sins" for married women that strictly rendered women voiceless and powerless. Until quite recently, women's subjectivity was also severely limited by the Patrilineal Family Law (1948–1990), "which protected men's dominance over women in patrilocal marriage, patriarchal family, and patrilineage kinship in the inheritance of property" (Seungsook Moon 52). It has been changing drastically in contemporary Korean society, but historically the names of the daughters and wives were not specified in the *jokbo*, the book of family lineage. According to Korean cultural tradition, women do not change their last names to those of their husbands when they get married. Many foreigners and even some

Koreans take this as an exemplification of Korean women's autonomy. On the contrary, this signifies another affirmation of patriarchal lineage that does not allow women to be included in the clan bloodline symbolized by family name. It is another stark manifestation of exclusion of women.

Under this androcentric culture, abandoned women without male protectors, such as Chang-gook's mother and her illegitimate son, are relegated to the lowest social status. Chang-gook's mother challenges this stigma by repeating, "Don't ever call my son bastard." Harsh criticism is also given to the centuries-old caste system in the film. In the archery scene where townspeople gather together, Ji-hum's father calls Dog-eye a "butcher" and says, "Current times are good, so you are allowed to compete in archery, once only allowed for landowners." Traditionally butchers occupied the lowest social caste, and they were separated from the community, relegated to the outskirts of the town. By making Dog-eye a butcher, the director criticizes the class consciousness and class gap that is still persistent, despite public denial and negation. In addition, Kim further dramatizes the lowest social status Chang-gook is relegated to by making him Dog-eye's assistant.

Throughout history, the power disparity between colonizing nations and the colonized is very often represented metaphorically in gendered and sexualized terms. This is true of Korea under both Japanese colonialism and U.S. neocolonialism after the Korean War, symbolized by the issues of "comfort women" and military sex workers.[9] In a patriarchal culture that strictly controls women's sexuality under an ideology of chastity and allows women's position and existence only within a space related to men, the colonized Korean female body is taken as "a sign of shame and humiliation" that damages the self-image and masculinity of the Korean male. The same mentality that silenced and effaced the issue of the "comfort women," as Katharine H. S. Moon rightly points out, stigmatizes and also ostracizes military sex workers as social and moral outcasts.[10]

In *Address Unknown*, the director thematizes the racialized and sexualized relationship of the U.S. neocolonial domination over South Korea with the image of a white dog and a yellow one mating on the street. It is also represented by the image of James's military boots, a symbol of colonial military forces, placed side by side on the stepping stone with Eun-ok's small white shoes. The contrast in their size and color becomes a powerful metaphor of the relationship between the masculine military colonizer and the commodified, exploited female body of the colonized.

The prejudice against racial mixing also has deep historical roots in Korean nationalism. Claiming a "single nation" and a "single ethnicity," Korea was traditionally called "a nation of white clothes" symbolizing racial and ethnic purity. As a result, Korean nationalism is basically an exclusionary ideology that does not tolerate others, especially those of other races. This explains the strong clanship and regionalism in Korean society. People show strong resentment against military sex workers and their mixed-race children as the embodiment of the transgression of not only sexual, but also racial taboos, since they imply the sensual meeting of Korean women with the Western masculine power. This resentment is also deeply related to the negative image of U.S. military forces stationed in Korea, which are often associated with race and sex crimes against Koreans. The body of Yun Kum-yi, a Korean military sex worker who was murdered and mutilated by an American GI[11] for example, became "a symbolic site for the violent victimization of the Korean nation and Korean women." Ironically enough, as Hyun Sook Kim points out, "Yun's image was reshaped from the despised 'Western princess' to the national symbol of 'violated woman'" (189).

This case enflamed Korean national consciousness and prompted an ongoing forceful demand for changes in the unequal terms of the United States of America–Republic of Korea Status of Forces Agreement (SOFA), including the terms under which accused American military personnel could be subject to trial in Korean court. It is also worth noticing the changing attitudes of Koreans toward American troops from passive endurance to assertive defiance.[12]

In this film, the sexual violence against women's bodies is symbolically represented by the vivid tattoo on the breast of Chang-gook's mother that reads, "U.S. Army Captain, Michael." Later, James attempts to inscribe his name on Eun-ok's body, too. This symbolic act of permanently marking women's bodies as possessions and commodities is another form of sexual violence and assault that exploits and humiliates women. This is deeply related to the white male fantasy of dominance over submissive Asian women as easily accessible. The hyperfeminized and fetishistic image of Asian women that populates American culture from *Madame Butterfly*, *The World of Suzie Wong*, and *Year of the Dragon*, to *Miss Saigon* is another manifestation of the traditional Orientalist attitudes of Western superiority over the East.[13] This reminds me of an episode I experienced with a shop owner in midtown Manhattan several years ago. After asking where I was from, he said that he knew Korean women very well. His eyes revealed a yearning nostalgia for those years when he was stationed in Korea. His gaze suggested a sort of "I know your kind" look. In his fantasy world, the body of every Korean woman must have been objectified as prostituted. Koreans are deeply concerned that "GIs are getting a distorted and erroneous impression of Korea through their interactions with the Korean nationals in kijichons, i.e., prostitutes, pimps, drug dealers, and other social pariahs" (Moon 153).

Given the historical and cultural origins discussed thus far, it is easy to see how mixed-race children have become the targets of discrimination and prejudice regardless of their color. Many of them leave Korea either by adoption or by acquiring American citizenship.[14] Elizabeth Kim, a white/Korean mixed-raced woman, in her book *Ten Thousand Sorrows: The Extraordinary Journey of a Korean War Orphan*, describes her traumatic early life before she left Korea, adopted by a white American family. Black/Korean mixed-race children, however, experience more severe discrimination. The negative perception Koreans have of African Americans has no doubt been influenced by various means: the negative images of African Americans represented in globalized media around the world today, imported racism and the racial hierarchy from Western imperial powers, and misconceptions through the lack of opportunities for cultural or personal exchange.

In addition, the racial discrimination and the racial tension between whites and blacks within the U.S. military stationed in Korea affect the racial prejudice and attitudes of local Koreans. The segregation in the U.S. military forces is notorious. Even when discrimination was abolished with respect to military jobs, segregation still existed in the U.S. Army. As late as 1951, 30% of U.S. field troops in Korea were segregated. The racial tension and hierarchy between white and black Americans is transferred to the social stratification and self-identities of the military sex workers in camp towns: "Women who fraternized with or sold sexual services to black men were themselves labeled 'black' by Americans and Koreans, and such women faced severe social condemnation and stigmatization by others, including prostitutes who catered to white men" (Moon 144–45).

Cruelty as a Means of Returning Humanity to a Predefiled State

In the archery scene noted earlier, the director also represents collective historical anti-Japanese consciousness by making the shooting target the Japanese national flag, making the film not only a treatise on U.S. imperialism but also one on the longer history of colonialism in Korea. As Kim Ki-duk states, he was quite antagonistic toward U.S. neocolonialism at the beginning, but his attitude toward individual U.S. soldiers changed as he saw the barren and dilapidated environment of the camp town while hunting for shooting locations. The director believes that "the deep-seated military culture and the imperialist sentiments . . . cannot be a matter of one or two U.S. soldiers" (interview). This explains his sympathetic depiction of James' adjustment problems within the army from which he sought an outlet in sex and drugs.

The director's attitude toward U.S. cultural colonialism is more clearly represented in his treatment of the English language in the film. Since the birth of Western imperialism, the study of English is closely related to political and cultural indoctrination, not just "at the level of simple utility" but to "the unconscious level of constructed values" that prioritizes both English and English-speaking people as the "privileging norm" (Ashcroft, Griffiths, and Tiffin 3). In this film, as in Korean society in general, English is a symbol of both power and resentment: Ji-hum's refusal to learn English reflects the director's own attitude. The reason behind this is revealed in Dog-eye's advice to Chang-gook: "Don't be proud of your English fluency too much. If you know it too well, you have to do whatever they want you to do." Eun-ok eventually changes her attitude toward English and eagerly begins to study it as a means to getting an eye operation. When two boys molest Ji-hum and rob him, their "superiority," based on their knowledge of English, is beset by Chang-gook's even better fluency. But in the case of Chang-gook's mother, English becomes proof of her insanity and humiliation when she insists on speaking *only* in English. She represents the internalized psyche of the politically and culturally colonized people in that they believe that they become "more American" or "whiter" if they speak English well. Her pose as superior and her insistence that she is "going to America soon" evoke only ridicule and resentment from the neighbors and from her son. For Chang-gook's mother, English is the only means for her and her son's survival and for achievement of their American dream.

Kim Ki-duk is often compared with Antonin Artaud, "who introduced the theater of cruelty as a means to find a cure for himself and others at the beginning of the 20th century" (biography). His rough and charged visual style is often compared to "prehistoric cave paintings," and he is said to "translate the inner desire of marginalized people into images where shivering self-destruction and sublime lyricism co-exist" (untitled). Filled with destruction, rape, murder, and sadomasochistic cruelty, Kim's films make viewers uncomfortable, one of the main reasons for the extremely divided reactions of critics and audiences. The violence in *Address Unknown*, treated in long and medium shots and sometimes offscreen, is extremely harsh on viewers' emotions, increasing rather than lessening feelings of discomfort. Understandably, in *Address Unknown*, the director wants to dramatize Chang-gook's daily miseries of psychological and physical violence through images of cruelty, and Kim does so unblinkingly. It is extremely harsh on our emotions and the fact that images of violence are often treated in long or medium shots, or sometimes offscreen rather than in detailed close-ups does not lessen our feelings of discomfort.

Even though it is not clear whether the director borrowed the idea of dog beating from the big cultural controversy surrounding the issue,[15] the director repeatedly and graphically depicts Dog-eye and his cruel treatment of dogs as an example of the further degradation of human nature. This explains the why he is represented by only his degrading nickname. By juxtaposing man and animal side by sided, Kim creates a visual metaphor, using various images of animals and juxtapositions of man and dog, to lay bare the dark, animalistic side of human nature. Ji-hum's dying dog, freed by Chang-gook, returns home to the master who sold him to the dog butcher dies, suffering from an arrow fired into his back by Dog-eye. Even a rusted, unburied gun, which symbolizes the fratricide of the Korean Civil War, now ironically becomes a weapon for the war hero to shoot his chicken and for Dog-eye to chase dogs down. These human beings as depicted are less than animals.

In this cultural and economic wasteland, stigmatized as a *kijichon* left behind the "progress" of modernization and industrialization, dogs and dog meat are exchanged as important capital, objects of exploitation for people who are the epitome of the ugliness of snobbery and blind, materialistic greed. The films of Kim Ki-duk are full of the diabolic desire and bloody violence that represent the cruelty of our lives and of the world we live in. They have to be taken, according to the director, as "a sacrifice for returning humanity to a state before being defiled by a cruel reality" (biography). In *Address Unknown*, the only hope for humanity remains in the hearts of the younger generation, whose attitudes toward animals show quite a contrast to those of the adults. All three teenagers show genuine care and love for dogs: Ji-hum loves his dog dearly; Chang-gook frees Ji-hum's dog after it was sold to Dog-eye (a good deed, for which Chang-gook is severely beaten and chained by Dog-eye); and Eun-ok finds comfort from her complex-ridden circumstances in play with her puppy, which sinisterly extends to masturbation, a scene that is much criticized by Korean feminists. Their criticism is justified in the sense that the director tends to describe every woman as a nymphomaniac or promiscuous in his films. But this problematic scene could be taken as one of a rite of passage, a girl reaching toward an exploration of her own sexuality. Moreover, the scene is not loaded with any sexual implication for the audience, since it is composed as a frame with frames, seen through Ji-hum's peeping eyes. Most sexual scenes in the film do not allow much voyeuristic pleasure for viewers, as they are long shots or offscreen. The vinyl house, a green house, which is common in the countryside of Korea, is utilized as a place of secret romance when Ji-hum tries to express his love for Eun-ok, but soon transforms itself into a site of violent crime when Eun-ok is raped by two boys who have tormented Ji-hum. The vinyl house provides an effective visual masking by blurring and cutting off sight but not sound. In the scene where Eun-ok chases the boys who ridicule her, she catches not only the boys by surprise but the viewers as well, by violently breaking through the vinyl wall. It is one of the most grotesque scenes in the film. She terrorizes the boys with the image of her uncovered, exaggerated, and blind white eye.

The depictions of violence in Kim Ki-duk's films are not just visual and aural. Instead, they often disturb all of our sensory and nerve mechanisms in a form of synesthesia. By tormenting all our five senses they sometimes seem to test the limits of our sensitivity. For example, the falling drops of blood in the dog-beating scene in *Address Unknown* and the live fish with flesh cut out in *The Isle* are images beyond the entertaining visual violence of American commercial cinema. Sometimes these images provoke a much more bizarre sense of grotesqueness since they are placed in settings full of sublime beauty and lyricism. The image of water so clean and clear, traditionally symbolizing life and rebirth, is spoiled by hidden violence and death in *The Isle*. Similarly, in *Address Unknown* water is soiled, a blood-thick, muddy, and rotten puddle reflecting the distorted image of a beaten dog and, later, the tragic/comic image of Dog-eye, hung by the dogs. In this film, degraded human nature does not need even the disguise of surface beauty and purity.

The director is particularly talented in transforming the colloquial expressions of the folk into his own imagery. For example, he utilizes common expressions such as *hooked on love* and *hooked on men* and transforms them into the images of an actual fishhook that is repeatedly utilized by the voiceless female with violence in *The Isle*. In *Address Unknown* he translates the expression *live like a dog, and die like a dog* to describe the life and death of Dog-eye. When Dog-eye is persecuted by the dogs, his image is the exact replica of the dogs he has beaten to death.

Almost all the female characters in Kim Ki-duk's filmography are prostitutes or, if not, made into them as in the case of *The Villain* (2002). This is the main reason why he is despised by Korean feminist film critics, who describe him as "a specter of misogyny" and a "good-for-nothing filmmaker" (biography). Does his attitude simply represent the totality of the Korean male chauvinism against women? Instead of simply criticizing Kim Ki-duk for his degraded representation of female characters, it might be more interesting and meaningful to observe him from a different, if not more subversive, angle.

The director's reaction to the harsh criticism against him and his work as an "anxiety the mainstream tends to have towards the non-mainstream" (interview) is significant. In his attempt to separate his ideology and aesthetics from those of mainstream commercial directors, he attempts to deconstruct the middle-class ideology taken for granted and challenges the fixed, rigidly defined moral and ethical "norms" of Korean society. The nameless and voiceless female characters in *The Isle* (she does not speak a single line throughout the film) and in *Address Unknown*

(Chang-gook's mother does not have her own name and is only identified as mother) both show symptoms of hysteria and madness. What forces turn them into monstrous, violent, dangerous, and grotesque figures—one putting fishing hooks into her own vagina and the other eating her dead son's flesh? What do their symptoms of female hysteria imply socially and politically? The mad women and their hysterical symptoms may reprise a long-repressed history of female subjectivity and sexuality in Korean society. The prostituted women in Kim Ki-duk's films can be read as mocking the ideology of chastity and the respectability Korean culture has cherished and imposed on women for so long.

Culturally and socially marginalized and ostracized, these women remain nameless and invisible through a history of subjugation and exploitation. As cheap laborers and sex workers, they endure deep-rooted prejudices against their commodified and objectified bodies. Through the representation of these characters, Kim seems to deconstruct the dichotomies of moral/immoral, good/evil, chaste/promiscuous, college girl/prostitute. Exerting the twisted and displaced power of madness and grotesqueness, they desperately attempt to turn themselves into self-determined individuals of their own autonomous subjectivity and sexuality. In this sense, Kim's films can be interpreted as antiheroic farces, criticizing the dehumanizing cultural assumptions against marginalized women. As Hyun Sook-kim explains in her study of *yanggongju*, we need to deconstruct "the totalizing, uni-dimensional images" of these women and acknowledge them as working women. To do so, we have to free ourselves from "middle-class cultural and political norms" (180).

The Vicious Circle: Fallacious Reasoning of Marginalization

The U.S. military camp town as represented in this film creates its own microcosm within the larger social systems and functions outside of mainstream society, with its own historical and cultural background. The individual lives of the three forlorn teenagers are predetermined by factors that affect not only how they live but also how their identities are constructed in the public and private spheres. None of them can escape the inevitable tragedy of his or her condition as hinted by the director's statement: "To me the three characters in this film are just like the abandoned letters of my childhood. They are the children of an era which is yet to be received" (interview).

Ji-hum, the filmmaker's persona, is a feminized and vulnerable high school dropout who is alienated and isolated from his peers. He is overshadowed by his war-hero father whose present is completely dominated by his past. Lacking courage and articulation, he quietly observes the social injustices around him without commenting or taking action. He cannot articulate his love for Eun-ok except by watching her through a peephole. His only means of self-expression and communication is through painting. The humiliation and the guilt of helplessly watching Eun-ok raped and transformed into a prostitute brings a sudden change in him that makes him violently retaliate against his tormentors and Eun-ok's lover/benefactor James. Ji-hum has to pay for his regained manhood and violence-defined masculinity, however, and finally ends up in jail.

For Eun-ok, the vicious circle starts with her brother's wooden gun, a relic of military culture, which damages Eun-ok's eye, turning her into a version of young Chang-gook's mother. Her scarred body becomes an object of exchange through her sexual relationship with James, an American soldier who has problems adjusting to the military life abroad, often expressed in his violence toward Eun-ok. The painted eye that James places over Eun-ok's blinded one represents the fantasy of Western beauty and the implied American dream for her. James represents the typical colonizer, a benefactor with political and economic power who can provide an eye operation. Ironically, Eun-ok regains her insight into her identity and subjectivity through self-mutilation of her newly healed eye in one of the film's most violent scenes. Will there be any hope for Ji-hum and Eun-ok? Such is suggested by their brief encounter before Ji-hum is put into jail. The scene in which Ji-hum makes peace with his father by pinning the military medal back on his father suggests that Ji-hum may endure and prevail through his humanity and his suffering, like the director himself.

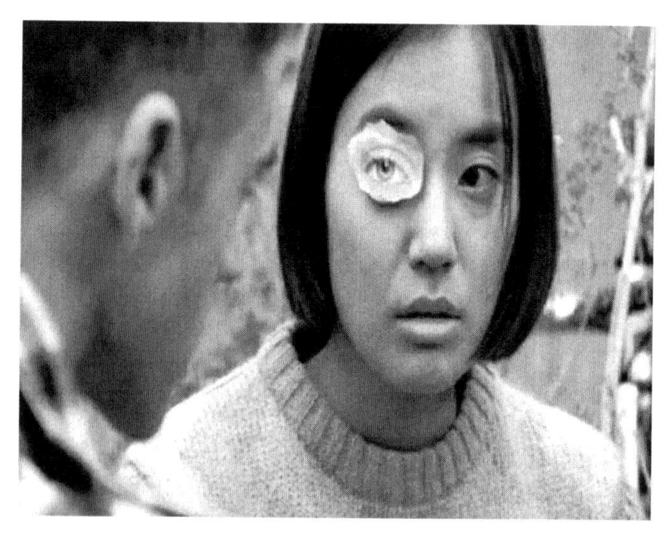

Figure 12.2. The Western ideal of beauty clashes with wounds of neocolonialism.

For Chang-gook, there is no escape from the inevitable circle that must be completed. The image of Chang-gook confined to a dog cage on the back of Dog-eye's motorcycle early in the film is a powerful signifier of the inhuman treatment he has to endure and the low social status to which he is relegated. It also foretells his fate as a permanent victim. No matter where he runs or how many times he tries to escape, he comes back to Dog-eye. As a social outcast, he is "a problem" or causes problems because of his "difference." Dog-eye and Chang-gook are bound together with a vicious karmic chain, and neither can break free without destroying the other. The circle that Chang-gook tries to break is powerfully represented by the image of the motorcycle wheel to which he is later handcuffed.

The murder of Dog-eye has multiple implications for Chang-gook. It could be seen simply as revenge for the inhuman cruelty and violence inflicted upon him and dogs. The ironic mirroring of Dog-eye's death, in the same manner as the dogs he butchers, proves this assumption. But many viewers remain puzzled about the true motive behind the violent murder. Literally and symbolically, Dog-eye, as the militarily clothed boyfriend of Chang-gook's mother, is a father figure for Chang-gook. Even though a violent villain himself, he shows genuine tenderness and sympathy for Chang-gook's mother and understands her pain. He chides Chang-gook: "Don't you have any pity for her, the poor wretched woman who has to raise you?" As a father figure, he tries to teach Chang-gook how to cope with the world, such as how to win in an eye-to-eye confrontation,

Figure 12.3. Chang-gook symbolically constrained by race and class.

even with dogs. Though he brutally retaliates against Chang-gook when the boy sets Ji-hum's dog free, Dog-eye does show some concern for the boy: "Poor kid, how can you live in this world, soft-hearted like that?" Through the murder of Dog-eye, his surrogate father figure, Chang-gook kills his own American father who abandoned him and his mother. As he repeatedly states to his mother in the film: "Don't mention him to me. I will kill him when I meet him."

Chang-gook is very much criticized for his violence toward his mother, but we need to be reminded of his humanity. He always protects Ji-hum and cannot beat the dogs as he is ordered to, even though he is beaten up by Dog-eye because of it. His violence toward his mother is always related to her quasi-insane actions, as when she continually takes pictures of him to send in letters to his American father, letters that keep coming back stamped "address unknown" or when she is involved in street fighting, stealing the neighbor's vegetables, or insisting on speaking in English. His final act of violence inflicted on his mother before he commits suicide puzzles many viewers. In this scene, the bloody violence shocks many viewers too much for them to realize the real intention of Gang-gook's action. He performs the act with a pathos of heartbreaking love and sympathy, which suggests it is the only thing he can do for his mother before he leaves her alone in the world. Cleansing his mother's body before he cuts "U.S. Army Captain, Michael" away is a symbolic baptizing for a rebirth of his mother as a new and different woman, unburdened by an illegitimate mixed-race son. He knows that the only way she can go on living is by literally cutting her ties to and her yearning for his black father. Out of his desperate love for his mother, he wants to restore her sanity and secure her place in the world of reality.

Chang-gook's suicide attempt is successful, and the image of his dead body pitched headlong, half buried in a frozen rice paddy, is so tragic that it is becomes rather comic. It is precisely this kind of image that has become one of the director's trademarks. We see the same tragic/comic image when earlier all three teens walk together, white bandages on their eyes. The real tragedy is represented by Chang-gook's mother's grief-stricken, seemingly endless search for Chang-gook's body, expressed through the image of the water in the rice paddy going from water, to snow, and finally to ice. Chang-gook's mother has to thaw the frozen earth to dig him out. As the sole family member, she cannot allow even Ji-hum to touch or be near her son. This absolute refusal of Ji-hum's help heightens the tragedy of their lives. According to the director, the inverted half-ditched image is expressive of "Chang-gook's wish to belong to this land and at the same time rejecting it" (interview), but this interpretation seems too elaborate. Rather, it seems to me that Chang-gook has been completely violated and is now finally ditched in the desolate plains after being thrown away all his life. As an unwanted bastard son, claimed neither by his father's country nor accepted by his mother's, he is swept away by the wind and thrust into the bottom of the rice fields just like his mother's returned letters stamped "address unknown."

Even though throughout the film Chang-gook is determined not to show his sorrow through tears, his mother still understands him: his love and violence toward her, his love and hate toward his father, and his despair. She also understands that she is the only person he can hit back and the only way he knows to deal with his frustrations is with violence. She keeps saying to Dog-eye: "That poor little kid, don't ever hit him. I'll kill you first." Her grotesqueness owes much to the last scene, which implies that she eats the flesh of her dead son. The image of Chang-gook's mother as a literal "devouring mother" has several implications. For her, Chang-gook's body is part of her own. Like Eva in Toni Morrison's *Sula*, who burned her beloved son whom she could not "get back in" her womb again, Chang-gook's mother, by devouring her son's body, symbolically unbirths him. She subconsciously may not want to leave any trace of him on the land that refused to accept him. By setting fire to the bus they live in, she erases all traces of them both.

Saying the Unspeakable and Touching the Untouchable

The historical records show that the phobia and discrimination against miscegenation is not limited to Korea and Korean people, as Gary Nash discusses in his search for the hidden history of mixed race in America:

> We read in amazement that before World War II, the Australian government systematically tore the children of European-Aboriginal marriages away from parents in the belief that placing the children in orphanages was the only hope of salvaging doomed and probably defective children of ill-advised interracial love. We shake our heads at new books describing the sterilization of hundreds of thousands of women not just in Nazi Germany but in the United States, Sweden, Norway, Denmark, Finland, Canada, and Britain in this century in order to protect the racial purity of these nations. (ix)

In modern times, we are relieved to see that the antimiscegenation sentiment is not so blatant, but we also know that it continues in subtler forms. But in the case of Korea, discrimination is still persistent because of its specific historical and cultural background, rather than indigenous racial dynamics. The corrosive effect of the multiple prejudices, ostracism, and marginalization experienced by mixed-race children is not their individual problem but is related to the whole structure of Korean society.[16]

To survive in this globalized world, we cannot isolate ourselves any more by sticking to the age-old, rigid, nationalistic ideology, and Koreans are no exception. In Korean society, Confucian ethics still consciously or unconsciously govern daily lives in both public and private spheres. Recently Korean scholar Kim Kyung-il strongly stated that "Confucius must die for this country to live," in his very controversial book of the same title. As he rightly points out, Confucian morality is basically meant for politics rather than human beings, and results in political deceit and hypocrisy that encourages factionalism and regionalism, patriarchy that stifles women and youth, authoritarian hierarchy and an educational system that erases creativity in youth, and class stratification that marginalizes the powerless and the dispossessed (7–8). To be a citizen in a new era that increasingly requires exchanges across national, cultural, racial, and ethnic borders we have to cultivate cosmopolitan consciousness and acceptance for others with "difference." Instead of insisting on a single unitary identity, Korean society has to welcome the diversity within it. Prejudice against a marginalized group, whether it is related to class, race, ethnicity, or gender, is another projection of the psyche of the colonized victim, signifying the need for the other.

Most of the characters in Kim Ki-duk's filmography are people bruised by various systems of oppression that relegate them to poverty, obscurity, and even death. By representing those whom he calls "his own people," the director dares to air the dark side of Korean society people want to ignore. Through his rough and shocking sociocultural analyses, Kim succeeds in forcing people to face the problems hidden behind the myths of egalitarianism and economic and social development. By addressing the issue of miscegenation and mixed-race children, a symbol of the legacy of the Korean War, in *Address Unknown*, Kim is sending a clear message that history is not the past but the present; and, without a real confrontation with history, especially the dark and shameful past, we will just repeat it in the future.

By unveiling the fallacious reasoning of those who seek to marginalize others, the director challenges the ideology and cultural assumptions of middle-class, mainstream Korean society. For Kim Ki-duk, filmmaking is a process of "kidnapping the mainstream into his own space, then introducing himself as a fellow human being who asks to shake hands" (biography). The mainstream does not seem to be willing to shake hands with him, however, as proven by the commercial failure of *Address Unknown* and his other films. Ironically, the very reason he was rejected makes him one of the most important film directors in contemporary Korean cinema. He says the unspeakable and touches the untouchable.

Notes

1. Refer to www.kimkiduk.com for the information cited in the text as biography, filmography, interviews, and untitled document.

2. The characters in Kim's films are usually defined as marginal or social misfits, a life the director has shared. His adolescent life had nothing to do with the refined culture of the mainstream society. His early life was filled with poverty and alienation: born and raised in a small mountain town, he moved to Seoul at the age of nine. After he was forced to quit junior high, he had no formal education. After working in factories, he joined the marines and served for five years as a noncommissioned officer, which provided material for the rich details of brotherhood in his films. Different from other filmmakers, Kim is familiar with the mass of people who hardly know a path to self-redemption because they are so used to despair and degradation. Yet the director tries to find hope for them, evidenced in his films full of imaginative and attractive graphic images. It is interesting to note that the filmmaker's personas in his films are artists, all carrying a symbol of fragile hope such as a bird, a goldfish, or a turtle (biography).

3. Throughout human history incest and miscegenation are regarded as *the* most horrible sexual taboos in most cultures: "Incest proper, and its metaphorical form as the violation of a minor, even combines in some countries with its direct opposite, inter-racial sexual relations, an extreme form of exogamy, as the two most powerful inducements to horror and collective vengeance." Claude Levi-Strauss, *The Elementary Structures of Kinship* rev. ed. trans. James Harle Bell, John Richard von Sturmer, and Rodney Needham (Boston: Beacon, 1969) 10.

4. Section 69 of California's Civil Code refused marriage licenses to whites and "Mongolians, Negroes, mulattoes and persons of mixed blood." *Asian American Studies: A Reader*, ed. Jean Yu Wen, Shen Wu, and Min Song (New Brunswick: Rutgers University Press, 2000) xxv.

5. "Venice Film Festival Pays Attention to 'Address Unknown' " UP, August 31, 2001, quoted in www.kimkiduk.com.

6. For the political and historical details of this period of Korean history, refer to chapter 18, Carter J. Eckert, Ki-baik Lee, Young Ick-lew, Michael Robinson, Edward W. Wagner, eds., *Korea Old and New: A History* (Seoul: lchokak, Pub. For Korea Institute, Harvard University, 1990).

7. General Yi Song-gye founded the Yi Dynasty against Koryo in 1392, which ended in 1910 after the Japanese takeover. During this period Chinese cultural influence represented by neo-Confucianism, more than any other period, came into Korea. In some ways, Korea became even more Confucian than China, and Buddhism, which was the main political and cultural influence during the Koryo Dynasty, declined greatly. For the details, refer to Rhoads Murphey, *East Asia: A New History* (New York: Longman, 2001) 182–87.

8. Quoted in Han Kyung-ah, "The Realities and Problems on the Amerasians in Korea," master's thesis, Hyosung Women's University, 1994, 8.

9. For detailed discussions and analyses of the issue of the comfort women, see Chungmoo Choi, "Nationalism and Construction of Gender in Korea," and Hyunah Yang, "Re-membering the Korean Military Comfort Women: Nationalism, Sexuality, and Silencing," both in *Dangerous Women: Gender and Korean*

Nationalism, ed. Elaine H. Kim and Chungmoo Choi (New York and London: Routledge, 1998) 9–32, 123–40.

10. Since they arose under completely different historical circumstances, we cannot associate the comfort women who were forcibly drafted under the Japanese imperialistic colonial state with the military sex workers driven into the job driven by financial need, as Katharine H. S. Moon points out: "To make the analogies between the dominated and conquered state of a nation and the bodies of individual women makes sense in the case of Japanese imperialism in Korea and 'comfort women' of the 1940s. The Japanese did have effective, 'colonialized' control over Korea. The Japanese military did 'recruit' and deploy tens of thousands of Korean women, which was humiliating and shameful to Koreans. But in the case of U.S. camptown prostitution, such an analogy is not accurate" (167).

11. See also "Great Army, Great Father," Ahn Il-soon, in *A Report on the Violation of Human Rights on Women and Children by U.S. Military Forces in Korea.*

12. Oh Yon-ho in "Make Us Sad No More!" (1990), "describes the changing attitudes of Koreans toward American troops between September 1945, the end of Japanese colonialism and the beginning of American occupation of Korea. In 1945, those Koreans injured or assaulted by U.S. soldiers quietly endured the military crimes. During the 1960s and 1970s, victimized Koreans began to challenge soldiers verbally and shout back: 'Why do you hit instead of talking?' since 1987, with the rise of strong anti-American sentiments, Koreans have begun to cry out, 'Yankee Go Home!' " Quoted in Hyun Sook-kim, 188.

13. For the images of Asian women in American films, see Marchetti.

14. See "Is Mixed Blood a Curse?" *Sisa Journal*, April 27, 1995.

The citizenship for mixed-race children was legally sanctioned by the Amerasian Immigration Law, passed in October 1982 under the Reagan administration, but it was limited by birth date.

15. Since around the time of the Olympic Games, held in Seoul in 1988, Korean people became the targets of severe criticism for eating dog meat and for dog beating. Some Koreans do eat dog meat, although traditionally forbidden for Buddhists, a practice shared by some other cultures.

16. For more details, see "Different Blood . . . It was a Curse!" *Hangyorae* 21.360 (May 31, 2001): 39 published by Hangyorae News.

Works Cited

Ahn Il-soon. "Great Army, Great Father," *A Report on the Violation of Human Rights on Women and Children by U.S. Military Forces in Korea.* Seoul: Doo Rae-bang, 1995. 13–25.

Anzaldua, Gloria. *Making Face, Making Soul, Haciendo Caras: Creative and Critical Perspectives by Women of Color.* San Francisco: Aunt Lute, 1990.

Ashcroft, Bill, Gareth Griffiths, and Helen Tiffin, eds. *The Empire Writes Back: Theory and Practice in Post-colonial Literatures.* London and New York: Routledge, 1989.

Chung Hee-sang. Is Mixed Blood a Curse?" *Sisa Journal* (Apr. 27, 1995): 50–55.
Chungmoo Choi, "Nationalism and Construction of Gender in Korea." *Dangerous Women: Gender and Korean Nationalism*. Ed. Elaine H. Kim and Chungmoo Choi. New York: Routledge, 1998. 9–32.
Eckert, Carter J., Ki-baik Lee, Young Ick-lew, Michael Robinson, and Edward W. Wagner, eds. *Korea Old and New: A History*. Seoul: lchokak, Publication for the Korea Institute, Harvard University, 1990.
Han Kyung-ah. "The Realities and Problems on the Amerasians in Korea." Master's thesis, Hyosung Women's University, 1994.
Jean Yu-wen, Shen Wu, and Min Song, eds. *Asian American Studies: A Reader*. New Brunswick: Rutgers University Press, 2000.
Kim, Elaine H., and Chungmoo Choi, eds. *Dangerous Women: Gender and Korean Nationalism*. New York and London: Routledge, 1998.
Kim Ki-duk Web site. www.kimkiduk.com.
Kim, Hyun-sook. "Yanggongju as an Allegory of the Working-class Women in Popular Radical Texts." (See intro in *Dangerous Women* below.) 175–202.
Kim, Kyung Il. *Confucius Must Die for This Country to Live*. Seoul: Bada, 1999.
Levi-Strauss, Claude. *The Elementary Structures of Kinship*. Rev. ed. Trans. James Harle Bell, John Richard von Sturmer, and Rodney Needham. Boston: Beacon, 1969.
Marchetti, Gina. *Romance and the Yellow Peril*. Berkeley: University of California Press, 1994.
Moon, Katharine H. S. "Prostitute Bodies and Gendered States." In *Dangerous Women: Gender and Korean Nationalism*. Ed. Elaine H. Kim and Chungmoo Choi. New York: Routledge, 1998. 141–74.
Moon, Seong-suk. "Begetting the Nation: The Androcentric Discourse of National History and Tradition in South Korea." *Dangerous Women: Gender and Korean Nationalism*. Ed. Elaine H. Kim and Chungmoo Choi. New York: Routledge, 1997. 33–66.
Murphey, Rhoads. *East Asia: A New History*. New York: Longman, 2001.
Nash, Gary B. *Forbidden Love: The Secret History of Mixed-Race America*. New York: Holt, 1999.
Oh Yon-ho. *Make Us Sad No More!* Seoul: Paeksan Sodang, 1990.
Won Jae-son. "Different Blood, . . . It was a Curse!" *Hangyorae* 21.360 (May 31, 2001). Published by Hangyorae News. 38–41.
Yang Hyunah. "Re-membering the Korean Military Comfort Women: Nationalism, Sexuality, and Silencing." *Dangerous Women: Gender and Korean Nationalism*. Ed. Elaine H. Kim and Chungmoo Choi. New York: Routledge, 1998. 123–40.

13

DIANE CARSON

Transgressing Boundaries

From Sexual Abuse to Eating Disorders in *301/302*

DESPITE THE DISTINGUISHING details of this and an array of other culturally specific narratives discussed in illuminating analytical studies of diverse national cinemas, women's exhibition of eating disorders as one response to sexual trauma crosses borders and cultures. As resonant with overarching metaphoric content and tropes of nationalism as it is closely focused on personal worlds gone awry, *301/302* extracts and explores a rich, revealing spectacle of gender resistance and collapse without sacrificing more far-reaching implications of a national identity in crisis. Myopically preoccupied with their own *pas de deux*, the characters known by their apartment numbers 301 and 302 reverberate symbolically as an unsettling revelation of the boundaries of contemporary resistance to personal (or national) subjugation. The exhilarating achievement of *301/302*, resides, however, in the deeply moving, often claustrophobic interaction of the principals in their dramatic encounters and their immovable, even obsessive-compulsive, positions. Ultimately, the visceral and emotional impact of the collision of genders, and by implication between cultures, undulates with personal and political force. The personal is political in both an individual as well as a national sense.

In *301/302*, his twelfth feature film, producer/director Park Chul-soo highlights the divergent dysfunctional responses of two women living in adjoining apartments in a Seoul housing complex. Though they react to significantly different, humiliating sexual events, both women display an internalized psychological and emotional destabilization that prompts self-destructive behavior: one woman cannot eat anything without gagging and vomiting, and the other obsesses over cooking and eating until it defines her life. One woman remains passively incapable of defense; the other expresses her rage through violent action. To locate the film in South Korea's rich context, each woman's internalization of her trauma invites historical analogies with varied South Korean events. *301/302* presents, then, a specific narrative focused on the powerlessness of two sexually victimized women who displace their neuroses into eating disorders and a metaphorical commentary on the counterproductive consequences of a victimization legacy.

The Film: Its Content and Context

Winner of the 1995 Grand Bell Award for Best Film in Korea, an official selection for both the 1996 Sundance Film Festival and the 1996 Berlin International Film Festival, and the South Korean nominee for a foreign-language film Academy Award,[1] *301/302* carries impressive endorsements merited by daring content and unique style. Moreover, it employs a disjointed narrative, which requires the viewer, like the investigating detective who serves as the catalyst for unraveling the story, to piece together the causes and effects of the central characters' behavior. In so doing, *301/302* involves the viewer in deeply disturbing ways, making it difficult, if not impossible, to watch casually. For as intriguing as the intellectual participation to organize and understand the catalyst for each woman's obsessive-compulsive behavior is the visceral impact. While the interrogation of 302 by 301 piques viewers' curiosity, the equally intense preoccupation with food effects a reaction as personal as it is unusual; that is, so often plots stage character transactions during meals. But the food seldom becomes the means whereby neuroses are painfully probed and power (to accept or refuse food) nakedly wielded. In addition, each viewer's own functional or dysfunctional relationship to food factors into the equation or lurks in the background. Especially for American audiences, given the fixation on achieving and maintaining desirable weight, healthy and unhealthy food fads, and debates about matters as basic as nutritional requirements, it is difficult to imagine anyone indifferent to the central subject matter, and choices in art direction intensify the impact.

The claustrophobic confinement of most of the film's action to sterile apartments (the husband and wife's apartment as well as apartments 301 and 302) complements, as it emphasizes, the lives of the abnormally isolated women. Within this restricted and restrictive environment, snippets of memory occasionally intrude into consciousness, immersing the viewer in the women's interactive stimulus-response, stream-of-consciousness pattern as the film's unrelenting focus on food parallels the women's obsessions. And for the duration of the film, viewers will share this fixation with apprehensive anticipation. One of the most basic of all human needs—nutritional sustenance—becomes *the* catalyst for self-destructive behavior. And whoever we are, our own more or less satisfactory association with food implicates our deepest psychological and emotional nature. What could be, under quite different circumstances, delectable dishes become unappetizing by the conclusion of the opening credit sequence. By contrast, films as diverse as *Tampopo* (Itami Juzo 1985), *Babette's Feast* (Gabriel Axel 1987), *Like Water for Chocolate* (Alfonso Arau 1992), *Eat Drink Man Woman* (Ang Lee 1994), and, to reach back to a legendary example, *Tom Jones* (Tony Richardson 1963) trade on the food-sex association with appetizing indulgence and riotous joyfulness, exploiting the visceral reaction easily prompted. However, none of these films, as good as they are, implicates sexual dysfunction as *301/302* thoroughly and assuredly does.

In *301/302* our emotional involvement is initiated in the opening seconds of the film. Beginning before and interrupting the credits, tantalizing visual teasers encapsulate the fuller explanation parceled out in succeeding confessional encounters. Through the brief narrative flashbacks for 301 and 302 and an additional prolonged flashback for 301 (a nearly thirty-minute sequence that begins one hour into the film), memories intrude to reveal gradually but inexorably the physical events precipitating the psychological neuroses. Director Park lays out ingredients of the psychiatric problems with the measured care of a gourmet chef. He probes the underlying cause of 302's anorexia and the guilt of 301's bingeing.

Cinematically, the distortion of several fish-eye lens shots signals the abnormal perspective of each woman. A slyly moving camera that reframes shots encourages slight readjustments of our own perspective as the story unfolds in its nonlinear fashion. In a precise and careful translation of content to style, with camera moves as controlled and calculated as the women's behavior, Park mixes extreme close-ups with high-angle long shots, direct address to the camera with disembodied voiceover interpretation. The self-conscious art direction highlights the women's emotional register with 301's exceedingly organized kitchen an indication of her control fixation and 302's orderly office a sign of her sexual destitution. Consistent in enforcing this revealing color design, the sterile white of 301's husband's office mirrors his unresponsiveness. The blood red glow of 302's parents' butcher shop and the raw meat roughly handled express the elemental animal action taking place there. Balancing the visual regime with aural reinforcement, background music, and sound, consistently forceful and seldom inconspicuous, heightens emotion. Never mindlessly conventional or calculatingly invisible in his style, Park refuses to let us relax into a complacent spectatorial position or to follow a reassuring, predictable narrative line.

His challenge to and involvement of the viewer begin with the extremely fragmented opening credit sequence. This introduction, containing close-ups of food being aggressively prepared and discarded, announces the focus and style of the film through disjointed shots with food as the unifying theme. On our initial viewing of *301/302*, as the plot unfolds, we may gradually realize that the opening foreshadows in tone and content the major theme—the intense emotional connections between sex and food, food and control. But it is more likely, so obtuse are the connections among the abrupt shots, each separated from the succeeding shot with white credits on a black background, that only upon a second or even a third viewing will we realize we have witnessed a virtual synopsis of the film in the first few minutes.

This credit sequence begins with a white wall and a tilt down to a girl, facing forward, sitting with knees bent, intoning in a singsong voice, "My refrigerator is always filled with food, but I never eat it cold." As proof of her words, a shot of the refrigerator shows food cramming the shelves. The subsequent tilt up shows this girl (we will learn she is 301) standing on a stack of books to reach the table, slicing a cucumber with a large knife, an action echoed late in the film again by 301.

Figure 13.1. *301/302* (Park Chul-soo 1995).

The quick cut to and sound of a meat saw shearing through bright red meat jarringly follows, with another voice (that of 302) announcing that her huge refrigerator is always full of red meat. In addition to her gender and age connecting her with the previous girl, she is similarly squatting against a wall. After a person we presume is her mother (we do not see the face) walks past her and comes back with meat, the girl walks off camera in the direction of the meat locker. A fade to black ends these very brief introductions to two girls and their monologues about food. Foreshadowing more dire associations to come, even at this early stage, little of the food looks appealing. Further, neither the insistent music accompanying the first credit nor the broken egg that falling onto a knife and a cleaver relieves the mood so quickly established. Our curiosity and a growing tension are sustained through shots of a boiling pot, prepared food, sterile shelves of dishes, leftovers tossed into the garbage, a knife thrown into a sink, and other close-up shots, including one of what might be dripping blood. Only in retrospect, at the film's end, do we understand the two girls have become women whose lives intertwine with food as problematic anchor.

As the credits conclude, the story proper begins. A police detective arrives at Kang Song-hee's apartment 301 to announce his investigation of the disappearance of Kim Yoon-hee, the resident of apartment 302. Through a series of dialogues with 301 (they are most often referred to by their apartment numbers, another powerfully dehumanizing element), the detective elicits details of the relationship between 301 and 302. Brief flashbacks and flashbacks within flashbacks reveal the reasons for their present situation. 301 keeps a food diary, cooks gourmet meals, obsesses over her weight gain, and uses food as a weapon. Recently divorced, she struggled to keep her husband emotionally attentive and sexually interested through elaborate meals. When she discovered he was having an affair, feeling angry and trapped, she killed and cooked their dog, Chong Chong, an appalling and offensive retaliation. For Chong Chong, her husband showed unwavering affection even as his irritation with 301 increased. On several occasions, treating Chong Chong as a substitute child, he directs his wife to bathe the dog since she "has nothing else to do all day." 301 transforms the object of his affection into food, completing a disturbing rivalry for her husband's affection into a production of her own obsession. For 301, as for many gourmet cooks, the very act of cooking takes on fetishistic importance of its own. The activity becomes divorced from anything but its own intrinsic and symbolic meaning. Killing Chong Chong, making him part of her culinary creations, is 301's way of communicating. Cooking becomes her voice, killing and preparing a taboo dish her protest.

Knowing none of this, the investigator begins his interrogation in 301's kitchen, where he eats the best "chicken" he's ever had and drinks 301's wine. Responding to his question about male guests of 302, 301 immediately establishes the food/sex parallel, saying, "Yoon-hee refused sex as well as food." As the detective searches 302's apartment, Yoon-hee appears, or more accurately, her presence is visualized (since the detective does not see her), in several shots.

After he discovers a bottle of pills while searching apartment 302, we hear a male voiceover explaining that the pills are for a mental eating disorder, that the patient relates love or sex with food, and that food is a tool for controlling love. The clear message is imaginatively interjected through the densely layered information: a detective investigates, Yoon-hee appears in 302, an unidentified knowledgeable man (perhaps a psychiatrist) relates a conventional interpretation of sex/love and food. Explicitly and implicitly, the sex/food connection is established and then embellished. Sex, illness, and food conflate into dysfunctional behavior with the proposed solution a pharmaceutical prescription. However, the equation lamentably does not include the myriad of other variables affecting the disorder.

The intensity of the yin-yang personalities and the unflinching depiction of the unsavory elements make *301/302* a courageous, even astonishing, presentation. Its streamlined focus benefits from the exclusion of diversions while, arguably, suffering for its narrowness of purpose; that is, it is microscopic but also myopic. The film steadfastly refuses to succumb to the titillating or voyeuristic aspects of sex or the sensory appeal of food. By contrast with the more familiar use of food as an enticement to and enhancement of sexual pleasure, *301/302* follows a rare agenda. If films as different as *Tom Jones* (British), *9 1/2 Weeks* (1986, American), *Like Water for Chocolate* (Mexican), and *Strawberry and Chocolate* (1994, Cuban) exploit the sexually seductive aspects of food, where are the films dramatizing the behavior channeled as a result of sexual abuse into dysfunctional eating habits? In the international cinematic arena, most filmmakers prefer to ignore the disturbing material Park confronts through the dynamic interaction of 301 and 302 and through its unnerving intensity.

To signal and heighten the unconventional friction between 301 and 302, Park uses offbeat angles, overhead shots, camera tilts and arcs, and fish-eye shots through 302's keyhole as Song-hee moves into 301. In the next sequence, as Yoon-hee and Song-hee pass, going in opposite directions, outside the apartment building, we hear their internal monologue as voiceover. Song-hee notes 302's excessive thinness, "She's like a mannequin," while 302 thinks 301's breasts could "feed a hundred men. Such a pig." In other words, one is perceived as a lifeless body; the other is insulted as mammary excess. Neither is accidentally or inconsequentially so perceived.

Figure 13.2. A view from behind the door.

Working at her computer, 302 remembers a sexual attack, presented in a suffused red light. Neatly arranging her dishes, 301 looks off camera as we cut to a thematically motivated flashback. We again see 301 packing her plates and cups in preparation for leaving her husband as he calmly says he will miss her cooking and remembers, "I even ate a dog." Like pieces of a jigsaw puzzle, 301's and 302's dichotomous associations for food and sex will intensify but change little from the memories revealed in the first fifteen minutes of the film. What will change is the cat-and-mouse interaction between 301 and 302, 302's attempts to avoid and repulse 301, and 301's aggressive intrusion.

Song-hee is completely aware of the food-sex interdependency and explicitly identifies it early in her interaction with 302. In one of her early attempts to entice 302 to eat, she offers her sausage mignon. When 302 says, "No, thank you. Especially not sausage," 301 replies, "You must not like sex. Were you raped? Not me. I crave it as much as cooking. I enjoyed having sex with my ex-husband even without love." As 301 speaks off camera, 302 gags and convulses on screen. Walking back into the background, 301 continues to eat the sausage until 302 takes one more look at her and, choking, hurries out of her office. The next shot continues our disorientation. There are no immediate indications that 301 is now alone and back in her apartment as she addresses the camera and counters, "Sex isn't disgusting, love is." Thus inverting the usual judgment that idealizes love over sex, 301 asserts a surprising physical preference. Such an endorsement is as provocative as it is consistent for 301 to assert for she struggles to seduce her husband through her food's sensory appeal. She embodies the physical aspects of food and sex. She persists with her modus operandi. She prepares a particularly disgusting-looking meal of organ meats, but the nature of the food is completely irrelevant to 302. All of the gourmet meals 301 carefully prepares get thrown wholesale into the garbage with 302 gagging into the toilet even though she has not eaten a morsel.

The point-counterpoint continues. Stunned when she accidentally discovers 302 has not eaten a bite of her carefully designed creations (the second momentous failure for 301), 301 takes control. Taking the garbage bag full of uneaten food, she arranges the food on plates, voraciously eats several bites herself, and tries, again unsuccessfully, to force 302 to do the same. Instead, the red sauce prompts 302's painful flashback to her repeated rape, the butcher shop, and her predatory stepfather in scenes suffused with an alarming red light. They are painful to watch and lead to 302's imagining slashing her stepfather in several shots that alternate her pubescent girl's face with her adult one. Thematically, both women associate violence and abuse with sex, and both entertain brutal, vengeful retaliation.

Sharing traumatic experiences goes only so far. As 302 gradually reveals, her problem is the opposite of 301's. As a young girl whose family ran a butcher shop, a victim for years of incestuous rape by her stepfather, 302 literally cannot stomach eating. When 301 forces food upon her, 302 flees to the bathroom to vomit. Rather than finding that, as 301 says, "Eating is everything," 302 explains, "I just can't eat things. I just can't take in anything." It is not unusual for a victim of any sexual abuse to feel dirty and violated, and 302 takes the idea further, connecting anything she takes into her body with phallic violation.

Figure 13.3. Forcing food and friendship.

Ironically, 302 writes an advice column and books on the subject of love, a mind-body dichotomy. Expressing a common sentiment of some sexually abused women, 302 says, "My body is so full of dirty things. How can I stuff food or men in my body?" The curious answer by 301 is to place a pale blue glass between the camera and 302, directly over 302's face, and to fill it with water. Symbolically, she overlays 302's pained facial expression with a clear, cool, life-sustaining liquid.

Metaphoric and Sociocultural Contexts

Statistics are notoriously unreliable in studies of sexually abused women, and it is only with the greatest reservation we hypothesize that women in U.S. studies reliably reflect Korean experiences. But the story's explanation of 302's avoidance of food is not without foundation. In fact, Dr. Arthur Crisp found that "about 30% of female anorexics seem to have been subjected" to childhood sexual abuse (252). In another extensive study, for women "a perceived negative interpersonal response to the disclosure of their childhood sexual abuse predicted higher levels of vomiting" (Fallon and Wonderlich 398). Analysis of such data suggests behavior consonant with 302's and, however qualified the application of these studies, scriptwriter Lee Shu-goon reinforces such behavior as legitimate responses to sexual abuse and infidelity.

Not unexpectedly, these problems occur more often in industrialized countries (Daniels). The U.S. statistics on eating disorders long ago reached staggering proportions, signaling the complicated interrelationships among emotional, psychological, and physical forces. Five to 10 million women and 1 million males struggle with eating disorders (Weber). But while women exhibit more symptoms of anorexia and bulimia than men do, both genders explain that food is not the issue. In effect, control of food is a base line attempt to exert power over their lives. For the anorexic "the daily routine of self-denial is a form of self assertion" (Gidday). However, the effects of starvation on the mind as well as the body include depression and escalating isolation.[2] Individuals increasingly shut themselves off from interaction with others, further eroding self-esteem. And before long, the eating disorder controls daily routines, disrupts all normal life patterns, and threatens any already precarious stability.

However, even after 302 has been pressed to explain the repulsion she feels when she attempts to eat, 301 will not surrender and continues her failed attempts to reach and control her through food. For 301, this is an act of compassion, one she will take to a shocking extreme. Initially 301 believes 302 needs her encouragement, perhaps even assistance, to gain or regain her appetite. Since 301 uses food as her tool to attempt to insinuate herself into the affection of her husband, she resorts quickly to food as her avenue to repairing 302. But the traumas 302 has experienced extend beyond her own abuse. Attempts to hide from her stepfather resulted in another unexpected tragedy when a young neighbor girl who wanted to play hide and seek with 302 ended up frozen to death in the meat locker where she hid. Adding additional destructive force, 302 made a plaintive cry for help to her materialistic mother. Though her mother knows of the stepfather's abuse, she turns a blind eye, preferring instead to count and recount her money: capitalism trumps care. Doubly betrayed and abandoned, 302 explains to 301 that it is not just food her body refuses "but everything that has to do with this world." With a slowly building, inexorable pull reinforced through sinuous camera moves, Park clearly communicates but never graphically shows 301 doing to 302 what she did to the dog, killing and cooking her.

Through a jigsaw puzzle series of shots, Park establishes 302's past. Through flashbacks, we have learned a few details of 301's situation, but Park maintains their distinct difference by presenting 301's full story in an extended interlude (just under thirty minutes one hour into the film) rather than choosing the more jagged approach used with 302. Scenes with 301 and her husband trace the deteriorating relationship from its sexually satisfying stage to the husband's growing disaffection and 301's use of food in a desperate attempt to win him back. As the marriage continues to fail, food becomes 301's substitute for the sex her once delectable food instigated. This series of events culminates in her killing the dog offscreen. After unwittingly eating the dish prepared with the dog, the husband discovers its head boiling in a pot. Throughout this extended break, without cutting back to the detective or scenes with 302, we feel an increasing disgust with the food and a growing irritation over 301's inability to cope. However objectionable the husband's behavior, and it is insensitive and obnoxious, the retaliation through the dog confirms beyond a doubt 301's mental instability. But having learned of 301's execution of the dog, 302 does not react with her own horror. Instead, she obliquely suggests her own murder. "Wouldn't I taste good?" she asks. And 301 obliges. The extreme measures 301 takes, with 302's implied agreement, are sufficient to cause visceral feelings of revulsion even though, in contrast to the dog visually depicted in the pot, 301's murder of 302 and cooking her takes place through small details sufficient to turn most viewers' stomachs.

What are we to make of this yin/yang of sex and food, mind and body so directly confronted? If such extreme measures—killing and cooking her dog and her neighbor—do not exceed her strategy, to what extent should we interpret this film on a symbolic level? That food functions as a means of opening communication channels and as a weapon to destroy them comes as no surprise. The complex psychological dimensions of food continue to astonish and fascinate. Long a vehicle for ritualization and manipulation, it provides an available and powerful cinematic vocabulary for symbolic commentary as well as for cultural expression.

Because food is a vital and usually enjoyable part of a functional day, we all relate to it with varying degrees of interest or indifference. Academic attention prompted the University of California Press to introduce *Gastronomica: The Journal of Food and Culture* in February 2001, a quarterly marketed as "a vital forum for ideas, discussion, and thoughtful reflection on the history, literature, representation, and cultural impact of food."[3] In America where our ways of dealing with food also express our psychological neuroses on a daily basis, we may be tempted to project our experience onto 302's neurosis. After all, she shares characteristics of anorexic patients who struggle to maintain control through their refusal to eat. However, 302's behavior has more alarming origins. Her gagging in response to any food comes directly from repeated sexual trauma, not a loathing of her body provoked by the negative self-image shared by many anorexic and bulimic individuals lured by our media to subscribe to the thin ideal, to which few can measure up.[4] Additionally, other factors that create a low self-image find their expression through attempts to control what the body takes in. The hatred of her body comes, as explicitly revealed in flashbacks, as a result of 302's repeated rape by her stepfather.

In the course of the film, food figures in every scene—an extreme obsession in its own right. Because of the relatively subdued, reserved acting style of Pang Eun-jin (301) and Hwang Shin-hye (302), the viewer's own response may be more thoughtful and meditative. The omniscient point of view further distances the viewer from anchoring firmly in one actress. Though sympathetic to 302 for the inhuman treatment she endures from her mother and her stepfather, we remain distanced by her passivity and inaction. Appalled at 301's behavior, we step back from her unthinkable and truly nauseating action.

Knowing that often Korean's films (and those from many other countries) comment obliquely and more safely on historical or contemporary events through a distinctly different narrative vehicle, we might be encouraged to consider the action as an illustrative equivalent to Korean events. Knowing the Korean struggle for independence from colonizers and occupiers, the viewer quickly perceives the rape, greedy preoccupation, unfaithfulness, and obsessive fixation as rather transparent metaphors.[5] But the picture is more multifaceted than this and involves the achievement of South Korea and its recently heralded film industry.

We can date the energizing of the South Korean film industry to the 1985 lifting of excessively restrictive regulations. As if in response to the loosening of years of control, freer to express unsettling physical and psychological conflict, resourceful directors produced strong, confrontational fare. Even through the mid-1990s economic downturn, both established and relatively new talent continued to produce daring work, while, admittedly, routine action films shared the screen. Happily, this trend continues with, for example, writer/director Kim Ki-duk's *The Isle* stunning audiences at the 2001 Sundance Film Festival with its graphic and intense violence and breathtaking style. Similarly, writer/director Kwak Kyung-taek's *Friend* and writer/director Kim Sung-su's *Musa—The Warrior* led a stellar lineup of South Korean films at the 2001 Cannes International Film Festival where *Screen International*, among others, devoted several articles to the dynamic South Korean film industry. Undoubtedly, the South Korean requirement for cinemas to show South Korean films a minimum of 40% of the time each year fuels the industry.[6] Nevertheless, the style and content exceed any by-the-numbers meeting of quotas.

Within this context of support and revitalization, the film industry has employed its leverage to "remasculinize Korean Cinema," as Kyung Hyun Kim argues in his recent work, signaling its importance in his title, *The Remasculinization of Korean Cinema*. Finding the trope of masculinity embedded in South Korean films over the last twenty-five years, Kim considers film produced since 1980 as undisguised reflections of anxiety concerning male self-definition, a topic familiar in its various applications to many American films dating from the women's movement and male redefinition. But constructive scenarios will move beyond the dichotomous struggle between modernity and tradition, beyond the stereotypical gender struggles that offer grim options for contemporary women. Though Kim examines Korean men in works featuring them in recent films, his focus confronts the fact that, as Chungmoo Choi notes, South Korea's "national subjectivity has been exclusively a male subjectivity" throughout "Korea's long history of colonial and neo-colonial domination" (14). Further, Korean men have been constructed as "victims of the emasculation of the Korean nation" (13) in ways that have led them to become "complicit with the colonizer in disdaining Korean women" (17). As a result, the construction of a new nation "reinforced the patriarchal gender ideology of male domination" (20) in multivalent ways. A double bind resulted for women: the Confucian patriarchal ideology identified with tradition and the masculine discourse reinscribed as part of postcolonial nationalism. In essence, the male becomes the metaphor in a plot transparently reasserting his agency and rejuvenating his power, the woman the victim.

But they, "the sexualized feminine Other" (15) have not been silent as economic and sociocultural changes increased. For as this film confronts stereotypical expectations, *301/302* requires moving beyond its hermetically sealed world to acknowledge changes in the Korean social landscape to contextualize its surprising and extreme situations. As Hesung Chun Koh concludes about the late twentieth century depiction by Korean and Western writers, " 'Male dominance and female subordination' has been the recurring theme" (159). Furthermore, because family and household practices most need social change, "manifestations of Korean's women's emotional conflicts can best be seen in cases of hysterical neurosis" (160). Statistics show that 75.6% of such cases between 1958 and 1973 were women, a consequence of the pressure for Korean women to have a son, the emphasis on patriarchal and patrilineal principles, and the prejudice against women for child custody. "The attitude accorded women results in the haunting sense of regret," Korean *han* (168). Even with economic transformation, Marian Lief Palley notes that "though a nation's productive capacity may become modernized, it does not necessarily follow that its social and political values, which have evolved through the centuries, will be completely supplanted" (275). "While the material culture in South Korea has modernized and been affected by Western influences, its behavioral culture maintains and embraces some Confucian traditions, and it is slow to change. Part of this behavioral culture is reflected in the inequalities of women's roles" (275). Koh elaborates to explain that "neither the intellectuals nor the general public see social equality as a desirable or necessary goal, because they see no harmful effects from the present inequality" (159).

In several ways, the women known as 301 and 302 defy this entrapment, perhaps even to claim, as Joan Kee argues, "sites of independence" through the articulation of their hysteria (Claiming 449). In her detailed explication, she contends that "by developing a language of hysteria . . . the female protagonists evade patriarchally defined scripts" (450). But the site negotiated as a result of 301's and 302's traumatic experiences, the site seized by defiant challengers to the Korean context, offers severely restrictive spaces of refashioned and redefined liberation. For while they escape the cleverly designed and "increasingly sophisticated" sham of independence for these frighteningly resistant women, 302's self-destructive tyranny and 301's obsessive displacement onto perfecting her cooking amount to ambiguous, Pyrrhic victory.

This choice—preferable to capitulation to patriarchal definition with its concomitant surrender of agency and self, more viable than the erasure of desire—nevertheless offers only (and it could not be otherwise within patriarchy) compromised alternative space. And this is perhaps the most honest and painful, but crucial, understanding. It speaks directly, compellingly, to the contemporary woman for whom economic and emotional self-reliance exists as an attractive, perhaps the only acceptable, choice. For as Teresa de Lauretis concluded twenty years ago, "women *must either* consent *or* be seduced into consenting to femininity" (134). Then, as now, for the U.S. and South Korea, de Lauretis defines the project: "The real difficulty, but also the most exciting, original project of feminist theory remains precisely this—how to theorize that experience, which is at once social and personal, and how to construct the female subject from that political and intellectual rage" (166).

Park Chul-soo's *301/302* participates in the small, but important, body of films imagining this unaccommodating female subject and deserves enormous credit for doing so. More often, despite the increasingly visible, if struggling, independent woman in Korean films, "Recent cinematic examples of independent women never succeed in dislodging the woman from an ultimate dependency on men for validation. This failure is a fundamental one that circumvents the aspirations of many contemporary Korean films for being credible narratives of female independence" (Kee 450). At approximately the same time as *301/302*'s release (1995), other efforts to visualize cinematic feminist alternatives received attention. For example, Oh Byong-chul's *Go Alone Like a Rhino's Horn* and Lee Min-yong's *A Hot Roof.* In the melodramatic *Go Alone*, one of the three female protagonists, Kyong-hye, commits suicide after agonizing over her husband's affairs and her own retaliatory affair. Kyong-hye's success as a television announcer fails to suffice, and the other two thirtyish women also find the dreams of marriage wanting. By contrast, in *A Hot Roof* ten women accidentally beat an abusive husband to death and lead feminist supporters in their arguments of self defense. Female audience members at screenings have burst into spontaneous applause and cheers "when the three heroines cracked jokes about their husbands' incompetence and sexual clumsiness" (Shin 28). *Go Alone*'s writer, Kong Ji-young says, "In Korean movies, women have always been depicted to fit men's tastes, but *Go Alone* has no such characters. Here, the women are unyielding and self-reliant" (28) She maintains that not economic but "mental independence is more important" (28) for women to find contentment and happiness.

But while feminism has increasingly found supporters in contemporary South Korea (over forty organizations with some affiliation with the women's movement), while South Korea has succeeded in many facets of modernization, "its behavioral culture maintains and embraces some Confucian traditions, and it is slow to change" (Palley 275). In the 1990s, failure to adhere to the tenets of filial piety and self-sacrifice has led to criticisms of such women "as confused and misled by the charges brought about by modernization-cum-westernization" (Lee 69). The crucial and central concept is '*han*,' the fundamental concept conveying the trauma of Korean history. As "the essential national experience, han is constituted from sentiments of loss and rage at the severance of wholeness and continuity between self and history. . . . and—inevitably in a strict Confucian patriarchy—especially of women" (James 19). Metaphorically, then, 302 embodies the symbolic and enervating starvation while 301 the attempt to coax her to rejuvenation with irresistible offerings and design. Neither is satisfied as both hurtle toward collision and further trauma.

For its nervy presentation of the impact of grotesque sexual abuse and its honesty about the pain of infidelity, *301/302* outshines the standard and gratuitous films that fill American cinemas. For its boldness in upsetting our own equilibrium, it merits the awards it has earned and then some. And for its promise that there is much more to consider and tease from its metaphoric suggestiveness, it is a treasure.

Notes

1. It was not selected by the Motion Picture Arts and Sciences Academy to compete in the foreign film category but was South Korea's official nominee. Kee notes *301/302* was the first internationally distributed South Korean film and received positive critical reviews both domestically and internationally. Nevertheless, "the film was unsuccessful at the local box office when it was released in April 1995, earning roughly 350 million won (approximately $391,000 as of 1 December 1995)." Kee 464 note 2.

2. The opposite side of the coin is the grotesquely obese patients who eat uncontrollably. Recent estimates define 5 million Americans as morbidly obese, that is, an average man is one hundred or more pounds overweight. Atul Gawande, "The Man Who Couldn't Stop Eating," *The New Yorker*, July 9, 2001: 74–75.

3. Publicity literature from University of California Press, January 2001. The associated website is http://www.gastronomica.org. For context, see also Claude Levi-Strauss, *The Raw and the Cooked*, trans. John and Doreen Weightman (New York: Harper & Row, 1969) for a landmark discussion of cultural context.

4. In 2000, the average American woman was 5'4" and weighed 140 pounds. The average model was 5'11" and weighed 117 pounds. *Eating Disorders: The Inner Voice*, Cambridge Educational Videos, 2000. It is estimated that three of every one hundred women will develop an eating disorder.

5. In this context, see, for example, David E. James, "Im Kwon Taek: Korean National Cinema and Buddhism," *Film Quarterly* 54.3 (Spring 2001): 14–31, for a convincing analysis of embedded values and parallels to current and past events.

6. John A. Lent, *The Asian Film Industry* (University of Texas Press, 1990) 122–45, and "South Korea Territory Focus," *Screen International*, Cannes International Film Festival, 2001. Certain provisions do permit a reduction in the 40% requirement. See also Joan Kee, "The Image Significant: Identity in Contemporary Korean Video Art," *afterimage*, July/August 1999, 8–11, discussing the equally vibrant South Korean video art world.

Works Cited

Choi, Chungmoo. "Nationalism and Construction of Gender in Korea." *Women of Japan and Korea: Continuity and Change*. Ed. Joyce Gelb and Marian Lief Palley. Philadelphia: Temple University Press, 1994.

Crisp, Dr. Arthur H. "Anorexia Nervosa as Flight from Growth: Assessment and Treatment Based on the Model." *Handbook of Treatment for Eating Disorders*. Ed. David M. Garner and Paul E. Garfinkel. 2nd ed. New York: Guilford, 1997. 252.

Daniels, Anna. *Anorexia and Bulimia*. Time-Life Medical video, 1996.

de Lauretis, Teresa. *Alice Doesn't: Feminism, Semiotics, Cinema*. Bloomington: Indiana University Press, 1984.

Fallon, Patricia, and Stephen A. Wonderlich. "Sexual Abuse and Other Forms of Trauma." *Handbook of Treatment for Eating Disorders*. Ed. David M. Garner and Paul E. Garfinkel. 2nd ed. New York: Guilford, 1997. 398.

Gawande, Atul. "The Man Who Couldn't Stop Eating." *The New Yorker*, July 9, 2001: 74–75.

Gidday, Katherine. *The Famine Within*. Video, Los Angeles, Direct Cinema, 1990.

Shin Hye-son. "Feminism Gaining Ground in New Novels and Movies." *Newsreview*, November 11, 1995: 27–29.

James, David E. "Im Kwon-Taek: Korean National Cinema and Buddhism." *Film Quarterly* 54.3 (2001): 14–31.

Kee, Joan. "Claiming Sites of Independence: Articulating Hysteria in Pak Ch'ol-su's *301/302*." *positions* 9.2 (2001): 449–66.

———. "The Image Significant: Identity in Contemporary Korean Video Art." *afterimage*. July/August 1999: 8–11.

Kim, Kyung Hyun. *The Remasculinization of Korean Cinema*. Durham: Duke University Press, 2004.

Koh Hesung Chun. "Korean Women, Conflict, and Change: An Approach to Development Planning." *Korean Women: View from the Inner Room*. Ed. Laurel Kendall and Mark Peterson. New Haven, CT: East Rock, 1983.

Lee, June J.H. "Discourses of Illness, Meanings of Modernity: A Gendered Construction of Songinbyong." *Under Construction: The Gendering of Modernity, Class, and Consumption in the Republic of Korea*. Ed. Laurel Kendall. Honolulu: University of Hawaii Press, 2002.

Lent, John. A. *The Asian Film Industry*. Austin: University of Texas Press, 1990.

Levi-Strauss, Claude. *The Raw and the Cooked*. Trans. John and Doreen Weightman. New York: Harper and Row, 1969.

Palley, Marian Lief. "Feminism in a Confucian Society: The Women's Movement in Korea." *Dangerous Women: Gender and Korean Nationalism*. Ed. Elaine H. Kim and Chungmoo Choi. New York: Routledge, 1998.

Weber, Amy S. *Eating Disorders: The Inner Voice*. Cambridge Educational Videos, Cambridge Research Group, 2000, http://www.gastronomica.org.

14

ROBERT L. CAGLE

Taking the Plunge

Representing Queer Desire in Contemporary South Korean Cinema

IN 1999, FOR THE FIRST TIME EVER, domestically produced motion pictures garnered nine spots in the list of the twenty top-grossing movies of the year in South Korea. The culmination of this massive economic and cultural accomplishment was that *Shiri* (Kang Je-kyu 1999), a story of loyalties and love divided between the North and South, outsold U.S. blockbuster *Titanic* (James Cameron 1999) at the box office and went on to become, for a time, the highest grossing film in Korean history (Leong 24).[1]

This explosion of South Korea's entertainment industry occurred at and because of a critical moment in the divided nation's history. A serendipitous chain of events brought about monumental changes in both the motion picture industry and more important in the socioeconomic and political climates as well: First, the lift of a long-standing freeze on the export of Korean products opened new avenues for international theatrical and home video distribution and created a demand for higher quality productions with international appeal (Atkinson 112). Second, the corporate investors, or *chaebol* (e.g., Daewoo and Samsung), whose money had virtually run the Korean cinema industry during the previous decade, pulled out of the business during the recession of 1997. This allowed for increased opportunities for private funding—a move that favored edgy, daring productions over tried-and-true formulas, because as actual audience members, individual investors were more closely involved (and interested) in seeing challenging material presented on the big screen (Leong 11). Third, the Korean Council for Performing Arts Promotion, established after the dissolution of the arch-conservative Korean Performing Arts Ethics Committee, relaxed restrictions imposed by federal censorship laws (Lee 279).

This combination of radical change, rapid expansion, and marked liberalization transformed South Korea's film industry overnight into an amalgamation of both a developing industry—driven by the potential and the need for self-representation, redefining or completely rejecting conventions, and reshaping established genres—and a fully developed institution—capable of producing features that rival (or surpass) Western products in their reliably sophisticated storylines and consistently high production values. This split identity clearly echoes Korea's status as divided nation(s) as well as South Korea's own dilemma of being pulled in one direction by modernization and in the other by tradition.

One striking feature of a number of recent productions is their surprisingly frank and yet aesthetically discriminating depiction of sexuality. *Happy End* (Jung Ji-woo 1999); *Marriage Is a Crazy Thing* (Yoo Ha 2002); *Summer Time* (Park Jae-ho 2001); and *Sweet Sex and Love* (Bong Man-dae 2003) all deal unapologetically with a subject still not widely discussed in polite Korean society. Attendant to this trend toward openly depicting sexual behavior has been an increased willingness to broach other such morally charged but decidedly different themes as incest—*Old Boy* (Park Chan-wook, 2003); *Wanee and Junah* (Kim Young-gyun 2001); sadomasochism—*Lies* (Jang Sun-woo 2000); prostitution and sexual violence—Kim Ki-duk's entire oeuvre—most notably *Bad Guy* (2002) and *The Samaritan Girl* (2004); voyeurism and internet pornography—*Asako in Ruby Shoes* (E. J-young 2000); lesbianism—*Memento Mori* (Kim Tae-young and Min Kyu-dong 1999); and male homosexuality—*Wanee and Junah*, *Flower Island* (Song Il-gon 2001); *Desire* (Kim Eung-su 2002); and *Road Movie* (Kim In-sik 2002). Even more remarkable about films in these final two categories is that according to film scholar Lee Joo-ran, gay men and lesbians have remained unaccounted for, save for a very small number of references, in Korean cinema. Lee writes, "Discussing Korean gay and lesbian films is like drifting in space without sunlight or oxygen" (273).

It is, perhaps, not surprising that most of the films that treat these touchy subjects are melodramas, given that the genre has long been a staple of Korean popular film. Indeed, with its readily adaptable conventions and stock situations, the melodrama has a long history of serving different political purposes at different historical moments and has illustrated in its various incarnations, as film critic Yoshimoto Mitsuhiro has noted of Japanese melodrama, the "conflict between old and new social structures and modes of production" (106).

In her essay "South Korean Film Melodrama and the Question of National Cinema," for example, Kathleen McHugh reads changes in the representation of women in melodramas of the 1950s and 1960s as symbolic of cultural shifts experienced by the nation. In their extensive study of the history of Korean film, Min, Joo, and Kwak explain how the melodrama of the 1920s and 1930s used depictions of the tyranny of the rich and powerful over the poor and weak to comment upon the life under Japanese occupation (32–33). They later document how the democratic movement that arose after the end of the Third Republic allowed filmmakers to address social issues that had formerly been considered off limits. The melodrama provided a medium through which themes that had remained repressed throughout previous decades could now be expressed (62–63).

Bungee Jumping of Their Own (Kim Dae-seung 2001) is a contemporary example of this phenomenon, even going so far as to incorporate the rift between past and present into its narrative. The film tells the story of a man who experiences true love twice in his life: once with a woman, and later, with a much younger man. The shock associated with the controversial subject of homosexuality is reduced by the film's explanation that the younger man is, in fact, the reincarnation of the man's (female) first love. Although this trope for representing male-to-male desire might seem conservative, the mere fact that this film could be made and distributed in South Korea signals unmistakable progress toward recognizing marginalized voices in a culture forced to choose between maintaining long-standing traditions or plunging headlong into the twenty-first century.

Homosexuality is still considered a taboo subject, requiring Korean gays and lesbians to remain closeted (Hartzell), so the film utilizes ambiguity—a kind of "don't ask, don't tell" approach—to articulate queer desires. Furthermore, because of the social commentary it attempts to incorporate, it can be seen as a latter-day "plea for tolerance" film, like works such as the German film *Different from the Others* (*Anders als die Anderen*, Richard Oswald 1919) that signaled the very beginnings of gay and lesbian self-representation in Western film (Dyer 11–15, 212; Russo 19–22). Even though the male couple ends up committing suicide—a distressing element that directly echoes a similar trend in Western cinema, past and present—the action is transformed into something metaphoric, suggesting

Figure 14.1. *Bungee Jumping of Their Own* (Kim Dae-sung 2001).

a beginning rather than an end.[2] Thus, although the film finds ways of subsuming queer desires into a normative narrative of heterosexuality, the action serves merely to disavow them rather than negate them.

Bungee Jumping accomplishes this in different ways: First, the film employs a rather elaborate system of repetition and difference to tell its two parallel stories, underscoring the similarities between heterosexual and homosexual love. This has two results: On the one hand, it serves as narrative support for the film's project of heterosexualization, providing evidence that the two love stories are, in fact, one and the same. On the other hand, though, it delivers a more progressive message, showing viewers that there is very little that separates heterosexual from homosexual relationships.

Second, the film does its best to break down widely held stereotypes that link male homosexuality and femininity by focusing on characters whose behavior fits comfortably into dominant notions of (heterosexual) masculinity. Of course, the absence of any "true" homosexual characters (with the possible exception of the student falsely blamed for stealing cigarettes), is somewhat problematic but understandable, especially given that Wong Kar-wai's *Happy Together* (1997) was banned because of its depictions of homosexuality.[3] *Bungee Jumping* gets around this sticky issue by stressing that these characters have heterosexual pasts, and indeed, perhaps share a heterosexual future.

Finally, the film features a decidedly open ending, a move that transforms the film from an otherwise closed (like other realist films) to open text—rendering it a work that suggests an elliptical rather than linear narrative form, to be repeated, reviewed, and reinterpreted. The film, thus, creates a system that provides for the simultaneous experience, disavowal, and repetition of perverse pleasure. This process invites the spectator to surrender to forbidden desires (in this case, queer desires), but "saves"[4] him (in that it is heterosexual masculinity that is at stake here) from homosexuality by allowing him to redirect his desires toward more a socially acceptable end: the reestablishment of the law and the reconstitution of a heterosexual couple—a "marriage."[5] However, because the film's conclusion is anything but conclusive, linking, as it does, the film's ending with its beginning, the implied message seems to be one favoring endless repetition (not unlike reincarnation) over linear development and resolution.

This cyclical process of disavowal and repetition clearly shares a great deal with the three related psychoanalytic concepts of splitting, disavowal, and fetishism, whereby the subject "who cannot bear another's totality will fragment . . . that object [and] then isolate a neutral fragment . . . that more safely represents that person" (Stoller 132). The subject, then, when faced with desires he cannot bear, reduces the object of desire to one manageable aspect (and one that writes out those qualities that the subject finds problematic or unbearable)—a symbol of sorts—upon which he may then focus and find satisfaction. The result is a splitting of the ego that allows the subject to enjoy his perverse pleasures and yet disavow them, too—fulfilling the drive of fantasy while at the same time conforming to the demands of reality and by extension, dominant culture (Laplanche and Pontalis 427).

As the work of psychoanalytic critics such as Raymond Bellour and Stephen Heath has illustrated, just as the psychoanalyst interprets symptoms, so the film theorist identifies and analyzes filmic interruptions, interpreting cinematic strategies of desire and representability at work in the body of the text. This approach seems especially applicable to a text such as *Bungee Jumping* because the film bears the marks of two divergent desires—one to represent and one to repress homosexuality—and thus replicates, in a master narrative form, the same conflicts faced by the lead character.

A detailed synopsis of the film follows, given that some readers may not have had the opportunity to see the film: The film opens on a rainy afternoon in 1983, as In-woo (Lee Byung-hun) and Tae-hee (Lee Eun-ju), two college students, bump into one another on a busy sidewalk. Tae-hee asks In-woo to share his umbrella while they wait for the bus. In-woo is so completely smitten that he returns to the bus stop, umbrella in hand, to wait for Tae-hee's eventual return. After he finally spots her again on campus, he even stops attending one of his own courses so he can sit in on an art class in which Tae-hee is a student. The two spend a great deal of time together, and on a mountain climbing trip, Tae-hee stands at the edge of a cliff and announces that it is her dream to go to New Zealand, where one can jump off a cliff and live. Things seem to be going smoothly until In-woo dares, at the urging of his friends, to suggest that the two of them sleep together, and once again, they end up standing in the rain. The two eventually reconcile and spend a few hours together at a seedy love motel. They profess their love for one another and make plans to meet at the Yongsan station before In-woo leaves for the military. In-woo waits patiently at the train station, but Tae-hee never arrives.

The film then jumps ahead seventeen years to the year 2000. In-woo is now happily married and working as a Korean language instructor at a high school. A number of uncanny interactions with one of his male students, the popular Hyeon-bin (Yae Hyeon-soo), remind In-woo of events from his own past with Tae-hee, and the teacher becomes romantically fixated on his student. As infatuation turns into an obsession, rumors of an improper relationship between the two spread through the school. After an outburst in which the students in In-woo's class cover the blackboard with homophobic graffiti, the teacher is dismissed from duty. Separated from one another, the two find themselves inconsolable. In-woo leaves his wife and child and wanders aimlessly, ending up again at the train station where he waited for his lost love seventeen years before. As Hyeon-bin, evidently driven by some supernatural power, rushes to the train station to meet his teacher, the film reveals, though cross-cutting, striking parallels between past and present. Just as Tae-hee rushed across the street to reach the train station she was hit by a truck. Now, in the present, Hyeon-bin suffers the same fate, but survives. Injured, but determined, he keeps Tae-hee's appointment with In-woo on the platform, and the two embark on a life together. In fulfillment of Tae-hee's desire, the two make a trip to the Taupo bungee jumping site in New Zealand. They hold hands, look into one another's eyes, and leap off of the platform, *sans* bungee cords, explaining, in voiceover, that they are ready to be reincarnated together again, perhaps as a heterosexual couple, or perhaps not.

The film is divided into two distinct stories that are punctuated by a set of repeated images and actions. Its overall form is, save for its open ending, a classical realist text. Of course, establishing patterns of repetition is a common feature of the classical narrative film, lending an illusion of structural integrity to the events presented onscreen and laying the groundwork for and eventually being subsumed by the film's eventual resolution by creating a system of cause-and-effect relationships.[6] But what is particularly noteworthy of this film is the manner in which these repetitions, often aided by such devices as sound bridges and voiceovers, serves both to obscure and at the same time underscore discontinuities and interruptions in the representation. The overall effect of this strategy is an uncanny one,[7] leaving spectators wondering if they have missed something of importance (narrative material), caught sight of something they should not have (the cinematic apparatus), or experienced some combination of both. This uncertainty, paired with the film's willfully obscure resolution—of the very type that has come to define the Korean melodrama—enacts a cinematic version of the return of the repressed, luring the spectator into a *mise-en-abyme* of possible repetitions and rereadings.

This perverse strategy would seem to be directly at odds with the film's somewhat more conservative storyline, which, in its insistence upon demonstrating links between the film's first and second love stories, and devaluing differences between them, does its best to obliterate the spectre of gay desire that drives the film's second half. The second (homosexual) love story, thus, ostensibly becomes nothing more than a reworking of the same (heterosexual) relationship that opened the film. In rewriting what is an unmistakably homosexual relationship as a heterosexual one, the film adroitly avoids having to deal with the political ramifications of depicting male/male desire. At the same time, it rescues these images from being censored. Beyond this manifest content, however, there exist a number of fascinating gaps and imperfections that punctuate the narrative and can be read as the filmic equivalent of symptoms—irregularities or glitches in an otherwise smooth textual system that point toward a misalignment of desire and representability.

This process starts with the opening the credits and extends to the final frames. The film opens with a spectacular "flying camera" shot of a deep chasm with a river flowing through it. As the theme song plays, the opening credits appear superimposed over this dizzying vista. This shot is retroactively revealed to be the very chasm where the lovers of the second half of the film leap to their deaths and, if one is to believe the reincarnation story, their eventual rebirths. This "flying" shot fades to black and then cuts to a close-up shot of a bicyclist framed from the waist down. The image track cuts again to an overhead shot of the cyclist, back to a similar street-level close-up, and back again to an overhead shot, this time of the bicyclist nearly running into In-woo, who is carrying an umbrella. As In-woo jumps to avoid colliding with the cyclist, Tae-hee ducks under In-woo's umbrella, bumping into him in the process. Tae-hee asks, in voiceover, if In-woo will share his umbrella with her as they walk to the bus stop. The two pause at the corner, where, framed in a long shot, Tae-hee suggests that In-woo move closer to her under the umbrella, because his hesitancy to stand too close to her has resulted in his being exposed to the torrential downpour. He replies that he is fine. The bus arrives, Tae-hee boards it, and In-woo, in close-up, stares as it pulls away. The image track cuts away from his gaze to black as the film's title appears in luminous gold lettering. The title fades, and the image track cuts back once again to a long shot of the bus stop where In-woo stands waiting. A series of dissolves suggests that In-woo spends the next several days here (judging from the changes in light and in costume), at one point cutting to a close-up of In-woo who remains in focus, nearly still, as the people around him blur into abstraction. Eventually, he gives up and leaves.

This series of shots, a seemingly unimportant collection of images, becomes charged with a completely different kind of narrative value when viewed again after watching the rest of the film. The opening shots from the perspective of the flying camera that seem to mean nothing at the film's start are, at its end, shown to be the visual representation of the paths of the freed spirits of In-woo and Hyeon-bin/Tae-hee. The appearance, then, of this footage at the beginning of the film supports a reading of the film as cyclic and even suggests that the collision of the two main characters represents a moment of initial (re)birth, with their discovery of one another being part of some supernatural plan. The cyclist, who remains conspicuously unidentified, serves as an agent of fate, creating a situation that will bring the two lovers together. It is interesting to note, too, that when Hyeon-bin appears at the start of the second half of the film, he is shown riding a bicycle (notably in the *opposite* direction of the first bicyclist) in an almost identical fashion. Instead of cutting to In-woo (and Tae-hee) as the opening does, the cut is to a luminous close-up of the teen's smiling face and then shows him purposefully running into two of his male friends. This similarity, considered in light of In-woo's amorous fixation on the teen, suggests that Hyeon-bin is both the object of In-woo's desire and the agent of that desire, like the bicyclist in the earlier sequence.

This is further underscored in a later scene in which it is revealed that Hyeon-bin asks to be paired with In-woo in the three-legged race at the school's sports day. The sequence is presented twice: First In-woo is shown discussing the upcoming sports day with the school's physical education teacher. The teacher informs In-woo that he will pair the teacher with the fastest student in his class for the three-legged race. In-woo shyly agrees and leaves. When the scene is shown later, presented as a female teacher's memory of what she sees as "strange" behavior on the part of Hyeon-bin, the sequence begins at the point at which it ended the first time around. In this replay, it is revealed that In-woo asks to be paired with Hyeon-bin, but his request is denied. The camera then pulls back to reveal that Hyeon-bin has been present all along, standing just outside of the frame. The student walks over to the PE teacher after In-woo leaves and asks to take part in the three-legged race, explaining, somewhat unconvincingly, that since one of his friends wants to play basketball, he will sacrifice his spot on the team and run with In-woo in the race. This sequence is significant in that it both shows reciprocity of desire on the part of Hyeon-bin and, at the same time, stresses his agency in establishing and developing a relationship with his teacher.

Significantly, it is through Hyeon-bin that Tae-hee's role in meeting In-woo is revealed as well. Although the first half of the film clearly illustrates that she is, as her friend points out, "so organized" that it is unlikely that she would ever forget her umbrella, it is not until the second half of the film that the secret behind her chance meeting with In-woo is revealed. As Hyeon-bin sits staring at a lighter with Tae-hee's image etched on it, the image track cuts to the scene of the film's opening. This lighter comes to function as the film's fetish object *par excellence*—in that it is the material representation of a narrative of desire and loss. Hyeon-bin's possession of the Tae-hee's prized lighter, promised to the only man she ever loved, is proof positive, to In-woo, that he is Tae-hee reincarnated. It also provides the impetus for what proves to be *the* pivotal sequence in the film: the moment at which Hyeon-bin "becomes" Tae-hee by experiencing her flashback of the rainy day, thus recontextualizing all that has come after this first, defining sequence.

In the flashback Tae-hee is shown watching out a window (just as In-woo does in later scenes) for In-woo's arrival on the street below. When he passes by, she rushes out the door and into the street, casually bumping into him as he jumps out of the way of the oncoming bicyclist. While this replay of the film's opening scene does serve to illustrate Tae-hee's agency in making contact with the object of her secret admiration, it is, I think, not insignificant that the revelation comes not as a mere flashback (as it might in standard Korean melodramas) but rather filtered through the figure of Hyeon-bin, already established as an agent of desire. In other words, Tae-hee's desire for In-woo only finds expression when it is articulated through the figure of Hyeon-bin. Similarly, In-woo's desire for Hyeon-bin, and Hyeon-bin's for In-woo, must be mediated through the figure of Tae-hee.[8]

This gap in the story of Tae-hee and In-woo's initial meeting is, in fact, alluded to at the beginning of the film when Tae-hee is heard speaking in voiceover, that is, without "speaking" in the scene itself. This strategy does double duty, suggesting that the two have some sort of deep psychic bond (as though she is communicating to him without speaking) and at the same time, signaling the fact that some material (the scene of speaking) is already missing. This displacement, given that the audience does not see from when and where Tae-hee speaks, but instead, only hears her voice both establishes the gap that Hyeon-bin will later fill in,

Figure 14.2. The three-legged race.

and, at the same time, begins the process of naturalizing the film's covering over of such gaps using various techniques.

Worthy of note in this opening sequence, too, is the fact that the bus bears the number 131, a symbolic representation of the relationships that the film presents. On either side of the three is a one, suggesting the two halves of a couple, divided. The three calls to mind the fact that there are three members of this love affair: In-woo, Tae-hee, and Hyeon-bin. It also foreshadows both the first and second instances of involuntary memory that occur in the film: the waltz lesson on the beach and the aforementioned three-legged race, by echoing both Tae-hee's and Hyeon-bin's counting aloud and by showing how two ones, joined together, can make three. Of course, the overtones, too, of a "three-legged" race—the name suggestive of a vulgar slang term for the penis, further sexualizes what becomes the first romantic moment shared by In-woo and Hyeon-bin. The evidence that this is more than just a race comes in two forms: first, In-woo hesitates slightly before placing his hand on Hyeon-bin's shoulder, highlighting the act as one of extreme emotional or erotic value. Second, In-woo is suddenly seized by a fit of hiccups, the symptom that has already been established, in his interactions with Tae-hee, as a sign that he is nervous or excited. Of course, In-woo's hiccups, however, do not necessarily link, at least directly, Hyeon-bin and Tae-hee but merely illustrate that as he was with Tae-hee, In-woo is now excited and nervous when he is near Hyeon-bin.

This similarity gets played out in a scene that provides the first direct link between past and present. It occurs when In-woo is wandering through the classroom and hears Hyeon-bin's cell phone ring. The ring tone, a waltz, triggers an involuntary memory of an afternoon spent learning to dance at the beach with Tae-hee. As the telephone plays an electronic version of the second waltz from Shostakovich's Jazz Suite number 2, the image track shifts from present (the classroom) to past (a scene at the beach), with the tune providing a sound bridge between the two temporalities and, more important, between Hyeon-bin's and Tae-hee's identities. The music condenses the two identities into one. A group of young people is seated around a bonfire on the beach. Tae-hee gets up and walks away, and In-woo, who, as the scene later reveals, has not spoken to Tae-hee since their initial meeting, gets up and follows her. The two flirt shyly with one another, and Tae-hee mentions that she is learning to waltz. She offers to teach In-woo, and humming the tune and counting, the two waltz along the seashore at sunset. When the image track cuts back to the present, In-woo is looking at the text message screen on Hyeon-bin's cell phone. It reads, "I love you." In-woo erases the message and then appears to be shocked at his actions. A student enters the room, asks if In-woo is coming to class, and the two exit. The student glances back for a moment at the cell phone lying on Hyeon-bin's desk.

This sequence is particularly striking for a number of reasons: Its function seems to be to establish a key association between In-woo's past and present, inextricably linking Hyeon-bin with Tae-hee. However, the scene's symbolic value, its function as evidence, is at least potentially weakened by the fact that the memory of this particular afternoon and this particular song has been thus far withheld from the spectator. In other words, because the memory has not yet been introduced in the film, and thus, is not part of the spectator's shared past with In-woo, it holds no established authenticity at the time of its presentation. The film attempts to ease the gloss over the gap by using a sound bridge to ease the shift from present to past and back again.

Indeed, the film makes liberal use of such sound bridges and voiceovers throughout, displacing sound from other scenes and in so doing providing external commentary on diegetic actions, as when In-woo's friend refers to him (in a conversation that occurs later in the film) as a "dumb lumberjack," while he is shown sawing logs for Tae-hee's art class, or filling in material elided in the process of montage, as when In-woo hears Tae-hee, in voiceover, asking him to wait at the train station for her, just in case she is late.

The overall effect that this has is to naturalize, narratively speaking, the film's extensive project of covering over the irregularities that insistently illustrate the differences between the first and second love stories. In other words, by creating a system that tutors the viewer, through subjecting him/her to repetitions, to experience narrative ellipses as normal—to draw attention away from the fact that information is missing but suggested—the film facilitates the development of the associations necessary to collapse the heterosexual romance onto the homosexual one and, thus, obscure, at least in part, the second. Conversely, however, this same process opens up possibilities for representing the ostensibly gay relationship on and in the same terms as the heterosexual one.

In closing, I would like to make mention what amounts to the film's most explicit (save for the homophobic comments of the students in In-woo's class) reference to homosexuality: In-woo's visit to the hospital. No longer able to make love with his wife, and increasingly drawn to Hyeon-bin, In-woo goes to a clinic for psychiatric testing. There, the psychologist, notably a woman, reassures In-woo that his test results are "quite normal," adding that his responses suggest that he is "proud of his sexuality" and that he is "normally attracted to women." She adds, however, that more tests might be necessary. Her final comment to In-woo is that it is her opinion that his interest in a member of the same sex "should be seen comfortably as part of human nature."

This sequence is particularly powerful, not only because it virtually undoes the clinicalization (and pathologization) of sexuality through shifting the discussion of desire into the doctor's office, but also because it functions as a pivotal moment in the film's discourse around difference and pathology: In-woo is shown as suffering from impotence with his wife. He visits the clinic. Then the film cuts to a shot of Hyeon-bin leaving a gallery with his girlfriend. She chatters away annoyingly about this and that as Hyeon-bin stares off into the distance, apparently uninterested in her or her conversation. The two stop at a roadside antiques stall where she picks up a spoon, looking at it first from the front and then from the back, and he picks up a lighter—Tae-hee's lighter. These two objects have already been established as being symbolic in In-woo's relationship with Tae-hee, and, I would like to suggest, it is with this sequence and the one that follows it that they illustrate just how easily In-woo's desires shift from hetero- to homosexual.

During In-woo and Tae-hee's mountain climbing expedition the two stop at a cafe for bibimbap. In-woo is nervous, and as a way of making conversation observes that if one stares into one side of a spoon, the viewer sees his own face reflected right side up; however, if he looks into the other side, the opposite is true—his reflection is upside-down. The conversation soon shifts, as Tae-hee asks In-woo (who has claimed to be a Korean major) why it is that *cheotkkarak* (chopstick) is spelled with an *s* (*shiot*), while *sutkkarak* (spoon) is spelled with a *t* (*tiguet*) since both are pronounced the same (as *t*). In-woo makes a joke instead of providing a real answer, saying that the logic behind the spelling is that the *shiot* resembles chopsticks, and the *tigeul* resembles a spoon. The two laugh and continue to eat. The dualism represented by In-woo's observations serves to foreshadow what will eventually be the dual nature of In-woo's object(s) of desire: although one object appears to be the opposite of (or different from) the other, both are somehow the same.

In the later scene, it is Hyeon-bin's girlfriend who examines a spoon, this one far too corroded to reflect anything, but her actions replicate, almost exactly, those of In-woo and Tae-hee in the earlier scene. While she looks at the spoon Hyeon-bin is staring fixedly at the image (of Tae-hee) etched onto the lighter he has found. "Is this woman famous?" he asks. "She looks familiar." The implication here is that Hyeon-bin is seeing a distorted reflection of himself as Tae-hee, not unlike the inverted images on the spoon's reflective surface.

The following sequence takes place in the classroom, where In-woo is teaching the difference between "different" and "wrong," explaining that one would not say "I'm *wrong* from you," but rather, "I'm *different* from you." The message, when viewed in light of the two sequences that have preceded this one, is clear: differences in sexual desire are neither pathological nor wrong; they are merely different.

This reading frames the film's final images of In-woo and Hyeon-bin's happy days together in an even more progressive light. Their trip to New Zealand and their ultimate vault into the unknown becomes less an act of suicide and more an exhilarating plunge into uncharted territories of desire—a fall into love—visualizing a lasting metaphor for romance, and, in going where none have dared go before, echoing the very project of the film.

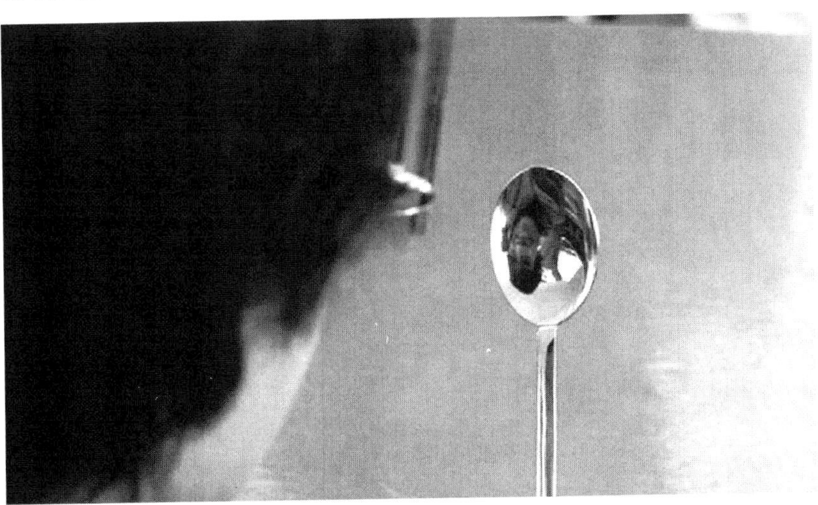

Figure 14.3. "Different, not wrong.'

Notes

1. For more on the success of *Shiri*, see "Storming the Big Screen: The *Shiri* Syndrome," by Shin and Stringer in this volume.

2. That the leads' final act is, in fact, a double suicide, is supported by both visual and verbal evidence. The two men ponder (in voiceover) what they will do if they are both reincarnated as women. The wild tracking shots that follow the jump suggest POV shots that could be attributed to the freed spirits of the characters. Most obviously, as the two jump from the bridge it is apparent that neither is attached to the bungee cords, which are clearly still attached to the bridge. Indeed, even the English-language title of the film, *Bungee Jumping of Their Own*, unambiguously indicates that the plunge taken by the two leads is unique: its participants survive not as corporeal beings but rather as eternal spirits. In their analysis of the film, Grossman and Lee interpret these final images in radically different terms. They write, "[T]he two journey to New Zealand to engage in life-affirming bunjee [sic] jumps that permit them rapturously to enjoy feigned deaths without being further inconvenienced by the gender-bending determinisms that real deaths, in this film, apparently entail" (188). Such an interpretation fails to recognize the film's formal integrity and subsequently undervalues its cultural import.

3. Lee provides an overview of the controversy surrounding Wong's film in her essay. See 279–80.

4. This process, like fetishism, allays the subject's fears that he is somehow not "normal" through disavowal. For discussions of this process see Freud, "Fetishism" (1927), and "The Splitting of the Ego in the Process of Defence" (1940).

5. Raymond Bellour has observed that resolution often takes the form of a marriage, at least in the classical Hollywood text. See Bellour, quoted in Bergstrom, 87.

6. For an overview of how this process works, see Lapsley and Westlake, chapter 5.

7. J. Hillis Miller discusses this phenomenon as it applies to literature in his *Fiction and Repetition*.

8. This situation calls to mind a similar one mapped out by Luce Irigaray in her "Commodities among Themselves," *This Sex Which Is Not One*, trans. Catherine Porter (Ithaca, NY: Cornell University Press, 1985).

Works Cited

Atkinson, Michael. "Leaps of Bliss." *The Village Voice*. August 14–20, 2002. 112.

Bergstrom, Janet. "Alternation, Segmentation, Hypnosis: An Interview with Raymond Bellour." *Camera Obscura* 3–4 (Summer 1979): 71–103.

Dyer, Richard. *Now You See It: Studies on Lesbian and Gay Film*. London: Routledge, 1990.

Freud, Sigmund. "Fetishism." (1927) *Standard Edition* 21 (1961). London: Hogarth, 1953. 152–57.

———. "The Splitting of the Ego in the Process of Defence." (1940) *SE* 23 (1964): 275–78.

Grossman, Andrew, and Jooran Lee. "*Memento Mori* and Other Ghostly Sexualities." *New Korean Cinema*. Ed. Chi-Yun Shin and Julian Stringer. New York: New York University Press, 2005. 180–92.

Hartzell, Adam. "Queer Pal for the Straight Gal—Wanee & Junah and Queer Friendship." http://www.thefilmjournal.com/issue7/wanee.html.

Irigaray, Luce. *This Sex Which Is Not One*. Trans. Catherine Porter. Ithaca, NY: Cornell University Press, 1985.

Jung Jae-hyung. "Road Movie: Queerish Reasonableness of Nomadic Existence." *Film Critiques* 3 (2004): 171–76.

Laplanche, J., and J.-B. Pontalis. *The Language of Psycho-analysis*. Trans. Donald Nicholson-Smith. New York: Norton, 1974.

Lapsley, Robert, and Michael Westlake. *Film Theory: An Introduction*. Manchester: Manchester University Press, 1988.

Lee, Juran. "Remembered Branches: Towards a Future of Korean Homosexual Film." *Queer Asian Cinema: Shadows in the Shade*. Ed. Andrew Grossman. Binghamton, NY: Haworth, 2000. 273–81.

Leong, Anthony C. Y. *Korean Cinema: The New Hong Kong*. Victoria, BC: Trafford, 2004.

McHugh, Kathleen. "South Korean Film Melodrama and the Question of National Cinema." *Quarterly Review of Film and Video* 18.01 (2001): 1–15.

Miller, J. Hillis. *Fiction and Repetition: Seven English Novels*. Cambridge: Harvard, 1982.

Min, Eungjun, Jinsook Joo, and Jan Ju Kwak. *Korean Film: History, Resistance, and Democratic Imagination*. London: Praeger, 2003.

Rist, Peter Harry. "Korean Cinema Now: Balancing Creativity and Commerce in an Emerging National Industry." *cineAction*! 64 (2004): 37–45.

Russo, Vito. *The Celluloid Closet: Homosexuality in the Movies* (revised edition). New York: Harper and Row, 1985.

Stoller, Robert. *Perversion: The Erotic Form of Hatred*. London: Maresfield, 1986.

Yoshimoto, Mitsuhiro. "Melodrama, Postmodernism, and Japanese Cinema." *Melodrama and Asian Cinema*. Ed. Wimal Dissanayake. Cambridge: Cambridge University Press, 1993.

Contributors

CHRIS BERRY teaches in the Department of Media and Communications, Goldsmiths College at the University of London. He is the editor of *Chinese Films in Focus: 25 New Takes and Perspectives on Chinese Cinema*; coauthor of *China on Screen: Cinema and Nation* (Columbia University Press); and translator of *Ni Zhen, My Memoirs from the Beijing Film Academy: The Origin of China's Fifth Generation Filmmakers*.

ROBERT L. CAGLE writes about national cinemas and cultures. His essays have appeared in such journals as *Cinema Journal*, the *Velvet Light Trap*, and *CineAction*, as well as in various anthologies. A recipient of a Korean Film Council Research Grant for Overseas Studies on Korean Films, he is currently at work on a project on melodrama as a transnational entertainment form.

DIANE CARSON is a professor of Film at St. Louis Community College at Meramec. She is editor of *John Sayles: Interviews* and coeditor of *Sayles Talk: New Perspectives on Independent Filmmaker John Sayles*, *More Than a Method: Trends and Traditions in Contemporary Film Performance*, *Shared Differences: Multicultural Media and Practical Pedagogy*, and *Multiple Voices in Feminist Film Criticism*. She enjoyed Fulbright studies in South Korea, China, and Japan and work as associate producer on the documentary *Remembering* Bonnie and Clyde.

DAVID DESSER is professor of Cinema Studies, Comparative Literature, and East Asian Languages and Cultures at the University of Illinois. He is the author and editor of nine books, including *The Samurai Films of Akira Kurosawa*, *Eros Plus Massacre: An Introduction to the Japanese New Wave Cinema*, *The Cinema of Hong Kong: History, Arts, Identity*, and *Ozu's*

Tokyo Story. He also provided commentary on the Criterion Collection DVDs of *Tokyo Story* and *Seven Samurai*.

David Scott Diffrient earned his PhD from the Department of Film and Television at UCLA and is currently assistant professor of Film and Media Studies at Colorado State University. His essays have appeared in several journals and anthologies, including *Cinema Journal, Historical Journal of Film, Radio, and Television, South Korean Golden Age Cinema* (Wayne State University Press), and *New Korean Cinema* (New York University Press). He is presently coediting a forthcoming volume on the television series *Gilmore Girls*.

Linda C. Ehrlich, associate professor of Japanese, World Literature, and Cinema at Case Western Reserve University, has published articles on world cinema in *Film Quarterly, Cinema Journal, Literature/Film Quarterly, Cinemaya, Ethnomusicology*, and *Journal of Religion and Film*, among others. She has coedited (with David Desser) *Cinematic Landscapes* (University of Texas Press; 2nd edition) and authored *An Open Window: The Cinema of Víctor Erice*, which appeared in the Scarecrow Press Filmmakers' Series (72).

Frances Gateward is professor of Film Studies at Ursinus College. Her work has been published in a number of journals and anthologies, including *Multiple Modernities: Cinemas and Popular Media in Transcultural East Asia* (Temple University Press) and *Chinese Connections Critical Perspectives on Film, Identity, and Diaspora* (Temple University Press). She is the editor of *Zhang Yimou: Interviews* (University Press of Mississippi) and coeditor of *Sugar Spice and Everything Nice: Cinemas of Girlhood* (Wayne State) and *Where the Boys Are: Cinemas of Masculinity and Youth* (Wayne State). She is also a recipient of the Korean Film Council Research Grant for Overseas Studies on Korean Films.

Hye Seung Chung is visiting assistant professor in the Department of Comparative Literature at Hamilton College. Her writing has appeared in *Asian Cinema, Cinema Journal*, and other journals, as well as in anthologies such as *East Main Street: Asian American Popular Culture* (New York University Press), *South Korean Golden Age Melodrama* (Wayne State University Press), and *New Korean Cinema* (New York University Press). She is the author of *Hollywood Asian: Philip Ahn and the Politics of Cross-Ethnic Performance* (Temple University Press) and is currently writing a book on transnational Korean cinema.

MYUNG JA KIM has been teaching African American studies at Boston University and the Catholic University in Seoul. Kim's work focuses on American ethnic literature and the promotion of transracial and transcultural understanding between different groups.

SUK-YOUNG KIM is an assistant professor of Theater and Dance at the University of California at Santa Barbara. Her research interests include East Asian performance, gender, and nationalism, Korean cultural studies, Russian literature, and Slavic folklore. Her research has been acknowledged by the International Federation for Theatre Research New Scholar's Prize (2004), the American Society for Theater Research Fellowship (2006), and the Library of Congress Kluge Fellowship (2006–07). She is currently working on a book project titled *Illusive Utopia: Theater and Film in North Korea*, which explores how the state-produced propaganda performances intersect with everyday life practices in North Korea.

DARCY PAQUET, a former faculty member of Korea University, currently writes for *Screen International* magazine and is a program consultant for the Far East Film Festival in Udine, Italy. He frequently writes subtitles for Korean feature films and is the English language editor for the Korean Film Council.

SEUNG HYUN PARK is an assistant professor of Communications at Hallym University, South Korea. His research has been published in *Asian Cinema*, *Cinema Journal*, and the *Korean Journal of Journalism and Communication Studies*.

ANNE RUTHERFORD teaches Cinema Studies in the School of Humanities at University of Western Sydney. Her recent work includes essays on affect and embodiment in cinema spectatorship, including in the work of Angelopoulos and in documentary film. Her publications include essays and interviews in *UTS Review*, *Senses of Cinema*, *Independent Film and Video Monthly*, *Real Time*, *Metro*, *Artlink*, and several anthologies.

CHI-YUN SHIN is a lecturer in Film Studies and is currently the BA Film Studies course leader at Sheffield Hallam University, UK. She is a coeditor of the anthology *New Korean Cinema* (Edinburgh University Press) and contributor to journals such as *Paragraph* and *Scope: The Online Journal of Film Studies*.

JULIAN STRINGER is associate professor of Film Studies at the University of Nottingham, England. He is editor of *Movie Blockbusters* (Routledge), coeditor (with Chi-Yun Shin) of *New Korean Cinema* (New York University Press/Edinburgh University Press), and author of forthcoming monographs on film festivals and on Hong Kong cinema. He is also coordinating editor of *Scope: An Online Journal of Film Studies.*

HYANGSOON YI is an assistant professor of Comparative Literature at the University of Georgia. Her book *Buddhist Nuns and Korean Literature* and her edited volume *Buddhist Nuns in East Asia* are now in press. Her research interests include Korean literature and film, Korean Buddhist nuns, and Irish Traveler drama. She is currently working on a book-length manuscript on Korean Buddhist films.

Index

12 Gates of Hell (*Jiok 12 gwan mun*, Lee Hyuk-soo 1979), 195
18 Amazons (*Mulim 18 Yuhgol*, Kim Chung-yong 1979), 195
2009: Lost Memories (Lee Si-myong 2002), 201
20th Century Fox, 28
301, 302 (*Samgong-il samgong*, Park Chul-soo 1995), 9–10, 143, 265–75, 277–79
9½ Weeks (Adrian Lyne 1986), 270
Abenko Airborne Corps. See *Avengo Flying Rangers*
Academy Awards, 214n9, 266
Achas, Nan, 4
Act for the Prevention of Domestic Violence and Victim Prevention, 205
action films, 20, 63–64, 198–99, 202
Address Unknown (Kim Ki-duk 2001), 9, 243, 244–47, 249–60
Affair, An (*Jeongsa*, E.J. Yong 1998), 10
A.F.R.I.K.A. (Shin Seung-soo 2002), 76, 82, 84, 85, 87–88
Ahn Byung-sup, 5, 168
Ahn, Sung-ki, 79, 93
Aimless Bullet (*Obaltan*, Yoo Hyeon-mok 1961), 116
Allen, Michael, 62
Anarchists, The (Yoo young-sik 2000), 201
Anderson, Benedict, 239n9
Andrei Rublev (Andre Tarkovsky 1966), 132
Anemic Cinema (Marcel Duchamp 1926), 138n15
Anzaldua, Gloria, 246
Arabian Nights, 133
Arahan (Ryo Seung-wan 2004), 194
Arirang (Lee Kang-cheon 1954), 239n10
Arirang (Na Un-gyu 1926), 45
Armstrong, Charles, 239n7
Artaud, Antonin, 252
Asako in Ruby Shoes (*Soon Ae Bo*, E J-young 2000), 284
Ashes of Time (*Dung che sai duk*, Wong Kar-wai 1994), 172n18
Asian Film Festival, 117
Association of Korean Women's Unions, 206
Attack the Gas Station (*Juyuso seubgyuksageun*, Kim Sang-jin 1999), 76, 82, 84, 92
Austin Powers: International Man of Mystery (Jay Roach 1997), 52
Avengo Flying Rangers (*Abengo gongsugundan*, Im Kwon-taek 1982), 19

Babette's Feast (Gabriel Axel 1987), 267
Bachelard, Gaston, 179
Bad Guy. See *The Villain*
Bae Doo-na, 93
Bae Yong-kyun, 175, 186n1
Bakhtin, Mikhail, 133, 149, 240n18
Ballet Mécanique (*Fernand Léger* and *Dudley Murphy* 1924), 138n15
Barthes, Roland, 136n5
Battlefield, The (Lee Man-hee 1974), 19
Battleship Potemkin (*Bronenosets Potyomkin*, Sergei Eisenstein 1925), 161
Batvia Military Tribunal of 1948, 216n15
Bauman, Zygmont, 135
Bazin, Andre, 103
Beat, 73–75, 82–83, 85–86, 87, 88
Because You Are a Woman (*Danji geudaega yeojalaneun iyumaneulo*, Kim Yu-jin 1990), 24, 195
Bee Gees, The, 160
Beijing International Women's Conference of 1995, 208
Bellour, Raymond, 287, 296n5
Benjamin, Walter, 157, 161, 169
Berlin Film Festival, 11, 12n1, 214n9, 216n16, 243, 266
Berlin Wall, 61, 221, 226
Berry, Chris, 59, 61
Betrayal (David Hugh Jones 1983), 89
Beyond the Mountains (*Sansan-i buseojin ileum-i-yeo*, Chung Ji-Young 1991), 184
Bhabha, Homi, 115, 129–30
Bichunmoo (Kim Young-jun 2000), 48, 59, 88
Birdcage Inn (*Palandaemun*, Kim Ki-duk 1998), 243
Black Cat, The series, 62
Black Republic (*Guedeuldo ulicheoleom*, Park Kwang-su 1990), 79
Bordwell, David, 119, 137n5, 184
Box of Death (*Jugeom-ui sangja*, Kim Ki-young), 101
Boyarin, Jonathan, 223
Brent Plate, S., 184
Bresson, Henri Cartier, 168
Bride Born in the Year of the Horse (Kim Ki-deok 1966), 195
Bride Stripped Bare by Her Bachelors, 7
Brooks, Peter, 169, 173n25
Brussels International Film Festival, 216
Bullock, Sandra, 2
Bungee Jumping of Their Own (*Bungeejumpreul hada*, Kim Dae-Seung 2001), 10, 48, 87, 285–95
Bush, George W., 219
Butcher's Wife, The (*Sam-yang-dong jeong-yugjeom*, Shin Jeong-gyun 1999), 195
Byun Young-joo, 8, 206, 208, 211–13

Cage, Nicolas, 94n1
Cagle, Robert, 194
Calla (Song Hae-Seong 1999), 89, 214n3
Cameron, James, 92
Cannes Film Festival, 11, 12n1, 39, 59, 118, 175, 214n9, 276
Canterbury Tales, The (Chaucer), 133
Carnivore, 99–100
Carrey, Jim, 94n1
Carrie (Brian De Palma 1976), 130
censorship, 10, 16–18, 28–30, 46, 214n9–215, 221, 284
Chabrol, Claude, 80
Chan, Fruit, 4
Chatterjee, Partha, 62
Chen, Joan, 4
Cheung, Cecelia, 197
Chihwaseon (Im Kwon-taek 2002), 60
Chilsu and Mansu (Park Kwang-su 1988), 77
Chinese Box (Wayne Wang 1997), 117
Chinese Connection (*Jing wu Men*, Lo Wei 1972), 200

Cho, Francisca, 181
Cho Hae-jong, 203
Choi Bae-dal (Oyamu Masutatsu), 201
Choi, Chungmoo, 5, 137n7, 276
Choi Eun-suk, 103
Choi Min-sik, 63, 93
Choo Sang-mee, 93
Chosun Dynasty, 20, 150
Chosun-Japanese War, 20
Christmas in August (8wol-ui Keuliseumaseu, Hur Jin-ho 1998), 6, 37–40, 47–52
Chun Doo-hwan, 16, 32n3, 123, 146
Chun Tae-il, 216n18
Chun Tae-il Literary Award, 210
Chung Ok-nim, 137n12
Chung Sung-il, 103
Chungmuro, 22, 66
Chunhyang (*Choon hyang jun*, Im Kwan-taek 2000), 44, 134
Chunking Express (*Chung Hing sam lam*, Wong Kar-wai 1994), 172n18
Citizen Kane (Orson Welles 1941), 89
Coachman (*Mabu*, Kim Dae-jin 1961), 116
Cold War 4, 6, 9, 61, 221–22, 233, 236
colonialism, Japanese, 6, 245
Columbus, Chris, 92
Come Come, Come Upward (*Aje aje bara aje*, Im Kwon-taek 1989), 184
comfort women, 8, 206–13
Communism, 16, 19
Comolli, Luc, 151
Confucianism, 24, 44, 106, 144, 150–51, 154n5, 186n11, 276, 277, 278, 203, 204, 248–49, 260
Consolidated Fight Committee, 206
Contact, The (*Jeobsog*, Chang Yoon-hyun 1997), 39, 47
Contreras, Cynthia, 177
Corman, Roger, 7
Corset (*Koleuses*, Jeong Byung-gak 1996), 30
Crack of the Halo (Kim jin-han 1997), 49
Crisp, Arthur, 273
Crocodile (*Ag-eo*, Kim Ki-duk 1996), 243
Crouching Tiger, Hidden Dragon (Ang Lee 2000), 60
Cruise, Tom, 94n1
Cummings, Bruce, 16, 238n6
Currie, Mark, 155n17

Daewoo, 26, 64, 283
Daffodil, A (*Suseonhwa* Choi Hun 1973), 20
Day a Pig Fell into the Well, The (*Doejiga umul-e ppajin na*, Hong Sang-soo 1996), 24, 77, 129, 132
De Certeau, Michel, 128
De Lauretis, Teresa, 278
De Palma, Brian, 80
Decameron, The (Giovanni Boccaccio), 133
DeNiro, Robert, 94n1
Desire (*Yok-mang*, Kim Eung-su 2002), 10, 284
Deuchler, Martina, 154n8
Die Another Day (Lee Tamahori 2002), 220, 238n2
Die Bad (*Juk go na Ho gun Na puh go na*, Ryoo Seung-won 2000), 82, 85
Die Hard series, 29, 62
Different from the Others (*Anders als die Andern*, Richard Oswald 1919), 285
Dissanayake, Wimal, 42, 43, 44
Double Agent (*Yi-jung Gan-cheop*, Steve Kim 2003), 236
Douglas, Kirk, 220
Doyle, Christopher, 171n14
Dream of a Warrior (*Cheonsamong*, Park Jee-hoon), 88
Dreamworks, 11
Dredge, C., 154n5
Dreyer, Carl Theodor, 184
Duchamp, Marcel, 7, 130

Eat Drink Man Woman (Ang Lee 1994), 267
Eisenstein, Sergei, 8, 161, 169, 170n5, 171n6, 173n24
Eliot, T. S., 168
Elsaesser, Thomas, 42, 43, 202
Emmerich, Roland, 92
Equal Opportunity Employment Act, 204
E.T. The Extra-Terrestrial (Steven Spielberg 1982), 184
Eve of Strike (Lee Yong-bae and Kim Myong-gon 1990), 206

Failan (Song Hae-sung, 2001), 81, 197
Fallen Angels (*Duo luo tian shi*, Wong Kar-wai 1995), 166, 171n14
Farewell, My Darling (*Hagsaengbugunsin-wi*, Park Chul-soo 1996), 8, 141–53
Festival (*Chukje*, Im Kwon-taek 1996), 135
Fighter in the Wind (*Ba-ram-eui Pa-i-teo*, Yang Yun-ho 2004), 201–02
Final Witness, The (*Choihui jeungin*, Lee Doo-yong 1980), 19
Fine Windy Day, A (*Balambuleo joheun nal*, Yi Chang-ho 1980), 77
Fire Woman. See *Woman of Fire*
Five Fingers of Death (*Tian xia di yi quan*, Chen Chang-ho 1973), 200
Flame, The (*Bulkkoch*, Yoo Hyun-Mok 1975), 19
Flashbacks, use of, 89, 193–94, 214n3, 267, 271, 272, 274
Flaubert, Gustav, 168
Flower Island (Song Il-gon 2001), 284
Ford, Harrison, 94n1
Forrest Gump (Robert Zemeckis 1994), 92, 94n1
Foul King, The (*Banchig-wang*, Kim Jee-won 2000), 2
French New Wave, 80
Frequency (Gregory Hoblit 2000), 89
Friend (*Chingu*, Kwak Kyung-taek 2001), 55, 78, 81, 85, 89, 92, 276
Full Monty, The (Peter Cattaneo 1997), 124
Fuller, Samuel, 7

Gabriel, Teshome, 118, 134
Gagman (Lee Myung-se 1988), 24
Gargantua and Pantagruel (Rabelais), 149
Gastronomica: The Journal of Food and Culture, 275
General in Red (*Hong-uijanggun*, Lee Du-Young 1973), 19
General Who Wears Red Clothes, The. See *General in Red*
Gen-X Cops (*Dak ging san yan lui*, Benny Chan 1999), 68n2
Ghost in Love (*Jaguimo*, Lee Kwang-hoon 1998), 55
Gibson, Mel, 94n1
Gillete, Phillip L., 201
Gillispie, Michael, 182, 187n21
Gilsottom (*Gilsoddeum*, Im Kwon-taek 1986), 135
Ginko Bed, The (*Eunhaengnamu chimdae* Kang Je-kyu 1996), 26, 39, 60
Glory of Night, The (*Bam-ui change*, Kim Ho-sun 1979), 21
Go Alone Like a Rhino's Horn (*Musso-ui ppulcheoleom honjaseo gala*, Oh Byong-chul 1995), 278
Godard, Jean-Luc, 80
Godfather, The (Francis Ford Coppola 1972), 184
Golden Age, 2, 4, 25, 116, 195
Golden Harvest, 3
Grand Bell Awards, 18, 19, 33n5, 118, 266
Green Fish (*Chologmulgogi*, Lee Chang-dong 1997), 81, 118
Gwangju Uprising, 16, 32–33n3, 123–24, 126, 137n11

Habitual Sadness (*Naj-eun mogsoli 2*, Byun Young-joo 1997), 8, 208, 209–10, 211–13, 216n16

han, 43–44, 277, 279
Han Seok-gyu, 39, 63, 93, 236
Hana-bi (Kitano Takeshi 1997), 214n9
Hanks, Tom, 94n1
Hansen, Miriam, 8, 169, 172n21
Happy End (Cheong Ju-wu 1999), 10, 124, 125, 195, 284
Happy Together (*Chun gwong cha sit*, Wong Kar-wai 1997), 286
Harry Potter and the Sorcerer's Stone (Chris Columbus 2001), 80, 92, 94n1
Hart-Landsberg, Martin, 239n11
He Said She Said (*Ken Kwapis* and *Marisa Silver* 1991), 89
Heat (Michael Mann 1995), 62
Heath, Stephen, 287
Heavenly Homecoming to the Stars (*Byeoldeul-ui gohyang*, Lee Jang-ho 1974), 20
Henderson, Gregory, 222
Hi, Dharma (*Dalmaya Nolja*, Park Cheol-kwan 2002), 11
Hicks, Emily D., 228
Hidden Hero, The (*Gisbal-eobneun gisu*, Im Kwon-taek 1979), 19
Higson, Andrew, 5, 203
Hitchcock, Alfred, 7
"Holiday," 160
Hollywood Renaissance, 80
Holocaust, 202
Hong Kong cinema, 78, 94n2, 172n18, 198
Hong Sang-soo, 132–35
Hook, The (George Seaton 1963), 220
Hot Roof, A (*Gaegat-eun nal-ui ohu*, Lee Min-yong 1995), 195, 278
Hou Hsiao-hsien, 4
Housemaid, The (*Hanyeo*, Kim Ki-young 1960), 7, 101–09
Hui, Ann, 4
Huizinga, Johannes, 183
Human Market (*Ingansijang O-haneunim*, Jin yu-young 1989), 30
Hur Jin-ho, 38–39, 49–50
Hwa byung, 191–92
Hwang Shin-hye, 275
Hyun Sook-kim, 255
Hyundai, 26, 64

I Will Never Cry Again (*Ulji aneuri*, Im Kwon-taek 1974), 19
I Wish I Had a Wife (*Nado Anega isseosmyeon joketa*, Park Heung-sik 2001), 48
I Won't Cry. See *I Will Never Cry Again*
Il Mare (Lee Hyeon-seung 2000), 2, 11, 89
Im Kwon-taek, 24, 38, 79
Imamura Shohei, 4, 7
In the Mood for Love (*Fa yeung nin wa*, Wong Ka-wai 2000), 171n14
Indecent Proposal (Adrian Lyne 1993), 29
Independence Day (Roland Emmerich 1996), 92
Insect Woman, 104, 106
International Commission of Jurists, 208
International Labor Organization, 208
International Monetary Fund (IMF), 34n10, 124–25, 132
Interview (Daniel H. Byun 2000), 89
Irigary, Luce, 296n8
Isle, The (Kim Ki-duk 2000), 243, 247, 254, 276
Ito Hirobumui, 201

Jackson, Peter, 79, 92
James Bond series, 62
James, David, 5
Jameson, Fredric, 170, 173n26
Jang Dong-kun, 79, 93, 94
Jang Hyuk, 94
Jang Jin-young, 93
Jang Sun-woo, 5, 18, 22, 80, 116, 158
Japanese cinema, 94n2, 238n6
Japanese New Wave, 80
Japanese Occupation, 45–46, 101, 127–28, 200–02, 238

Jeffords, Susan, 203
Jeon Do-youn, 79, 93
Jeon Ji-hyun, 93
Jin Hee-kyung, 93
Joint Security Area (*Gong dong Gyung bee Koo yuck*, Park Chan-wook 2000), 9, 55, 61, 67, 68, 89, 92, 198, 225, 231–37, 240n17, 241n19
Jon Byohng Je, 86
jopok, 81, 193
"Journey, The" (Hwang Chhiu), 143
Jung Woo-sung, 93
Jurassic Park (Steven Spielberg 1993), 61, 92
JVC, 64

Kang Duk-kyung, 210, 213
Kang je-kyu, 60–61, 92
Kang Woo-suk, 25, 92
Kee, Joan, 277
Kick the Moon (*Sila eu Dalbam*, Kim Sang-jin 2001), 81–82, 87, 92
Kid, Carol, 57
kijichon, 248, 250, 253
Killer Butterfly (*Sal-innabileul jjochneun yeoja*, Kim Ki-young 1978), 103, 111n7
Kim Dae-jung, 61, 123, 239n12
Kim Dong-ho, 49
Kim Don-won, 206
Kim Hak-soon, 208
Kim Ha-neul, 93
Kim Hee-seon, 79, 93
Kim Hye-soo, 93
Kim Jin-han, 49
Kim Ji-seok, 106
Kim Jong-il, 61, 239n12
Kim Ki-duk, 4, 9, 243–44, 251, 260
Kim Ki-young, 7, 38, 101–10
Kim Kyeong, 106
Kim Myong-gon, 206
Kim Sang-jin, 92
Kim Shin-rak, 202
Kim Soyoung, 5, 52n5, 110, 197
Kim Sun-hyuk, 238n4
Kim Yoon-jin, 62
Kim Yoon-shin, 210–11
Kim Young-sam, 224
Kim, Elizabeth, 251
Kim, Kyung Hyun, 5, 78, 123, 172n15, 197, 240n17, 276
King Hu, 95n3
Kirby, Lynne, 127
Klinger, Barbara, 198
Ko So-young, 93
Koh Hesung Chun, 277
Kong Ji-young, 278
Korean Academy of Film Arts, 3, 39
Korean Council for Performing Arts Promotion, 284
Korean Council for the Women Drafted as Sexual Slaves by Japan, The, 207
Korean Film Archive, 3
Korean Film Council (KOFIC), 3, 67
Korean Motion Picture Promotion Corporation (KMPPC), 3, 17, 18–19, 52, 78
Korean New Wave, 22–25, 30, 80, 116, 158
Korean Performing Arts Ethics Committee, 284
Korean War, 9, 32n3, 46, 69–70n3, 221–22, 223, 231, 233, 245, 249, 260
Kracauer, Siegfried, 157, 162
Kukai, 182
Kundun (Martin Scorcese 1997), 184
Kurosawa Kiyoshi, 4
Kwak Jae-yong, 92
Kwak Kyung-taek, 92
Kwan, Stanley, 4

L'origine du XXIéme siécele (Jean Luc Godard 2000), 136n4
Lai Ming, Leon, 88
Lake House, The (*Alejandro Agresti* 2006), 2
Landy, Marcia, 163
Last Witness, The (*Heuk Soo Seon*, Bae Chang-ho 2001), 195
Law, Clara, 4

Lawrence, Martin, 94n1
Lee, Bruce, 200
Lee Byung-hun, 79, 93, 94
Lee Chang-dong, 4, 7, 118
Lee Eun-ju, 93
Lee Hyangjin, 5, 238n5
Lee Joo-ran, 284
Lee Jung-jae, 94
Lee Man-hee, 221
Lee Mi-youn, 93
Lee Myung-se, 24, 158–59, 164, 167–69, 172n17
Lee Sung-jae, 93
Lee Tae-won, 18
Lee Yong-kwan, 103
Lee Yong-soo, 210
Lee Youn-bae, 206
Lee Young-ae, 93
Lee Young-il, 16
Lee Yo-won, 93
Legend of Ginko, The (*Dan Jok Bee Yon Soo*, Park Jae-hyun 2000), 55, 67
Lent, John, 34n12
Lesage, Julia, 211
Letter, The (*Pyeonji*, Lee Jeong-Kuk 1997), 97
Libera Me (Yang Yun-ho 2000), 67
Lies (*Geojismal*, Jang Sun-woo 1999), 284
Life and Death of the Hollywood Kid, The (*Hollywood kid-ui saeng*-ae, Chong Chi-young 1994), 45, 77
Like Water for Chocolate (*Como agua para chocolate*, Alfonso Arau 1992), 267, 270
Lim Eun-joo, 195
Little Buddha (Bernardo Bertolucci 1993), 184
Locarno Film Festival, 175
Lock Stock and Two Smoking Barrels (Guy Ritchie 1998), 88
Long Kiss Goodnight, The (Renny Harlin 1996), 196, 214n6
Lord of the Rings trilogy, 80
Lord of the Rings: Fellowship of the Ring (Peter Jackson 2001), 92, 94n1
Lord of the Rings: The Two Towers (Peter Jackson 2002), 92
Lucas, George, 80, 92
Lucía (Humberto Solás 1968), 138n17

Madame Butterfly (*Giacomo Puccini*), 250
Madame Freedom (*Jayu buin*, Han Hyong-mo 1956), 46, 125, 126
Manchurian Candidate (John Frankenheimer 1962), 238n3
Mandala (Im Kwon-taek 1981), 184
Mao-ying, Angela, 95n3
Marchetti, Gina, 199
Marines Who Never Returned, The (*Toraoji annun haebyong*, Lee Man Hee 1963), 239n10
Marriage Is a Crazy Thing (*Gyeol-honun, Mi-chin-jisida*, Yoo Ha 2002), 284
Marriage Story (*Gyeolhon-i-yagi*, Kim Eui-suk 1992), 24, 26
Martial arts films, 95n3, 199–202
Mayumi: The Female Terrorist from North Korea (*Mayumi*, Shin Sang-ok 1990), 25
McHugh, Kathleen, 285
melodrama, 6, 20–21, 37–38, 40–49
Memento (Christopher Nolan 2000), 89, 118, 136n4
Memento Mori, 78, 89, 284
Memories, 194
Memories of Murder (*Sa-rin-eui Chu-eok*, Bong Jun-ho 2003), 60
MGM, 11
Ming Dynasty, 199
Minjung, 24, 116, 123, 124, 126, 136n2, 204, 213
Miramax, 11, 59
Mishra, Sudhir, 4
Miss Saigon, 250
Missing in Action (Joseph Zito 1984), 203
Mizoguchi, Kenji, 166
Moment to Remember, A (*Nae_Meori_Sok_ui_Jee_woogae*, John H. Lee 2004), 193

Monet, Claude, 167
Moon Jae-chol, 103
Moon, Katherine H. S., 249, 262n10
Mother, The (*Eomeoni*, Lim Wok-sik 1976), 20
Murmuring (*Najeun moksori*, Byun Young-joo 1995), 8, 208, 209, 211–13, 216n16
Murphy, Eddie, 94n1
MUSA—The Warrior (Kim Sang-su 2001), 88, 197, 199, 276
My Beautiful Girl Mari (*Mari Iyagi*, Lee Sung-gang 2001), 88
My Last Memory of Heungunam (*Naega majimak bon heungnam*, Ko Young-nam 1983), 19
My Life to Live (*Vivre Sa Vie*, Jean Luc Godard 1962), 132
My Love My Bride (*Na-ui salang na-ui sinbu* 1990), 24
My Own Breathing (*Najeun Moksori* 3, Byun Young-joo 1999), 8, 208, 210–11, 212, 213, 216n16
My Sassy Girl (*Yupgijugin Geunyu*, Kwak Jae-yong, 2001), 11, 87, 92
My Wife is a Gangster (*Jopok Manura*, Jo Jin-kyu 2001), 11, 81, 92, 196–97
My Wife is a Gangster 2 (*Jopok Manura 2: Dolahon Jeon-seol*, Chung Hung-soon 2003), 193

Nabi: The Butterfly (Moon seung-wook 2001), 193
Nan Achnas, 4
Napoleon (Abel Gance 1927), 130
Narboni, Jean, 151
Nash, Christopher, 233
Nash, Gary, 245, 259
Neal, Steve, 8, 163
Neo-Confucianism, 8, 106, 125, 154n8
New Wave, Korean, 5, 8, 16, 22–25, 30, 47, 158
Nikita (Luc Besson 1990), 62, 64
No Blood No Tears (Pido Noon-muldo Upshi, Ryoo Seung-wan 2002), 2, 84, 194, 214n7
North Korea, People's Republic of, 9, 61, 63, 219–37
Notting Hill (Roger Michell, 1999), 52
Nowhere to Hide (Injeongsajeong bol geos eobsda Injeongsajeong bol geos eobsda, Lee myung-se), 8, 52, 60, 88, 130, 158–70

Oasis (Lee Chang-dong 2002), 10
Officer and a Gentleman, An (Taylor Hackford 1982), 126
Official Story, The (*La historia oficial*, Luis Puenzo 1985), 29
Oh! Dream Country (Yoo In-taek and Hong Ki-son 1997), 206
Oh, Happy Day (Yoon Hak-ryul 2003), 195
Old Boy (Park Chan-wook 2003), 11, 284
Old House, The (*Goga*, Cho Mun-Jin 1977), 20
On Yon-ho, 262n12
Ordet (Carl Dreyey 1955), 183
Oshima Nagisa, 80
Our Twisted Hero (*Ulideul-ui ilgeuleojin yeong-ung*, Park Jong-won 1992), 135
Over the Rainbow (Ahn Jin-woo 2002), 193
Ozu, Yasujiro, 184

Paik Nak-chung, 239n7
Palley, Marian Lief, 277
Panahi, Jafar, 4
Pang, Danny, 4
Pang, Eun-jin, 275
pansori, 43, 44, 133–34, 203
Park Chong-Chul, 123
Park Chul-soo, 141–42, 143
Park Chung-hee, 16, 31–32n1, 102, 103, 106, 108, 110, 122
Park Jiye, 109
Park Joong-hoon, 93
Park Jung-hee, 240n13
Park Kwang-su, 5, 80, 116, 125, 158
Park Shin-yang, 93

Parquet, Darcy, 162
Partisans of South Korea (*Nambugun*, Jeong Ji-yeong 1990), 224
Passage to Buddha (Chang Sonu 1994), 184
Peppermint Candy (*Bakha Sa-tang*, Lee Chang-dong 2000), 7, 81, 116, 117–29, 136n4
Petal, A (*Kochip*, Park Kwang-su 1996), 24, 137n11
Picasso, Pablo, 171n10
Picnic (Song Il-gon 1999), 124
Pihl, Marshell R., 134
Plate, S. Brent, 184
Point of No Return (John Badham 1993), 62
Policeman (*Gyeongchalgwan*, Lee Du-yong 1978), 20
Ponette (Jaques Doillion 1996), 184
Popular Memory Group, 205, 209
Power of Kangwon Province, The (*Gang-wondo-ui him*, Hong Sang-soo 1998), 129, 130, 132
Promise, A (*Yagsog*, Kim Yu-jin 1998), 48
Public Enemy (*Gong-gong-eui Juck*, Kang Woo-Suk 2002), 92
Public Performance Ethics Committee, 28
Public Performance Promotion Association, 30
Pulp Fiction (Quentin Tarantino 1994), 88
Purn, 206, 215n13
Purple Storm (*Ziyu fengbao*, Teddy Chan 1999), 68n2
Pusan International Film Festival, 3–4, 11, 39, 78, 102, 103, 117, 216n16
Pusan Promotion Plan, 4

Quiet Family, The (*Jo-yonghan gajok*, Kim Ji Woon 1998), 52

Raging Bull (Martin Scorcese 1980), 166, 172n16
Raimi, Sam, 92
Rambo (George P. Cosmatos 1985), 203
Rashomon (Kurosawa Akira 1950), 89, 129, 130
Ratanaruang, Pen-ek, 4
Ray, Nicholas, 7
Rayns, Tony, 16
Reagan, Ronald, 203, 219
Real Fiction (*Shilje sanghwang*, Kim Ki-duk 2000), 243
Reeves, Keanu, 2
Remaining Spy, The (*Anlyucheobja*, Kim Si-Hyeon 1975), 19
Resnais, Alain, 89
Resurrection of the Little Match Girl (*Sungnyangpari Sonyue Jaerim*, Jang Sun-woo 2002), 76
Rhim Hye-kyung, 179
Rikidozan: A Hero Extraordinary (*Yeok-do-san*, Song Hae-sung 2004), 202
Rimbaud, 171n10
Riza, Riri, 4
Road Movie (Kim In-shik 2002), 284
Roberts, Julia, 79, 94n1
Rock, The (Michael Bay 1996), 68
Rooster, A (*Sutalg*, Shin Seung-su 1990), 24
Rub Love (Lee Seo-soon 2003), 193
Rush (Lee Sang-in 1999), 82
Russo-Japanese War, 215n12

Sakamoto Inji, 4
Salvador (Oliver Stone 1986), 29
Samaritan Girl (*Samaria*, Kim Ki-duk 2004), 243, 284
Samsung, 26, 64, 66, 283
Saulabi (Mun Jong-geum 2004), 200
Schraeder, Paul, 184
Scorcese, Martin, 80
Se7en (David Fincher 1995), 64
Secret Tears (*Bee mil*, Park Ki-hyung 2000), 193
Seinfeld, 136n4
Seoul Raiders (*Han cheng gong lüe*, Jingle Ma, 2005), 2
September 11, 2001, 68n2
Seven Women Prisoners (Kim Shi-hyeon 1965), 221

Shim Eun-ha, 39, 79, 93
Shim Hye-soo, 93
Shin Eun-kyung, 93
Shin Ha-kyun, 94
Shin Sang-ok, 102
Shinoda Masahiro, 80
Shiri (Kang Je-kyu 1999), 6, 48, 52, 55–68, 78, 88, 92, 130, 195 199, 225, 226, 227, 236, 283
Shoppa, Leonard, 204
Short, Stephen, 10
Siddhartha (Conrad Brooks 1972), 184
Silence of the Lambs (Jonathan Demme 1991), 63, 64
Silence, The (*Sokout*, Moshen Makhmalbaf 1998), 117
Silmido (Kang Woo-suk 2003), 55, 67
Silver Stallion, The (*Eunma-neun oji anhneunda*, Jang Gil-su 1992), 24
Sin Chang-heui, 111n10
Singhae udong, 203–04
Single Spark, A (*Aleumda-un cheongnyeon Jeon Taeil*, Park Kwang-su 1995), 38
Soil, The (*Toji*, Kim Soo-yong 1974), 20
Sol Kyung-gu, 94
Song for a Ressurection, The (*Buhwal-ui nolae*, Lee Chong-gook 1990), 24, 137n11
Song Kang-ho, 63, 94
Sony Pictures Classics, 60
Sopyonje (Im Kwon-taek 1993), 2, 24, 41, 44, 79, 92, 134, 203
Soul Guardians (Park Kwang-chun 1998), 55
Southern Communist Guerillas (Jeong Ji-young 1990), 24, 25
Special Law on Sexual Violence, 204
Speed (Jan de Bont 1994), 62
Spider Forest (Geo_mee_soop, Song Il-gon 2004), 193
Spider-man (Sam Raimi 2002), 80, 92
Spielberg, Steven, 80, 92
Spin Kick (*Dol-lyeo-cha-gi*, Nam Sang-kook 2004), 200
Spinning Wheel, The (*Yeoin janhoksa moulleya moulleya*, Lee Doo-yong 1984), 12n1
Sports films, 199, 202
Spring in My Hometown, 78
Spring, Summer, Fall, Winter... Spring (*Bom, Yeo-reum, Ga-eul, Gyeo-ul, geu-ri-go... Bom*, Kim Ki-duk 2003), 60, 243
Spy Li Cheol-jin, 9, 225, 226–31, 232, 233, 237
Stallybrass, Peter, 150
Standish, Isolde, 28
Star Wars (George Lucas 1977), 92, 184
Star Wars I: Phantom Menace (George Lucas 1999), 80, 92
Star Wars II: Attack of the Clones (George Lucas 2002), 80
State of Siege (Coasta-Gavras, 1972), 29
Strawberry and Chocolate (*Fresa y chocolate*, Tomás Gutiérrez Alea and Juan Carlos Tabío 1994), 270
Suh Joon-sik, 206
Sul Kyong-su, 48
Summer Time (Park Jae-ho 2001), 284
Sundance Film Festival, 266, 276
Sunshine Policy, 128, 225
Sweet Sex and Love (*Ma-sit-neun Sek-seu Geu-ri-go Sa-rang*, Bong Man-dae 2003), 284
Sympathy for Mr. Vengeance (*Boksooneun Na-eui Gut*, Park Chan-wook 2002), 2, 60, 84

Taebaek Mountains (*Taebaeksanmaek*, Im Kwon-taek 1994), 19, 25, 224
Taeguki: Brotherhood of War (Kang Je-kyu 2004), 55, 67, 135, 197, 237, 241n19
Take Care of My Cat (*Goyangyirul butakhae*, Jeong-jae-Eun 2001), 60, 76, 78, 85, 87
Tampopo (Itami Juzo 1985), 267
Taussig, Michael, 157, 159, 170n1, 171n7

Tears (*Noon mool*, Im Sang-soo 2000), 10, 82, 83
Tell Me Something (Chang Yoon-hyun 1999), 195
Teo, Stephen, 78
Terminator (James Cameron 1984), 29
Terminator 2: Judgment Day (James Cameron 1991), 29
Testimony (*Jeung-eon*, Im Kwon-taek 1973), 19
That Man That Woman (*Geu yeoja geu namja*, Kim Eui-suk 1993), 30
Thesz, Lou, 202
Thirty-Two Short Films about Glenn Gould (François Gerard 1993), 132
Three (Kim Jee-woon 2002), 194
Three Friends (*Sechingu*, Lim Sun-Rye 1996), 2, 78
Tian Zhuangzhauang, 4
Timeless Bottomless Bad Movie (*Nappun yeonghwa*, Jang Sun-woo), 7, 76, 82–83, 86, 87
Titanic (James Cameron 1997), 6, 57, 58, 80, 92, 283
To the Starry Island (*Geu seom-e gago sipda*, Park Kwang-su 1993), 38, 135
Tokyo Raiders (*Dong jing gong lüe*, Jingle Ma 2000), 2
Tom Jones (Tony Richardson 1963), 267, 270
Too Young to Die (*Jukeodo Jo A*, Park Jin-pyo 2002), 10
Total Recall (Paul Verhoeven 1990), 29
Truffaut, François, 80
Turner, Victor, 152, 185
Two Cops (Kang Woo-seok 1993), 77
Typhoon (Kwak Kyung-taek 2005), 11

Union of Korean Film Promotion, 18
United States of American-Republic of Korea Status of Forces Agreement, 250
Universal, 11

Vacant House (Kim Ki-duk 2004), 243
Van Gennep, Arnold, 185
Venice Film Festival, 11, 214, 243, 245
Vienna Human Rights Conference of 1993, 208
Vietnam War, 1, 24
Village in the Mist (*Angae maeul*, Im Kwon-taek 1983), 12n1
Village Road Show, 3
Villain, The (*Nabbeun namja*, Kim-Ki-duk 2002), 254
Virgin Stripped Bare by Her Bachelors (*Oh! Soo-jung*, Hong Sang-soo 2000), 7, 78, 89, 116, 130–36
Volcano High (*Hwa San Goh*, Kim Tae-kyun 2001), 88
Volken, Vanick, 222

Wanee and Junah (*Wanee wa Junah*, Kim Yong-gyun 2001), 284
Wang, Xiaoshuai, 4
Warner Bros., 11
Washington, Denzel, 94n1
Watt, Ian, 103
Waugh, Patricia, 155n17
Way Down East (D. W. Griffith 1920), 46
Way Home, The (*Jiburo*, Lee Jeong-Hyang 2002), 92
Whale Hunting (*Goraesanyang*, Bae Chang-ho 1984), 77
What Are You Going to Do Tomorrow? (Lee Bong-won 1987), 29
"When I Dream," 57
Whispering Corridors (*Yeogogoedam*, Park Ki-hyeong 1998), 78
White Badge (*Ha-yanjeonjaeng*, Jeong Ji-Young 1992), 2, 24
White Paper of Unification, 224–25
White, Allen, 150
White, Hayden, 194
Why Has Bodhidharma Left for the East? (*Dalmaga dongjjok-euro gan kkadakeun?*, Bae Yong-kyun 1989), 8, 26, 175–85
Wild Animals (*Yasaeng dongmul bohoguyeog*, Kim Ki-duk 1997), 243

Williams, Linda, 42, 46–47, 48
Willis, Bruce, 94n1
Winter Sonata, 198
Winter Woman, The (Gyeol Buin, Kang Dae-jin 1977), 20
Woman of Fire (*Hwanyeo*, Kim Ki-young 1971), 104, 106
Woman of Fire '82 (*Hwanyeo*, Kim Ki-young 1982), 104
Woman-Being in Asia, A (Byun Young-joo), 206
Women of Yi Dynasty (1969), 195
Won Bin, 94
Wong Kar-wai, 80, 166
Wood, Ed, 7, 103
World of Suzie Wong, The (Richard Quine 1960), 250
World War II, 46, 222

Yamagate International Documentary Festival, 216
Yanggongju, 125, 248, 255
Year of the Dragon (Michael Cimino 1985), 250
Yesterday (Jung Yun-su 2002), 193
Yi Dynasty, 204, 247, 261n7
Y.M.C.A. Baseball Team (*Y.M.C.A. Yagoo-dan*, Kim Hyun-seok 2002), 201
Yokdong udang, 204
Yonggary (Shim *Hyung-rae* 2001), 55
Yoo Ji-tae, 94
Yoo Oh-seong, 79, 93, 94
Yoo Young-kil, 49, 50
Yoon Doo-ri, 191, 206, 213, 213n1
Yoshida Yoshishige, 80
Yoshimoto Mitsuhiro, 285
Yosong haebang, 204
Yu, Gina, 44, 45
Yu Gwan-sun, 20
Yu Hyun-mok, 102
Yun Kum-yi, 250
Yushin Kaehyuk, 16, 32n2, 122, 137n6

Zemekis, Robert, 92
Zen Buddhism, 8, 168, 175–77, 179, 180, 182, 184–85, 186n11
Zhang Ziyi, 88, 197